For a BETTER WORLD

THE WINNIPEG GENERAL STRIKE & THE WORKERS' REVOLT

Edited by
JAMES NAYLOR, RHONDA L. HINTHER,
JIM MOCHORUK

UNIVERSITY OF MANITOBA PRESS

For a Better World: The Winnipeg General Strike and the Workers' Revolt

26 25 24 23 22 1 2 3 4 5

University of Manitoba Press
Winnipeg, Manitoba, Canada
Treaty 1 Territory
uofmpress.ca

Cataloguing data available from Library and Archives Canada
ISBN 978-0-88755-299-1 (PAPER)
ISBN 978-0-88755-017-1 (PDF)
ISBN 978-0-88755-021-8 (EPUB)
ISBN 978-0-88755-088-1 (BOUND)

Cover images: L.B. Foote photographs, Winnipeg, 1919.
Cover design by Mike Carroll
Interior design by Karen Armstrong

Printed in Canada

The University of Manitoba Press acknowledges the financial support for its publication program provided by the Government of Canada through the Canada Book Fund, the Canada Council for the Arts, the Manitoba Department of Sport, Culture, and Heritage, the Manitoba Arts Council, and the Manitoba Book Publishing Tax Credit.

Funded by the Government of Canada | Canada

CONTENTS

ACKNOWLEDGEMENTS

An edited volume is, by definition, a collective endeavor—this one is particularly so. The approach of the centenary of the 1919 Winnipeg General Strike created a wave of interest in commemorating the event in ways that both explored the past and spoke to the present. Historians were, of course, immediately on side, but the labour movement, too, was excited by the unique opportunity to explore their past and to tell their story. As 2019 approached, labour and community projects proliferated in Winnipeg and, as writers, actors, curators, and others set to work, the city's working-class past and present took on a newfound prominence.

This book is self-consciously a part of these events. The three editors participated in helping organize a conference held in May 2019 entitled "Building a Better World, 1919–2019." The goal was to bring academic and public historians, trade unionists and other activists, as well as the broader public together to re-examine the Workers' Revolt of 1919 and its relevance to the present. Over the three years spent planning the event, the organizers discussed and debated the ways in which we could critically commemorate the past and tie it to modern-day struggles. This book is the product of those debates and the themes of the conference that followed—the challenges of inadequate pay and precarious work, the struggle to overcome divisions within the working class, and the possibilities that arose when labour came together to imagine a better world. We want to thank the other members of the organizing committee: David Camfield, Victor Dobchuk, Janita Froese, Jodi Giesbrecht, Tim Gordienko, Gordon Goldsborough, Julie Guard, Paul Jenkins, Esyllt Jones, Krishna Lalbiharie, Greg McFarlane, Paul Moist, Amber Ostermann, Scott Price, Sarah Reilly, Sharon Reilly, Dave Sauer, Yaza Shapata, Wendy Sol, Basia Sokol, Jeff Taylor, Janis Thiessen, and

Shannon Winters. The conference itself, which featured presentations by historians and labour studies scholars, activists, artists and poets, attracted well over 300 participants. While several of the chapters of this book originated with papers presented at the conference, the character of the book was deeply influenced by the conference as a whole. We wish to thank all of those who spoke or simply attended; you brought insights about the past and the present and helped us produce, we hope, a more insightful and inclusive book. The conference received considerable material support from a range of sources which we wish also to thank: the Canadian Association for Work and Labour Studies, the Canadian Committee on Labour History, the Canadian Union of Public Employees (Local 204), the Canadian Society for Ukrainian Labour Research, the Faculties of Arts at Brandon University and at the Universities of Manitoba and Winnipeg, the office of the Provost at the University of Winnipeg, the H. Sanford Riley Fellowship in Canadian History, the Manitoba Federation of Labour, the Professional Institute of the Public Service of Canada, the Social Sciences and Humanities Research Council of Canada, the University of Manitoba Faculty Association, and the Winnipeg Labour Council. As well, we want to thank the staff at the University of Winnipeg, Diversity Food Services, the Ukrainian Labour Temple, the Good Will Social Club, and Khao House restaurant. Collectively, all the participants and supporters provided an outstanding intellectual and social arena and were instrumental in encouraging the research, discussion, and debate which is reflected in this volume. The commemorations and discussions of 1919 were clearly infectious and we had little trouble attracting others to contribute to the book.

We also want to thank Sean Carleton, who read and commented on the editors' contributions to the book, as well as the anonymous reviewers whose insightful and helpful comments have contributed to a much stronger collection. We wish, as well, to recognize Nolan Reilly and Tom Mitchell, whose enthusiasms and deep knowledge have contributed considerably to many of the insights we have about the events in Winnipeg in 1919. The Manitoba Federation of Labour, and specifically through the efforts of Kevin Rebeck and Anna Rothney, was a generous and tolerant supporter of the conference as well as a large number of events commemorating and discussing the General Strike. Their encouragement, along with that of a raft of unions and union locals, made this conference a particularly inclusive event and has helped spur a renaissance of public labour history.

The University of Manitoba Press has been a supportive partner from early in the process. Jill McConkey and David Carr recognized the potential of this volume immediately, and David Larsen and Glenn Bergen helped shepherd it along efficiently and professionally. Gretchen Albers was a proficient and insightful copyeditor. Mike Carroll created a beautiful book cover. The Press, under the direction of David Carr, has been enjoyable to work with and we wish David well on his retirement.

Rhonda thanks her family—especially Aaron Floresco, Sebastian Hinther-Floresco, Evelyn Hinther, the late Sophie Skolny, Glen Ash, Lynne Onofreychuk, Helen Floresco, George Floresco, and Cathy Kennedy—for their continual cheerleading of this and her other projects. Elementary school student Sebastian was especially patient and willing to work independently during COVID home/remote schooling when he couldn't have Mom's full assistance because she had to "jump on a Zoom meeting" with "the Jims" or had to attend to other aspects of the manuscript's development. Rhonda is also grateful to her many friends for their interest in and support of her work, for COVID walks, and other outdoor diversions during this book's creation. Finally, she'd also like to acknowledge "the Jims"—Naylor and Mochoruk—for the many times they picked up so much of the slack of the editorial process as she attempted to juggle 24-7 pandemic parenting, online teaching, and this book and other projects. She couldn't have wished for better or more understanding—and fun—collaborators.

Jim Naylor's thanks go out not only to those who encouraged and, in one way or another, helped with this book, but particularly to those who were key to the success of the Strike centenary conference and, by extension, this volume. He particularly wishes to mention Jeff Taylor for encouraging and facilitating our ability to think big about the anniversary, and Amber Ostermann who, in countless practical ways, ensured its success. Although the conference was held at the University of Winnipeg (and thanks to everyone there who helped) its administration was undertaken by Brandon University where Demetres Tryphonopoulos, Sally Spiss, Jan Chaboyer, and particularly Jan Mahoney, were supportive and endlessly helpful. Jim's sister Karen provided both occasional shelter and a sympathetic ear during trips to Winnipeg for conference planning while his children, Adrie,

Keir, and Rhys (and in the final stretches, grandson Robin), provided a welcome mix of interest in—and distraction from—all of this. Molly Rozum deserves special thanks for her interest, insights, and support throughout the project. Finally, he wishes to thank the coeditors and coauthors; working with Rhonda and Jim proved to be more enjoyable and enriching than could have been imagined at the outset.

Jim Mochoruk wants to thank the members of the conference planning committee (listed above) and the conference participants who made the event itself such a wonderful and intellectually enriching experience. He is also deeply appreciative of his coauthors and coeditors Jim Naylor and Rhonda Hinther. Working and writing together has been both enjoyable and—truly remarkable in academic terms—painless. He also wants to thank his family—most especially Mary, who has put up with his prolonged absences and pre-occupations for over four decades; his children, Kaitlin, Brendan and Colleen—who have always supported and encouraged their father, no matter what; their partners Ryan, Hayley, and Tyler, who have rounded out the family in so many wonderful ways; and finally, Braylynn, Sage and Luca, whose mere presence makes Jim believe that we are headed "for a better world."

Introduction

James Naylor, Rhonda L. Hinther, and Jim Mochoruk

Anniversaries are a time to take stock. The centenary of the Winnipeg General Strike in 2019 sparked a rash of commemoration, celebration, reflection, and reevaluation among a remarkably broad and diverse array of people. For many of us who participated in the events of that year there was a sense that the Strike was both remote in time and relevant in the present. For the labour movement in particular, battered by neoliberalism for decades, the relevance of a mass working class–led response to the predations of capital was unmistakable. Not only had it been possible to dream of a world—in the language of 1919—where human needs trumped the soulless pursuit of profit, it was possible to fight for it—in the language of 2019—by at least beginning to construct an intersectional movement across deeply etched divisions of gender and ethnicity. Whatever its achievements and shortcomings, the Winnipeg General Strike provided (in the language of a generation of historians who came of age in the 1960s and 1970s) a "useful history." It was a tool for rethinking the present.[1]

Nonetheless, 100 years is a long time. The Strike is as close to the present as it was to the close of the Napoleonic Wars, to a time when, in the words of E.P. Thompson, the English working class—the world's first—had only just embarked on its own "making." It would be another three or four decades until industrialization firmly took root in Canada, and another couple until the Knights of Labor exploded across North

America, proclaiming the arrival of an oppositional class imaginary to the world constructed by robber barons and "parasites." One hundred years before the Strike, the forks of the Red and Assiniboine Rivers were only just becoming the focal point of the continental fur trade and the first colonial settlers had just arrived from the Scottish Highlands. The Métis resistance to colonialism at Red River was a mere half-century before 1919; indeed, several of the leading bourgeois opponents of the Strike in Winnipeg had participated in 1885's military suppression of what they saw as Indigenous hindrances to the unbridled expansion of settler colonialism and British Canadian capital.[2] The settlement and transformation of the Northwest enabled by the forced dispossession of Aboriginal and Métis peoples in tandem with massive immigration from Europe—processes that led to the emergence of Winnipeg as a commercial and industrial centre—predated the Strike by only two decades. In this same stretch of time, the small city of under 40,000 grew more than fourfold to become Canada's third-largest metropolis.

This context explains the place and its people in 1919. Long a site of important Indigenous meaning, of trade and diplomacy, it had been transformed into the major beachhead of white settler colonialism in the Northwest. Winnipeg's "civic leaders" were capitalists confident and triumphant in the conquests of trade and industry both locally and much more broadly in a long "gilded age" that celebrated and rewarded avarice. Overwhelmingly, Winnipeg was populated by a working class shaped by empire, or rather empires. The most privileged—privilege being a relative term at a time when labour of any sort was increasingly debased and controlled—were those who could claim "Britishness" and marketable skills. Less so were those enticed from eastern and central Europe, notably the Austro-Hungarian, Russian, and German empires, often driven here by an emergent agricultural and industrial capitalism that undermined the value of their agricultural labour in the old world. Mostly—though not entirely—absent were racialized imperial subjects from Africa and east and south Asia. The labour of these groups was useful in British colonies in Africa and the West Indies but was judged to be undesirable (except when other, more "preferred" options were unavailable) in the "White Dominion" of Canada. Indigenous people were seen through a similarly racialized lens, largely confined to reserves or residential schools typically beyond the ever-expanding limits of white settlement. Their labour was usually harnessed in areas considered more remote, where profit demanded utilization of labour power closer to hand—as in the fishing, lumber, and mineral exploration fields, as well as the still important fur trade.

The processes of Indigenous dispossession, of capital accumulation, of the creation of transportation infrastructure, and the massive immigration that had created the Winnipeg of 1919 were all, in different but connected ways, deeply wrenching experiences. And they were all exacerbated by the trauma of the First World War. Variously described as a crusade to defend and vindicate the British Empire or, in Woodrow Wilson's reinterpretation, a war to make the world safe for democracy, an increasing number of workers internationally saw it as the outcome of capitalism itself. In the late nineteenth century capitalist European empires had claimed the world in their frenzied race for resources and markets; in the twentieth they had turned on each other to secure these and future prizes. Already understanding that their labouring bodies were deemed expendable in "dark satanic mills," factories, and mines, millions arrived as cannon fodder in the trenches of Europe. Even on the "home front," far from exploding shells, the bodies of workers and their families were threatened by deprivation as the "high cost of living" left pantries bare while "plutocrats" and "profiteers" gorged. The descent of the "civilized" European world into barbarism was rapid and confusing as contradictory notions of patriotism and class consciousness mixed chaotically among workers everywhere. However one understood the war, few would dispute that its sacrifices were shared unequally. Workers' sense of injustice was inflamed as was their skepticism of a social order that threatened hardship in "good times" and delivered catastrophe in bad times. At the same time, the war had demonstrated—in a gruesome manner—alternative possibilities. The impressive mobilization of the nation's resources in total war as well as an astounding willingness to sacrifice for a common goal suggested what might be achieved if directed toward a better world. The result was an explosive mixture of working-class anger, solidarity, and hope.

Such sentiments were readily apparent at the Walker Theatre in downtown Winnipeg on Sunday afternoon, 22 December 1918—in the midst of the influenza pandemic—at a meeting sponsored by the Winnipeg Trades and Labor Council (WTLC) and the Socialist Party of Canada (SPC). The 1,700 present, representing both "British" and immigrant workers, decried the way that the federal government was continuing to restrict civil liberties with the clear intent of restraining workers, their unions, and their increasingly anticapitalist ideas. The meeting also expressed its support of the workers' revolution in Russia and opposed Canada's military support of pro-Tsarist forces fighting it. The Russian Revolution that had taken that country out of the war and overthrown capitalism had an electrifying effect internationally. The great experiment there demonstrated that a different future was possible, fuelling workers' imagination and hope internationally. Just as importantly, the mere mention of revolution galvanized capital's opposition to even a hint of radicalism. Whether or not workers saw Russia as a model, the possibilities, and the stakes, had increased immeasurably.

Many of the same ideas were present in Calgary in March 1919—in ways that were increasingly consequential. Along with the rhetoric of the Walker Theatre meeting came a strategy developed by a body that believed it had the capacity to carry it out. The Western Labour Conference brought together 237 representative union leaders and activists from throughout western Canada intent on building upon what was already happening. They were aware that workers were already coming together, coordinating the actions of their individual unions, which were based on specific craft skills, via federations that increasingly functioned as industrial unions—a move that dramatically increased workers' ability to put pressure on bosses. At Calgary these men and (handful of) women proposed building a new movement where all workers would combine their power in One Big Union (OBU). And, recognizing the limited power of isolated groups of workers, they proposed a broader implementation of labour's most potent and sweeping weapon—the general strike. This had already proven its potential, as the previous year a burgeoning general strike movement had forced the City of Winnipeg to recognize and bargain with its civic employees. Such militancy (this was one of four occasions when Winnipeg workers had threatened to strike in sympathy with other unions in 1918) was matched by a growing radicalism. The attendees at the Calgary Conference unanimously called for "the transformation of capitalistic private property to communal wealth," referencing, once again, the recent revolution in Russia.[3] Indeed, such ideas were already taking firm hold in the WTLC as witnessed by that body's election of delegates to the Calgary Conference—R.B. Russell and R.J. Johns—leading advocates of the both the OBU and socialism.

Matters came to a head in Winnipeg at the start of May 1919. Reflecting the growing movement toward more effective unity, workers in both the metal and building trades went on strike, insisting that their employers negotiate with federations of unions, rather than with individual union locals representing specific trades. This demand met a solid wall of opposition from the employers. The strikers took their case to the WTLC. That body had both grown in confidence over the past few months as the city's labour movement soared in size (about 5,000 workers joined unions in just the first nineteen days of May) and moved solidly to the left.[4] Unionists old and new were well aware of wider discussions about transforming the labour movement and the fight for socialism. Over 4,000 of them crammed the city's Industrial Bureau building in early May to hear about the OBU.[5] Those who were not present could still read about the OBU and socialism in the WTLC's *Western Labor News*, which was edited by the radical preacher William Ivens and had recently displaced the staid labour organ, *The Voice*.

The WTLC unanimously decided to conduct a strike vote among its affiliated unions about going out on a general strike. On 13 May, the results were in: 11,112 workers had voted yes, only 524 were opposed. It is worth noting that this procedure ignored the practices and regulations of individual national and international unions. Winnipeg workers had taken matters into their own hands. They set 11:00 a.m., 15 May, as the beginning of the great strike.

The Strike began when telephone operators, popularly known as "hello girls," failed to show up for their 7 a.m. shift. By noon, the city was shut down. Streetcars returned to their barns, shops and restaurants closed, factories emptied, mail delivery ground to a halt. The precipitant action of the "hello girls" symbolized the ways in which the Strike potentially challenged hierarchies of gender and skill in the labour movement. And very quickly the ethnic order appeared upended as well, as thousands of immigrant workers joined the walkout. Only a few months earlier, the city had seen anti-immigrant riots aimed at preserving jobs for "British" workers and returned veterans of the Canadian Expeditionary Force. Soon, as many as 35,000 workers were on strike. More than half of them belonged to no union; many were poor immigrant workers in precarious jobs who, in normal times, would simply have been fired for the slightest hint of activism and thrown into life-threatening destitution. Overall, the strikers represented members of perhaps half of all the households in Winnipeg. This was an unexpected, and unprecedented, level of solidarity. Small wonder that strikers felt that this would all be over in a matter of days. What else could the bosses do but capitulate?

The fact that the employers did not concede defeat was, ironically, a product of labour's strength. While the leadership of the Strike—a very large Central Strike Committee made up of delegates from each striking union, which elected a smaller body of fifteen to provide day-to-day direction—kept its focus on the central demands around collective bargaining and living wages, the city's propertied elite recognized much more was at stake. The latter formed a "Citizens' Committee of 1000" to defend a social and economic order that they felt was very much under siege. Declaring themselves guardians not just of capitalism, but of "British" constitutional democracy (with all of its implied colonialist privileges, hierarchy, and racism—many of which they articulated in furious attacks on the "enemy aliens" they saw as instigating events) they approached the Strike as an existential threat. Under the guidance of lawyer and former mayor A.J. Andrews, they determined that negotiation would only broadcast their weakness; the Strike must be clearly and demonstrably broken.

The Strike leadership certainly recognized the dangers. Civil disorder would increase the likelihood of military intervention by the federal government. In any case, labour's most powerful tool was the withdrawal of its labour power; deprived of their source of profit, capitalists would be forced to come to the table. In the meantime, it was safest, and sufficient, to "do nothing." Aided by the warm late spring weather, almost daily mass gatherings were organized in Victoria Park by the Red River, not far from City Hall. There, and in workers' and ethnic halls around the city, workers met, listened to speakers, and discussed the progress of the Strike. The estimated 171 mass meetings held in the city during the Strike represented a participatory democracy, in itself a challenge to a parliamentary order in which workers had, at best, a modicum of input.[6]

The challenge of Winnipeg workers was amplified by the fact that Winnipeg was but one front in a national (indeed international) challenge to the social order that Canadian labour historians have come to call the Workers' Revolt. Few of the catalysts that prompted the Winnipeg General Strike were unique to that city; from Victoria, British Columbia, to Amherst, Nova Scotia, workers participated in general, or near-general, strikes to force employers to ameliorate the often desperate conditions of workers and their families in the immediate term, but also to reset, in one way or another, the deep imbalance of wealth and power in Canada. Often they were led by the same group of workers; it was those from the metal trades—in many ways at the vanguard of industrial society—who led the charge not only in Winnipeg, but in Toronto and in the labour hotspots of Europe at the end of the First World War. Most astounding—and most troubling for the authorities—was the degree of solidarity between workers across considerable distances. This had already been presaged in impressive strikes and protests in many countries to prevent their governments from waging war against the revolutionary workers' government in Russia. In several cities in western Canada general strikes were organized in active support of Winnipeg's striking workers. In some centres such as Saskatoon and Brandon these general strikes were solid and prolonged even when local workers had already succeeded in winning important concessions. In this remarkable late spring of 1919, thousands of workers were willing to put their own victories, and indeed their own livelihoods, on the line to support their class comrades hundreds of kilometres away.

The Canadian government, then, faced an even more daunting challenge than did Winnipeg's business elite. If the "contagion" of Winnipeg spread across Canada, the federal authorities could do little to stop it. Already Canadian soldiers had mutinied rather than be sent to Russia to fight the Bolsheviks;[7] Prime Minister Borden would not want to test their loyalty if ordered to fight Canadian workers. The federal government would do much to build its arsenal of weapons to confront such challenges: they amended the Criminal Code to include a sweeping definition of sedition, they streamlined and broadened their ability to deport under the terms of the Immigration Act, and they revamped and strengthened the federal police forces by creating the Royal Canadian Mounted Police. Still, the federal government realized it needed to proceed with caution. Broader powers would be used carefully and surgically, at the same time nurturing conservative labour leaders who felt their own powers challenged by the radical ground shaking beneath their feet. The federal government was already well aware of the growing working-class strength and radicalism that had been developing during the war and had determined that the best immediate strategy was to nurture the support of "safe and sane" union leaders. Borden had brought Conservative trade unionist Gideon Robertson into his cabinet, eventually making him minister of labour (and put him to good use in dealing with the general strike movements in Winnipeg in both 1918 and 1919), and he had signalled the government's intentions by honouring the antiradical president of the American Federation of Labor, Samuel Gompers, with an invitation to address Parliament. By the time of the springtime wave of general strikes, a Royal Commission on Industrial Relations was crossing Canada, listening to workers' concerns (and to a remarkable extent their hopes for a social system based on human needs). Given the federal government's constraints, Winnipeg's Citizens' Committee of 1000 increasingly took matters into its own hands.

Among the Citizens' first goals was to ensure its hold on the instruments of power, specifically the police. The police were unionized and openly sympathetic to the strikers, although they had, at the request of the General Strike Committee, promised to remain at their posts. This provided little solace to civic authorities who demanded that they not only individually forswear striking but also break all connections with the broader labour movement. Overwhelmingly rejecting the "ultimatum," almost the entire police force was fired on 9 June and replaced by untrained antistrike "special" police. This did not go well. The following day, in an attempt to demonstrate their control of the city, these "thugs" (as they were described in the banner headline of the *Western Labor News*) provoked and lost a three-hour battle near the iconic downtown intersection of Portage and Main. Along with the ability of residents of working-class neighbourhoods to effectively challenge strikebreakers, it was clear that civic authorities and, in particular, the Citizens' Committee, had lost control of the city's streets.

The story was similar among a particularly important sector of the city's population: the large number of recently returned soldiers. Two days after the start of the Strike, a meeting of 3,000 returned soldiers rejected a proposal from the executive committees of the veterans' organizations to remain neutral. Like the city's population as a whole, they appear to have split along class lines with a majority of enlisted men recognizing their affinity to the strikers and their interest in collectively bettering their own working-class lives. No doubt much of the Citizens'

Committee's furiously bigoted propaganda was aimed at just this audience. Given the overrepresentation of those of British birth or ancestry in the Canadian military, the Citizens felt that a relentless denunciation of "enemy aliens" and of "traitors" to the British constitutional order would undermine the soldiers' support of the Strike. Whatever the veterans might have thought about the city's immigrant population, the Citizens' campaign flopped; clearly the leadership of the Strike was just as "British" as the Citizens' Committee and working-class soldiers' hopes for the future differed little from the strikers.

This broadening of the struggle in Winnipeg reflects the fact that the conflict was much more than a strike. Those at the heart of it—those in the metal and building trades—were only the catalyst. They had unleashed a wave of anger and hope that cannot be explained by a relatively small group of workers' demands for the right to collective bargaining. The thousands of immigrant workers in the North End, toiling in precarious jobs, where the chances of forming and sustaining a union were remote, readily joined in a battle alongside skilled "British" workers who had, in many ways, effectively collaborated in their marginalization both before and during the war. Returned soldiers, who might be assumed to feel alienated from those who had avoided the horrors of Flanders and who had, in many cases, taken their jobs, readily sprang to the support of the struggle. This was, in effect, an urban working-class uprising, uniting people across divides old and new—across distinctions of skill, ethnicity, and (particularly important at this moment) activity during the war. Just as importantly, as an uprising of working-class families and neighbourhoods, it reached across genders. The participation of women both as wage workers and as nonwage workers was crucial to the success of the Strike. Women activists such as Helen Armstrong and Edith Hancox organized on many fronts, from building new unions, to helping feed strikers and speaking to diverse audiences explaining and advancing the broader struggle. In mid-June, the "Soldiers' Parliament" lauded the women strikers. Recognizing the struggle for "equal pay for equal work," J.S. Woodsworth, who had just arrived in Winnipeg to support the Strike, declared that "this strike was part of the great movement for the emancipation of women."[8] Without pretending that the Strike overcame racism or misogyny, the social disruption of the Strike, the breaking of quotidian practices, the assumption of new roles, and the possibility of a working-class future opened up such hierarchies to new questions. In this way, the Strike represented a truly revolutionary moment.

The Citizens' Committee definitely saw a revolutionary threat. While their use of the word was certainly hyperbolic, they were not wrong in thinking their world was threatened. Under the direction of A.J. Andrews, they set out in the third week of June to extinguish the threat. Acting under dubious legal authority, Andrews organized the arrests of R.B. Russell, William Ivens, John Queen, A.A. Heaps, Roger Bray, and George Armstrong in the early hours of 17 June; R.J. Johns was arrested shortly afterwards in Montreal and W.A. Pritchard in Calgary. All were charged with seditious conspiracy. Although all were well-known radicals, only Russell was an official member of the Strike leadership. Also arrested were five non-British immigrants: Mike Verenczuk (a victim of mistaken identity), Michael Charitonoff, Moses Almazoff, Oscar Schoppelrei, and Samuel Blumenberg. For Andrews, it seems, they served to validate the Citizens' narrative that "aliens" were behind the uprising.

On the evening of 20 June, the returned soldiers' committee (now deprived of its chairperson, Roger Bray) met and determined to stage a "silent parade" on Main Street the following afternoon . . . "Bloody Saturday." As the crowd gathered in preparation to march, members of the Royal North West Mounted Police (RNWMP) charged on horseback. On their third foray through the crowd, they fired their revolvers, killing two. They were soon backed up by "Specials," armed with batons, who advanced on the crowd trapping and beating marchers. Soon, army vehicles carrying Lewis machine guns were stationed through downtown Winnipeg. James Winning, the WTLC president, dubbed the attack "another Peterloo," referencing the murderous assault on unarmed working-class protesters in Manchester, England, who were calling for the expansion of democratic rights in the summer of 1819—exactly a century earlier.[9]

Within days, the Strike was called off and attention turned to the closing scene of the drama: the trials. A.J. Andrews had successfully lobbied the Borden government to change the Immigration Act to allow for the rapid deportation of British subjects born outside of Canada, but in the end opted for a public, criminal trial on the charge of seditious conspiracy. The intent was to publicly try and condemn those arrested, not for their role in the Strike, but for their radical ideas. Houses and offices were raided across Canada, books and letters seized, all to provide evidence of treasonous intent. The defendant—in what was to amount to show trials aimed at public consumption—would be socialism.

The prosecution was successful in obtaining guilty verdicts,[10] in large part due to a tainted rural jury that had been secretly screened by the RNWMP and the McDonald Detective Agency, and the defendants received prison sentences, in most cases, of one year. They failed to convict prostrike member of the provincial legislature Fred Dixon on charges of seditious libel for his role in editing the *Western Labor News* following the arrest of William Ivens; similar charges against J.S. Woodsworth were subsequently dropped. Despite the convictions, the attempt to demonize the defendants' ideas failed badly. The accused used the trials to mount a spirited and erudite defence of labour radicalism, socialism, and traditional "British" rights and liberties. The lengthy addresses to the jury by William Pritchard and Fred Dixon were published as pamphlets and found their way into countless working-class homes in Winnipeg and beyond. So too did a book-length history of the Strike, published by the defence committee established to support the accused, which publicized not only the events of the Strike, but the radicalism that echoed at the Calgary Western Labour Conference and in the Walker Theatre. On the streets of Winnipeg, labour continued to march, reminding the bosses: "Prison Bars Cannot Confine Ideas."

Now working-class heroes, George Armstrong, William Ivens, and John Queen were elected to the Manitoba legislature while still in prison, joined there by Fred Dixon and seven other Labour members. Not all labour activists agreed on the lessons of the Strike, or the way forward, and former strikers set out in a number of directions: the One Big Union, the nascent Communist Party, and the new Independent Labour Party (as well as the established unions) all became significant forces in attempting to forge a new direction for Winnipeg workers. Collectively, working-class families and neighbourhoods proudly claimed the legacy of the Winnipeg General Strike as they built upon their experiences in 1919 to construct the diverse working-class cultures and struggles that would come to define Winnipeg.

......

As an important and singular event in Canadian and world history, the Winnipeg General Strike sits at the centre of this volume. It can only be understood, though, in the context of a vastly broader wave of mass strikes and revolutions that exploded in the closing days of the First World War. In this context, Europe commands the lion's share of attention. The Russian Revolution, of course, deeply shaped the entirety of the twentieth century. As well, events such as revolutionary uprisings in Germany and Hungary, the Biennio Rosso—the Two Red Years—in Italy, as well as the rise of mass Communist Parties on that continent collectively redefined working-class politics and activism. The literature regarding these developments is vast and continues to grow. We have chosen to examine the Winnipeg Strike in the context of the Americas, considering ways in which our understanding of the city, the nation, and the hemisphere can combine to pose new questions and suggest new ways forward in our exploration of both the Winnipeg Strike and the broader Workers' Revolt.

To this end, the editors have chosen to begin the volume with a careful reconsideration of the historiography of the Winnipeg General Strike (Chapter 1), exploring the evolution of the perceptions of the event and the ways in which evolving research, insights, and perspectives have enriched our understanding over the course of a century. As Canada's largest and most famous event of class confrontation, the Strike's meaning is important to the understanding of the nature and politics of class in the country's history. As we explain in this chapter, the long tendency to categorize the events of 1919 Winnipeg in a "strike or revolution" binary inhibited more complex analyses of the ways in which working-class ideas were in rapid flux and what this meant for systems of gender, race, and ethnicity. In the closing decades of the twentieth century, historians broadened the lens through which they viewed the Strike but, as this volume hopes to demonstrate, there remains much to be done. The contributions here point—each in their own way—to significant and promising avenues forward.

Very importantly, considering the Strike in its hemispheric context makes visible the common history of settler colonialism. As we hoped to emphasize in the brief overview with which we began this Introduction, the events of 1919 took place within a contested space, only recently subject to imperial expropriation and even more recently urbanized and industrialized. This has not, and still does not, inform writing on the Workers' Revolt. Adele Perry (Chapter 2) seeks to begin to correct this, raising the issue of Indigenous peoples' labour and placing the event within the context of settler–Indigenous relations.

Historians of the Winnipeg General Strike have long acknowledged the crucial and volatile role played by large numbers of recently demobilized soldiers returned from the battlefields of Europe, as well as the importance of "immigrant" (meaning, in early twentieth-century Canada, non-British) workers in the Strike. In narratives of the Strike, both groups are identified as important, but remain marginal and somewhat out of focus. David Thompson's (Chapter 3) careful study of several prostrike soldier activists helps to explain the motivations and nature of their participation in the struggle. His insights identify the nuanced and shifting sentiments of the soldiers, a process that was apparent everywhere as working-class people reevaluated their worldviews and felt their own collective power. Of course, one of the key issues for veterans—certainly one which the Citizens' Committee and some of the conservative leaders of some veterans' organizations pushed to the forefront in hopes of winning the returned men over to the antistrike side—was the place of non-British "dangerous foreigners" in both the labour movement and the workplace. On this front, Henry Trachtenberg (Chapter 4) examines the dynamics of Winnipeg's Jewish community during the Strike, providing valuable insight into the intersection of class and ethnicity at a moment when the significance and meaning of both were being contested. The very notion of the "Workers' Revolt" implies that battle lines were drawn across lines of class. We know that, in practice, class does not exist in isolation from other social identities and hierarchies, and Trachtenberg allows us to view this dynamic as, in this case, class came to prevail over allegiances of religion and ethnicity within an important active and politicized community.

As the editors explain in the first chapter, the past few decades have brought an increased understanding of Winnipeg's place within the broader labour uprising of this period. While an earlier generation of historians attributed the revolt to specifically Western Canadian conditions, close examinations by Mikhail Bjorge of developments in Edmonton (Chapter 5) and by Tom Langford of the Crowsnest Pass (Chapter 6) demonstrate the complexity of the region. In each case, large numbers of radicalized workers vocally identified with the struggle in Winnipeg, but they also faced difficult challenges both from within and without the labour movement. These studies allow us to understand both the remarkable nature of solidarity and its points of vulnerability. In the end, they act as implicit counterpoints to Winnipeg; large numbers of workers shared many of the same sentiments, but their enemies proved capable of stifling the movement.

Two chapters on Montreal—by Geoffrey Ewen (Chapter 7) on a civic workers' strike in 1918 and Benoit Marsan (Chapter 8) on unemployed workers' struggles—similarly invite fruitful comparisons to Winnipeg. On one hand, the parallels are obvious; Winnipeg's 1918 civic workers' strike is well understood as setting the stage for the grander confrontation the following year, and unemployment, or the fear of unemployment, was an overwhelming, if understudied, feature of demobilization at the end of the war. But the chapters help us look at these common features in a different manner. Most notably, the stories Ewen and Marsan tell are about crowd activity; the stage, in Montreal, is overwhelming the street, a place controlled neither by business nor labour leaders. The streets of Winnipeg were alive too, from the "riot" of 10 June, to the marches of the returned soldiers, to regular street confrontation in working-class neighbourhoods like Weston. How can we read such activity and what role did it play in the mass strike in Winnipeg?

Working-class struggles exploded in the United States in this same period as massive strikes swept the nation, including by 400,000 coal miners and almost as many steel workers. About four million U.S. workers struck that year. The uprising was met with waves of repression led by Attorney General A. Mitchell Palmer and stringent immigration restrictions. As well, the deadly and widespread white-supremacist violence against African Americans in the summer of 1919 cannot be separated from the anxieties of postwar unemployment and rising anti-radicalism. Certainly, connections with and comparisons to the United States can provide insight. Jeff Stilley's study of the 1918 Kansas City Strike (Chapter 9) is particularly useful in this regard as he draws out questions of gender and race in ways that have not been adequately explored in Canada. He also provides interesting perspectives on the breakdown of alliances between middle-class Progressive-era reformers and the working class when the latter took dramatic action on its own behalf. Cal Winslow visits the other truly monumental general strike (besides Winnipeg's) in this period—Seattle's. Even in 1919, Seattle and Winnipeg were often spoken of in the same breath, and it is important not to think of them in isolation. Joel Wolfe's sweeping assessment of workers' movements throughout the Americas (Chapter 11) ties much of this together. He leads us to view the ideology, strike activity, racial tensions, and the war-induced social dislocations through a refreshing lens that brings to light several important connections.

As all of these contributions recognize, class conflict is never just about the workers. Gregory Kealey (Chapter 12) and Myer Siemiatycki (Chapter 13) explore the ways in which capital and the state restructured themselves to deal with the challenge of labour. Kealey sees the Workers' Revolt as provoking a rethinking and reorganization of Canada's police powers while Siemiatycki delves into the various ways in which business and government manoeuvred to defeat the uprising through less directly repressive means, particularly through the co-optation and support of more conservative trade union leaders. While the focus of the best studies of labour in this period seek to explain how the working-class was remade, these two studies provide a glimpse into the processes by which the state evolved in response to the challenges from below.

A historic confrontation such as the Winnipeg General Strike, of course, has significant meaning in social memory. The centenary of the event in 2019 demonstrated clearly how its meaning has shifted over time and within different contexts. This has never been carefully charted and explained. Sharon Reilly (Chapter 14) traces the public history of the Winnipeg General Strike, touching on local and national manifestations and interpretations, while David Frank (Chapter 15) focuses on specific productions and installations marking the 100th anniversary to consider how the Strike is portrayed on a wider stage today. Together they demonstrate the ways in which the Strike does not solely reside in the past.

The various chapters in this volume each make important contributions to our understanding of the Winnipeg General Strike and the wider Workers' Revolt. In many cases, the themes overlap, as contributors consider the unevenness and complexity of workers' radicalization, the legacy of older divisions of gender, ethnicity, race, Indigeneity, and skill, the relative power of rank-and-file, street-level militancy, and the ability of capital and the state—along with conservative labour leaders—to remake themselves in the face of new challenges. In a final chapter (Chapter 16), the editors take stock and look ahead. Where do we stand in our understanding of the Strike? How can we incorporate the insights of the scholars in this book and elsewhere to better understand the events of 1919, the ways in which social hierarchies were challenged (or not), and their consequences for Winnipeg and beyond? What will the history of the great uprising of 100 years ago look like in the twenty-first century?

Notes

1 For a detailed discussion of the ways in which historians have interpreted the Strike, see Chapter 1, infra. Readers will note that what follows in this introduction has been only lightly referenced. This is by design. Those seeking detailed information on sources—both primary and secondary—will find them in abundance in the following chapters.

2 Any such list would include Hugh John Macdonald, son of Canada's first prime minister, John A. Macdonald. Hugh John briefly served as premier of Manitoba in 1899 and, at the time of the Strike, as a police magistrate who played an active role in policing "aliens" and strikers. He had participated in the Wolseley Expedition of 1870 to put down the Red River Rebellion. He moved to Winnipeg permanently in 1882 and then served as an officer in the 90th Battalion, Winnipeg Rifles during the North-West Resistance. In the same vein, A.J. Andrews, the undisputed leader of the antistrike forces in 1919, had come to Winnipeg in 1880 and took a break from his law studies in 1885 to serve in the 95th Manitoba Grenadiers during the North-West Resistance. Another interesting example was James Ashdown, one of Winnipeg's first millionaires, one-time mayor of the city and one of the leaders of Winnipeg's social, political, and economic elite. He had participated in the Red River Rebellion as a vociferous foe of Riel in 1869–70.

3 Norman Penner, ed., *Winnipeg 1919: The Strikers' Own History of the Winnipeg General Strike* (Toronto: Lorimer, 2019), 29.

4 "Wonderful Organizing Wave Sweeps City," *Western Labor News*, 19 May 1919.

5 "4,000 Workers Hear Cassidy Talk on the O.B.U.," *Western Labor News*, 9 May 1919. The text of the article reports between four and five thousand present.

6 Michael Butt, "'To Each According to His Need, and From Each According to His Ability. Why Cannot the World See This?': The Politics of William Ivens, 1916–1936" (MA thesis, University of Winnipeg, 1993), 113.

7 Benjamin Isitt, *From Victoria to Vladivostok: Canada's Siberian Expedition, 1917–19* (Vancouver: UBC Press, 2010).

8 Cited in Penner, *Winnipeg 1919*, 142.

9 Penner, *Winnipeg 1919*, 199.

10 The only individual charged with seditious conspiracy who was not convicted was Alderman A.A. Heaps, who had conducted his own defence.

1

"Strike or Revolution" Redux: The Historiography of the Winnipeg General Strike

James Naylor, Rhonda L. Hinther, and Jim Mochoruk

How do we make sense of the Winnipeg General Strike? Strikers, opponents, scholars, activists, public historians, and community members have all documented and proffered varied impressions and interpretations of "the Strike." This is a much-deserved level of attention given the event's scope and significance, both at the time and beyond. In addition to being the most substantive singular demonstration of working-class resistance in Canadian history, the Strike would rapidly become (and continues to be) one of the moments (if it can be reduced to a "moment") most discussed, debated, and commemorated in Canadian labour history. In this chapter, we explore the contours of the 1919 Winnipeg General Strike's scholarly and popular historiography.

Two of the core interpretations and historiographic traditions surrounding the events in Winnipeg in 1919 were enshrined early; indeed, just days after the Strike commenced. From the first edition of the *Western Labor News'* (*WLN*) "Special Strike Edition" (17 May 1919), the leaders of the Strike put forward their view that this dramatic, city-wide withdrawal of labour was just that: a strike for clearly identifiable, and traditional, trade union demands—the right to collective bargaining, a living wage, and improved working conditions.[1] Within two days the Strike Committee's major opponent, the Citizens' Committee of 1000, began publishing its own paper—the *Citizen*—which offered up the vision of the Strike as an incipient revolution, launched by a cadre of dangerous radicals and foreigners in order to (mis)lead Canadian workers into supporting a "Bolshevik" style revolution that would overthrow the existing social order if not stopped immediately.[2]

Winnipeg's daily newspapers, the *Free Press*, the *Tribune,* and the *Telegram,* all joined the interpretive fray once they had been able to restart publication after the initial shutdown of their operations on 15 May. They, and the vast majority of the Canadian and American newspapers who provided coverage of the Strike, tended to echo the tone and views of the antistrike *Citizen*—adding colour and depth to the portrayal of the Strike as a revolutionary situation linked to radicals and enemy aliens.[3] Just as importantly, the successors to both the General Strike Committee and the Citizens' Committee deepened their respective interpretations of the "real" meaning and purposes of the Strike in a flurry of poststrike publications. On behalf of the strikers' "side" there were several publications put forward by the Winnipeg Defence Committee (essentially the reconstituted leadership of the Central Strike Committee). Most significant among these was *"Saving the World From Democracy": The Winnipeg General Sympathetic Strike, May–June, 1919.*[4] Published in the aftermath of the trials of the Strike leaders—but in time for the provincial election of 1920—this substantial work joined several other Defence Committee publications: Fred Dixon's *Address to the Jury in Defence of Freedom of Speech*; Bill Pritchard's *Address to the Jury*; and W.H. Truman's, *The Russell Trial and Labour's Rights.*[5] All three were published in 1920 and, like the speaking tours of the Strike leaders before their trials began and the lengthier *Saving the World From Democracy*, the purpose of these pamphlets was severalfold. First, they disseminated the core interpretation of the Strike as a peaceful and appropriate withdrawal of labour power occasioned by difficult economic times and wartime sacrifices by workers—problems which had been ignored by uncaring and authoritarian governments and profit-mongering employers. Second, they also stressed the violation of core British civil and legal rights by the authorities and the Citizens' Committee both during and after the Strike. Finally, they were sold in order to raise money for the legal costs of the defendants and to provide funding for the support of the imprisoned men's families.

The Citizens' Committee of 1000, having broken the Strike—with more than a little aid from the federal government—were less inclined to take up the pen in the aftermath of the Strike. There was only one publication forthcoming from the "victors" in the battle against revolution and dangerous foreigners: *The Activities and Organizations of the Citizens' Committee of One Thousand, in Connection with the Winnipeg Strike, May–June, 1919.*[6] Perhaps it was felt that the less said the better; in this work only the most prosaic of details on fighting this "apprehended revolution," and certainly few names of antistrike leaders, were given—this was always a tightly kept secret. Besides, in the aftermath of the Strike, many of the Citizens' Committee's most articulate voices were too busy drawing up the prosecution plans for the Strike trials and then actually leading the (largely) successful prosecutions (for which they were handsomely compensated)[7] to spend much time writing about the Strike.

The original newspaper reports and the follow-up publications of the Winnipeg Defence Committee and the Citizens' Committee have provided much of the grist for the historian's mill. They, along with the preliminary hearing and trial reports of those arrested for their roles in the Strike, constituted the most important set of readily accessible primary sources for what had happened in Winnipeg in May and June of 1919.[8] But there were two other sources that quickly became available. The report of the Mathers inquiry into industrial relations in Canada—which had held hearings in Winnipeg just before the Strike began in May—was released in July of 1919 and can be viewed as a type of background report on the grievances of the working classes in Winnipeg and elsewhere.[9] Its findings certainly offered considerable support for the key complaints of Winnipeg workers, even though Winnipeg's organized labour movement had declined to attend or testify at the hearings. Even more significant is the Robson report, the result of the provincially appointed *Royal Commission to Enquire into and Report upon the Causes and Effects of the General Strike Which Recently Existed in the City of Winnipeg.*[10] Released in 1920—but delayed until after the trials of the Strike leaders had been concluded—this report and its attendant testimony has been a treasure trove for historians.

Unlike the newspaper pieces and the court proceedings, both of these reports were far less polemical in nature. To be sure, the two judges who headed these inquiries were not without strong views—neither could tolerate the One Big Union (OBU) and overtly radical labour leaders—but overall, they conducted their work with considerable open-mindedness. What is interesting about these two reports, however, is that neither received much attention when they were first delivered. As Tom Mitchell has recently pointed out, the Robson report in particular was largely ignored by the press when it was first released in 1920 and was not really utilized to any great extent until the late 1940s.[11] But it is worthwhile noting that both of these reports came down on the interpretive side of the Winnipeg General Strike as an action aimed at securing labour's right to collective bargaining, a living wage, and improved working conditions.

It is not very often that the core historiography of such a major event remains so consistent—and so tightly linked to the newspapers' "first draft of history"—for such a long time. It is quite remarkable that the rhetoric of the leadership of the two opposing camps should so completely dominate the interpretation of this event for so long. Indeed, it is no exaggeration to say that the strikers' and the Citizens' Committee's overtly polemical and partisan newspapers set forth the interpretive framework that would define the historiography for fifty years. It is not surprising, then, that when the first scholarly work on the Strike was published in 1950, its penultimate chapter was simply entitled "Strike or Revolution." And even when scholarly interest in labour history in general, and Winnipeg's great sympathetic strike in particular, took off in the 1960s and 1970s, the core question still seemed to be: was the Winnipeg General Strike a strike or an apprehended revolution?

The answer to this question seemed straightforward enough to the historians who first seriously approached this topic. The scholarly consensus—constructed by D.C. Masters in 1950,[12] and built upon in the early 1970s by Kenneth McNaught,[13] Norman Penner (precisely echoing the Strike leaders by republishing their 1920 history of the Strike),[14] and most notably, David Bercuson[15]—was that this was a strike conducted primarily for the "traditional" goals of organized labour: the right to collective bargaining, a living wage, and improved working conditions. So, for more than half a century, the core historiographic debate had shifted very little. To be sure, these scholars added much to our knowledge of the Strike, its context, and particularly the views and beliefs of the leaders on both sides. Bercuson's work was especially rich in detail and not only became the go-to work on the Strike but added (along with Ross McCormack's separate work on the western Canadian radical movement[16]) the trope of western exceptionalism to the interpretive framework. In essence, western exceptionalism maintained that class relations on the "frontier" were immature and rougher than those in more established regions. The assumption behind this was that mature societies naturally developed institutions that eased social functions, thereby creating a stable social order—a common belief among mainstream social theorists in the 1950s and 1960s. This led historians like Bercuson to reify and exaggerate regional distinctions in class relations.[17]

Thus, we come again to this basic point: from May 1919 until well over half a century later there was really only one major debate over the Strike—and that was resolved in favour of "moderate" labour's view of the Strike being all about winning the right to collective bargaining and decent wages and working conditions. There was, of course, at least one other interpretive strain that had developed (in addition to the trope of western exceptionalism), revolving around another seemingly simple question: was the Winnipeg General Strike a total failure? On the one hand it was hard to deny that when the Strike was called off on 26 June, Winnipeg's working class, and the entire Canadian working class for that matter, had sustained serious losses. The core demands that had precipitated the Strike vote in the first place were not met: the right to collective bargaining was not extended to more workers; many strikers were blacklisted and were never allowed to return to their places of employment; some of those who did return to their old jobs found that they had lost their seniority, their pension rights, and other benefits, and were often required to sign "yellow-dog" contracts. Beyond this, in 1920–21 several of the Strike's leaders were imprisoned and the labour movement was engaging in renewed internecine quarrels between traditional craft unionists and those who believed in industrial unionism. Meanwhile, immigrant workers, particularly radical ones—be they eastern European or British born—could now be more easily "shovelled" out of the country owing to the federal government's strike-related decision to amend the Immigration Act. By the same token, a strike-related amendment to the Criminal Code of Canada (originally Section 97a and 97b, but later combined into the infamous Section 98) dramatically curtailed the civil liberties of all Canadians, but particularly those who challenged the existing social order.[18] Emboldened by the "victory" of the Citizens' Committee and the federal government in Winnipeg, and determined to prevent another apprehended revolution from breaking out in their backyards, governments and businesses all across Canada launched a new labour relations regime that would work against the interests of the working class throughout the interwar period. But was it possible that there was some sort of silver lining? For Bercuson the answer was simple: the Winnipeg General Strike was a major defeat, pure and simple. However, that conclusion—and certainly a sound one from the standpoint of an industrial relations analysis—would soon be challenged.

But before considering this academic challenge, something of an anomaly needs to be noted. It is a truism that Winnipeg's political life was deeply bifurcated along geographic and class lines both before and particularly after the Winnipeg General Strike and would remain so for the next quarter century. In some narratives the intellectual and political descendants of the Strike Committee and of the Citizens' Committee of 1000 waged a symbolic reenactment of the Strike every election season throughout this entire period. The "North End" of Winnipeg became synonymous with a strong left-wing orientation, including electoral support for Communist candidates at every level of government.[19] But there was also continuous support for other overtly pro-labour candidates in the working-class enclaves of the city, including former Strike leader A.A. Heaps and, most famously, the (briefly serving and quickly arrested) replacement editor of the *Western Labor News*, J.S. Woodsworth. Meanwhile, another former Strike leader, John Queen, would go on to become the mayor of Winnipeg for several terms, and labour representatives came very close to controlling Winnipeg City Council—prevented from doing so only by the most overt gerrymandering imaginable. Historian J.E. Rea studied this phenomenon with considerable care in the 1970s[20] and, along with a cadre of talented University of Manitoba graduate students such as Brian McKillop and David Hall,[21] documented the political ethos of Winnipeg proving, among other things, that the truism was in fact true: in the aftermath of the Strike the politics of class dominated the city's political life.

However, despite the profound and long-lasting divide between the inheritors of this class-based political struggle, something rather peculiar needs to be observed: one could grow up in Winnipeg well into the post–Second World War era and never have the Winnipeg General Strike impinge upon one's consciousness. For many decades, there were no statues, no plaques, and no physical reminders left in place. Both the James Street Labour Temple, where the Strike Committee met, and the adjacent Victoria Park, where the strikers and returned soldiers held their large open-air meetings and where the Labour Church held massive services during the Strike, were physically removed from the cityscape—the park in 1924 and the labour temple in 1966. In effect, no form of commemoration whatsoever was left to help tell the tale of this signal event in the city's history. Not until 1969—the fiftieth anniversary of the Strike—was there any sort of recognition of the Strike in a public space—and that was a simple plaque donated by the United Steelworkers of America that was grudgingly placed at Winnipeg's City Hall. It said, quite simply: "In Honour of the People of Winnipeg Whose Sacrifice for Union Recognition Helped Millions of Canadians Win the Benefits of Collective Bargaining." Meanwhile, one could attend school and proceed from kindergarten to Grade 12 in either official language in Manitoba (as did all three editors of this collection) and never learn that the province's capital city had been the site of North America's greatest general strike, or that mounted police had charged into a crowd on Main Street, or that machine-gun-bearing vehicles had patrolled the streets of downtown Winnipeg. Unless one came from a labour or socialist family—where memories of this event were kept alive—the odds were that you never heard a word about the Winnipeg General Strike until—or rather if—you got to university and happened to take a class in Canadian history where the Strike received mention. Clearly, the people who ran the city, the inheritors of the mantle of the Citizens' Committee of 1000, wanted all memory of what they would have viewed as "negative heritage" erased—and they were incredibly successful at this for many years.[22] It has often been observed that despite the losses associated with the Strike, the verdict of history has been quite kind to the striking women and men of 1919—reversing the dictum that the victors always write the history. And that is certainly true in an academic sense, as almost every scholarly contribution on the history and legacy of the Strike has tended to be quite favourable to the strikers and equally hostile to the Citizens' Committee of 1000. But for many decades the political, economic and social descendants of the Citizens had succeeded in suppressing the public memory of the Winnipeg General Strike just as effectively as their ancestors had suppressed the Strike itself.

But this brings us back to the academic interpretation of the Strike, and particularly to David Bercuson's contribution to this interpretation. Although virtually everyone acknowledged the excellence of his research, not everyone was satisfied with either his approach or all of his conclusions. Just as his monumental *Confrontation at Winnipeg* was published in 1974, a new group of Canadian scholars was arising: a group whose goal was to present a nuanced set of accounts of working-class life and culture in Canada.[23] Inspired by the social and cultural history approaches that had been developing in Great Britain and the United States in the 1950s and 1960s, most notably the work of the British Marxist historians and American historians of both labour and African-American slavery,[24] these historians wanted to move away from the older industrial relations model of labour history.[25] And, while few of them specialized in Winnipeg or even western Canadian history, they recognized in Bercuson's work a continuation of a much older tradition of writing labour history; a tradition that did not fit well with their desire to write about more than the history of trade unions, their leaders, and labour's place in a capitalist society. At the risk of extreme reductionism, those who were engaged in the new labour history wanted to write about the entire working class—male and female, skilled and unskilled, organized and unorganized, Anglo-Celtic and "other." For many of these practitioners the goal was to write history from the bottom up and to focus upon the formation of a distinct working-class culture—not only in the workplace or on the picket line, but in working-class homes and neighbourhoods, in the formal and informal gathering places of working-class families, and in the broader associational lives of workers and their kin.

But this was not the limit of their interpretive differences with the older approach. Collectively the new labour historians rejected the parochialism they believed to be inherent in a western exceptionalist argument (i.e., that western Canadian workers were less conservative than their eastern counterparts and more inclined to radicalism at least partly because the western capitalists with whom they had to contend were so much more aggressive and uncompromising than their better-established eastern counterparts). As several of these scholars specialized in central Canadian and Maritime labour history, they were well equipped to challenge the notion that eastern Canadian workers were inherently more conservative than their western counterparts. They were also more likely to place working-class history in a much broader context; indeed, in an international context. And to say the least, the broader context of the dying days of the First World War and the immediate postwar era was truly remarkable: the October Revolution in Russia, the rise of the Spartacists in Germany, a revolution in Hungary, the growing radicalization of the Italian workers' movement, the rapid development of worker discontent and strikes all across North America—including a General Strike in Seattle and the policemen's strike in Boston—and growing clashes between workers and authorities everywhere (or so it seemed) in the Americas and Europe. Revolution and worker militance seemed to be the order of the day: America's "Red Scare" didn't need to spill over the border—it was already here. No wonder the Citizens' Committee and federal government were so worried!

What did all of this mean for the historiography of the Winnipeg General Strike? Well, in the first instance the Strike was put into a different national context. Winnipeg, while certainly an important case, was not the only site of contestation; rather, it was argued that the events in Winnipeg needed to be seen as part of the great postwar "Workers' Revolt" that stretched not only across much of Canada and the United States but throughout much of the capitalist world. This was already apparent, in 1969, to the University of Manitoba economic historian Clare Pentland who, writing in the radical Winnipeg-based magazine *Canadian Dimension*, recognized the city's General Strike as "one of the great class-confrontations of capitalist history . . . even without counting the . . . often massive" general strikes across the country that spring.[26] As Nolan Reilly put it, describing the outcome of a 1983 symposium (held in the lead-up to the sixty-fifth anniversary of the Strike): "a consensus emerged that Winnipeg was only the tip of an iceberg of class conflict that stretched from Nova Scotia to British Columbia. Although the intensity and institutional form of conflict varied somewhat across the country, workers in no one region were found to be exceptionally radical or conservative in their response to the post–First World War crisis. This line of reasoning marked a significant revision of the historiography and popular thinking on the 1919 General Strike."[27] Reilly's comments were a clear-cut rebuke to the western exceptionalist argument that had been used to explain why Winnipeg's workers had taken such dramatic—and potentially costly—action in May and June of 1919.

But just as importantly, even as the broader "Workers' Revolt" theme was being developed with considerable success,[28] several other avenues of research were opened up. Ironically, the question of who "won" and who "lost" in this strike was not really the central issue that Professor Bercuson would later make it out to be.[29] Indeed, although he would argue that the Marxist labour and social historians who had come to dominate the writing of Canadian labour history by the early 1980s saw Winnipeg 1919 as a worker's victory, one would be hard pressed to find any such conclusion in the works of the historians who examined the Strike. Rather, there was a notable tendency to see the very real defeats of the Strike balanced by a growth in working-class solidarity (if only for a few brief moments), by important working-class challenges to the ethnic and gender exclusivity that had characterized the prestrike labour movement and by a growing awareness of the power of the working class in a political and economic sense. These were, however, far from claims of an overt working-class victory.

What was really happening was that even though the broader context of a workers' revolt was taken as a given by most scholars, many historians were engaged in drilling down into ever greater levels of detail and complexity, often taking as their focus not necessarily the Strike itself, but examining the event as part of broader histories of labour migration and "ethnic" community formation, activism, and worker solidarity. From the 1970s and 1980s onward, scholars such as Donald Avery, Orest Martynowych, Roz Usiskin, Henry Trachtenberg, Morris Mott, Art Grenke, and several others were paying careful attention to the ethnic communities which supplied the so-called "dangerous foreigners" who were so reviled by the Citizens' Committee of 1000, by the mainstream press, and by not a few of the Anglo-Celtic strikers and "returned men."[30] Others, meanwhile, were busily revisiting the ideas of several of the most prominent male Strike leaders and their strategies. For example, Gerald Friesen wrote on R.B. Russell and the Socialist Party of Canada while Allen Mills produced important works on F.J.

Dixon and J.S. Woodsworth.[31] Mildred and Harry Gutkin's *Profiles in Dissent: The Shaping of Radical Thought in the Canadian West* included profiles of several of the key Strike leaders. And MA student Eric Angel made a fascinating contribution to the literature when he analyzed the role of picketing—and certain forms of violence and threatened violence—in order to challenge the traditional narrative of the Strike as a completely peaceful event (on the side of the strikers, that is).[32]

By the mid-1980s, the field of women's history began influencing the Winnipeg General Strike's historiography as feminist labour historians began asking different questions about the event, as they were elsewhere about other historical moments and their impact on, and the involvement of, women. As such, women and their engagement with the Strike began receiving some specific, albeit still relatively scant, attention. In 1986, Mary Horodyski published the first and, to date, still the most detailed analysis of the role of women—on both sides—in the Strike.[33] Linda Kealey's work has been likewise important, examining women's labour activism as part of the more expansive labour revolt of 1919 (and well before). Though not her main focus, Kealey provides some specific treatment of women's participation in the Winnipeg General Strike, carefully and usefully situating it within the broader context of women's socialist and labour activism in Canada in the late nineteenth and first two decades of the twentieth centuries. Because of Kealey and others, especially well-documented is Strike leader Helen Armstrong. Mildred and Harry Gutkin's 1997 *Profiles in Dissent* includes a chapter on Armstrong, the only one in the book expressly focused on a woman.[34] Paula Kelly's work for her engaging and important 2001 film, *The Notorious Mrs. Armstrong*, has helped to illuminate further Armstrong's practical and intellectual leadership and labour for the Strike effort. Kelly has noted the difficulties of carrying out research on Armstrong, a circumstance that underscores broader challenges inherent to investigating women's history of the Strike. Armstrong, despite her seemingly larger-than-life presence during the Strike, "had devolved into little more than a footnote in the pages of Manitoba history" while "much scholarship and popular opinion had been expended on an analysis of the male leadership of the Strike and their subsequent role in provincial and federal politics."[35] David Thompson agrees, noting in his 2020 article on Strike leader Edith Hancox that "in spite of their pivotal roles in the confrontation . . . the pro-strike heroines of those tumultuous six weeks have largely remained anonymous . . . hidden by the very repressions of the capitalistic patriarchy they challenged." Thompson's work on Hancox makes another much-needed contribution to the still relatively limited historiography of women and the Strike. His study is one with broader implications, offering "a reminder that Canada's interwar Left was not monolithically male and that we ought to re-examine the diversity of women who, notwithstanding considerable restraints, thrived there."[36] Arguably, in spite of what we know about "women worthies" like Armstrong and Hancox, the opening paragraph of Horodyski's 1986 piece still rings true today: "The historiography of the Strike has been male-centered, and like all history which refuses to include women and renders them invisible, it has been severely biased and incomplete."[37]

Clearly, beginning in the 1970s much new work has been done that has enhanced our understanding of the Winnipeg General Strike and the broader milieu in which it occurred. It is also the case that in addition to the works cited above on political matters, ethnic groups, women, ideology, and the role of the state, one could see by the 1990s that once again new approaches were being applied to the Strike. For example, in 1993, Chad Reimer's Gramscian analysis of the discourses of the strikers and their opponents challenged us to reexamine the language of nationalism, of patriotism, of "war time sacrifice" and of "Britishness" as it was utilized by participants and observers on both sides of the Strike.[38]

By the 1990s, a much broader and more nuanced understanding of both the Winnipeg Strike and its place in a pan-Canadian context found its place in *The Workers' Revolt in Canada, 1917–1925*. Edited by Craig Heron, the volume brought together historians from across the country to carefully explore workers' activity both regionally and nationally and confirmed Gregory Kealey's arguments first made at the 1983 Winnipeg symposium regarding the national breadth of the uprising.[39] More than that, the authors revealed much regarding the ways in which the experience of these events, although differing significantly by locality, gender, industry, and much more, also displayed remarkable similarities. Many of the elements explored in Tom Mitchell's and James Naylor's chapter in the book, entitled "The Prairies: In the Eye of the Storm," which largely focused on the Winnipeg Strike, were apparent almost everywhere. These included the construction and augmentation of more unitary working-class organizations including local Trades and Labour Councils, the willingness of many workers to push—or bypass—their established union leaderships if they were deemed inadequate to the task of effectively channelling workers' militancy, as well as an almost ubiquitous desire—expressed with varying degrees of political clarity—to remake society on the basis of human needs. Outcomes and experiences, of course, varied from place to place, but Mitchell and Naylor's identification of the emergence of a common class identity and vision in Winnipeg could be seen in countless locations in 1919. The words of Winnipeg's *Western Labor News* would not have sounded out of place in any industrial centre that year: "We have a historical mission to perform . . . Our basis of organization must broaden still further and develop until it establishes . . . a system where usefulness and not profit will be the basis of production."[40]

A notable feature of the historiography of the Strike had been its almost singular focus on the strikers. Legal scholars have begun to address this and, in doing so, have been helping to nuance our understanding of the Strike, making important contributions to the literature—most notably Jack Walker's 2004 work on the Strike trials.[41] Begun in the 1990s, Tom Mitchell's research on the Citizens' Committee of 1000 and its driving force, A.J. Andrews, would culminate in what is the single most important monograph on the General Strike since Bercuson's—2010's *When the State Trembled: How A.J. Andrews and the Citizens' Committee Broke the Winnipeg General Strike*, coauthored with Reinhold Kramer.[42] Of perhaps equal importance was the work that Gregory Kealey undertook to unlock the files of the mounted police. These files, obtained after changes to Canada's Freedom of Information Act in the 1980s, provided a treasure trove of spy and informers' reports as well as considerable data on the state's view of radicals.[43] And, although it was not specifically about the General Strike, Esyllt Jones's crucial work on the influenza epidemic in Winnipeg in the year prior to the Strike is absolutely germane to the topic. Her richly textured analysis of the course and impact of this pandemic not only makes clear how class and ethnic divisions intensified as a result of the pandemic, but also how the experience of the flu pandemic (paradoxically) strengthened the labour movement in Winnipeg on the eve of the Strike.[44]

To be fair, it must be highlighted that, with the exception of some of the works on "dangerous foreigners" and ethnicity noted above, most of what we know about the Winnipeg General Strike and its participants skews heavily Anglo-Celtic. Increasingly more and more scholars are challenging this. Sarah-Jane Mathieu's broader work on Black sleeping car porters includes important commentary documenting the members' of their union, the Order of Sleeping Car Porters, overt support for and participation in the Strike. This was done at great risk both for these men and their families, subject as they were to patterns of oppression wrought by the intersections of race, gender, and class. Nonetheless, as Mathieu notes in her 2010 book, "the Winnipeg General Strike emboldened black railroaders and confirmed their racial and working-class consciousness."[45] Recent work of scholars such as Adele Perry, Owen Toews, Evelyn Peters, and many others have begun to bring to bear not only the question of how one writes labour history in a city that included significant (though often seemingly invisible) First Nations and Métis populations (and where they have never been included in that history), but in particular how one writes that history in the context of a white settler colonialism in which non-Indigenous folks—capitalist and worker alike—never doubted for a moment terra nullius and "nation-building" narratives that justified a perceived inherent right to appropriate and use First Nations' lands and resources.[46] Clearly, much more research is needed to assess the everyday encounters of a variety of the rank-and-file women and men, especially Black, Indigenous, and peoples of colour, with the events of 1919. And, across all communities, more investigation of the roles of children and youth (many of whom would have been workers themselves) in the Winnipeg General Strike is crucial, as most of our knowledge of this sizable group in a demographically "young" city like Winnipeg is sorely limited and mostly anecdotal.

Because 2019 was the centennial of the Winnipeg General Strike, it is not surprising that a few new publications set out to synthesize the events of the Strike. Following in the tradition of some fine popular histories of the Strike, most notably Jack Bumsted's 1994 illustrated history,[47] long-time labour activist and writer Dennis Lewycky has published a new popular history of the Strike—*Magnificent Fight: The 1919 Winnipeg General Strike.*[48] And, in a truly innovative departure, the Graphic History Collective and David Lester have produced a graphic history of the General Strike that has already reached a large and diverse demographic—offering an easy-to-digest and yet hard-hitting analysis of Winnipeg in 1919.[49] Beyond these there have been scores of short pieces appearing in magazines, newspapers, and labour and socialist journals, outlining the events and offering interpretations of the ongoing legacy of this event for a broad, nonacademic audience.[50]

In much the same vein, with demands and support from labour organizations and several other agencies, the public history of the Winnipeg General Strike has exploded. Whereas Winnipeg had but one public acknowledgement of the Strike as late as 1969, fifty years later the same cannot be said: Winnipeg now has a series of plaques indicating key sites in the struggle—one commemorating the former James Avenue Labour Temple in the Concert Hall (which is roughly where the Labour Temple was located), one at the Provincial Legislature, and another at City Hall. Similarly, public historians, museum professionals, archivists, community activists, and others have worked to ensure artifacts and archival materials documenting the Strike are carefully preserved. Major collections of significance exist at the Manitoba Museum, the University of Manitoba Archives and Special Collections, the Winnipeg Fire Fighters Museum, the Winnipeg Police Museum, Library and Archives Canada, and the Canadian Museum of History (CMH). Numerous artifacts are also held privately; Paul Moist, retired national president of CUPE, has amassed perhaps the most significant collection outside a heritage institution. These collections have supported both temporary and permanent exhibitions on the Strike at the Manitoba Museum, the CMH, and elsewhere, engaging broad audiences by highlighting the events of the Strike through the display of special constable batons and armbands, "Permitted by Authority of Strike Committee" placards, labour songs, soundscapes, theatrical performances, period costumes, photographs, and recreated immersive environments (like the CMH's reconstructed Meeting Room #12 from the James Street Labour Temple), along with other elements.

Artists have also played critical roles in memorializing the Strike. Robert Kell's celebrated series of paintings on 1919 have been exhibited in venues across the country and individual works can be found in numerous private and public collections.[51] Public art installations also mark the event in important and dynamic ways. A massive steel structure commemorating the Strike and Winnipeg's workers was installed in 2017 at Lily Street and Market Avenue—a site of considerable significance and violence on Bloody Saturday. And, in conjunction with the 100th anniversary of the Strike, Noam Gonick's and Bernie Miller's sculpture of the famed overturned streetcar (from Bloody Saturday, 21 June) was unveiled on 21 June 2019 at the corner of Main Street and Market Avenue. These forms of memorialization symbolically take possession of some of Winnipeg's public space, and, instead of commemorating the "usual suspects"—military leaders, business people, and mainstream politicians—seek to celebrate the courage and accomplishments of those "ordinary" Winnipeggers who, in 1919, sought to make Winnipeg and the world a better place for all.

The public history and collective memory of the Strike is manifest and accessible in numerous other ways as well. Janis Thiessen's recent work, using oral history interviews with descendants of 1919 participants that she conducted in the lead-up to the Strike's 100th anniversary, explores intergenerational memories of the event and their subsequent impact on social justice perspectives in families and communities.[52] The popular (and recently massively updated) Winnipeg General Strike walking and driving tour leads participants past key sites of the Strike.[53] Plays, novels, graphic histories, and films about the Strike likewise help to enrich public understanding and awareness of the Strike.[54] Beyond this, the popularity of Danny Shur's musical *Stand!*—now a film released in 2019—ensures that the events of 1919 will be in the public's consciousness for some time to come.[55] Taken together, these public histories go some distance toward reclaiming the heritage and legacy of 1919 for future generations, helping to solidify the Winnipeg General Strike's place as the most commemorated event in Canadian labour history.

As readers will note, in the following chapters several of the issues raised above are still being debated. But astute readers will observe that contributors to this volume are also striking out in some new directions and attempting to fill in some of the historiographical gaps. Most ambitiously, we hope to be able to further expand the ways in which the Strike can be viewed through a wider lens. While class, of course, is at the centre of the story we are exploring here, historians have become increasingly cognizant of the interconnected ways in which colonialism and capitalism structure a multitude of intersecting oppressions including those of ethnicity, race, and gender, all of which shaped how the conflicts of 1919 were experienced and fought. We shall return to the question of what has been accomplished in this collection and what needs to come next in the book's concluding chapter.

Notes

1 This reference to the strikers' newspaper includes not only the *WLN*'s daily strike bulletin, but also F.J. Dixon's *Western Star* and *The Enlightener.* These were published clandestinely after the arrests of editors William Ivens (17 June) and his successor, J.S. Woodsworth (23 June), and the *WLN's* official closure by the authorities on 23 June.

2 Reinhold Kramer and Tom Mitchell, *When the State Trembled: How A.J. Andrews and the Citizens' Committee Broke the Winnipeg General Strike* (Toronto: University of Toronto Press, 2010), 16, 24.

3 As Michael Dupuis has noted, the *Toronto Star* was a notable exception to this rule among mainstream newspapers. See Michael Dupuis. "The Toronto Star and the Winnipeg General Strike," *Manitoba History* 49, no. 49 (2005). See also Dupuis, "William R. Plewman, *The Toronto Daily Star*, and the Reporting of the Winnipeg General Strike," *Labour / Le Travail* 57 (2006): 167–81, and Dupuis, *Winnipeg's General Strike: Reports from the Front Lines* (Charleston, SC: The History Press, 2014). An interesting selection of newspaper reports is readily accessible in J.E. Rea, *The Winnipeg General Strike*, Canadian History through the Press Series (Toronto: Holt, Rinehart and Winston of Canada, 1973). Even more fulsome is the collection to be found in Canada, Labour Canada Library, *Winnipeg General Strike Clippings* (Ottawa: Central Microfilm Unit, Public Archives of Canada, 1969).

4 Winnipeg Defence Committee, *"Saving the World from Democracy": The Winnipeg General Sympathetic Strike, May–June, 1919: Trial by Jury Destroyed by Stampede Forty-Five Minute Legislation—Workers Arrested and Rushed to Penitentiary to Smash Strike—Leading Lawyers, Members of Employers' Committee of 1000—Engaged by Federal Government to Prosecute Workers: Strike—Arrests—Trials—Penitentiary* (Winnipeg: Winnipeg Defence Committee, 1920). This was republished, with a lengthy introduction by Norman Penner, in 1973 as *Winnipeg, 1919: The Strikers' Own History of the Winnipeg General Strike* (Toronto: James Lewis and Samuel, 1973).

5 F.J. Dixon, *Address to the Jury in Defence of Freedom of Speech* (Winnipeg: Winnipeg Defence Committee, 1920); W.A. Pritchard, *Address to the Jury* (Winnipeg: Winnipeg Defence Committee, 1920); and W.H. Trueman, *Russell Trial and Labour's Rights* (Winnipeg: Wallingford Press, 1920). The Defence Committee also published a version of the charges against J.S. Woodsworth, which were eventually dropped by the Crown. See Manitoba, Court of King's Bench, *The King vs. J.S. Woodsworth: Indictment for Publishing Seditious Libels, Six Counts, and Speaking Seditious Words* (Winnipeg: Winnipeg Defence Committee, 1920).

Because Dixon's trial occurred before the omnibus trial of the so-called "Winnipeg Seven" (A.A. Heaps, William Ivens, John Queen, W.A. Pritchard, Roger Bray, George Armstrong, and Dick Johns)—and because he was acquitted, largely on the basis of his articulate address to the jury— his speech was printed and distributed as both a defence of the strikers and as a fundraiser for those still facing trial. It is also of some note that it was in the face of Dixon's successful self-defence against the charge of seditious libel that the charges against J.S. Woodsworth were effectively dropped.

6 Citizens' Committee of One Thousand, *The Activities and Organizations of the Citizens' Committee of One Thousand, in Connection with the Winnipeg Strike, May–June, 1919* (Winnipeg: Citizens' Committee of One Thousand, 1919).

7 Reinhold Kramer and Tom Mitchell, *When the State Trembled: How A.J. Andrews and the Citizens' Committee Broke the Winnipeg General Strike* (Toronto: University of Toronto Press, 2010), 287–92.

8 D.C. Masters, for example, made heavy use of the extensive reportage of the hearings and trials that appeared in the mainstream press and the *Western Labor News,* as well as official records of the trials.

9 Canada, Department of Labour, *Report of the Royal Commission appointed under Order-in-Council (PC 670) to enquire into Industrial Relations in Canada together with a Minority Report* (Ottawa: King's Printer, 1919). See also Canada, Department of Labour, "Evidence Presented at the Royal Commission on Industrial Relations at Winnipeg, May 10 and 12, 1919."

10 Manitoba, *The Royal Commission to Enquire into and Report upon the Causes and Effects of the General Strike Which Recently Existed in the City of Winnipeg for a period of six weeks, including the methods of calling and carrying on such strike*, Report of H.A. Robson, KC, Commissioner (Winnipeg: 1920).

11 Tom Mitchell, "Strike or Revolution?: H.A. Robson's Inquiry and the Winnipeg General Strike," *Manitoba Law Journal* 42, no. 2 (2019): 56–84.

12 Donald C. Masters, *The Winnipeg General Strike*, Social Credit in Alberta 2 (Toronto: University of Toronto Press, 1950).

13 Kenneth McNaught and Allen Mills, *A Prophet in Politics: A Biography of J.S. Woodsworth* (1959; repr., University of Toronto Press, 2017). See also McNaught, *The Winnipeg Strike, 1919* (Don Mills, ON: Longman Canada, 1974).

14 Norman Penner, *Winnipeg, 1919: The Strikers' Own History of the Winnipeg General Strike* (Toronto: James Lewis and Samuel, 1973).

15 David Bercuson, "The Winnipeg General Strike, Collective Bargaining, and the One Big Union Issue," *The Canadian Historical Review* 51, no. 2 (1970): 164–76. See also Bercuson, *Confrontation at Winnipeg: Labour, Industrial Relations, and the General Strike* (Montreal and Kingston: McGill-Queen's University Press, 1974).

16 A. Ross McCormack, *Reformers, Rebels, and Revolutionaries: The Western Canadian Radical Movement, 1899–1919* (1977; repr., Toronto: University of Toronto Press, 1991).

17 Although S.D. Clark had criticized both Frederick Jackson Turner's environmentalism and the Talcott Parson's structural functionalism that dominated mainstream North American social theory in the 1950s, critics point out he was not immune, as evidenced in his western exceptionalist argument in his foreword to Masters's *The Winnipeg General Strike* (although that might have been at least partially so that he could justify including a work on the Winnipeg General Strike in a series dedicated to understanding the Social Credit phenomenon in Alberta). See David A. Nook, "S.D. Clark in the Context of Canadian Sociology," *Canadian Journal of Sociology* 8, no. 1 (Winter 1983): 79–97.

The echoes of Turner and Parsons can be heard the works of Bercuson and McCormack. For both of them, the exceptionalist argument maintained that western Canadian workers were less conservative than their eastern counterparts and more inclined to radicalism at least partly because western capitalists were so much more aggressive and uncompromising than their better-established eastern counterparts. Consequently, workers built more combative unions, as opposed to "the East" where both employers and unions were more accommodating, and workers more effectively socialized to the status quo. Labour historians in the 1970s and beyond demonstrated that this was an oversimplification, and sometimes flatly wrong.

18 See Barbara Roberts, *Whence They Came: Deportation from Canada, 1900–1935* (Ottawa: University of Ottawa Press, 1988). And for a significant new analysis of the implementation of this new legislation, see Dennis Molinero, *An Exceptional Law: Section 98 and the Emergency State, 1919–1936* (Toronto: University of Toronto Press, 2017).

19 For a fuller recent treatment of this post-Strike history, see Stefan Epp-Koop, *We're Going to Run This City: Winnipeg's Political Left after the General Strike* (Winnipeg: University of Manitoba Press, 2015); James Naylor, *The Fate of Labour Socialism: The Co-operative Commonwealth Federation and the Dream of a Working-Class Future* (Toronto: University of Toronto Press, 2016); and "Whatever Happened to Labourism?," *Left History* 21, no. 1 (Spring/Summer 2017): 51–62.

20 J.E. Rea, "The Politics of Conscience: Winnipeg after the Strike," Canadian Historical Association, *Historical Papers*, 1971. See also J.E. Rea, "The Politics of Class: Winnipeg City Council, 1919–1945," in *The West and the Nation*, ed. Carl Berger and Ramsey Cook (Toronto: McClelland and Stewart, 1976).

21 Brian McKillop, "Citizen and Socialist: The Ethos of Political Winnipeg, 1919–1935" (MA thesis, University of Manitoba, 1970); and David Hall, "Times of Trouble: Labour Quiescence in Winnipeg, 1920–1929" (MA thesis, University of Manitoba, 1983).

22 See, for example, James Naylor, "The Winnipeg General Strike," http://newsocialist.org/the-winnipeg-general-strike/, 11 February 2010.

23 We intentionally avoid the phrase "new generation" as there was little age difference between Bercuson and McCormack, for instance, and those who would engage in an academic battle against their interpretive framework.

24 For Canadian scholars the primary inspiration was E.P. Thompson. His groundbreaking work, *The Making of the English Working Class,* and his many articles on the development of plebian and working-class culture, influenced social historians throughout the English-speaking world. The work of several other of the British Marxist historians was also of great importance to the intellectual formation of these young Canadian scholars—Eric Hobsbawm in particular, with his studies of popular revolts, "primitive rebels," "Labouring Men," and large-scale works on the development of capitalism and industrialism was essential reading—but scholars such as Dorothy Thompson, George Rude, Rodney Hilton, Raphael Samuels, and those associated with the innovative *History Workshop Journal,* and journals such as *Past and Present* and *The New Left Review* were also influential. However, for all of the undoubted impact of these British scholars, there is no question that leading American historians also played a role in the thinking and training of Canada's "new labour historians." Scholars such as Herbert Gutman, who wrote extensively on slavery and the peculiarities of the American working class, David Brody with his pioneering work on steelworkers in the preunion days, Melvin Dubofsky with his work on the International Workers of the World and the "culture of poverty," David Montgomery with his early work on American labour in the age of Reconstruction, and Eugene Genovese's work on the economics and culture of slavery are but a few of the American scholars whose work helped to shape the Canadians.

25 This is an extensive group—and by no means completely cohesive—but would definitely include Greg Kealey and Bryan Palmer, both of whose early work focused upon the working class in Ontario; Linda Kealey, Russell Hann, Peter Warrian,

Wayne Roberts—and then soon after the students that these young scholars helped to train or influence such as Craig Heron, Joan Sangster, David Frank, and Nolan Reilly (among many others).

26 H.C. Pentland, "Fifty Years After," *Canadian Dimension* 6, no. 2 (July 1969). Pentland's article was republished in *Canadian Dimension*, 52, no. 2 (Summer 2018), along with a commentary by James Naylor, "One Hundred Years After: the Winnipeg General Strike." Pentland was an important transitional figure in Canadian labour history. See Gregory Kealey, "H.C. Pentland and Working-Class Studies," *Canadian Journal of Political and Social Theory* 3, no. 2 (Spring/Summer, 1979): 79–94.

27 Nolan Reilly, "Introduction to Papers from the Winnipeg General Strike Symposium, March 1983," in *Labour/Le Travail* 13 (Spring 1984): 8.

28 See Gregory Kealey's contribution to the symposium, "1919: The Canadian Labour Revolt" in *Labour/Le Travail* 13 (Spring 1984): 11–44.

29 David Bercuson, *Confrontation at Winnipeg*, rev. ed. (Montreal and Kingston: McGill-Queen's University Press, 1990), 196–205.

30 See, for example, Donald Avery, '*Dangerous Foreigners': European Immigrant Workers and Labour Radicalism in Canada, 1896–1932* (Toronto: McClelland and Stewart, 1979); Avery, "The Radical Alien and the Winnipeg General Strike of 1919," in *The West and the Nation*, ed. Carl Berger and Ramsay Cook (Toronto: McClelland and Stewart, 1976.); Avery, "Ethnic and Class Tensions in Canada 1918–20: Anglo-Canadians and the Alien Worker," in *Loyalties in Conflict: Ukrainians in Canada during the Great War*, ed. Frances Swyripa and John Thompson (Edmonton: Canadian Institute of Ukrainian Studies, University of Alberta, 1983), 79–98; Roz Usiskin, "A Theoretical Reformulation of the Relationship between Political Ideology, Social Class, and Ethnicity, 1905–1920" (MA thesis, University of Manitoba, 1978); Usiskin, "The Winnipeg Jewish Radical Community: Its Early Formation 1905–1918" in Jewish Historical Society of Western Canada, comp., *Jewish Life and Times: A Collection of Essays* (Winnipeg: JHSWC, 1983); Usiskin, "The 'Alien' and the 'Bolshevik': The 1919 Winnipeg General Strike," *Canadian Jewish Outlook*, July/August 1983 (Vancouver: Canadian Jewish Outlook Collective, 1983); Art Grenke, "The German Community of Winnipeg and the English–Canadian Response to World War One," *Canadian Ethnic Studies* 20, no. 1 (1988): 21–44: Grenke, *The German Community in Winnipeg 1872 to 1919* (New York: AMS Press, 1991); Henry Trachtenberg, "The Winnipeg Jewish Community and Politics: The Inter-War Years, 1919–1939," in *Historical and Scientific Society of Manitoba Transactions*, series III, no. 35, 1978–79 (Winnipeg: Manitoba Historical Society, 1981); Trachtenberg, "The 'Old Clo' Move': Anti-Semitism, Politics, and The Jews of Winnipeg, 1882–1921" (PhD. diss., York University, 1984); Morris Mott, "The Foreign Peril: Nativism in Winnipeg, 1916–1923" (MA thesis, University of Manitoba, 1970); Orest Martynowych, "The Ukrainian Socialist Movement in Canada, 1900–1918," *Journal of Ukrainian Graduate Studies* 1, no. 1 (Fall 1976): 27–44 and Ibid., 2, no. 1, (Spring 1977): 22–31; Martynowych, *Ukrainians in Canada: The Formative Years, 1891–1924* (Edmonton: Canadian Institute of Ukrainian Studies Press, University of Alberta, 1991).

31 Gerald Friesen, "Bob Russell's Political Thought: Socialism and Industrial Unionism in Winnipeg, 1914–1919," in *River Road: Essays on Manitoba and Prairie History* (Winnipeg: University of Manitoba Press, 1996); Allen Mills, *Fool for Christ: The Political Thought of J.S. Woodsworth* (Toronto: University of Toronto Press, 1991);

and "Single Tax, Socialism and the Independent Labour Party of Manitoba: The Political Ideas of F.J. Dixon and S.J Farmer," *Labour/Le Travail* 5 (Spring 1980): 33–56.

32 Eric Angel, "Workers, Picketing and the Winnipeg General Strike of 1919" (MA thesis, Queen's University, 1995).

33 Mary Horodyski, "Women and the Winnipeg General Strike of 1919," *Manitoba History*, no. 11 (Spring 1986).

34 Linda Kealey, "'No Special Protection—No Sympathy': Women's Activism in the Canadian Labour Revolt of 1919" in *Class, Community, and the Labour Movement: Wales and Canada, 1850–1930*, ed. Dean R. Hopkin and Gregory S. Kealey (Aberystwyth: Llafur/CCLH, 1989), 134–59; Kealey, *Enlisting Women for the Cause: Women, Labour, and the Left in Canada, 1890–1920* (Toronto: University of Toronto Press, 1998); Harry Gutkin and Mildred Gutkin, *Profiles in Dissent: The Shaping of Radical Thought in the Canadian West* (Edmonton: NeWest Press, 1997).

35 Paula Kelly, "Looking for Mrs. Armstrong," *The Beaver: Exploring Canada's History* 82, no. 3 (June 2002): 20; Paula Kelly, *The Notorious Mrs. Armstrong* (Documentary, Buffalo Gal Productions, 2001).

36 David Thompson, "More Sugar, Less Salt: Edith Hancox and the Passionate Mobilization of the Dispossessed, 1919–1928," *Labour/ Le Travail* 85 (Spring 2020): 127–63, quotes at 127, 129.

37 Mary Horodyski, "Women and the Winnipeg General Strike of 1919," *Manitoba History*, no. 11 (Spring 1986).

38 Chad Reimer, "War, Nationhood, and Working-Class Entitlement: The Counterhegemonic Challenge of the 1919 Winnipeg General Strike," *Prairie Forum* 18, no. 2 (Fall 1993): 219–37.

39 Craig Heron, ed., *The Workers' Revolt in Canada, 1917–1925* (Toronto: University of Toronto Press, 1998).

40 Tom Mitchell and James Naylor, "The Prairies: In the Eye of the Storm," in Heron, *Workers' Revolt in Canada*, 215.

41 Jack Walker, *The Great Canadian Sedition Trials: The Courts and the Winnipeg General Strike, 1919–1920* (Winnipeg: Legal Research Institute of the University of Manitoba and the Canadian Legal History Project, 2004).

42 Reinhold Kramer and Tom Mitchell, *When the State Trembled: How A.J. Andrews and the Citizens' Committee Broke the Winnipeg General Strike* (Toronto: University of Toronto Press, 2010). For examples of his earlier work on this, see Tom Mitchell, "'To Reach the Leadership of This Revolutionary Movement': A.J. Andrews, the Canadian State and the Suppression of the Winnipeg General Strike," *Prairie Forum* 18, no. 2 (Fall 1993); and Mitchell, "'Legal Gentlemen Appointed by the Federal Government': The Canadian State, the Citizens' Committee of 1000, and Winnipeg's Seditious Conspiracy Trials of 1919–1920," *Labour / Le Travail* 53 (Spring 2004): 9–46.

43 See, for example, Gregory S. Kealey, "The Royal Canadian Mounted Police, the Canadian Security Intelligence Service, the Public Archives of Canada, and Access to Information: A Curious Tale," *Labour / Le Travail* 21 (1988); and Kealey, "State Repression of Labour and the Left in Canada, 1914–1920," *Canadian Historical Review* 73, no. 3 (September 1992): 281–314.

44 Esyllt W. Jones, *Influenza 1918: Disease, Death, and Struggle in Winnipeg* (Toronto: University of Toronto Press, 2007).

45 Sarah-Jane Mathieu, *North of the Color Line: Migration and Black Resistance in Canada, 1870–1955* (Chapel Hill: University of North Carolina Press, 2010), 130.

46 Adele Perry, *Aqueduct: Colonialism, Resources, and the Histories We Remember* (Winnipeg: ARP Books, 2016); Evelyn Peters, Matthew Stock, and Adrian Werner, *Rooster Town: The History of an Urban Métis Community, 1901–1961* (Winnipeg: University of Manitoba Press, 2018); Owen Toews, *Stolen City: Racial Capitalism and the Making of Winnipeg* (Winnipeg: ARP Books, 2018).

47 J.M. Bumsted, *The Winnipeg General Strike of 1919: An Illustrated History* (Winnipeg: Watson and Dwyer, 1994).

48 Dennis Lewycky, *Magnificent Fight: The 1919 Winnipeg General Strike* (Winnipeg: Fernwood, 2019).

49 The Graphic History Collective and David Lester, *1919: A Graphic History of the Winnipeg General Strike* (Toronto: Between the Lines, 2019).

50 Examples include Allan Levine, "The 1919 General Strike Was a Battle for Winnipeg's Soul," *Globe and Mail*, 10 May 2019; Tom Jokinen, "What the Winnipeg General Strike Can Teach Us about Class, Capitalism, and Greed," *The Walrus*, June 2019; and Tom Jokinen, "The 1919 Winnipeg General Strike: 100 Years Later," *CBC Ideas*, 15 May 2019, https://www.cbc.ca/1.5136887; James Naylor, "Standing Together," *Canada's History*, April–May 2019; Bryan D. Palmer, "1919: Recovering a Legacy," *Canadian Dimension*, Summer 2019; Paul Moist, "Winnipeg 1919: Causes and Consequences," *CCPA Monitor*, March 2019; Manitoba Building Trades, "The 1919 General Strike: A Hundred-Year Journey," *Manitoba Building Trades Journal*, April 2019.

51 S. Reilly, "Robert Kell and the Art of the Winnipeg General Strike," *Labour / Le Travail* 20 (1987): 185–92.

52 Janis Thiessen, "Remembering 1919: The Winnipeg General Strike," *Labour/Le Travail* 86 (Fall 2020): 159–76.

53 Nolan Reilly and Sharon Reilly, *1919 Winnipeg General Strike: Driving and Walking Tour* (Winnipeg: Manitoba Federation of Labour, 2019). The original version of this pamphlet was Gerry Berkowski and Nolan Reilly, *1919, the Winnipeg General Strike: A Driving and Walking Tour* (Winnipeg: Manitoba Culture, Heritage and Recreation, 1985).

54 See, for example, Lucius Dechausay, "David Lester Captures the Repression of 1919's Winnipeg General Strike in the Style of a War Artist | CBC Arts," CBC, 5 August 2020, https://www.cbc.ca/arts/david-lester-captures-the-repression-of-1919-s-winnipeg-general-strike-in-the-style-of-a-war-artist-1.5674168; Ann Maud Henry, *Lulu Street* (play, first performed at MTC in 1967); Jack Grey, *Striker Schneiderman* (play, first performed in Toronto in 1970); Margaret Sweatman, *Fox* (Winnipeg: Turnstone Press, 1991 and 2017); Rick McNair *Labour on Trial* (play, first performed at the Ukrainian Labor Temple, Winnipeg, 1994); The Winnipeg Labour Choir, *The Red Album* (labour music, recorded in Winnipeg, 1995); Doug Smith and Victor Dobchuk, *Six Weeks of Solidarity: Winnipeg 1919* (film, Winnipeg, 1994); Manitoba Labour Education Centre, *Telling Our Stories: Winnipeg 1919* (film, Winnipeg, 1994); Paula Kelly, *The Notorious Mrs. Armstrong* (documentary, Buffalo Gal Productions, 2001); Andy Blicq, *Bloody Saturday* (documentary, Canadian Broadcasting Corporation, 2007).

55 See Chapters 14 and 15 for a closer examination of the public history of the Strike.

2

In the Water: Race, Empire, and the Winnipeg General Strike

Adele Perry

This paper aims to reinterpret parts of the Winnipeg General Strike of 1919 through the analytics of Indigenous studies and critical race scholarship. I do so by examining links between Winnipeg's labour movement and the dispossession of Shoal Lake 40 First Nation in the interests of Winnipeg's water supply. Shoal Lake water began running in Winnipeg taps in March of 1919, about six weeks before the General Strike began. The arrival of Shoal Lake water and the Winnipeg General Strike occurred at the same time and in the same place. In a number of ways, the events were mutually constitutive or, to put it another way, part of the same story. Beginning within this recognition shifts how we understand the radical erasure of Indigenous people and issues from Winnipeg in 1919. The Strike and the labour and the left politics that helped produce and animate it were about Indigenous peoples, lands, and resources, including water, even when those topics were putatively absent from their public conversation. The striking absence of Indigenous peoples, lands, or politics from the robust and wide-ranging political conversation in and around the Strike was not simply an absence. It was part of a discursive, material, and political process that worked to construct labour and its imagined Canada as necessarily non-Indigenous, usually white, and often British. The reliance on languages of British rights doubled down on this erasure by imagining Winnipeg and its radical futurity as distinctly non-Indigenous, even when it was not always British, and not always white.

Putting questions of race and colonialism at the centre of how we read Winnipeg in 1919 should complicate triumphalist interpretations of what the Strike meant for relations amongst different groups of ordinary people. The Strike offered a different version of settler colonialism, but it did not challenge the basic terms of that colonial bargain. Historians repeat the erasures and elisions of early twentieth-century radical thinking when we treat the apparent absence of Indigenous people and issues from the Strike as commonsensical, beyond comment and analysis, or intellectually out of bounds. I'd like to suggest that we can make histories of Indigenous labour and the dispossession of Indigenous peoples, lands, and resources a central part of the story of Winnipeg in the interwar period, and of the General Strike in particular. To make this case I begin with Winnipeg, turn to Shoal Lake, and end with the connections between the two in the spring and summer of 1919.

Winnipeg

The space around the Forks of the Red and Assiniboine Rivers witnessed a range of important historical shifts over the course of the nineteenth century. This was an Anishinaabeg, Ininewak and Métis place, one connected by riverways and trade routes and networks to an expansive Indigenous world. From the second decade of the nineteenth century onward it was also the site of laboured experiment in forms of settler colonialism, most notably the scheme organized by Lord Selkirk in 1812. The society that became known as the Red River Settlement or Colony was overwhelmingly Métis by mid-century, and it remained as such for some time. After the so-called "transfer" of Rupertsland and the Red River Resistance of 1869–70, Manitoba entered Canada as a province. An 1870 census of Manitoba's "settled" population found over 90 percent of the population had been born in the Northwest. A little fewer than 10,000 of the 12,000 counted were described as half-breed, which the census defined as "any person having both white and Indian blood." A little more than 1,500 were described as "white," defined as "those who are white, or with no admission of Indian blood." A smaller number of First Nations people were "settled on land or living in houses." This was a snapshot of a variegated, Indigenous society, one where the modest number of non-Indigenous people were likely tied by patterns of kinship and economy to Indigenous peoples and institutions.[1]

The cumulative effect of Métis land loss and the development of the reserve and residential schooling systems worked to separate Indigenous from non-Indigenous in the 1870s and 1880s across western Canada.[2] But Winnipeg remained home to Indigenous people, and Indigenous workers. Population growth, and with it change, came in two waves: the first around the railway boom of the 1880s, and again in the first decade of the twentieth century. It was the latter that transformed the city. The population of the city grew from 42,430 in 1901 to 136,035 a decade later.[3] The amendment of the Indian Act to compel status Indian children to attend residential school or day school in 1920 and to make it illegal for bands to obtain funds or legal counsel to pursue claims makes clear how the carceral work of Canadian Indigenous policy tightened and became more restrictive in the interwar period.

For all of this Indigenous people, and Indigenous workers, remained a routine part of urban life in Winnipeg. Evelyn Peters, Adrian Stock, and Adrian Werner's careful study of the Métis suburb of Rooster Town reveals that there were more than 300 Métis living north of the Assiniboine River and in Fort Rouge in 1901, most of them in Métis households and tending to cluster around railway yards.[4] To the south of the city was the community of Rooster Town, one of a number of Métis and working-class communities on Winnipeg's outskirts. In 1911, most of the community's "household heads" were labourers, some were teamsters, and a few did the skilled and better paid work of switchman, tram driver, or carpenter. Three years before the General Strike, Rooster Town was made up of about thirty-four households and an estimated 190 people, and patterns of work, community, and poverty that had been established earlier in the century remained.[5]

The water easily accessible around the forks of the Red and Assiniboine Rivers had always been complicated for people to manage and use. A decade after Winnipeg was incorporated the city privatized the city's water supply, giving a company exclusive rights to supply the city with water in exchange for fire protection and twenty-five gallons of water per capita, per day. The Winnipeg Water Works minimally filtered water drawn from the Assiniboine River, and within a relatively short time the system had proven itself unworkable. In 1884 it was reported that "the water-supply of Winnipeg is attracting a great deal of attention."[6] With the exception of Main Street and a "few short lengths of other streets," Winnipeggers had to depend on "water carriers or upon fetching water in pails from public pumps." The "very poor and the squatters living in mere huts in certain parts of the city" were not even considered part of the discussion.[7] By 1900, the city bought the Water Works out of its contract for a substantial sum and turned to artesian well water and municipally owned mains. The well water had its own problems for ordinary people and for the business interests who sought to attract new enterprise to the city—it was "very hard, ruinous to boilers, plumbing and heating apparatus, costly in soap and washing compounds, injurious to fabrics and unsuitable for many manufacturing industries which might be attracted to Winnipeg by the cheap hydro-electric power and plentiful supply of soft water."[8] Officials and their hired experts regularly proclaimed the well water safe, but the city remained troubled by typhoid that broke out when river water was mixed with municipal water supply.[9] Access to this water supply also varied, and did so in ways that revealed and perpetuated class division. Fewer than half of the houses in Wards 5 and 6, which made up the city's North End, were connected to the municipal system.[10] It was hard to avoid connecting poor and limited access to municipal water with greater rates of epidemic disease, especially typhoid, in the city's working-class neighbourhoods.

The idea that water might be brought to Winnipeg from the Lake of the Woods watershed had been raised at least since 1884.[11] It found its champion in Thomas Russ Deacon, whose biography tied together northwestern Ontario's resource frontier, anti-labour politics, and the Winnipeg's business elite. Deacon was southern Ontario born and trained as a civil engineer. He arrived in the Anishinaabeg territories of Treaty 3 as part of the 1890s resource boom, becoming managing director and engineer for the Mikado Gold Mining Company on Shoal Lake. Deacon was perhaps not much of a business success in these years: it was later "alleged" that "the Indians of the district still refer to him as 'Chief-No-Gold.'"[12] Early in the twentieth century Deacon relocated to Winnipeg, founded Manitoba Bridge and Iron Works, and became president of the Manitoba Steel and Iron Company and vice-president of the Manitoba Rolling Mill Company.[13]

Deacon was a ready example of Winnipeg's wealth, its anti-labour politics, and the ways these were imbedded in ongoing exploitation of Indigenous territories, knowledges, and resources, especially in Treaty 3 territory. Deacon's financial interests shifted from mining in northwestern Ontario to industry in Winnipeg, but he remained tied to Shoal Lake through the cottage his family kept there. Deacon lived in Crescentwood, refused to recognize unions, hired strikebreakers, constantly extolled the formative virtues of free enterprise, and represented what one-time Trades and Labour Council President F.G. Tipping called "the old paternalistic Ontario 'bush culture' of that period."[14] During the heat of the Winnipeg General Strike Deacon was a symbol of anti-labour local employers, one of what the *Western Labor News* called "the Flavelles, and the Andrews, and the Barretts, and the Deacons."[15]

Deacon also represented what historian Don Nerbas has called the "bourgeoisie's hegemony in civic politics."[16] Deacon was elected to the Winnipeg City Council in 1906, and in 1912 he ran for mayor on what was routinely described as a "Shoal Lake water" ticket. Deacon certainly had a limited platform, and it was to build an aqueduct that would connect the city of Winnipeg to the "soft" water of Lake of the Woods watershed. Deacon presented himself as "The People's Choice for Mayor," and explained that he was "in favor of providing at once for the people of Winnipeg an ample and permanent supply of pure soft water, which will forever remove the menace now hanging over Winnipeg of a water famine and the consequent danger of conflagration and sickness."[17] In a letter to the editor, Deacon pitched that his plan would particularly benefit "the poorer people": "The manufacturer and merchant can to some extent unload his extra cost on to the consumers; the well-to-do can provide ample tanks in their larger basements for a good supply of soft water with special pumping equipment to distribute it through the house, but the poorer man has less room in his cellar for tanks, less money to provide soft water tanks, and can less easily bear the additional cost of softening powders, extra soap, destruction of his clothing, extra repairs to his plumbing all of which add heavily to his cost of living."[18] Within a year, Deacon had this complicated and ambitious project well under way. It involved securing the permission from various bodies of the settler state, raising money by creating bonds which were sold on an international market, and taking support for the building of an aqueduct estimated to cost some $13 million to at least two plebiscites.

The historical scholarship on Winnipeg in the 1910s emphasizes the totality of class division, and the way that men like Deacon lived in and moved about a radically different world than those who worked in his shops, or worked to organize them. But in the years leading up to 1919 the city's elite and the mainstream labour movement worked together on questions on water supply. To galvanize support for his plan to build an aqueduct, Deacon led at least two "inspection trips" to Shoal Lake to see the prospective water supply.[19] One took place in September 1913, when Deacon took an "occasional turn at the wheel" of the borrowed Young Men's Christian Association camp boat. On board were more than forty men, a mix of provincial and civic politicians, leaders of community organizations, and at least two representatives of the labour movement, Edward McGrath from the Winnipeg Trades and Labor Council (WTLC) and A.W. Puttee, former member of Parliament, a labour moderate, and editor of *The Voice*.[20] A few years later, Puttee was sitting on the Greater Winnipeg Water District's (GWWD) Administration Board, and would chair the Colonization Scheme that the GWWD established in 1915, sponsored, and ran from 1915 onward.[21] Another inspection trip in 1914 took time to observe that this was Anishinaabeg space, noting "an interesting local exhibit, the Indian burying ground."[22] For the most part, these observations accessed Shoal Lake not for its people, but for the resources that the settler city wanted.

Following the 1913 trip, the organized labour movement clarified and amplified their support for the plan to build an aqueduct linking Winnipeg and Shoal Lake. The *Free Press* explained that McGrath "favored the Shoal Lake scheme from the start and he is more than ever convinced of its feasibility, after seeing the lake for himself and having the plans for the pipelines explained to him."[23] A few days later the WTLC held a meeting that "had a healthy appearance and energetic action about it." Roughly 100 were present as the bylaw authorizing the creation of a debt to build the aqueduct was discussed by the "municipal" committee and McGrath and Puttee reported on their "trip of inspection of the source at Shoal Lake." The WTLC declined Mayor Deacon's offer to attend a special meeting, in part because "the council was unanimous in support of the by-law" that would make the aqueduct possible.[24]

Shoal Lake

Shoal Lake lies about 150 kilometres to the east of Winnipeg, on the western edge of the Lake of the Woods watershed. In 1913, the Indian agent reported that Shoal Lake 40's members supported themselves by "trapping, hunting, fishing, working on steamers and in the lumber camps."[25] The building of Winnipeg's aqueduct used Indigenous labour and knowledge and set into motion the dispossession of important parts of the modest amounts of lands and resources recognized as belonging to Shoal Lake 40. In the fall of 1913, the GWWD wrote to the federal government's Department of Indian Affairs (DIA), requesting the right to build a camp and do survey work on the Shoal Lake 40 reserve. Ottawa readily agreed.[26] At Shoal Lake 40, Chief Pete Redsky did what Indigenous people around Lake of the Woods had done for centuries: he worked to turn this into an opportunity for trade and for wage work. When Ottawa got wind that Redsky was selling sand and gravel to a contractor, they made clear that this could only be done if Shoal Lake 40 "surrendered" their rights to gravel and sand. A surrender process was conducted in December 1913, and Shoal Lake 40 lost its rights to these resources.[27]

Photographic archives make clear the ways that Anishinaabeg men from Shoal Lake 40 worked in the early building of the aqueduct, documenting men clearing land around Falcon River and testing muck near the aqueduct's intake.[28] Questions of labour surfaced routinely in correspondence between the Indian agent, Ottawa officials, and Pete Redsky. As historian Mary Jane Logan McCallum explains, labour "was also part of a colonial apparatus meant to, among other things, extinguish Aboriginal title and status."[29] Amid the loss of their rights to resources and to land, Shoal Lake 40 was offered work. In late 1913 and early 1914 the contractor promised work to "all Indians wanting to work," something that the agent thought "will be a great benefit to them."[30]

It was a particularly heavy aspect of Canada's colonial law that would separate Shoal Lake 40 from critical parts of its reserve lands in the interests of Winnipeg's water. They were not the only First Nation that lost reserve lands in these years. In the fifteen years between 1896 and 1911, a remarkable 21 percent of lands reserved for prairie First Nations were lost to the process of surrender and, as Sarah Carter has shown, surrenders picked up speed during the war.[31] But by early 1914 it was clear that Shoal Lake 40 would lose the biggest and most significant and consequential part of its reserve lands through the particular mechanism of section 46 of the Indian Act.[32] This section laid out a process by which reserve lands might be taken for "any railway, road, public work, or work designed for any public utility" without the consent or approval of the First Nation.[33] In June of 1914 the City of Winnipeg paid the federal government $1,500 for approximately 3,000 acres of Shoal Lake 40's reserve, representing three dollars an acre for 355 acres of land and fifteen cents an acre for lakebed and islands.[34]

Chief Redsky would write, as he had before, requesting information and recompense for his community in the polite terms demanded in a colonial system that would, within a decade, formally ban First Nations from hiring lawyers or pursuing land claims. Late in December 1918, Redsky wrote to Ottawa: "This is asking the Government for the pay for the Reserve," explaining that "the place was the best part of our Reserve," land that was "very good Farming, Good timber, good hay land."[35] Redsky threatened to travel to Ottawa with an interpreter, and the local Indian agent tried to defuse the situation by promising "they could get all the satisfaction without his going down.[36] The federal government would pay out the paltry amounts owed Shoal Lake 40 sometime after, but the reserve was still trisected by the land loss and the GWWD's engineering works. Shoal Lake 40's main settlement was relocated to what became a kind of artificial island. It remained as such until Freedom Road, a long fought-for twenty-four-kilometre gravel highway connecting Shoal Lake 40 with the TransCanada highway, opened in the spring of 2019, 100 years after Shoal Lake water began to flow in Winnipeg taps.

Shoal Lake and Winnipeg, 1919

The plan to build the aqueduct was developed and galvanized in a prewar context of colonial and capitalist ambition. In 1914 Canada entered the First World War as a colony within the British Empire. Winnipeg's much vaunted population increase slowed, and the organized working class would question their support for an expensive and ambitious plan to deliver drinking water to the city. In February 1915 the city's labour newspaper, *The Voice,* asked whether Winnipeg really needed the costly new water supply, and whose interests it would really serve. The aqueduct no longer seemed like much of a bargain, especially to those whose stake was in health rather than industrial machinery: "To be sure, it won't corrode the steam boilers as much as the present supply does; but only a few of us own steam boilers, and we all have stomachs," they explained. "Fourteen million is a big price for 200,000 people to pay for a water supply of dubious value to persons not interested in machinery. The debt was assumed, of course, during the piping times of peace when a population of 500,000 seemed an imminent probability." But such objections never became resistance, at least in any legible fashion. "It is not for those who voted the money, or those who failed to register their opinion at the polls to grumble now."[37]

Here, the labour movement, or the parts of it that wrote in *The Voice,* rejects the class arguments that Deacon had made about water before the war began. Labour's stake in the building of the aqueduct was in the wage work that it required. The Anishinaabeg men who did the early work on the aqueduct were displaced as the massive public work moved west from Shoal Lake and slowly toward Winnipeg. This was a project that was nothing if not labour-intensive, and the work of laying track, digging trenches, pouring concrete, tunnelling, and more was done by the same people who were the critical labour force for most of the projects of early twentieth-century western Canada, to whom the Winnipeg General Strike would speak directly and in clear terms: young, mobile, and migrant men, disproportionately European. The "maximum number" of men working on the project was about 2,500. Relying on a non-Indigenous workforce for what was called "bush work" meant camps. In 1915, there were eleven work camps associated with the aqueduct and twenty-two in 1918.[38]

It was hard to recruit settler men to work in Indigenous space, which the officials of the GWWD called "the bush." A recruiter reported that "most of the men coming to his office do not want work outside the city; they prefer a job in town."[39] As the war went on labour recruitment became more difficult. "We know how difficult it has been to get men to go to the Bush to cut cordwood for the City and the District during the present winter," they reported in 1917.[40] In October 1918 one of the GWWD's main contractors complained about "our inability to obtain the proper amount of labor this season," even when they were paying 75 to 100 percent higher wages.[41] The GWWD's self-titled Colonization Scheme began in 1915, and was imagined in part as a way of making work along the aqueduct more attractive for urban men. "The usual objections of married men who are offered employment in bush camps can be overcome by providing shacks for families and school facilities for the children," explained a letter in 1924.[42]

Workers on the aqueduct organized in a range of ways. The mainstream labour movement kept an eye on the working conditions in the GWWD works. In June of 1916 the GWWD's board heard from representatives of the WTLC "regarding enforcement of the Fair Wage Schedule in respect to rates of wages for laborers and carpenters, and the adoption of a new schedule for future contracts."[43] Puttee used his position on the administration board to inquire if complaints about overcrowded camps were being properly responded to.[44] There do not seem to have been unions, but there were strikes. In the summer of 1916 there were "strikes and squabbles at several Camps," most of them reportedly about food.[45] One of them occurred at the Winnipeg Aqueduct Construction Company, where their bunkhouses were overcrowded with "double-decker double beds."[46] In May 1916 the men "struck work" and refused to return until a cook they suspected of having a skin disease was fired.[47]

In the summer of 1918, two teenaged cousins, Mike Podolczuk and Nick Podolczuk, were charged with murdering their coworker, a seventy-year-old "bushman" named Louis Marcie, at a lumber camp along the GWWD railway. The local press followed the case avidly. The local media's coverage of the trial provides a window into the world of wage work in GWWD camps. At the centre of this case was a seventy-year-old man who made his living clearing brush, and two boys barely into their teens whose eastern-European surnames marked them as members of the ethnic communities that teetered at the edges of claims to whiteness. The charges against Nick Podolczuk were dropped, and fourteen-year-old Mike Podolczuk's defence would argue that the boy had no choice but to use his axe against a man who was "a dangerous paranoic with homicidal tendencies." The judge thought otherwise, and explained that Podolczuk would have hung had he been an adult. The courts sentenced the fourteen-year-old to five years in a provincial youth facility for the murder.[48]

Labour on the first stages of the GWWD's work had been done by Indigenous men, but within a year or two this work had been defined as non-Indigenous. The GWWD required that their subcontractors follow a "fair wage schedule," and provide working men with what they called "good board and lodging" at the cost of five dollars per week.[49] This also required only hiring men who lived within the five municipalities that made up the Water District: Winnipeg, St. Boniface, Transcona, St. Vital, and Fort Garry, or, as it was explained in 1916, "all workmen employed upon the work contemplated in and to be executed pursuant to said contracts shall be residents of the District unless such residents are not available or that Emergencies or other special circumstances exist which would render it contrary to the public interests to enforce that provision." This would have included Indigenous men, especially Métis ones, but excluded the Anishinaabeg men who had cleared brush and tested muck around the Falcon River. When the pressure of wartime labour shortages prompted the GWWD's administration board to revise this, they did so in ways that kept its focus on racial and national membership, allowing that five contractors were allowed to "employ workmen (except interned aliens) from whatever source they can be obtained and whether they are resident of the District or not; provided that British subjects are given preference and labor available in the District first exhausted."[50] In effect, I think we can view the Fair Wage Schedule as a document reflecting elite anxieties about labour conflict, but also as a kind of white labour clause, and later one that tied right to work with categories of nation and loyalty.

It was presumably concern about where their workers came from that led the GWWD to create a detailed census of all their head office and field employees in January 1916. This census shows patterns of what kinds of people did what kind of work, and also suggests the employer's enduring interest in the origins and family circumstances of their workers. The head office employees were men, most married, living south of the Assiniboine River. A few women worked as stenographers. In the GWWD's works at Waugh the labour force was different: many men were Canadian, or British, but not insignificant numbers were Italian, or Polish, and they lived near their work or in the city's North End. If any of the fifty-six employees enumerated were Indigenous, it does not show from the description of their "nationality" or "citizenship."[51]

In the pages of the labour press the GWWD advertised their excursion trips that took people from Winnipeg to Shoal Lake and back for a day. In 1918 Winnipeg's labour newspaper, *The Voice*, let its readers know that the GWWD was holding a "public excursion" on Victoria Day, that particularly imperial holiday. For a dollar, people could travel by GWWD rail to "the terminus of the aqueduct pipe line," and have an opportunity to view camps "now in full operation" and "the work being done."[52] Excursions to Shoal Lake, marketed to working class people who had a dollar or two for train fare but not private cottages, continued during the Strike, though the GWWD did not advertise in the *Western Labor News*. In June of 1919 the Strike edition of the daily *Telegram* advertised the opportunity for "the citizens a chance to get away from the heat of the city and to the cooling breezes of the lake, and also let them see the work which has been done to secure the splendid supply of soft water for Winnipeg."[53]

The conversation about the present and the future that radiated outward from the Winnipeg General Strike was incisive and broad-ranging, showing us what Ian McKay has evocatively called a way of reasoning otherwise. But on questions of race, empire, and colonialism, those around the Strike reasoned in ways that were far from otherwise. Racialized workers teetered at an uncomfortable edge. Historian Sarah-Jane Mathieu examines how Black men organized as part of the Order of Sleeping Car Porters participated in the Strike. Later in 1919 white workers insisted on separate wage scales, essentially returning "to a prewar segregationist contractual model" and "belying any claim that the Canadian labor revolts of 1919 had transformed Canadian unionists' racialized views."[54] Whether Asian workers could and would participate in the Strike was up for discussion. At the Calgary conference of March 1919, delegates debated whether they should "go on the record as opposing the patronage of restaurants owned and operated by Asiatic and be it further resolved that this conference support the hotel and restaurant employees in establishing white help exclusively in all hotels and restaurants or other licensed premises where food and refreshments are served." This blunt anti-Asian racism was successfully challenged by delegates who argued that it ought to be possible for Chinese workers to be "brought into this One Big Union." But anti-Asian racism permeated all sides of the argument, with a Vancouver delegate declaring "I don't love the oriental any more than any other labor man, for the simple reason I have to compete with him." They would conclude by affirming the OBU's commitment to "organizing all the workers, irrespective of race, creed or colour."[55] By the middle of June, the striker's newspaper only saw "the Chinese quarter" as a place where employers went for strikebreakers.[56]

The newspapers and other public documents created by and around the Strike engaged loudly and at length in what Chad Reimer has called "a language of working-class entitlement which was largely structured by the previous four years of war" that "appealed to traditions of British law and justice" and "the strikers' rights as British-Canadian citizens.'"[57] Putting it differently, McKay explains that radicals in 1919 Winnipeg navigated a "racialized minefield, acutely conscious of the damage their enemies could inflict with the 'alien' card."[58] This was about whiteness as well. Languages of race circulated in multiple directions in and around the Strike: the embattled civic elite denounced the strikers as dangerous foreigners, despite the fact that, as Owen Toews notes, the leadership was overwhelmingly British-born and deeply invested in a language of legitimate white and British men.[59] Racial language hardened at particular moments. The agreement that city police were asked to sign was dubbed "THE SLAVE PACT" in June 1919. "No white man will sign away his liberty which generations of workers have earned with sweat and blood ... "ONLY A SLAVE COULD SIGN IT. A FREE MAN, A WHITE MAN—NEVER."[60]

Historian Kurt Korneski's study of race, nation, and reform ideologies in late nineteenth- and early twentieth-century Winnipeg tracks the ways that "the geopolitical settings of imperialism" structured reform thinking and activism, even when these settings were a poor fit with lived experience.[61] The readily available English language archive suggests that the Strike's leadership shared significant common ground with middle-class and elite reformers when it came to their thoughts about race, empire, and nation. By the time of the Strike, the labour newspaper had nothing to say about Indigenous people at all. The interest in Indigenous labour and land rights that David Goutor identifies in Canadian labour organizing in the 1880s and 1900s is not visible in Winnipeg in 1919.[62] The capacity to do keyword searches confirms the impression of radical silence and makes clear how infrequently the labour press in Winnipeg wrote anything about Indigenous people. One edition of *Strikers' Defense Bulletin* and about thirty-four issues of the *Western Labor News* for 1919 contain no references to Indigenous people at all. If, as Ian McKay argues, the Winnipeg General Strike was "an experiment in radical democracy," it was one that made clear that there were salient limits on who was included and who was excluded from that experiment.[63]

It may have been different outside of the English-language press, or among the more radical. If that was the case, it left no clear archival footprint in the records of the Communist Party of Canada. As Oleksa Drachewych has argued, the history of international communism and what it termed the national and colonial questions is understudied. In Canada, she continues, the national question of the CPC has revolved around foreign workers and French Canada, and Indigenous peoples "barely registered" in the interwar period. It was not until 1937 that the CPC "vaguely called for government assistance and equal rights for Indigenous people."[64] The timeline of the CCF's policy on Indigenous peoples is approximately similar.[65]

This particular and near total erasure was more than an omission or an oversight. It was not that there were no Indigenous people, and Indigenous workers, in Winnipeg, and it was not that Strike leaders were somehow unaware of Indigenous people or their local presence. We should not treat radical clergyman, reformer, and politician J.S. Woodsworth as synonymous with the Strike. But he was an important leader and became the coeditor of the *Western Labor News* toward the end of the Strike.[66] A decade before the Strike Woodsworth published *Strangers Within Our Gates: Or, Coming Canadians*. This short book is a revealing window into early twentieth-century racial thinking. Woodsworth framed his racial hierarchies around migration, and who was and who was not a desirable or possible immigrant for Canada. But Indigenous people are there at the bottom with "the Negro and the Indian." Woodsworth explained that he located them there since "neither the negro nor the Indian are immigrants, and yet they are so entirely different from the ordinary white population that some mention of them is necessary if we would understand the complexity of our problems." Woodsworth was shamed by the presence of Indigenous people in city and country and by the way that Indigenous and settlers shared, or did not share, space. "One of the most pathetic signs is that of an Indian stepping off a sidewalk to let a white man pass, or turning out of a prairie trail to give a white man the right of way." "Once the Indians were proud autochthones; now they are despised natives; aborigines, yet outcasts, belated survivors of an earlier age, strangers in the land of their fathers." Woodsworth quoted a colleague who urged "industrial schools," a subset of residential schools, and reminded his readers of the Christian obligations to Indigenous people.[67]

Woodsworth's 1911 book, *My Neighbor: A Study of City Conditions,* placed Indigenous people and history within a particular framework. Woodsworth illustrated "Winnipeg, Old and New" with an image of tipis, Red River carts, and low buildings and a contrasting image of streetcars and tall brick buildings. Woodsworth made nods to the city's Indigenous history. He noted that Winnipeg's location was selected "in order that it might capture the fur trade of the Indians, who paddled down these streams in their birch canoes" and that "half-breed 'freighters'" had essentially laid out the "great thoroughfares of a cosmopolitan city." Woodsworth's book placed the emphasis on migration, and the challenges that poor European migrants presented to what literary scholar Daniel Coleman would call Canadian white civility. But a chapter on "The Seamy Side or Social Pathology" revealed the layered connections between this and Indigenous people in Winnipeg. It included a long list of offences committed in Winnipeg in 1910, and an accompanying list of "Nationalities Represented in Above." Two hundred and sixty-one were "Halfbreed," and another five "Indian." An accounting of children who came under the auspices of Winnipeg's Children's Aid Society enumerated thirty "French Half-Breeds" among the 828.[68]

The room that Woodsworth accords to Indigenous people within these books is limited and generally disconnected from his critiques of Canada and urban life. It was in the years between 1915 and 1921 that, as Ian McKay explains, Woodsworth "transformed himself from an evolutionary liberal into an orthodox first formation socialist."[69] There was limited and condescending room for Indigenous people in the former, but seemingly none in the latter. By 1919, that Indigenous people might be part of radical future being called forth by the Strike was unthinkable.

There was a conversation between Indigenous organizers and the labour radicals in 1919, but it was largely if not entirely a one-sided one. Writing from Toronto in November of 1919, Haudenosaunee chief and veteran Frederick Loft explained that the League of Indians, formed the year before, had their first meeting in Sault Saint Marie, with representation from Ontario and Manitoba. Loft linked the project of organizing a national Indigenous organization to labour radicalism and unrest. "Union is the outstanding impulse of men today, because it is the only way by which the individual and collective elements of society can wield a force and power to be heard and their demands recognized by governments," he explained. "Look at the force and power of all kinds of labor organizations, because of their unions." Loft went on to call for a national organization that would "co-operate and work for each other as we should," and challenge those who were "depriving us of our lands and even deny of us the rights we are entitled to as free men under the British flag."[70] The Indian agent in Fort Frances, the agency east of Shoal Lake 40, got wind of the league's work and reported it to Ottawa. He enclosed Loft's letter, and associated it with radical organizing. "I do not know if you are aware of this movement but I am suspicious of it," the agent explained to Duncan Campbell Scott. "I don't like the tone of it. It looks like the I.W.W. or O.B.U. Or Balshevick." The agent got the letter from the chief of Couchiching, but thought "that nearly all the bands had received it."[71]

The connections between labour unrest and Indigenous organizing is clear both in Loft's letter and in Ottawa's fevered response to it. But this recognition seems to have been one-sided, and that is worth sitting with. The apparent absence of any discussion of Indigenous peoples or politics in and around the Strike should not be read as an accident, or as an unintended or meaningless consequence. Instead, we need to situate the particular silence, this unwillingness to see the Indigenous past and present of Winnipeg, as part of a wider and longer history of settler colonialism and whiteness. Examining the connections between labour radicalism and anti-Asian politics, American historian Kornel Chang argues that the "imagining of a transnational working-class community" in the interwar period was "not a statement of universal solidarity but a racialized vision predicated on white racial unity."[72]

There is no doubt that the Strike offered a sustained challenge to brittle and sharply political divisions between so-called aliens or foreigners and so-called citizens and those who might make ready claims to British justice. This was a significant move, and one that historians are right to emphasize. But we also ought not to misunderstand it. The expansion and contestation of claims to whiteness and British citizenship and the sustained efforts to wrest them from employers and the state were that, but they were not a challenge to hierarchies of race and colonialism. The claim that "for the workers of Winnipeg, the barriers of color, race and creed had been torn down are now beyond hope of being rebuilt"[73] was both made and heard within a context that rendered Indigenous people, and Indigenous workers, invisible.

The erasure of Indigenous people from the supple and expansive political language of the Winnipeg General Strike effectively disconnected it from the long history of struggles within the particular territory it occurred within. In *Stolen City,* Owen Toews points out that the events of the Winnipeg General Strike occurred within one generation of the North-West Rebellion, and two of the Red River Resistance. The temporal proximity of the Indigenous resistance of the late nineteenth century and the labour radicalism of the early twentieth century is made vivid by how many of "the key figures involved in suppressing the Winnipeg General Strike had themselves participated as young men in the conquest of the Metis and First Nations peoples of the North-West."[74] The life story of Honoré Jaxon, from the North-West Rebellion to the Industrial Workers of the World in Chicago, suggests how these connections were also present in the lives of the left and organized labour.[75] Surely some of the Indigenous people living in Winnipeg and St. Boniface participated in the Winnipeg General Strike. Peters, Stock, and Warner's work with the census of 1916 identifies a Chippewa servant, a Cree carpenter, a Mohawk brakeman, and an Indian labourer in a Cartage company.[76] There is much historians do not know about histories of Indigenous people, labour, and radicalism in twentieth-century Canada.

Beginning with the dispossession of Shoal Lake 40, the building of the Winnipeg aqueduct, and the General Strike allows us to see these complicated connections, and to register the Strike within an enduring history of settler colonialism. Shoal Lake water flowed in Winnipeg taps a few weeks before the Strike began, and these histories are part of the same story. Organized labour, and the left, were tied to colonialism, to the active and regularly repeated exclusion of Indigenous peoples from the category of worker, and on the dispossession of Indigenous lands and resources. The Winnipeg General Strike did not challenge settler colonialism as much as it fought for a different version of it. Indigenous people were no more present in the radical visions of a possible Canada that emanated from soapboxes, printing houses, and shop floors in Winnipeg than they were in the boosters' promises. In imagining a future without Indigenous people and without recognition of Indigenous territory and resources, the leaders of the Winnipeg General Strike accepted the core promise of settler colonialism as part of their wages of whiteness. An adequate history of the Strike and its enormous possibilities must also include recognition of this erasure, and what it meant for the social movements, scholars, and activists who have looked, and still look, to the Winnipeg General Strike.

I would like to thank Robin Neckoway for his research work on some related work, and the assistance of the City of Winnipeg Archive's Sarah Ramsden, and Jarad Buckwold. Cuyler Cotton provided important feedback. Ryan Eyford, Erin Millions, Mary Jane Logan McCallum, and Owen Toews all thought this along with me, in one way or another. I would also like to acknowledge the University of Manitoba's Centre for Human Rights Research, who provided a small grant for some of this work.

Notes

1 For the census definitions, see https://www.bac-lac.gc.ca/eng/census/1870/Pages/about-census.aspx#tab4; and for a discussion of the census, see "The Archibald Census," http://www.legislativeassemblyofassiniboia.ca/en/page/67/archibald-census-1870#_edn1.

2 For this argument, see Sarah Carter, *Aboriginal People and Colonizers of Western Canada to 1900* (Toronto: University of Toronto Press, 2007), Chapter 8; and Mary Jane Logan McCallum and Adele Perry, *Structures of Indifference: An Indigenous Life and Death in a Canadian City* (Winnipeg: University of Manitoba Press, 2018), Chapter 1.

3 Alan Artibise, *Winnipeg: A Social History of Urban Growth, 1874–1914* (Montreal and Kingston: McGill-Queen's University Press, 1875), 134 and Table 6.

4 Evelyn Peters, Matthew Stock, and Adrian Werner, *Rooster Town: The History of an Urban Metis Community, 1901–1961* (Winnipeg: University of Manitoba Press, 2018) 24–26.

5 Peters, Stock, and Werner, *Rooster Town,* 46, 56.

6 Niven Agnew, "Our Water Supply: A Practical Paper by Dr. Agnew on the Subject: Suggestions as to the Water We Drink, and Where to Get It From," *Transactions of the Manitoba Historical Society*, 1884 (Winnipeg: Manitoba Daily Free Press, 1884), 2. For a discussion of Winnipeg, water, and colonialism, see Adele Perry, *Aqueduct: Colonialism, Resources, and the Histories We Remember* (Winnipeg: ARP, 2016).

7 *What Shall We Do about Our Water Supply? A Conversation Between a Citizen and a Director of the Water Company* (Winnipeg: Manitoban Printing, 1887), 1, 2, 8.

8 *Greater Winnipeg Water District Aqueduct Construction Scheme: What It Is, What It Means* (n.p.: Administration Board, 1919) 5–6.

9 City of Winnipeg, Department of Public Health, *Annual Report, 1909,* City of Winnipeg Archives (hereafter CWA), Committee on Public Health and Welfare, A

711. Also see Artibise, *Winnipeg*, 215–16. For an analysis of the links between health and class in interwar Winnipeg, see Esyllt Jones, *Influenza 1918: Disease, Death, and Struggle in Winnipeg* (Toronto: University of Toronto Press, 2007).

10 Artibise, *Winnipeg*, 217.

11 See Agnew, "Our Water Supply."

12 Untitled, *Winnipeg Tribune*, 17 May 1913. Thomas Russ Deacon fonds, Archives of Manitoba (hereafter Deacon Papers, AM), MG 14 B1, "Clippings re Mayoralty."

13 See entry for Thomas Russ Deacon, *Memorable Manitobans*, located at http://www.mhs.mb.ca/docs/people/deacon_tr.shtml; J.M. Bumsted, *Dictionary of Manitoba Biography* (Winnipeg: University of Manitoba Press, 1999), 66.

14 See David Bercuson, *Confrontation at Winnipeg: Labour, Industrial Relations, and the General Strike*, rev. ed. (Montréal and Kingston: McGill-Queen's University Press, 1990 [1974]), 52.

15 "The Solider and the Alien," *Western Labor News*, 7 June 1919. Also see "A Passion for Justice," *Western Labor News*, 17 June 1919.

16 Don Nerbas, "Wealth and Privilege: An Analysis of Winnipeg's Early Business Elite," *Manitoba History* 47 (Spring/Summer 2004): 49.

17 Electoral ticket, "Vote for Deacon: The People's Choice for Mayor," in Deacon Papers, AM.

18 T.R. Deacon, letter to the editor, "Against the Bylaw," *Winnipeg Tribune*, 12 September 1912, in Deacon Papers, AM.

19 "Shoal Lake Ideal as Water Source," *Manitoba Free Press*, 15 September 1913; "Inspection Trip to Shoal Lake," *Manitoba Free Press*, 27 July 1914.

20 "Shoal Lake Ideal as Water Source," *Manitoba Free Press*, 15 September 1913. Also see untitled, *Winnipeg Tribune*, 17 May 1913, in Deacon Papers, AM.

21 *Greater Winnipeg Water District Aqueduct Construction Scheme: What It Is, What It Means* (n.p.: Administration Board, 1919), 4. For more on Puttee, see Stefan Epp-Koop, *We're Going to Run This City: Winnipeg's Political Left after the General Strike* (Winnipeg: University of Manitoba Press, 2015), 8–9; Bumsted, *Dictionary of Manitoba Biography*, 203.

22 "Inspection Trip to Shoal Lake," *Winnipeg Tribune*, 27 July 1914.

23 "Shoal Lake Ideal as Water Source," *Manitoba Free Press*, 15 September 1913.

24 "The Trades and Labor Council," *The Voice*, 19 September 1913.

25 "Shoal Lake Bands, Nos 39 and 40," in Annual report of the Department of Indian Affairs for 1913, Sessional Papers 1913, transcript at http://central.bac-lac.gc.ca/.item/?id=1906-IAAR-RAAI&op=pdf&app=indianaffairs.

26 S. Stewart to R.S. McKenzie, 27 October 1913, Indian Affairs, Library and Archives Canada, (hereafter IA, LAC) RG 10, volume 3178, file 447, 733-1; Memo, Hon Dr., Roche, 28 October 1913, IA, LAC, RG 10, volume 3178, file 447, 733-1A.

27 J.D. McLean to R.S. McKenzie, 5 December 1913, IA, LAC, RG 10, volume 3178, file 447, 733-1A; 11, draft Surrender Document, n.d. [15 December 1913], IA, LAC, RG 10, volume 3178, file 447, 733-1A.

28 See Greater Winnipeg Water District Photographs, 39 and 12, City of Winnipeg Archives, (hereafter COWA). Some of this collection is online at https://winnipeginfocus.winnipeg.ca/d00269.

29 Mary Jane Logan McCallum, *Indigenous Women, Work, and History: 1940–1980* (Winnipeg: University of Manitoba Press, 2014).

30 R.S. McKenzie to D.C. Scott, 20 December 1913; and R.S. McKenzie to J.D. McLean, 14 January 1914, both in IA, LAC, RG 10, volume 3178, file 447, 733-1A.

31 Richard Spaulding, "Executive Summary," in Peggy Martin-McGuire, "First Nation Land Surrenders on the Prairies, 1896–1911" (Ottawa: Indian Claims Commission, 1989), xiii; Sarah Carter, "'An Infamous Proposal': Prairie Indian Reserve Land and Soldier Settlement after World War I," *Manitoba History* 37 (Spring/Summer 1999): 9–23.

32 J.D. McLean to Thomas R. Deacon, 26 February 1914, IA, LAC, RG 10, volume 3178, file 447, 733-1A.

33 The Indian Act, 1906 (Ottawa: King's Printer, 1906), 15.

34 See M. Peterson to S.H. Reynolds, 20 June 1914, and M. Peterson to S.H Reynolds, 3 July 1914, CWA, GWWD, Administration Board Memos, 10 October 1913 to 3 October 1918; Thomas R. Deacon to Duncan C Scott, 6 May 1914, IA, LAC, RG 10, volume 3178, file 447, 733-1A. For a more detailed discussion, see Adele Perry, "Drinking Dispossession: Winnipeg, Shoal Lake 40, and Canada," in *Surviving Canada: Indigenous Peoples Celebrate 150 Years of Betrayal*, ed. Kiera Ladner and Myra Tait (Winnipeg: ARP, 2017), 261–73.

35 Chief Redsky to R.S. McKenzie, 19 December 1918, IA, LAC, RG 10, volume 3178, file 447, 733-1.

36 R.S. McKenzie to J.D. Mclean, 31 December 1918, IA, LAC, RG 10, volume 3178, file 447, 733-1.

37 "The Shoal Lake Water Supply," *The Voice*, 5 February 1915.

38 W.G. Chase, "Construction Features of the Water Works of the Greater Winnipeg Water District," *American Water Works Association* 7, no. 6 (November 1920): 938.

39 W. Campbell to Frank Kerr, License Inspector, 16 December 1916, COWA, GWWD Commissioners Reports, 1913–1915, temporary box 3.

40 Chairman of the Commissioners to Chair and Members of the Admin Board, 1 February 1917, COWA, GWWD Commissioners Reports, 1913–1915, temporary box 3.

41 William Smaill to Administration Board, 26 October 1918, COWA, GWWD Correspondence re: Administration Board Minutes, 1918, A1386, file 98.

42 William Davis to William Scott, 22 July 1924, GWWD Railway Settlement, Correspondence, 1916–1920, A1384, file 79.

43 Minutes of GWWD Administration Board, item 1618, 2 June 1916, 1913, COWA, GWWD.

44 9 April 1917, GWWD Administration Board Minute Book, 1917–1945, COWA, GWWD, temporary box 2.

45 BDW/BL/Chairman of the Commissioners to Chair and Members of the Admin Board, 1 February 1917, COWA, GWWD Commissioners Reports, 1913–1915, temporary box 3.

46 Harry Mead to R.D. Waugh, 23 January 1917 COWA, GWWD Commissioners Reports, 1913–1915, temporary box 3.

47 W.H. Lovatt to R.D. Waugh, 22 January 1917, COWA, GWWD Commissioners Reports, 1913–1915, temporary box 3.

48 See "Charge of Murder Faces Two Youths," *Winnipeg Free Press*, 7 June 1918; "Grand Jury Finds Bill for Murder," *Winnipeg Free Press*, 29 June 1918; "Charge of Murder Faces Two Youths," *Winnipeg Free Press*, 7 June 1918; "Boy Slayer Pleads Self Defense," *Winnipeg Tribune*, 5 July 1918; "Boy Slayer of Louis Marcie Given Five

Years at Portage," *Brandon Daily Sun*, 10 July 1918.

49 Brigadier-General R.N. Rattan, J.G. Sullivan, and R.S. Lea, *Report on the Aqueduct of the Greater Winnipeg Water District by the Special Board of Consulting Engineers* (Winnipeg: Greater Winnipeg Water District, 1916), 15.

50 M. Peterson to R.D. Waugh, 18 December 1916, COWA, Greater Winnipeg Water District, Correspondence re: Administration Board Minutes, 1916, A1386, file 96, COWA, GWWD; Chairman of the Commissioners to Chair and Members of the Administration Board, 1 February 1917, GWWD Commissioners Reports, 1913–1915, COWA, GWWD, temporary box 3. Also see David Ennis, "Not All Down Hill from There: The Shoal Lake Aqueduct and the Winnipeg Water District," *Manitoba History* 75 (Summer 2014): 42.

51 "Greater Winnipeg Water District, Statement of Employees," 1 January 1916, COWA. Thanks to Jarad Buckwold for tracking this down for me and making it available.

52 *The Voice*, 17 May 1915.

53 "Shoal Lake Excursion Leaves Here Tomorrow," *Winnipeg Telegram Strike Editions*, 20 June 1919.

54 Sarah-Jane Mathieu, *North of the Color Line: Migration and Black Resistance in Canada, 1870–1955* (Chapel Hill: University of North Carolina, 2010).

55 Report of Western Canada Labor Conference, Calgary, 13–15 March 1919, *Western Labor News*, 5 April 1919.

56 "Who Employs the Aliens?," *Western Labor News*, 15 June 1919.

57 Chad Reimer, "War, Nationhood, and Working-Class Entitlement: The Counterhegemonic Challenge of the 1919 Winnipeg General Strike," *Prairie Forum* 18, no. 2 (Fall 1993): 220, 228, 231.

58 Ian McKay, *Reasoning Otherwise: Leftists and the People's Enlightenment in Canada, 1890–1920* (Toronto: BTL, 2008), 476.

59 Owen Toews, *Stolen City: Racial Capitalism and the Making of Winnipeg* (Winnipeg: ARP, 2018), especially 91–92.

60 "Labor Demands," *Western Labor News*, 2 June 1919. Also see "A Significant Pact," *Western Labor News*, 11 June 1919.

61 Kurt Korneski, *Race, Nation, and Reform Ideology in Winnipeg, 1880s–1920s* (Madison, NJ: Fairleigh Dickinson University Press, 2015), 206.

62 See David Goutor, "Constructing the 'Great Menace': Canadian Labour's Opposition to Asian Immigration, 1880–1914," *Canadian Historical Review* 88, no. 4 (December 2007): 461–62.

63 McKay, *Reasoning Otherwise*, 482.

64 Oleksa Drachewych, "'The most exploited section of the working class': The Canadian Communist Party, International Communism, Nationality, and Racial Equality in the Interwar Period," *Beyond Borders: The New Canadian History* (blog) https://thenewcanadianhistory.com/2017/03/20/the-most-exploited-section-of-the-working-class-the-canadian-communist-party-international-communism-nationality-and-racial-equality-in-the-interwar-period/; also see Oleksa Drachewych, "Transnational Leftism: A Symposium on the Comintern and the National, Colonial, and Racial Questions," *Beyond Borders: The New Canadian History* (blog), https://thenewcanadianhistory.com/2017/09/11/transnational-leftism-a-symposium-on-the-comintern-and-the-national-colonial-and-racial-questions/.

65 See James M. Pitsula, "The Saskatchewan CCF Government and Treaty Indians, 1944–64," *Canadian Historical Review* 75, no. 1 (1994): 21–52.

66 Tom Mitchell and James Naylor, "The Prairies: The Eye of the Storm," in *The Workers' Revolt in Canada, 1917–1925*, ed. Craig Heron (Toronto: University of Toronto Press, 1998), 211.

67 J.S. Woodsworth, *Strangers within Our Gates: Or, Coming Canadians* (Toronto: F.C. Stephenson, 1909), 190, 192, 193, 194. On this, see Daniel Coleman, "J.S. Woodsworth and the Discourse of White Civility," in *Human Welfare, Rights, and Social Activism: Rethinking the Legacy of J.S. Woodsworth*, ed. Jane Pulkingham (Toronto: University of Toronto Press, 2014), 221–44.

68 J.S. Woodsworth, *My Neighbor: A Study of City Conditions; A Plea for Social Service* (Toronto: Missionary Society of the Methodist Church, 1913), 46, 47, 208–13, 226.

69 McKay, *Reasoning Otherwise*, 436. Also see Jane Pulkingham, "A Common Interest?: Reflections on the Social Legacy of J.S. Woodsworth and the Contemporary Politics of Social Change in Canada," in *Human Welfare*.

70 Frederick Loft to Chief and Brethren, 14 November 1919, LAC. Reprinted in *Strange Visitors: Documents in Indigenous-Settler Relations in Canada from 1876*, ed. Keith D. Smith (Toronto, University of Toronto Press, 2014), 129–31.

71 J.P. Wright to Duncan Campbell Scott, 20 December 1919, reprinted in Smith, *Strange Visitors*, 132. Thanks to Peter Kulchyski for reminding me of this.

72 Kornel Chang, "Circulating Race and Empire: Transnational Labor Activism and the Politics of Anti-Asian Agitation in the Anglo-American Pacific World," *Journal of American History* (December 2009): 678.

73 *Strike Bulletin*, 27 May 1919, reproduced in *Winnipeg, 1919: The Strikers' Own History of the Winnipeg General Strike*, ed. Norman Penner (Toronto: James Lewis and Samuel, 1973), 78.

74 Toews, *Stolen City*, 88.

75 See Donald Smith, *Honoré Jaxon: Prairie Visionary* (Calgary: Coteau Books, 2007).

76 This is from Matthew Stock, Table 5.1.3., "Aboriginal People Living in Winnipeg and Saint Boniface, 1916," found at https://roostertown.lib.umanitoba.ca/?page_id=468.

3

From Patriotism to Insurgency: The Shifting Allegiances of Winnipeg 1919's Striker-Soldiers

David Thompson

In 1919, an imperialist war arrived home as class war. Scholars are unanimous on the formidable and volatile role Great War veterans played during the Winnipeg General Strike yet, within the historiography, the striker-soldiers remain shadowy figures.[1] How did their engagement in imperial and class warfare reinforce, transform, and/or destabilize their fidelity to patriotism, authority, Anglo-Canadian privilege, and liberal capitalism? This chapter offers a reconnaissance of the politics and actions of twelve prostrike veteran organizers. Their histories complicate any one-dimensional reading of the striker-soldiers by accounting for the diversity and dynamism of progressive politics within their ranks. "Beneath the apparently solid surface" of veteran patriotism and reaction, ex-soldiers' fluid opinions "betrayed oceans of liquid matter, only needing expansion to rend into fragments" the edifice of liberal-capitalist modernity.[2] As the class war escalated so too did veteran perspectives and conduct. By mid-strike, their broad frontal attack on the state and capital drove a vulnerable salient deep into enemy territory.

Working-class Winnipeg veterans were overwhelmingly prostrike.[3] As a "third force," striker-soldiers pushed the Strike Committee past its strategy of "passive resistance."[4] If the milk-wagon placards, "by the authority of the Strike Committee," symbolized a constitutional crisis, the soldiers' parliament also signalled a challenge to state power. The burdens ex-servicemen carried from war and demobilization expanded the Strike beyond demands for union recognition and collective bargaining rights. War profiteering, military hierarchy and autocracy, trauma, grief, survivor's guilt, and a trained hatred of the enemy weighed heavily among them. Their return to civilian life was mired in broken promises—high unemployment, stingy war pensions, and the denial of rights were not the rewards democracy's defenders expected. The workers' revolt was also an ex-soldiers' mutiny.[5]

Veterans occupied "a position of great strategic importance," to both sides of the Strike.[6] By virtue of being the most talked about and talked to during the confrontation, veterans crowded out the influence of women, children, and immigrant strikers. The cabal of Winnipeg's business elite, the Citizens' Committee of 1000, through propaganda, bribes, and their ex-soldier front organization, tried to pit veterans "against foreign workers and their Anglo-Canadian allies."[7] It was the Citizens' failure to convert a class war into a race war that resulted in the state's show of force. Alternatively, the Strike Committee and their organ, the *Western Labor News* (*WLN*), expanded veteran support by utilizing a "war discourse, with its economy of sacrifice," to harness the ex-soldier's patriotism and weld it to a "working-class definition of citizenship and nationhood."[8] So interested in winning veterans' favour, the Strike Committee even denied striking immigrants adequate and visible representation. While generally appealing to class unity, the Strike's organizers also offered other racist concessions to soldier patriots, including the promise to investigate the problem of alien labour after the Strike.[9]

By portraying ex-servicemen as subjects to be won, and not as agents with their own history and competing values, the existing scholarship habitually collapses what is otherwise acknowledged as the complexity of striker-soldiers' politics. The Citizens wished, and the Strike Committee expected, ex-servicemen to behave in ways inimical to labour solidarity—but what about the veterans themselves? Neither side was wholly mistaken: patriotism, British values, antipacifism, and xenophobia did animate some striker-soldiers, just as they did many civilians.[10] However, veterans held multiple rival and evolving visions including views that qualified, questioned, and challenged both labour and capitalist jingoism.

Of the almost 12,000 ex-servicemen who returned to the city prior to or during the Winnipeg General Strike, the twelve veterans profiled in this chapter were among the most prominent striker-soldiers.[11] 1919's "dirty dozen" oscillated across a spectrum of opposing values: patriotism/perfidy, legality/illegality, racial discord/class solidarity, and reform/revolution. They played out these dialectics in the streets and within the soldiers' parliament. To differentiate, we might divide the twelve in half. On the one hand were the six *prostrike patriots*. William Bathie, Adam Hay, Frederick Law, Frank Lazenby, Arthur "Jack" Moore, and Charles Mounsey exemplify conventional portrayals of the striker-soldier. These veterans articulated a labour patriotism that positioned the Strike's demands and their rights and sacrifices as soldiers in the context of traditional British values. The patriots believed maintaining peace was commensurate with the legality of the Strike itself, that the working class could be defined in racial and exclusionary terms, and that the reforms demanded did not threaten liberal capitalism. On the other hand were the half-dozen *prostrike insurgents*—Roger Bray, Samuel Cartwright, Thomas Dunn, John Farnell, James Grant, and Joseph Martin. For the insurgents, mutiny could dislodge national and imperial allegiances. They decried constitutional law and order as morally bankrupt, leaned towards ethnically inclusive worker solidarity, and believed that the Strike's aims would fundamentally transform economic and state relations. The fluidity within and between the patriots and insurgents suggest that the Strike challenged untested assumptions, dislodged deeply held beliefs, and created opportunities to think and act otherwise.

To discover the dynamic values among the prostrike twelve requires an investigation of their war records and their fragmentary and often biased appearance in contemporary newspaper reports. This chapter begins by contrasting the prostrike twelve by nationality, age, marital status, occupation, rank, and war service. The second section traces the demobilized prostrike patriots and their relationship to veteran associations, labour, and antialien protest prior to May 1919. The third section reconnoitres the vulnerable salient which patriot and insurgent veteran leaders advanced during the revolt. The final section assesses the varying roles of the prostrike twelve in veteran and labour circles in the Strike's aftermath.

The Demographics of Winnipeg 1919's "Dirty Dozen"

The prostrike twelve were all born in the United Kingdom and immigrated to Canada prior to the Great War.[12] With their cross-Atlantic connection they remained tethered not just to the Empire, but also to a rich history of soldier uprisings. From the English Revolution to the nineteenth-century birth of the working class, ex-soldiers and sailors comprised an integral phalanx of popular resistance to modern political tyranny, enclosures, and economic and social inequity. Strike leader A.A. Heaps once contrasted the 1819 Peterloo massacre with "Bloody Saturday." Victorious at Waterloo and Vimy Ridge respectively, soldiers joined their working-class brethren to demand the franchise in Manchester and collective bargaining rights in Winnipeg. The veterans of the Napoleonic Wars, "were promised many things, just as today, and received nothing," Heaps reminded his audience. Instead, the "armed forces of the Law" violently attacked its heroes.[13]

At the time of the revolt, the prostrike organizers ranged in age from thirty to fifty years old, with a mean age of thirty-eight.[14] They were all married, and most were already fathers. A decade senior than the average veteran in 1919, they were the elder statesmen within their band of brothers.

To a certain extent, prewar occupations demarcate the patriots from the insurgents. Several of the patriots did not have obvious connections with the working class: Law, club manager; Mounsey, architect/civil engineer; and Lazenby, policeman. Alternatively, patriot Bathie was a precariously employed labourer/caretaker, Hay a low-level accounting clerk in the Canadian Pacific Railway (CPR) freighthouse, and Moore a Canadian National Railway (CNR) painter.[15] Among the insurgents only Grant, a real estate agent, held a white-collar job prior to the war. The other insurgents made a living with their hands, including: Bray, butcher; Cartwright, CPR mechanic; Dunn, street railway motorman; Farnell, railway switchman; and Martin, farmer/trapper. Three insurgents and patriot Moore were active in the prewar labour movement. Dunn was one-time president of the Street Railway Union; Cartwright once presided over the Brotherhood of Railroad Carmen, Jubilee Lodge, alongside vice-president Moore.[16] Bray's foray as a radical Methodist preacher suggests he held prewar labour sympathies.[17] The prostrike twelve knew the hardships of work as well as war. Deleterious health effects of working-class life marked their bodies—a rail injury had left

Cartwright blind in one eye, while others suffered from a variety of prewar ailments. Precarious labour was also common—Bray enlisted to escape unemployment and a soldier's pay enticed an injured Farnell to reenlist twice.

Those with a military resume prior to the Great War were less likely to evince radical sympathies. Five of the six patriots and only one of the insurgents were previously in uniform.[18] All of the patriots and four of the insurgents enlisted before 1916. All twelve averaged 140 weeks as soldier-workers. None were commissioned officers, but the patriots and insurgents contrast in the uniformity of rank and war record.[19] Patriots Law, Moore, and Mounsey were sergeants, Lazenby was a corporal, and Bathie and Hay were privates. Conversely, all the insurgents held the rank of private. Of the patriots, all but Mounsey saw the frontlines, whereas only insurgents Dunn, Farnell, and Martin experienced the horror of the trenches. A poor general physique kept Mounsey from France and Belgium. Only the visually impaired Cartwright did not serve overseas: the lone conscript, he was struck off strength five months after being drafted. Rheumatism and bronchitis kept Grant in England, while an injured thumb during training excused Bray from crossing the Channel. Although their adversaries singled out Bray and Cartwright's undistinguished military records, the prostrike dozen could all claim they were part of the soldier proletariat, swept up in the machinery of war.[20]

Four of the five patriots who fought in Flanders' fields sustained injuries. Law, Hay, and Bathie were medically discharged in 1916. Hay survived several gas poisonings before a shell buried him in a trench along the Ypres Salient in July 1915, crippling his feet. Law was scarred by bullet and shrapnel wounds, but bladder stones ultimately led to his release. "General overstrain" and gonorrhoea relieved Bathie of duty. After an injury during the Vimy offensive, a gunshot wound at Arras in April 1918 ended Moore's career as a machine gun sergeant. He demobilized in Winnipeg in January 1919. Lazenby returned later that month, having survived multiple injuries at Passchendaele and Vimy over the course of his service.[21]

Of the three insurgents who battled on the Western Front, only Farnell incurred injuries. A shrapnel wound at Armentières in February 1915 required the amputation of Farnell's toe. Prior heart problems and almost complete deafness ultimately made Farnell unfit for service by late 1916. Martin, only seven weeks on the front in 1915, spent the bulk of his service as a regimental barber. He was eventually discharged in September 1917 due to syphilis, a knee injury, and heart trouble. Furious that the doctors attributed his health issues to prewar ailments and offered him only a partial pension, Martin signed off on his discharge papers as "refus[ing] to accept 8 dollars per month as it doesn't cover one-third of my present disability." With his injured thumb, Bray butchered and cooked in the training camps until his return in January 1919. Dunn, who divided his war service between trench duty and camp carpentry, demobilized in Winnipeg physically unscathed in mid-June 1919 in time to participate in the General Strike's climax.[22]

Prostrike Patriots and the Origins of the Striker-Soldier

Patriots Hay and Law were the first to organize Winnipeg's ex-soldiers. The elite and charitable Returned Soldiers' Association (RSA) was not for them. The RSA's $5 membership fee annoyed Hay. Desiring an organization exclusively for Great War veterans that was neither the RSA's "association of businessmen," as Law put it, or a fee-based organization like the Army and Navy Veterans (ANV), the two inaugurated the Great War Veterans' Association (GWVA) on 17 September 1916.[23] In March 1917 GWVA president Hay and secretary Law appeared in front of the Special Committee on Returned Soldiers' Problems where they voiced frustration with war profiteers, the Pension Board (from its heavy bureaucracy to the inequality of rank-tiered pensions), the civilian-managed patriotic associations, and the stigma attached to accepting charity from the Patriotic Fund. A month later, at a national meeting of ex-servicemen in Winnipeg, Hay and Law played leading roles in expanding the GWVA into a national organization.[24]

The GWVA was the most important of veterans' associations prior to the 1925 consolidation of ex-servicemen organizations into the Canadian Legion. The GWVA was far from being a reactionary force; instead, it was a fluid site of class struggle. During its existence, GWVA members frequently overruled former commissioned officers. GWVA activists kept alive the calls for a war-service bonus and pension reforms that stood to benefit the poorest among them, and, in allegiance with larger working-class concerns, demanded union recognition and the right to strike. Rank-and-filers ensured the GWVA offered scathing critiques of war profiteering, inflation, and economic inequality. Taxing

Figure 3.1. Frederick Law, 1883–1960. Source: Great War Veterans' Association of Canada (Winnipeg Branch), *Year Book* (Winnipeg: Great War Veterans' Association of Canada, Winnipeg Branch, 1919), 15.

Figure 3.2. "Adam Hay, 1882–1940." Source: "Photograph of the Brotherhood of Railway Clerks," *San Francisco Chronicle*, 20 July 1919.

land speculation, breaking up the two-party system, and introducing proportional representation were among the GWVA's earliest political priorities. In 1918 Law warned Ottawa that labour and the returned soldier would align to "run the machinery of the government." "It is ridiculous for men to fight for their country and then return to have their patience exhausted by official negligence," said Law.[25]

Animus towards enemy aliens, anticonscriptionists, and the left complicated the GWVA's inner class struggle. In January 1917, Hay and Law took issue with Winnipeg MLA and labour social reformer F.J. Dixon, after he encouraged the burning of registration cards. Veterans chased Dixon out of a theatre and attacked him in an alleyway. Hay and Law organized a Dixon recall petition and held boisterous conscription meetings; riots were only narrowly averted.[26] Hay and Law also supported several resolutions during the first national GWVA meeting, including a call to disenfranchise enemy aliens and the sequestration of German-owned land. Yet Hay's patriotic animus also targeted the civilian elite. In May 1917, Hay accused and then refused to apologize to two upper-class women who, owing to ill health, failed to stand at a tribute to Great War soldiers; facing class censure, Hay was nudged out of the leadership of the GWVA.[27]

The GWVA's rebuke and class upheaval shifted Hay's allegiances and perspective. Hay signed a union card shortly after the Western Freight Handlers' Union expanded its membership to include clerks and station employees in June 1918.[28] Hay soon shared the stage with erstwhile adversaries—anticonscriptionists, pacifists, and labour radicals. At a gathering supporting striking metal trades workers in August, Hay suggested the Great War had caused an evolution in the class struggle. If "the aristocratic officer is a thing of the past," and the common soldier sought to "rid the world of the Kaiser and make for the world true democracy," why, asked Hay, "can't we get together here and help make it for democracy?" Strikes expose employer hypocrisy, believed Hay. "The masters are saying there is a war on and all must serve," he said. "But the masters do not serve . . . they are doing a lot of flag waving. That is all."[29] In October, Hay, as the newly elected president of the local Western Freight Handlers' Union, directed his coworkers to strike in sympathy with their picketing Calgary brethren—the action's relative success portended the 1919 revolt. The CPR took back all the workers, except Hay. Hay was fired after publicly "thank[ing] God that [he] did not scab during the recent strike." A threatened second work stoppage resulted in his reinstatement. The *WLN* opined that "this is 'SOME' treatment for a man who has done his 'bit' over there." In early 1919, Hay was elected as the vice-president of the Winnipeg Trades and Labor Council (WTLC), a position he would hold over the course of the Strike.[30]

Where Hay's patriotism pivoted towards labour insurgency, Bathie and Moore's arrival on the Winnipeg scene coincided with a new surge in xenophobia and antisocialism. They first came to prominence following the antialien violence that shook Winnipeg in January 1919, when 300 veterans, following provocations from the Citizens, rioted, attacked foreigners, and destroyed the Edelweiss Brewery, the German club, and socialist Sam Blumenburg's dry cleaning business.[31] Law acted as a "peacemaker" during the rampage, but later declared that had he not been a GWVA official he "would have helped 'clean out' the aliens."[32] Representatives of Winnipeg's labour movement immediately held meetings with veterans to assuage their reactionary violence; meetings where Bathie and Moore acted as de facto spokespersons for the rioters. James Winning, president of the WTLC and a friend of Hay, insisted that just as soldiers fought in Flanders alongside international allies, the workers who had remained in Canada fought profiteers in an "economic war," with allies from "all nations and all crafts."[33] For their part, Moore and Bathie riled the veteran crowds with attacks on the pacifist, Reverend William Ivens, editor of the *WLN* and future Strike

Figure 3.3. A.E. Moore, 1881–1950. Source: "Named to Test Loyalty of Aliens in Manitoba," *Winnipeg Tribune*, 8 February 1919.

Figure 3.4. William Bathie, 1869–1952. Source: Great War Veterans' Association of Canada (Winnipeg Branch), *Year Book*, 15.

organizer, who gently reminded them that the source of their economic hardship was the capitalist, not the pacifist.[34]

Outside of Winnipeg, engagement with anticonscriptionists also constrained Farnell's political allegiances. Following his final demobilization in 1917, the city of Brandon offered him work at $1.50 a day. In Brandon, Farnell joined the GWVA, attended political meetings, and wrote patriotic letters in which he deprecated civilian criticism of soldiers' drinking habits, and disparaged a sermon by anticonscriptionist and future Labour Church leader and communist A.E. Smith.[35] In 1918, he relocated to Windsor where he remained an active GWVA member.[36] Farnell's pre-revolt politics made him an unlikely insurgent, but as the Strike escalated his personal views were upended—where once he fired verbal volleys at teetotalling civilians and anticonscriptionists, he would soon sight capitalist elites in his crosshairs.

Persistent labour overtures to the returned veteran won many over to the necessity of worker solidarity, but the future prostrike patriots persisted in making enemy aliens and the Bolshevist threat central concerns. Law and Moore paraded to the provincial legislature in February 1919 urging the deportation of enemy aliens. Following the demonstration, as a newly hired employee of the provincial Alien Investigation Board, Moore demanded the registration of foreigners. On 14 May, two weeks after the building and metal trades workers had walked off the job, and on the evening before the Strike spread throughout the city, Bathie waited on Premier Norris to push for alien deportations. Underneath the fragile alliances between labour and ex-servicemen seethed significant ideological differences.[37]

Winnipeg 1919 and the Soldiers' Parliament

An untold number of striker-soldiers joined the 35,000 workers who participated in the Winnipeg revolt. Many were unemployed while others had just stepped out of their khakis. The GWVA, other veterans' bodies, the Citizens' Committee, and the authorities tried in vain to solidify veterans behind the banner of law and order and to stand in official neutrality, if not outright hostility to the Strike. They raised the spectre of enemy aliens, anarchists and Reds, but most of the rank and file would not be duped. During the Strike's early stages, the cautious prostrike patriots liaised with the Strike Committee and helped to maintain the peace. But by June, the police lockout, the induction of the specials, and the Citizens' misrepresentation of veteran direct actions polarized the prostrike camp. The six insurgent veterans, the soldiers' parliaments in Victoria Park where they held court, and their massive marches through the city's streets were among the lightning rods that led to "Bloody Saturday" and the Strike's tragic climax.

On 15 May, veteran organizations called a mass meeting to vow neutrality and to uphold "law and order" against a Bolshevik conspiracy. Instead, 2,500 veterans overwhelmed their conservative executives and resolved themselves in "full sympathy" with the Strike. They promised to uphold constitutional authority, and, only at the behest of GWVA vice-president J.O. Newton, added that labour and ex-soldiers should discuss the "deportation of the enemy alien" after the Strike had ended.[38] Hecklers accused the leaders of being capitalist sycophants. To allay reactionaries, three GWVA representatives—Law, Bathie, and Moore—were added to the Strike Committee.[39] Five days later, another veteran mass meeting declared neutrality, but at the same time endorsed workers' rights to union recognition and collective bargaining. The Strike Committee was under "clean, strong, white management," reported chauvinist Bathie.[40]

The GWVA organ, the *Manitoba Veteran*, was right to assume that by the end of May, the "influence of the returned man" would define the Strike's final stage, but perhaps not in the ways anticipated.[41] The posting of the yellow-dog police contract on 30 May sparked a new militancy among the ex-servicemen. Almost the entire force of 200 constables, many of them former soldiers, including Lazenby, would be locked out for refusing to sign the ultimatum. Thousands of veterans, organized by patriots Moore and Bathie and insurgent Bray, began their daily marches to the legislature and to city hall. Bathie told Premier Norris that the returned soldiers preferred a prostrike police presence to having the military "flood" the streets, but he would also voice misogynist displeasure that Helen Armstrong, the radical socialist, feminist, and anticonscriptionist, had dared to address the veteran crowds.[42] Moore called the police ultimatum an insult and promised the revolt would continue until they won the right to "collective bargaining, a living wage, and the sympathetic strike itself."[43] Protesting veterans tore Union Jack badges off parliamentary leaders, accusing them of "prostituting the flag" at the behest of "the plutocratic Committee of One Thousand."[44] During one march, ex-servicemen destroyed the Citizens' banner that hung over their Industrial Hall headquarters; in another, they paraded to Wellington Crescent and booed the homes of the wealthy.[45] Citizen A.L. Crossin felt that "these men only needed weapons to become an army."[46]

Over the course of these demonstrations, Bray usurped Moore as the chosen leader of the striker-soldiers. Although the antistrike press smeared Bray as not a "real soldier" and a debt-shirker who did most of his "fighting chasing round England looking at pigeons and fowls," the diminutive Bray, sporting a distinctive chevron moustache, galvanized striker-soldiers with his impressive oratorical skills.[47] Few elites escaped his harangues—he derided Senator G.D. Robertson, the federal government's negotiator—for his "disgraceful tactics" and unelected authority, and smeared federal parliamentarians as a "spineless bunch of incompetents."[48] Bray led calls for Premier Norris's resignation after he refused to enact compulsory collective bargaining. During the veterans' sieges on the provincial government Bray advocated socialist "control of industry by the worker."[49] Some ex-servicemen bristled at Bray's revolutionary pronouncements, but they did capture evolving veteran frustration over employer intransigence and government inaction. Bray insisted the sympathetic strike was the only "lawful weapon left to the worker," but he went far beyond the Strike Committee in promoting an escalation of tactics. Bray exposed the massing of troops and machine guns and publicized rumoured plots to plant bombs on Strike leaders. Bray told an undercover detective that several thousand ex-servicemen were prepared to seize the barracks. Historians have

Figure 3.5. Roger Bray, 1875–1952. Source: "Soldier Strike Leader's Revolt Boast is Quoted," *Winnipeg Tribune*, 5 August 1919.

called Bray's threat a tactically "unwise joke," that only confirmed to authorities that the Strike had become a "constitutional menace" that necessitated armed intervention.[50] However, Bray's threat was part of a rhetorical and material escalation of conflict in which striker-soldiers sought to break free of a stalemate that was almost certain to favour the state and capital.

The emergence of leaders like Bray and the growing militancy of the prostrike veteran forces dumbfounded the Citizens' Committee of 1000. Citizens' propaganda merely further estranged working-class veterans by casting aspersions that striker-soldiers could only be aliens, Bolsheviks, or conscripts. Grasping for legitimacy, the Citizens fronted the short-lived Returned Soldiers' Loyalist Association (RSLA), which mounted several demonstrations and served as a recruiting ground for the specials. Led by Captain Wheeler of the ANV and Frederick G. Thompson, an ex-Captain, lawyer, and Citizens' crony, the RSLA fanned the flames of xenophobia and promoted vigilante justice.[51] The Citizens financed a fleet of cars to bring in unwitting veterans from Tuxedo, while large firms, like Eaton's and Ford Motors, offered paid holidays for their ex-soldier staff to join the RSLA gatherings. Antistrike forces inflated both the support for the RSLA and the number of recruits sworn in as specials; after two days, fewer than 250 civilians and ex-soldiers were persuaded by the inducement of six dollars a day (a princely sum in postwar Canada) to enforce law and order.[52] At the soldiers' parliament, Bray mocked the RSLA, who despite bribes, "hadn't been able to muster a platoon." Many of the recruits, he contended, were not ex-soldiers at all, but white-collar clerks. He reported that striker-soldiers confiscated 300 gallons of beer, a gift to the RSLA by the Citizens, and poured it down the sewer. Bray accepted Wheeler's public challenge to a "personal fight," promising a battle "to the finish on any grass plot in town."[53] Violence was not limited to rhetoric. On 4 June, parades of the RSLA and striker-soldiers crossed paths and several skirmishes ensued.

By this point, the GWVA officer-class executives dropped all pretense of neutrality. They repudiated Bray and the direct actions of the ex-servicemen, and expressed support for the upstart RSLA.[54] A day earlier, a GWVA mass meeting was again overwhelmed by striker-soldiers who resolved that the GWVA go on record "giving their entire support to the present strikers."[55] The GWVA leadership embarrassingly declared the resolution illegitimate.[56] Bray retorted that it was the striker-soldiers who had "disowned the executives" of the city's veterans' organizations. Shortly afterwards, Bathie, Moore, and Law were expelled from the Strike Committee.[57] Neutrality was no longer a tenable veteran position. Bathie, Moore, and Law's diplomacy and competing allegiances were treated with suspicion by both the pro- and antistrike forces, leading to a polarization that isolated the prostrike patriots and ignited greater insurgency.

Upwards of 10,000 striker-soldiers continued to gather and parade daily. Their parliaments broke down the hierarchy of military command, as rank-and-file veterans lamented the costs of the war for democracy and the battles for freedom still to be waged. Hay, the patriot turned insurgent labour leader, took the stage to combine a critique of state tyranny with the freedoms won by labour. "The day of autocracy was past," he pronounced. "If it were not for organized labor all would be veritable slaves."[58] Meanwhile, Farnell was among those rounded up by Deputy Police Chief Chris Newton on 6 June after 6,000 veterans, replete with a brass band and pipers, disobeyed Mayor Gray's parade prohibition. Farnell invited the mayor to the soldiers' parliament and encouraged the "boys" to "fire so many questions at him that he will get himself so tied up that he won't know where he is at."[59] Gray's parade injunction held, but on 10 June, a day after the police dismissal, 200-odd specials provoked a three-hour riot in a failed attempt to recapture Portage and Main from the strikers. Citizen A.J. Andrews watched as predominantly "labour returned men," responded with bricks, stones,

Figure 3.6. John Farnell, 1889–1927. Source: www.ancestry.ca, n.d.

Figure 3.7. Charles Mounsey, 1874–1924. Source: "Has Labor's Support as Ward 2 Nominee," *Winnipeg Tribune*, 30 November 1920.

and glass bottles until the specials were forced to retreat.[60] Moore, Bray, and Farnell joined Rev. Major Frederick Scott, the senior chaplain to the 1st Canadian Division, to petition Mayor Gray to withdraw the specials. The beloved chaplain, after declaring himself in favour of collective bargaining to strikers in Victoria Park, attempted to broker peace, but was stymied by the intransigence of the Citizens and the RSLA.[61] Deemed too sympathetic to the Strike, on 14 June specials forced him out of the city, using what Reverend Scott would later call "Prussian methods."[62] Scott's cameo only served to legitimate the insurgents and embolden the striker-soldiers.

For some of the prostrike patriots, the radicalization of veterans proved difficult to stomach. Law made no effort to disguise his dislike of Bray and refused to comment on the riots.[63] Mounsey, an unemployed civil engineer, found the violence regrettable but also questioned the need for the specials and recognized that one could not avoid taking sides with either capital or labour, the two "mighty gladiators" of the era.[64] On 13 June Bathie wrote a letter to the GWVA that was published by the press and used as Citizens' propaganda. In it, Bathie claimed the "white management" of the Strike Committee had been usurped by a "foreign born" leadership that made returned soldiers "goats of a propaganda that seeks the destruction of everything constitutional."[65] Although anti-Red, racist, misogynist and obviously miffed by his ousting from the Strike leadership, Bathie would disapprove of the Citizens' "unwarranted liberty in advertising me and my letter," and rejected their attempt to "extol [his] loyalty." The patriotic Striker remained proud of

Figure 3.8. "Frank Lazenby, 1886–1970." Source: www.ancestry.ca, n.d.

Figure 3.9. Joseph Martin, 1886–1935. Source: "One Will Be Elected—Who?," *Winnipeg Tribune*, 23 October 1923.

his role as a "returned soldier movement worker," despite being assailed from both sides.[66]

On 16 June ten Strike leaders were arrested and sent to Stony Mountain penitentiary. Among those rounded up were Bray and two other ex-servicemen. The thousands who gathered in the soldiers' parliament were "electrified by the arrests" and "vibrant with emotion."[67] The ex-servicemen branded the arrests as a "dirty and despicable trick."[68] Farnell, Grant, Lazenby, Martin, and Dunn made up for Bray's absence. Lazenby, the discharged policeman, told the assembly: "Here we have, in the dead of night, a gang of people supposed to represent constituted authority, going to the homes of citizens, and tearing them out of their beds before their women-folk and children. As a citizen of this country I protest against such actions carried out in the name of constituted authority."[69] Patriot Lazenby's beliefs in law and order teetered in the wake of the Strike leaders' arrests as he crossed over, at least partially, into the insurgent camp. Veteran frustration in the Strike's trenches was palpable. They declared themselves willing to "fight against any body of men," who would seek to deny them the British right to free speech.[70] By 20 June, the parliamentarians refused to be "hidden away in Victoria Park and to be dictated to any longer."[71] Trained in the arts of war, not diplomacy, insurgent striker-soldiers imbued the revolt with the language and action of the militant.

On the eve of "Bloody Saturday," veterans gathered 5,000-strong in Market Square where they voted in favour of a silent demonstration. The crowd heckled the special police who observed the demonstration through the windows of city hall. "We'll hold that parade . . . and all hell will not stop us," said Grant; comrade Dunn agreed.[72] For his part, the now thoroughly radicalized Farnell promoted the proposed "indignation parade," as "the time has come when 1,000 men cannot dictate to the 200,000 citizens of Winnipeg." He also called for a siege on the Citizens' headquarters.[73] With "massed action" they had beaten the Germans, declared Martin, and their "brains and brawn" were required once again to defeat their capitalist foe. "A massed mob" was "the only weapon we have left," he said.[74] "Constituted authority has failed to produce results," Martin clarified on the morning of 21 June. He recommended the dismissal of all elected officials in the city.[75] Grant was equally unequivocal: "They are talking of soviets and revolution and if they don't watch out it will be a soviet government we'll establish." Grant aligned himself with the syndicalist upstart, the One Big Union (OBU), and declared that workers should be allowed to call "sympathetic" strikes, "whether the international [union] officers say so or not." He urged boycotting antiunion department stores and promised that "the time is coming when we labor men will dictate" work conditions.[76]

That afternoon, the striker-soldiers and their supporters gathered at Portage and Main. As the mayor read the riot act, Royal North-West Mounted Police (RNWMP), military forces, and the police specials descended on the strikers, drawing guns and swinging bats. Protesters overturned a streetcar and set it ablaze. For over two hours the battle raged—ninety-four protesters were arrested and countless were injured. Michael Sokolowski was shot dead and another striker died later of gunshot wounds. "They treated us worse than we ever treated Fritzy," declared one veteran survivor.[77] After the battle, Lazenby addressed a crowd of battered and bruised prostrike veterans. He lamented the "bloodshed," advised everyone to go home, but insisted they not give up. "If we are to be beaten down and trodden upon, we won't take it lying down," concluded Lazenby to "wild cheers."[78] In the days that followed, police arrested insurgent striker-soldiers—Farnell, Martin, and Grant—for allegedly inciting a riot.[79]

Prostrike Veterans in the Aftermath of "Bloody Saturday"

The winds of insurgency battered veterans' fidelity to capital, state, and Empire.[80] On 24 June, after Mayor Gray refused Farnell, Grant, and Lazenby's request to hold a veteran gathering, over 1,000 returned men journeyed outside of city limits to the St. Boniface baseball grounds.[81] Out of this last soldiers' parliament, veterans organized the Ex-Soldiers and Sailors Labour Party (ESSLP). It was at the March 1919 Western Labour Conference, the birthplace of the OBU, that a joint soldier/labour committee was first proposed.[82] Vancouver veterans started the first ESSLP; Winnipeg ex-servicemen delayed their own until the denouement of the Strike. Cribbing their organizational structure and constitution from their Vancouver comrades, the party welcomed all pro-labour veterans and called for sweeping economic and democratic reforms, including the confiscation of all capitalist profits over 7.5 percent since 1914; the reclamation of all land held by speculators; public ownership of a wide range of industries and utilities; unemployment insurance; free public education, including university; referendum and recall legislation; and proportional representation. The all-male gathering also demanded equal pay and full suffrage for women.[83]

Although the St. Boniface meeting included a Vancouver-centric call to deport Asian Canadians, it remained remarkably silent on the enemy alien "problem." The tragedy of Bloody Saturday signalled a loosening of racist attitudes. Veteran H. Mitchell and a half-dozen strikers testified to the innocence of the Polish-born Sokolowski, who died during the riots. Sokolowski threw no stones, said Mitchell, and in fact, the so-called "enemy alien" had a brother who had enlisted in the 49th Battalion at Edmonton and was wounded at Passchendaele.[84] The ESSLP's defence of Sokolowski narrowed the divide between soldier and immigrant strikers. The federal government's amendment to the Immigration Act, which expanded existing legislation to allow the state to deport not only radical enemy aliens but also British-born malcontents, helped provoke such cross-ethnic unity. Instead of demanding the expulsion of foreigners, the ESSLP subverted the rushed 6 June amendment to petition for their own deportation: "We, the Returned Soldiers and Sailors of Canada and His Majesty's forces, who fought for Freedom and Liberty, now resident in the City of Winnipeg, do demand the Government . . . to deport us to our mother countries according to [the] latest amendment to the Immigration Act. As we . . . find that this country is not governed in the Democratic spirit for which we fought."[85] A stinging rebuke to constituted authority, as many as 2,000 veterans signed the petition. The mainstream veterans' organizations condemned the ESSLP and promised to blacklist its recruits.[86]

While the ESSLP only lasted until 1922 and achieved little electoral success, for the prostrike twelve, the revolt remained a pivotal event in their lives. Most of the prostrike patriots continued their advocacy within the GWVA and its successor, the Canadian Legion. Hay, Moore, and Mounsey maintained close connections to the labour movement, while Bathie, Law, and Lazenby proved to be one-time interlopers. Racism, ardent nationalism, and anti-Bolshevism inflected the post-strike politics of the patriots, especially Moore. Shying away from both the GWVA and the Legion, all the insurgents but the imprisoned Farnell were active in the ESSLP. Four of them made the OBU home. Others supported the Independent Labour Party of Manitoba (ILPM). Increasingly, the insurgents identified as labour, not veteran, organizers. Imperial and class war took its toll; of Winnipeg's "dirty dozen," four did not live to witness the Second World War.

After his meteoric ascent into the house of labour, Hay remained a staunch labourist, at least until he disappears from the public record. At the National Industrial Conference held in September 1919, Hay declared he did not "believe in socialism." But, he added, he had enlisted to support his class, not the British Empire: "I did not go over there to fight for King and country . . . I went over to punish . . . your so-called German Socialists who betrayed the British labour movement." Although anti-Red, Hay knew "better conditions" for the working class would not be won without a fight.[87] Following the Strike, Hay sided with the internationalists against the OBU.[88] In the early 1920s, as grand vice-president of the International Union of Railway Clerks and Freight Handlers, Hay was involved in union raids against A.R. Mosher's more radical and nationalist rival, the Canadian Brotherhood of Railway Employees.[89]

Law proved the least labour friendly of the prostrike twelve. As the general manager of the Carleton Club, a male-only institution frequented by the Citizens, Law's allegiances were always suspect. As a witness during the Strike trials, Law was at a loss to describe why veterans who had previously rioted against pacifists and foreigners supported the Strike.[90] Law ran unsuccessfully for the provincial Liberal Party in 1920 and remained connected to the GWVA as its provincial organizer.[91] He managed the elite Carleton Club until his death in 1960.[92]

Like Law, Bathie could never quite embrace labour's cause. His equivocation and white male posturing helped him move up in the world; following the Strike, the former security guard landed a coveted job as a city licensing inspector, a position he held until his retirement.[93] A proponent for a soldier's gratuity into the 1920s, Bathie remained troubled by the incongruity between the promises made to Canada's heroes and their actual postwar treatment. But rather than accuse the government or capitalism for forgetting the veteran, Bathie blamed the returned man for "want of organising or too much organising."[94] Full of nostalgia, and sympathetic to those who survived the "hell-fire of Flanders," in 1924 Bathie presided over the St. James branch of the GWVA and likely continued to participate in Legion activities until his death in 1952.[95]

Despite Lazenby's incendiary speeches, the police commission reinstated the career soldier and police officer. His insurgency proved spasmodic; his solidarity collapsed into self-interest. Lazenby enforced capitalist law poststrike, arresting the poor on charges of begging and vagrancy.[96] In 1921 he left Winnipeg to become the police chief in Kamsack, Saskatchewan.[97]

"Jack" Moore built a political career as an ex-serviceman and friend of the workingman. Moore would say his benevolent activities were born from his promise to care for the orphaned sister of a soldier who died in the "muddy trenches of France."[98] But his charity had its limits, and he craved the attention of elites as much as his working-class comrades. Moore was elected as a labour MLA between 1920 and 1922, and served as president of the Manitoba command of the GWVA until 1925. To avoid having officers dominate the Canadian Legion, Moore was appointed as the Legion's national chairman in 1925, a figurehead position he held for the next twenty-five years.[99] "Wars are not brought about for the benefit of the working classes, but it is the working class that has to pay the price in blood and money," declared a class-conscious Moore in 1920.[100] While Moore advocated better treatment for poor widows and disabled ex-servicemen, including shell-shock sufferers, his appeals did not extend to immigrants.[101] In 1932, when CNR threatened to lay off veterans, Moore used his position in the Legion to call for the firing of all unnaturalized employees.[102] Just as he did in 1919, Moore disrupted communist organizing of ex-servicemen CNR employees by sewing racial division.

An outlier who fit uneasily in the patriot/insurgent paradigm, Mounsey found his political footing after the Strike. An executive member of the ESSLP, Mounsey spoke passionately for the veterans' bonus and ran unsuccessfully on the ESSLP ticket in the 1920 municipal elections.[103] Winnipeg "is run by the golden big stick, wielded from New York," the architect and civil engineer told the electorate.[104] Like Moore, Mounsey sought support for war-traumatized comrades. Mounsey never openly engaged in xenophobic rhetoric, nor was he active in the GWVA. The revolt had brought the insurgent out in Mounsey—when he died in 1924, he was remembered as a committed champion of labour.[105]

The most infamous of the prostrike insurgents, Bray participated in the ESSLP while awaiting trial. Criminal charges would not hold his tongue: "It is a capitalists' peace as it was a capitalists' war," he told a crowd of 2,000 in September 1919.[106] Bray served six months in prison for his role in the Strike. Between 1920 and 1923 Bray was on the OBU executive and a paid labour organizer. Relocating to Vancouver in the 1930s, Bray became involved in the Co-operative Commonwealth Federation (CCF). Among his CCF activities, Bray advocated extending the franchise to Asian Canadians.[107]

Dunn carried on the Strike's legacy within the ESSLP, ILPM, and the OBU. In October 1919, the ESSLP elected Dunn as their paid organizer.[108] Speaking out against Canada's military incursion in Soviet Russia, Dunn declared in 1920 that Canadian and Russian workers should stand "shoulder to shoulder." Formerly "patriotic" ex-servicemen would never "again go through the suffering they endured in the recent war," he told a cheering crowd.[109] As an ILPM candidate, he ran unsuccessfully in the 1922 federal by-election and in the 1932 provincial election.[110] His only successful candidacy was as a school board trustee in 1923.[111] Dunn, a street railwayman, held key positions in the OBU, including as secretary and as publisher of the *OBU Bulletin*. Defiant of state regulations, he was fined twice for his participation in the OBU's illegal sweepstakes contests.[112] Dunn's 1962 obituary noted his war record and membership in the Canadian Legion but made no mention of his lifelong involvement in the labour movement.[113]

Cartwright kept a low profile during the Strike, but he stood as one of its most ardent defenders in the interwar years. Elected as the ESSLP president in August 1919, the war conscript deflected charges against his war record and that the ESSLP was an OBU front.[114] He insisted the party welcomed no officers into its membership, explaining that

Figure 3.10. Thomas Dunn, 1884–1962. Source: www.ancestry.ca, n.d.

Figure 3.11. Samuel Cartwright, 1885–1961. Source: "Nominated Today to Contest Provincial Elections," *Winnipeg Tribune*, 8 July 1922.

"all the workers were not soldiers, but nearly all the soldiers were workers."[115] Cartwright stood unsuccessfully as the ESSLP candidate during the municipal election in 1919 and in the 1920 provincial election. After his second failed candidacy, Cartwright declared the "uselessness of veterans organizing for political purposes" and advocated a purely class-based party.[116] He briefly organized for the OBU in 1920.[117] Between 1923 and 1933 Cartwright served as the president of the ILPM.[118] Until he retired in 1955, Cartwright worked for the Winnipeg Electric Company. In his later years he supported the CCF.[119]

In February 1920, Farnell received a nine-month sentence for sedition. On May Day, Windsor protesters marched for the release of their former resident. Farnell became a father during the period of his arrest and conviction; his wife, despite periods of hospitalization, worked tirelessly with the ESSLP and labour across the country to lobby for his early release. A petition signed by 42,000 won him a commuted sentence; in August, 1920 Farnell received a warm welcome at a large gathering of Winnipeg workers.[120] Farnell continued to be active in veterans' circles until he succumbed to double pneumonia in January 1927—he was only thirty-seven years old.[121]

The sedition charges against Martin and Grant were quietly dropped in the fall of 1919. At Farnell's trial, Martin and Grant took credit for utterances attributed to their unlucky comrade.[122] In their poststrike involvement in the ESSLP, the two organizers led calls for the conscription of wealth and a tax on war profits. In 1923, Martin offered himself as an independent labour candidate in the federal by-election in North Winnipeg. Running against A.A. Heaps, the ILPM candidate and former Strike leader, Martin was accused of colluding with the Liberal candidate to split the labour vote. The reform of Ottawa's veteran bureaucracy and an elected senate were among Martin's campaign messages.[123] Despite making political capital of his role in the revolt, Martin mustered only forty-nine votes. He died in March 1936 after suffering for years from poor health.[124]

Until mid-1920, Grant served on the ESSLP executive and spoke at Labour Church gatherings in support of the Strike's leaders.[125] After managing the Vimy and Commercial Cafés, in 1924 the ex-trooper operated his own restaurant across the street from the former Citizens' headquarters.[126] In February 1926, three bandits held Grant at gunpoint for seventeen dollars from the till.[127] Grant could not stomach the "barbarous" sentence of five years and twenty lashes meted out to the petty criminals. In a letter to the press, Grant argued he suffered far worse a robbery after the Home Bank of Canada declared bankruptcy and he lost his life's savings. "The bank directors robbed for gain," Grant wrote, "these boys robbed for the price of a few meals—which should be supplied by the city to all [the] unemployed"—it was a "perversion of justice."[128] Five months later, Grant shot himself in the basement of his restaurant. Delusions of "imagined marauders" provoked his suicide, his friends claimed.[129] Seven years of soldiering in the Imperial and Canadian forces, the Strike's ignoble repression, and the "perversion" of capitalist justice might well have been additional traumas that brought Grant to despair.

Conclusion

A reconnaissance of the prostrike twelve reveals that the barrage of patriotic appeals directed at them concealed significant differences in how they exercised their privilege and reacted to their own subjugation. Victims and agents of imperial and class war, prostrike veterans displayed a dizzying array of perspectives on patriotic loyalty, justice, class solidarity, and the need for socio-economic reform. They were not all flag-waving bigots; far from it. There is evidence of a variety of labour patriotisms within the prostrike twelve. Hay declared he fought for neither king nor country but for "British labour." Alternatively, for Bray, a "capitalist's war and a capitalist's peace" made class, not national borders the only ones that mattered. In their public rejections of "constituted authority," and the poststrike call for their own deportation, some veterans evoked British values while others may well have rejected the very premise that the British Empire stood for freedom and liberty. The learned hatred of enemy aliens motivated the behaviour of some of the prostrike twelve. But the racist angst displayed by Law and Moore is absent in the final weeks of the soldiers' parliament and cannot be attributed to many of their other comrades. Veteran politics proved heterogeneous and mutable. Prior to the revolt and in its early weeks, prostrike patriots shaped much of the veterans' response to class struggle, but as the confrontation intensified the insurgents commanded attention.

The events of the Winnipeg General Strike transformed veterans' minds. Striker-soldiers profaned the sacred values of patriotism, legality, ethnic exclusion, and class inequity as they became radicalized by the Workers' Revolt. Such blasphemy was unthinkable when reactionary and patriotic veterans rioted in January 1919—but just four months later, the prostrike twelve publicly cursed their real conditions of life and showed solidarity with their kind.[130] Their patriotic violations were incomplete, variable, and far from universal but in their actions and words they drove a temporary salient into liberal-capitalism's defences. Winnipeg's striker-soldiers won the imperial war but lost the class war. Yet in their defeat, the "dirty dozen" and their supporters were confronted with new and invigorating—and sometimes frightening—possibilities that remade them.

Notes

1 On Winnipeg 1919's striker-soldiers see, in particular, D.C. Masters, *The Winnipeg General Strike* (Toronto: University of Toronto Press, 1950); Norman Penner, ed., *Winnipeg 1919: The Strikers' Own History of the Winnipeg General Strike* (Toronto: James Lewis and Samuel, 1973); Kenneth McNaught and David J. Bercuson, *The Winnipeg Strike: 1919* (Toronto: Longman Canada, 1974); David J. Bercuson, *Confrontation at Winnipeg: Labour, Industrial Relations, and the General Strike* (Montreal and Kingston: McGill-Queen's University Press, 1974); Donald Avery, "The Radical Alien and the Winnipeg General Strike of 1919," in *The West and the Nation: Essays in Honour of W.L. Morton*, ed. Carl Berger and Ramsay Cook (Toronto: McClelland and Stewart, 1976), 209–31; Chad Reimer, "War, Nationhood, and Working-Class Entitlement: The Counterhegemonic Challenge of the 1919 Winnipeg General Strike," *Prairie Forum* 18, no. 2 (Fall 1993): 219–38; Uduak Idiong, "The Third Force: Returned Soldiers in the Winnipeg General Strike of 1919," *Manitoba History* 34 (Autumn 1997); Tom Mitchell and James Naylor, "The

Prairies: In the Eye of the Storm," in *The Workers' Revolt in Canada, 1917–1925*, ed. Craig Heron (Toronto: University of Toronto Press, 1998), 176–230; Ian McKay, *Reasoning Otherwise: Leftists and the People's Enlightenment in Canada, 1890–1920* (Toronto: Between the Lines, 2008), 417–96; Reinhold Kramer and Tom Mitchell, *When the State Trembled: How A.J. Andrews and the Citizens' Committee Broke the Winnipeg General Strike* (Toronto: University of Toronto Press, 2010).

2 Karl Marx, "Speech at the Anniversary of the *People's Paper*," in Robert C. Tucker, *The Marx-Engels Reader*, 2nd ed. (New York: W.W. Norton and Company, 1978), 577.

3 Penner, *Winnipeg 1919*, 46; Bercuson, *Confrontation at Winnipeg*, 142; Reimer, "War, Nationhood, and Working-Class Entitlement," 224.

4 Idiong, "Third Force"; Masters, *Winnipeg General Strike*, 88–90; McNaught and Bercuson, *Winnipeg Strike*, 72.

5 "The Soldier and the Strike," *Western Labor News* (hereafter *WLN*), 2 June 1919, 3.

6 Masters, *Winnipeg General Strike*, 62.

7 Avery, "Radical Alien," 222.

8 Reimer, "War, Nationhood, and Working-Class Entitlement," 220, 224.

9 Kramer and Mitchell, *When the State Trembled*, 130; Mitchell and Naylor, "Prairies," 184.

10 A study of xenophobia among civilian strikers and their leadership would be a useful complement to the arguments presented here.

11 These twelve striker-soldiers were not chosen at random. They were selected after a close textual analysis of the Strike-era issues of *Western Labor News*, *Winnipeg Tribune*, and *Manitoba Free Press*. The twelve veterans profiled were the only prostrike ex-servicemen mentioned by name and war service in multiple press reports in May–June 1919. All twelve were identified as at least partially sympathetic to the Strike, and participated, in varying capacities, as Great War–returned soldiers.

12 Nine immigrated from England, two from Scotland, and one from Ireland. Over seventy percent of Canada's first contingent were born overseas. The following details of the prostrike veterans are gleaned from their personnel records, all of which are online at https://www.bac-lac.gc.ca/eng/discover/military-heritage/first-world-war/personnel-records. Personnel details were corroborated by *Henderson's Winnipeg City Directory*, http://peel.library.ualberta.ca/bibliography/921.3.html and census data. See: William Bathie, 21342, file 29086, box 507–48, Canadian Expeditionary Force (hereafter CEF), RG 150, Library and Archives Canada (hereafter LAC); Roger Ernest Bray, 829545, file 61757, box 1026–29, CEF, RG 150, LAC; Samuel Cartwright, 3346647, file 91523, box 1555–33, CEF, RG 150, LAC; Thomas Henry Dunn, 147087, file 369789, box 2753–45, CEF, RG 150, LAC; John Farnell, 865043, file 383419, box 2996–43, CEF, RG 150, LAC; James Grant, 14436, file 429364, box 3731–7, CEF, RG 150, LAC; Adam Cramond Hay, 684, file 449409, box 4174A–52, CEF, RG 150, LAC; Frederick William Law, 71012, file 518663, box 5451–57, CEF, RG 150, LAC; Frank Lazenby, 458, file 522105, box 5479–6, CEF, RG 150, LAC; Joseph Albert Martin, 155120, file 201968, box 5989–32, CEF, RG 150, LAC; Albert Ernest Moore, 622090, file 175065, box 6318–49, CEF, RG 150, LAC; Charles Herbert Mounsey, 425633, file 179903, CEF, RG 150, LAC.

13 "Monster Crowd Greets R.B. Russell," *OBU Bulletin*, 1 January 1921, 1.

14 Their mean age corresponds with those of the official Strike leadership. By birth: Bathie (1869–1952); Mounsey (1874–1924); Grant (1875–1926); Bray (1875–1952);

Moore (1881–1950); Hay (1882–1940); Law (1883–1960); Dunn (1884–1962); Cartwright (1885–1961); Martin (1886–1935); Lazenby (1886–1970); Farnell (1889–1927).

15 Moore was on the Winnipeg Trades Council legislative standing committee in 1912. See *The Voice*, 11 October 1912, 7.

16 On Dunn, see "Sunday Cars in Operation," *Winnipeg Tribune* (hereafter *WT*), 9 July 1906, 10; "Strike May Yet Result," *WT*, 13 April 1908, 1; "Coroner Says He Must Be Obeyed," *WT*, 16 June 1910, 7; "Charge against Mayor R.H. Webb Is Dismissed," *WT*, 3 July 1926, 1. On Cartwright, see *The Voice*, 1 January 1915, 2. Moore was on the Winnipeg Trades Council legislative standing committee in 1912. See *The Voice*, 11 October 1912, 7.

17 Harry Gutkin and Mildred Gutkin, *Profiles in Dissent: The Shaping of Radical Thought in the Canadian West* (Edmonton: NeWest Press, 1997), 193.

18 The most common previous service was as soldiers in the Boer War.

19 The patriots served an average of 140.5 weeks compared to 139.6 weeks for the insurgents.

20 All details drawn from the individual digitized military records at LAC.

21 All details drawn from the individual digitized military records at LAC.

22 All details drawn from the individual digitized military records at LAC.

23 "Form Society to Assist Soldiers Who Are in Need," *WT*, 18 September 1916, 3; Law, *WT*, 27 February 1917, 4.

24 Desmond Morton and Glenn Wright, *Winning the Second Battle: Canadian Veterans and the Return to Civilian Life, 1915–1930* (Toronto: University of Toronto Press, 1987), 64; *Returned Soldiers: Proceedings of the Special Committee . . .* (Ottawa: King's Printer, 1917), 849–62, https://archive.org/details/returnedsoldiers00canarich/page/n897/mode/2up.

25 Returned Soldiers Must Have Justice or Trouble Is Ahead," *WLN*, 15 November 1918, 7.

26 Gutkin and Gutkin, *Profiles in Dissent*, 27–29; "Petition out on the Dixon Affair," *Manitoba Free Press* (hereafter *MFP*), 23 January 1917, 7; "Near Riot at Dixon Meeting," *WT*, 31 January 1917, 1, 11.

27 "2 Women Patriots Are Hissed from Tribute Meeting," *WT*, 11 May 1917, 1, 16; "Hay Refuses to Take Blame for Ousting Women," *WT*, 12 May 1917, 1, 3.

28 "Freight Handlers Expanding," *The Voice*, 28 June 1918, 8.

29 "Sympathy Shown with the Strikers," *MFP*, 9 August 1918, 5.

30 Naylor and Mitchell, "Prairies," 181, 195; "Freight Men Here Favor C.P.R. Offer," *WT*, 19 October 1918, 5; *WT*, 5 November 1918, 14; "President Hay Reinstated," *WLN*, 15 November 1918, 5.

31 Mitchell and Naylor, "Prairies," 183.

32 "Socialist Propaganda Read at Russell Trial," *MFP*, 8 December 1919, 10.

33 "President Winning Addresses Soldiers," *WLN*, 7 February 1919, 11

34 "Returned Soldiers Address Labor Church," *WLN*, 14 February 1919, 1, 8.

35 Farnell, "Advice for Slanderers," *Brandon Daily Sun* (hereafter *BDS*), 15 January 1917, 7; Farnell, "Letters of Interest," *BDS*, 23 August 1917, 7; "Anti-conscriptionists," *BDS*, 19 November 1917, 3.

36 "Veterans Resent Juggling with P.M. Position," *Windsor Star*, 1 June 1918, 7.

37 "Government Officials Welcome Opportunity to Talk to Returned Men," *WT*, 3 February 1919, 1; "Alien Investigation Board to Sit First Time Friday Morning," *WT*, 11 February 1919, 1; "Veterans' Deputation Sees Government about Aliens," *MFP*, 15 May 1919, 5.

38 "Veterans Pledged to Uphold Law and Order," *MFP*, 16 May 1919, 1, 2; "GWVA Attitude," *WLN*, 17 May 1919, 2.

39 "Provincial GWVA Delegation," *WLN*, 20 May 1919, 4.

40 "Executive of the GWVA Gets Vote of Confidence," *MFP*, 21 May 1919, 1.

41 "Returned Men Dominate Third Phase of Strike," *Manitoba Veteran* (hereafter *MV*), 7 June 1919, 1.

42 "Returned Soldiers Wait on Government," MFP, 31 May 1919, 5. On Armstrong, see "Strikers Pay Third Visit to Premier," *MFP*, 3 June 1919, 8.

43 "Noisy Crowd of Returned Soldiers Again Wait on Premier Norris," *MFP*, 2 June 1919, 1, 2.

44 "Soldiers Mean Business," *WLN*, 3 June 1919, 1, 2.

45 Penner, *Winnipeg 1919*, 86–106.

46 Kramer and Mitchell, *When the State Trembled*, 109.

47 "Never Saw France," *MFP*, 5 June 1919, 3; "R.E. Bray Known in Various Localities," *MFP*, 16 June 1919, 10.

48 *MFP*, 31 May 1919, 5; "Crowd Pays Visit to City Council," *MFP*, 2 June 1919, 1, 2.

49 "Deputation Renews Demand That Government Resign," *MFP*, 4 June 1919, 12.

50 Kramer and Mitchell, *When the State Trembled*, 253.

51 "Committee of 1,000 Organize Opposition Soldiers' Parade," *WLN*, 5 June 1919, 4; "Vets Organize Loyalist Association to Put Down Reds and Guard Citizens," *WT*, 5 June 1919, 1; Kramer and Mitchell, *When the State Trembled*, 110, 125–30, 140.

52 Kramer and Mitchell, *When the State Trembled*, 139.

53 "Strike Parade in Defiance of the Mayor's Proclamation Is Abruptly Discontinued," *MFP*, 7 June 1919, 7. For Wheeler's challenge, see *WT*, 5 June 1919, 1.

54 Vet Delegation Is Repudiated," *WT*, 31 May 1919, 1; "All Associations of War Veterans Repudiate and Regret Parades," *MFP*, 2 June 1919, 1.

55 "Great War Veterans Endorse Strike," *WLN*, 5 June 1919, 1, 4.

56 "Vets' Executive Makes Strike Resolution Void," *WT*, 5 June 1919, 2.

57 "Proposal Is Put Up to Vet Meeting," *WT*, 3 June 1919, 1, 2.

58 "Soldiers Fool Opponents," *WLN*, 4 June 1919, 1, 4.

59 *MFP*, 7 June 1919, 7.

60 Kramer and Mitchell, *When the State Trembled*, 157.

61 "Returned Men Get Concessions, *WLN*, 12 June 1919, 1, 4; Mitchell and Naylor, "Prairies," 187.

62 "Heaps in Montreal," *OBU Bulletin*, 5 June 1920, 3; Bercuson, *Confrontation at Winnipeg*, 149–50.

63 "Hundreds Rush to Join Volunteer Force," *MFP*, 12 June 1919, 6.

64 Chas H. Mounsey, "Returned Soldier Suggests a 'Daniel' for Enquiry Job," *WT*, 11 June 1919, 4.

65 "Great War Veteran Exposes Strike," *MFP*, 14 June 1919, 5; "Bathie, Labor-veterans' Leader Exposes Inner Workings of Walk-out," *WT*, 13 June 1919, 1.

66 "Bathie Explains His Statement on Bolshevism," *WT*, 16 June 1919, 5.

67 Mitchell and Naylor, "Prairies," 210.

68 "Soldiers' Parliament Strong and Calm," *WLN*, 17 June 1919, 1.

69 "Returned Soldiers Condemn Arrests," *WLN*, 18 June 1919, 4.

70 "Soldier Strikers Plan Meeting to Flay Govt. for 'Russian Methods,'" *WT*, 20 June 1919, 1.

71 "With the Returned Soldiers," *WLN*, 23 June 1919, 4.

72 "Farnell Trial Is Expected to End Tomorrow," *WT*, 17 February 1920, 1, 2.

73 "Gray Asserts Parade Will Be Broken Up," *WT*, 21 June 1919, 1, 2.

74 "Strikers Parade Called for 2.30; Mayor Says 'No,'" *MFP*, 21 June 1919, 1.

75 "Hundred Arrests Following Riots," *MFP*, 23 June 1919, 2.

76 *WT*, 21 June 1919, 1, 2.

77 "Bloody Saturday," *WLN*, 23 June 1919, 1.

78 *MFP*, 23 June 1919, 2.

79 Kramer and Mitchell, *When the State Trembled*, 205.

80 Tucker, *Marx-Engels Reader*, 476.

81 "1,000 Returned Men Are Urged to Form League," *WT*, 25 June 1919, 9; "Plans for Soldiers and Sailors Labor League Discussed," *MFP*, 25 June 1919, 5.

82 Elizabeth Anne Lees, "Problems of Pacification: Veterans' Groups in Vancouver, 1919–1922" (MA thesis, Simon Fraser University, 1985), 44–46.

83 "Constitution of Soldiers' and Sailors Labor Party of Canada," *WLN*, 18 July 1919, 4.

84 *MFP*, 25 June 1919, 5. Sokolowski's brother's military record could not be confirmed.

85 "The Returned Men Circulate Petition," *WLN*, 27 June 1919, 1. The ESSLP promised to send the petition to Prime Minister Borden, British Prime Minister Lloyd George and "to the Government of every country from which any of the soldiers came." The contents of the petition were also reported on in the *WT*, 25 June 1919, 9.

86 *WLN*, 18 July 1919, 4.

87 *National Industrial Conference on Dominion and provincial governments with representative employers and labour men, on the subject of industrial relations and labour laws, and for the consideration of the labour features of the treaty of peace* . . . (Ottawa: King's Printer, 1919), 127–29, https://archive.org/details/nationalindustri00natiuoft/page/126/mode/2up.

88 "Strikers' Release Delights Labor Men," *Ottawa Journal*, 11 September 1919, 2.

89 "Winnipeg Man Speaks at Cincinnati Meeting of Railroad Clerks," *WT*, 17 July 1920, 8; "An Absolute Falsehood, Declares A.R. Mosher," *Ottawa Journal*, 11 March 1921, 13; "Canadian Labor Delegates at Cincinnati Request Executive Representation," *WT*, 17 June 1922, 1.

90 "Labor Temple Order for Dire Necessity," *MFP*, 26 July 1919, 6.

91 *MFP*, 22 June 1920, 1.

92 *MFP*, 8 April 1960, 23.

93 *Henderson's Winnipeg City Directory*, 1920–1938, http://peel.library.ualberta.ca/bibliography/921.4.html.

94 William Bathie, "The Returned Men and Their Needs," *MFP*, 8 October 1920, 15.

95 "St. James," *WT*, 25 December 1924, 9.

96 "Local Notes," *MFP*, 25 June 1920, 6.

97 *WT*, 18 March 1921, 6.

98 "Promise Made to War-Time Comrade Started Legion Chairman on Work," *MFP*, 11 September 1950, 3.

99 Morton and Wright, *Winning the Second Battle*, 199.

100 "Intervention Protest Endorsed by Veterans at Winnipeg Meeting," *WT*, 7 September 1920, 5; "Protest against Intervention by Allied Forces in Russia," *MFP*, 7 September 1920, 12.

101 "Immense Gathering Favors Unification of Returned Soldiers," *MV*, 24 April 1920, 1; "Com. A.E. Moore, M.L.A. Makes Eloquent Plea in Local House," *MV*, 15 March 1921, 6.

102 "Alien Workers in C.N.R. Shops Will Be Laid Off First," *WT*, 12 April 1932, 1; "Mayor Urges Seniority for Returned Men," *WT*, 31 December 1932, 22; "Worker Veterans' League Fight Legion Splitter," *Worker*, 30 April 1932, 2.

103 "Soldiers' Gratuity Mass Meeting—Strong Support," *WLN*, 26 September 1919, 1, 8; "Labor Candidates' Meeting in Ward Two," *MFP*, 24 November 1920, 7.

104 "Refers to Mall as Automobile Drive," *MFP*, 27 November 1920, 24.

105 "Deaths and Funerals," *MFP*, 20 March 1924, 23.

106 "Bray's Resolutions Endorsed by Crowd," *MFP*, 15 September 1919, 5.

107 Gutkin and Gutkin, *Profiles in Dissent*, 202–3; "Oriental Vote Is CCF Plan," *Victoria Daily Times*, 26 September 1935, 6.

108 "Ex-Soldiers and Sailors to Appoint a Paid Organizer," *MFP*, 14 October 1919, 7.

109 "Intervening in Russian Affairs," *MFP*, 16 August 1920, 2; "Workers Voice Opposition to War on Bolshes," *WT*, 16 August 1920, 12. Dunn also chaired the Canadian Friends of Soviet Russia in 1923. See "Labor Repeats Protest against Immigration," *WT*, 21 March 1923, 7.

110 "West Kildonan Laborites Name New Candidate," *WT*, 5 November 1921, 6; "Three Selkirk Candidates to Forfeit Deposits," *WT*, 10 January 1922, 8; *WT*, 20 June 1932, 3.

111 "West Kildonan School Board Elects Trustees," *WT*, 3 February 1923, 1.

112 "Publisher of Guessing Coupon Is Fined $1,000," *WT*, 20 October 1926, 1; "Jail Term for Editor of OBU Is Considered," *WT*, 6 December 1933, 1; "Court Takes Drastic View of Competition," *WT*, 7 December 1933, 1.

113 "Thomas Henry Dunn," *WT*, 29 November 1962, 31.

114 "Pay $2,000 Gratuity from Excess Profits," *MFP*, 22 September 1919, 6; "Soldiers' Gratuity Mass Meeting—Strong Support," *WLN*, 26 September 1919, 1, 8.

115 "Farmer Cheered by 5,000," *OBU Bulletin*, 22 November 1919, 1; "Labor-radicals Hold Big Campaign Meeting," *MFP*, 17 November 1919, 3.

116 "Labor Victory Gains Two Seats in Council," *WLN*, 5 December 1919, 1; "How They Stand in City Returns," *WT*, 30 June 1920, 1; "Urges Vets to Avoid Politics; Sam Cartwright Sees Moral in Defeat of All Soldier Candidates," *WT*, 5 July 1920, 5.

117 *WT*, 21 February 1920, 5.

118 "ILP Honors S. Cartwright for Service," *WT*, 23 January 1933, 4.

119 *MFP*, 30 August 1961, 32.

120 "Nab Farnell on Seditious Talk Charge," *WT*, 24 July 1919, 1; "John Farnell on Trial for Uttering Sedition," *MFP*, 13 February 1920, 5; Petition for Farnell," *MFP*, 2

March 1920, 4; "To Stage Protests against Sentences Passed at 'Peg," *Windsor Star*, 24 April 1920, 20; "John Farnell to Be Released from Jail," *MFP*, 5 August 1920, 12; "Thousands Turn Out to Hear Debate on Labour Organization," *MFP*, 7 August 1920, 6.

121 "Active Worker in Vet. Circles Here Is Dead," *WT*, 12 January 1927, 8.

122 "Farnell Trial Is Expected to End Tomorrow," *WT*, 17 February 1920, 1, 2.

123 "New Candidate Enters Contest," *WT*, 9 October 1923, 1; "McMurray Endorsed as Solicitor-General," *WT*, 25 October 1923, 7; "North Winnipeg Campaign Ends," *WT*, 22 October 1923, 17.

124 *WT*, 12 March 1936, 7.

125 "Ex-soldiers', Sailors' Labor Party Meets; Growth Is Reported," *WT*, 1 August 1919, 5; "Soldiers' and Sailors' Labor Party," *WLN*, 12 September 1919, 1, 8.

126 Grant's restaurant advertised to its customers that it employed only "all white help"—not even the insurgent Grant was immune from displays of racism. See, for example, *WT*, 2 November 1925, 8.

127 "Daring Midnight Hold-up at Store of Harold Snell," *MFP*, 12 February 1926, 1; "Three Youths Admit Part in Hold-Up Series," *WT*, 19 February 1926, 1.

128 James Grant, "In a Comparative Evil," *WT*, 2 April 1926, 5.

129 "Café Keeper Shoots Himself through the Head," *MFP*, 9 July 1926, 1, 2.

130 Karl Marx and Friedrich Engels, "Manifesto of the Communist Party," in Tucker, *Marx-Engels Reader*, 476.

4

"Adapt to the Institutions and Manners of this Country": Winnipeg Jews and the General Strike

Henry Trachtenberg

"The feeling against Jewery [*sic*] is becoming more bitter [*sic*] as people are realizing the removal of Jews from responsible positions will not only be the salvation of the country but a final victory over Bolshevism." So wrote a Royal North-West Mounted Police (RNWMP) agent in a report forwarded by A.A. McLean, comptroller of the national police force (and deputy minister to the president of the Privy Council, Newton W. Rowell) to George Yates, the private secretary to Prime Minister Sir Robert Borden, in June 1919. McLean advised Yates of the "general unpopularity of Jews" at the time. The agent rather convolutedly also claimed that rich Jews, members of the Citizens' Committee of 1000, were meeting twice weekly in the Rural Municipality of West Kildonan to financially support the strikers and thereby "fulfill a mission for the higher up Bolsheviks." As a result, according to this logic, allowing Jews to be Citizens' Committee members was very "unwise" and "dangerous."[1]

The following month, McLean informed Yates that Jacob Penner, a bookkeeper for the Canadian Candy Manufacturing Company, who was described incorrectly as a Russian Jew and influential member of the Jewish branch of the Social Democratic Party (SDP) in Winnipeg, and his associates were controlling developments behind the scenes during the Strike. As well, RNWMP Sergeant Albert Reames, who was in attendance at the meeting called by the Socialist Party of Canada (SPC) at the Majestic Theatre on 10 January 1919, claimed that 50 percent of the audience consisted of foreigners, many of them—"judging from the appearance"—Jews.[2]

Jews had been active in Marxist, social democratic, and anarchist movements for social, economic, and political change in the Russian Empire before and after the revolution of 1917. Given this situation, after Russia "betrayed" the Allied cause by signing a separate peace treaty with Germany in 1918, Winnipeg Jews from eastern Europe became the subjects of suspicions and allegations that they served foreign powers with an "anti-Canadian" ideology. Moreover, Yiddish was related closely to German, the language Canadian newspapers associated with Bolshevism and anarchism. It was easy, therefore, for governmental and police authorities to conclude that Jews were revolutionaries, Jewish socialists were a singular threat to national security, and Yiddish was a vehicle for the violent overthrow of Canadian society. Several reports of undercover RNWMP operations in Winnipeg had a distinctly anti-Semitic tone, and the force was convinced the Strike was the result of the "hard work of Jews and a few blind Britishers [*sic*]."[3]

Although there may have been more antiforeign than specifically anti-Jewish sentiment during the events of May–June, 1919, in an atmosphere of increasing paranoia and xenophobia sweeping North America, a "Jewish-Bolshevik" conspiracy as a reason for the Strike was a popularly held misconception. The widespread acceptance of this view led Wallis Lefeaux, who visited Russia in 1920 and had been an assistant to the defence counsel during the trials of the Strike leaders, to comment that he could not find "any justification whatever" for reports that the Bolshevik movement was a "Jewish promotion." He denied the claim that the labour walkout was an overt act in a Bolshevist conspiracy, asserting it had been used as a weapon to condemn the Strike leaders. Even so, some fifty years later, historian James Jackson found it necessary to deny that the Strike was a conspiracy directed from Moscow, a "pluto-Bolshevik Jew" plot to take over the world.[4]

Local, national, and international events immediately preceding and concurrent with the Strike, the Strike itself, and its immediate aftermath were seminal events in the history of the Winnipeg Jewish community. They directly shaped the political life, identity, and ideological perspective of a very large part of Winnipeg Jewry. A significant majority of the city's Jews were Orthodox in religious practice. Nevertheless, class orientation, accompanied by a strong ethno-cultural solidarity in the face of both a very considerable antiforeign and anti-Semitic attack amid the severe economic crisis of the Strike, became the central determinant in Jewish individual and communal responses.[5]

Most Winnipeg Jews, including the emergent small business community, were openly on the strikers' side during the labour conflict, a fact manifested in subsequent elections at all levels of government. The support was very clearly demonstrated in the civic election of 1919, when two Jewish candidates associated with the Citizens' Committee, Max Steinkopf and Harry Wilder, were overwhelmingly repudiated by their co-religionists. Furthermore, the profiles of several Jews associated with the Strike, particularly Abraham Albert Heaps, Marcus Hyman, Joseph Alter Cherniack, and arrested alien Solomon Moses Almazoff, were greatly enhanced, and they emerged as far more important individuals than they had been before May 1919.[6]

While in 1919 there were a small number of Jewish professionals and businessmen of note, Winnipeg Jews, numbering about 14,000, were socially and economically marginalized from the larger society. Almost 70 percent were born in eastern Europe, and about 90 percent, self-employed and working class, lived in small homes, boarding houses, and tenements in the North End, particularly between Main and McGregor Streets and centring on the busy commercial and residential thoroughfare of Selkirk Avenue. Nearly all Jewish religious and secular institutions and organizations, and businesses, were located in this district.[7]

As noted, Winnipeg Jews, who came from the Russian Pale of Settlement and Romania, overwhelmingly were Orthodox. However, a new immigrant group consisting of "ethnocultural" Jews, many convinced socialists and some having served apprenticeships in Czarist Russia's revolutionary movements, came to Winnipeg after the failed revolution of 1905. They cherished Yiddish, promoted their history, traditions, and culture in a secular manner, and rejoiced in the overthrow of the Czar. Although they were always a minority among Winnipeg Jewry, their political background, high literacy rate, and residential concentration in the North End facilitated radicalism and meant they became influential beyond their numbers. As a result, they established "one of the most dynamic and complex" radical communities in Canada.[8]

The radicals' arrival led to the establishment in Winnipeg of left-wing organizations, such as the Poale Zion (Socialist Labor Zionists, 1906); the Jewish branches of the Marxist-oriented SPC (1906) and the Marxist-inspired SDP (1910); the Socialist-Territorialists (1906), who believed in Jewish cultural autonomy within a socialist state; and the Young Jewish Labour League and the three branches of the Arbeiter Ring Sick Benefit Association (the Workmen's Circle, 1907), which combined working class fraternal mutual aid with a desire to replace the capitalist system. In 1917, the Arbeiter Ring, and particularly Branch 169, the Internationalists or Revolutionary Marxists, founded the Liberty (Freiheit) Temple at 410 Pritchard Avenue, which became the political, educational, social, and cultural headquarters of the Jewish left wing, and then specifically the Marxists. As a result, radicalism in the Winnipeg Jewish community became perhaps even more deeply rooted and diverse than among Ukrainian Winnipeggers. Indeed, for the members and supporters of the above-mentioned organizations and institutions, being Jewish meant being a radical.[9]

With extended family and friends in eastern Europe, throughout the First World War Winnipeg Jewry was apprehensive about the fate of thousands of their displaced co-religionists in the war zones of the Russian Pale. This situation was compounded when, in the wake of the Russian Civil and Polish–Russian Wars, in 1918–19 widespread and devastating pogroms broke out in Ukraine, Poland, and western Siberia. The eastern European Jews' physical survival was a matter of existential importance to the community, and led to the creation of the Western Jewish Fund for the Relief of War Sufferers. Just four days before the Strike began on 15 May 1919, thousands of Winnipeg Jews attended two emotional meetings at the *Talmud Torah* (Hebrew Free School) to protest the pogroms and passed resolutions which were sent to the Borden government.[10]

While Jews who were aliens of enemy nationality did not have to register with the police in the numbers that Ukrainians did, and were not interned as were Ukrainians in the thousands during the First World War, both were widely disenfranchised by the Wartime Elections Act of 1917. Certainly by the fall of 1918, many Jews were made anxious by the passage by the Dominion government of repressive orders-in-council covering censorship, sedition, and criticism of the war effort which affected them as individuals and groups; some of them were placed under RNWMP surveillance and their organizations raided. In Winnipeg, the Jewish branch of the SDP was banned.[11]

Given the situation of their co-religionists in eastern Europe, and the potential of Canada as a safe haven for them, Winnipeg Jewry viewed with apprehension the hurried amendments to the Immigration Act of 6 June 1919, particularly the deportation provisions of section 41. The Winnipeg Yiddish newspaper *Dos Yiddishe Vort* (*The Israelite Press*, *DYV*), which since 1915 had to meet with the approval of Canada's chief press censor, Lieutenant Colonel Ernest Chambers, reflected the Jewish community's anguish over this matter. *DYV* asserted that if Canada engaged in deportation, the country would become the "symbol of terror and outcast." This fear was only reinforced, a few days after the Strike ended, by the passage as an amendment to the Criminal Code of section 98.[12]

At the local level, in addition to dealing with daily occurrences of anti-Semitism and the catastrophic influenza epidemic of 1918–19, sometimes the physical security of Winnipeg Jews was threatened. For example, in 1917, a mass meeting called by the Jewish and Russian branches of the SDP to celebrate the fall of the Czar was held at the Queen's Theatre on Selkirk Avenue. Pro-monarchist Slavs chanting "down with the Jews, we do not need the Jews" arrived to attack the organizers and scheduled speakers. When a brawl ensued, the police had to be summoned before order could be restored and the meeting could proceed.[13]

The riot of returned soldiers and civilians on 26–27 January 1919 was a traumatic experience for the Jewish community. After destroying the SPC headquarters, they vainly searched for Samuel Blumenberg, the leading Jewish Marxist orator in the party and a featured speaker at the SPC-called protest meeting at the Walker Theatre on 22 December 1918, and at the Majestic Theatre. Ironically, Blumenberg was a member of the petite bourgeoisie; the mob vandalized his cleaning establishment, the Minneapolis Dye House, and another of his businesses, forcing his wife, Libby, to kiss the Union Jack. Other attacks on the same days resulted in the destruction of many other Jewish-owned businesses on north Main Street and Selkirk Avenue, and their proprietors also being forced to kiss the flag. The bloodiest battle, involving hundreds of people, lasted three hours and resulted in casualties and arrests. For all these combined reasons, Winnipeg Jewry was tense and fearful when the General Strike began.[14]

The Strike impacted some of Winnipeg's Jews in different ways. Sarah Moscovitch's brothers, who bought jitneys and charged people five cents a ride, saw the Strike as an opportunity to provide a service and make money. Movie theatres remained open at the Strike Committee's request and with its permission; therefore, the business of Ben Bloom, manager of the Famous Players Film Service, and one of the owners of the Dominion Theatre, continued uninterrupted. Merchant tailor Hyman Gunn maintained a pleasant relationship with two of his striking employees, who daily relieved him for two hours so he could go out for something to eat. Entrepreneur Solomon Bricker, in the process of establishing a wholesale clothing business with Joseph Nozick, did not let the Strike deter him from that goal. Pharmacist Joseph Wilder, while sympathetic to the working class, was not in favour of the Strike, believing it would bring "destruction and misery." Young mother Rose Berman Cohen, who needed a doctor for her baby daughter, was fearful about going outside, especially after Bloody Saturday.[15]

It has been contended that many in Winnipeg's Jewish community opposed the Strike, and that Jews were on both sides of the struggle. Not surprisingly, however, a large majority of North End Jews, probably equalling that of other eastern European immigrant communities, as stated, supported the strikers. Working-class Jews, such as cloak maker Shia (Samuel) Feldman, an employee of Western Cloak Manufacturing Company, and Fred Narvey's father, Casril Narvolansky, a nonunion labourer at Brown and Rutherford, a lumber and millwork company, were striking unionized and nonunion workers. Furthermore, many Jewish small business owners were keenly aware that their customers and neighbors were strikers. Narvey, for instance, recalled that as a child he went with his father, whose low pay meant the family lived from payday to payday at the best of times, and who was on strike for six weeks with no pay, to ask for credit from Mrs. (Jacob) Greenberg, who operated the corner grocery store at Stella Avenue and Parr Street.[16]

On the very day members of the building trades went on strike, the Poale Zion held a gathering to celebrate May Day, 1919 with musical entertainment and speakers, including the principal of the left-wing Yiddish I.L. Peretz *Folk Schule* (People's School), Joseph Hestrin, at

Steiman's Hall; and the Social Democrats held a concert and ball at the Liberty Temple. As well, the vote in favour of a general sympathetic strike presumably was discussed on 13 May at a meeting of the women's section of the Jewish branch of the SDP, also held in the temple.[17]

While many Jews, ardent believers in socialism and enthusiastic supporters of working-class militancy, may have been active in the union movement, they rarely achieved high positions in Winnipeg unions or trade councils. If, however, the Jewish labour movement played little role in the Strike, some individual Jews did have a prominent role. The most important of them was Abraham Albert Heaps.[18]

Born in 1885 into a working-class family in Leeds, England, Heaps learned the upholstering trade. Arriving in Winnipeg in 1911, he found employment in the coach shop of the Canadian Pacific Railway, and then with department store Robinson and Company. Through his union activities, Heaps became friends with two fellow British immigrant trade unionists: John Queen, a cask and barrel maker, advertising manager for the *Western Labor News* (the newspaper of the Winnipeg Trades and Labor Council), and Winnipeg alderman, and John Blumberg, a Jewish immigrant from England and motorman with the Winnipeg Street Railway Company. Heaps was elected as a Winnipeg alderman in a 1917 by-election, joining Queen as a representative for the "Jewish ward (5)" on City Council. During the election campaign, Heaps advertised in *DYV*, identifying himself as a Jew and "Jewish citizen" and appealing for support from his fellow Jews, a large majority of whom voted for him. He was reelected by acclamation in 1918.[19]

During the Strike, Heaps was a leading member of the General Strike Committee and chairman of the Committee's Central Relief Committee, which oversaw an assistance program for strikers in dire financial circumstances. He also was a member of some ad hoc committees. Already a member of the Winnipeg City Council committee responsible for overseeing the civic welfare program, Heaps sometimes dealt with more than 200 individual cases a day. With Queen, he also continued to advance the strikers' case on the Council, an effort that proved futile.[20]

To the Citizens' Committee, though, Heaps was the "stormy petrol" of the Winnipeg Labor Temple and City Council chamber who made a "great noise," worked on occasion as an upholsterer, made "lots of bullets" for Queen to fire, and was a "dangerous revolutionist." Along with Queen, who was staying with him, Heaps was the first Strike leader to be arrested for seditious conspiracy in the early morning hours of 17 June. His home was ransacked by the police as they searched for subversive materials.[21]

Released on bail, Heaps continued to participate on the City Council, and was one of the speakers who addressed large crowds in Toronto, Montreal, and elsewhere, attempting to raise funds for the strikers' defence committee. Acting as his own lawyer, he mounted an eloquent and passionate defence at his trial in March, 1920, and was found not guilty. Heaps's heroic status during and after the Strike was the foundation of his political career and of his majority support in the Jewish community for the next twenty years as an Independent Labour Party alderman for Wards 5 and then 3 (to 1925) and then Labor-Co-operative Commonwealth Federation member of Parliament for Winnipeg North (1925–40).[22]

While Heaps was a Jew, he was also British, and even as a trade unionist and social democrat was much more easily acculturated to the larger society than to eastern European Jewish immigrants. He also was a member of the English, not Jewish, local of the SDP, and he was neither an observant Jew nor was he conversant in Yiddish, Jews' *mamaloshen* (mother tongue). As a result, in 1919 Heaps may have been distant from Jewish culture, although Allan Levine was inaccurate when he concluded that Heaps was "never truly embraced" by Yiddish-speaking Winnipeg workers.[23]

Winnipeg Jews also knew that if Heaps was to have been deported with or without trial in the summer of 1919, at worst it would have been to Great Britain, and not the charnel house of eastern Europe or western Siberia. Nevertheless, North End Jewry was very relieved by the Dominion government's decision not to attempt to deport him and the other Strike leaders, and by his acquittal on the charge of seditious conspiracy.[24]

M. Temenson, a participant in the 1905 Russian Revolution, was a representative of the Metal Trades Council on the General Strike Committee. Fellow metal worker Harry Gale was secretary of the Jewish metal workers' union, a socialist, and union organizer of thirty Jews working in small metal shops, the largest of which was the Winnipeg Metal Company. He also was on the Strike Committee, for which he conducted research and wrote materials. Gale not only attended, but spoke at, several strikers' meetings at Victoria Park, and was part of the crowd that fled to the North End after the streetcar was overturned and set on fire on Bloody Saturday. Jewish representatives of the garment workers' and fur trade unions very likely were also on the committee. Several Jews were on subcommittees, including one Korman (probably Israel, a tailor) on the strikers' press committee, one Simkin (possibly Feivel or Frank, the assistant manager of *DYV*) on their censure committee, and one Sharret-Levy on another committee. Two Jews, Heaps and Radis (probably Ely, a plumber) were among the speakers appointed by the General Committee in response to a request from the "Jewish workingman's paper," most likely the left-wing *Die Volk Shtimme* (*The People's Voice*).[25]

The General Committee made some decisions negatively impacting Jews. Several requests for permits to hire individuals and to conduct their businesses were not granted. A communication from a packing house asking for a permit for four butchers to slaughter kosher meat was simply filed. The committee refused to publish a Yiddish leaflet for distribution in the North End, apparently to counter one circulated by the Citizens' Committee. Moreover, there was some nativist sentiment on the General Committee, which was sensitive to the charge of domination by foreigners. It not only endorsed a report from William Ivens that non-Anglo-Saxon speakers stay away from the Labor Temple, ordering Blumenberg and labourer Jacob Kaplunovitch to stop making speeches, but also agreed to support the civil authorities' efforts to deport all undesirable aliens and to restrict future immigration to Canada. These decisions, and any discomfort and loss from the Strike, however, did not diminish the overall strong support in the Jewish community for the strikers.[26]

The pressmen of *DYV*, including linotype operator Solomon Simkin, struck and from 16 May to 20 June 1919 shut down the newspaper, published twice weekly. Unlike its president and manager Harry (H.E) Wilder, Feivel Simkin was very sympathetic to the strikers. Following a request from the Strike Committee, with Simkin's approval and participation, the employees published materials in Yiddish and English for the strikers. As well, at night Simkin allowed the strikers at no cost to use *DYV*'s printing press to publish *The Strike Bulletin*.[27]

Several Jews offered the Strike Committee assistance: Robert Steiman, owner of Steiman Hardware and Furniture Company, the use of his (Steiman's) hall; Nathan Portnoy of Perth Dye Works, an automobile; and Dr. Avram (Abraham) Moyse, free medical services in his office in the Steiman Block. Grocer Isaac Colish, a Jewish councillor in West Kildonan and also a Manitoba police magistrate, prevented police from arresting strikers during some of their meetings in his municipality, and the superintendent of Kildonan Park from disrupting an assembly of strikers there. Colish also collected money for the strikers at that meeting and gave them free groceries at his store.[28]

The business manager of the People's Printing Company, Abraham Gutnick, was the publisher of *Die Volk Shtimme*. He allowed City of Winnipeg police and others to hold Strike meetings in his premises. With his involvement, his typesetting and other employees actively supported the Strike and published other prostrike materials, including the Yiddish newspaper *Die Volkszeitung* (*The People's Times*). An RNWMP undercover agent who surreptitiously visited *Die Volk Shtimme* reported that the employees stated that they were helping the Strike as effectively as the *Western Labor News*, and were doing "propaganda work" in Yiddish, which the Strike Committee wanted.[29]

Businessman Jacob Rosenthal agreed to a request from Helen Armstrong and the socialist Women's Labor League to allow them to establish a soup kitchen, the Free Lunch Room or Labor Café, in the large dining room of his Strathcona Hotel at Main Street and Rupert Avenue. As a result, from 24 May to 14 June, volunteers in the hotel kitchen prepared three meals daily for both female and male strikers. On 27 May, the Jewish Dramatic Society, which mounted major literary works at the Queen's Theatre, put on a performance for those in attendance at the Café, raising $329.29 for the cause.[30]

The attitude of a majority of Jews during the Strike was illustrated by Casril Narvolansky who, when the Mounted Police paraded by his house on Selkirk Avenue, muttered in Russian at them "Swine, Cossacks." In a similar vein, striking Canadian Northern Railway air-brake inspector Isaac Adleman described the Special Police as "hoodlums with clubs" whose purpose was "to make us lose our strike." Jewish support for the Strike certainly was reflected in an article by journalist and Jewish community leader Aaron Osovsky in *DYV*. He agreed with the "rightfulness" of the labour walkout, sympathized with the strikers' grievances, praised workers for their solidarity, endurance, and discipline, and condemned the "enmity and hatred" of the Citizens' Committee.[31]

Winnipeg Jews' overall sympathy with the strikers was perhaps best exemplified by Moses (Moishe) Jacob, an agent of the Canada Life Assurance Company. He took out a paid advertisement in *DYV* demonstrating his support for the strikers, and in an accompanying letter protested the "libel" that he was a member of the Citizens' Committee, stating that he had never belonged to it, his full sympathy was for the workers, and his "greatest wish" was that they would win the Strike.[32]

Regardless of Jacob's disclaimer, some prominent Jews, successful business and professional men, were alleged to be members of the Citizens' Committee. Among them were: Charles Tadman, president and managing director of two hardware stores; the Weidman brothers, Hiram and Mordecai, wholesale grocers; Harry Wilder, lawyer and businessman; Max Steinkopf, whose City Dairy would lose an estimated $10,000 during the Strike because he refused to allow his delivery vehicles to display "By Permission of the Strike Committee" placards; Dr. Abraham Bercovitch; Moses Finkelstein, president of the Northwest Fur and Hide Company and former Winnipeg alderman for the North End; and captain in the Canadian Army, Military District No.10, and lawyer Sidney Goldstine, who subsequently served as an assistant counsel in the prosecution of the Strike leaders.[33]

During the Strike, Wilder claimed that Jews should have been pleased that they were on both sides of the dispute, thereby averting a "catastrophe" for them in the larger society. However, once it began its "unclean racial struggle" against Jewish and other eastern European aliens, Wilder left the Committee of 1000. He then strongly denounced those Jews among the "tens" of foreigners on the committee who did not speak up in protest and continued to spread "awful propaganda" against other foreigners. Those Jews who remained members should have resigned, he argued, and the "'I Jew' should not have surrendered to the 'I capitalist.'"[34]

According to Wilder, the committee's antialien daily newspaper advertisements and pronouncements in their organ, the *Winnipeg Citizen*, were allowed to stand unchallenged, and remained as evidence available for anyone who wished to use them against foreigners, and this naturally meant Jews. Furthermore, reflecting the Jewish community's alarm, after the Strike he was indignant at the reactionary Winnipeg daily press and their "scandalous, cheap" journalists for inflaming anti–eastern European, and especially anti-Jewish, sentiment. The press had called Winnipeg Labour alderman Ernest Robinson, secretary of the Winnipeg Trades and Labor Council, "Rubenstein"; claimed that Solomon Almazoff, arrested with the Strike leaders, had been born in the Prussian, not Russian, Ukraine; and asserted that Blumenberg, also arrested, had been born in Russia, when he had been born in Romania.[35]

Winnipeg Jews were made apprehensive on 17 June by RNWMP raids on the offices of socialist and labour organizations in the Liberty Temple, where doors were smashed down, desks overturned, files scattered, and papers stolen. Their anxiety was reinforced by police raids on Jewish individuals' homes at 3:00 a.m. on Dominion Day, including those of Michael Charitonoff, another Jewish alien arrested along with the Strike leaders; men's clothing tailor Max Tessler, who had arrived in Winnipeg in 1904, joined the Jewish branch of the SDP in 1913, and become active in socialist politics; Yude Austin; Jacob Penner (whose wife Rose Shapack was Jewish), who represented the Retail Clerks' Union and the Bakery and Confectionary Workers' Union on the General Strike Committee, was a member of the strikers' Defence Committee, and served as secretary of the English-language branch of the SDP; and Harry Geller, business agent of the United Garment Workers' of America Union, Local No. 35. Geller's safe in the Labor Temple also was pried open and its contents taken.[36]

The following month, ten mounted police raided the People's Book Store at 824 ½ Main Street, owned by socialists Berl (Benjamin) Miller, former secretary of the Young Jewish Labor League, who came to Winnipeg in 1905, and his wife Bertha. Since 1910, the small, cramped store with wooden crates serving as seats had been a centre of "heated and spirited" debates among all Jewish radical groups. Searching for prohibited newspapers and books in Yiddish, German, and Russian, the Mounties found only a copy of *Die Volk Shtimme*.[37]

Police suspicion of Jews was manifested in other ways also. Louis Rosenberg had been a teacher in the Jewish farming colonies of Lipton and Cupar (Qu'Appelle) in Saskatchewan from 1915 to 1919, and now was the western Canadian agent of the Jewish Colonization Association. In Winnipeg for business purposes during the Strike, he was "visited" in his room by the RNWMP. Rosenberg had been born in Poland and immigrated with his family to Great Britain, coming to Canada in 1915. Only the fact that one of the policemen was a former member of a boys' group that Rosenberg had established in Leeds,

England, saved him from further problems. In the military, Maurice Bregman, stationed with the Canadian Army at the McGregor Street Armoury, was overheard expressing favorable comments about the Russian regime. As a result, he was cross-examined by his major about his political leanings, placed on a suspicious persons list, and was the last man in his unit to be demobilized in 1920.[38]

Winnipeg Jewry was made very fearful by the arrest on 17 June of five aliens, and especially the three Jewish Marxists among them: Charitonoff, twenty-seven; Blumenberg, thirty-three; and Almazoff, thirty, who wrote under the nom de plume Samuel Pearl. They faced deportation to, and certain death in, eastern Europe or a port in western Siberia under the control of White Russian commander Admiral Aleksandr Kolchak. This was a result of their also being charged on 26 June by the RNWMP under section 41 of the Immigration Act, in addition to the Criminal Code charges of seditious conspiracy and seditious libel of 17 June.[39]

The aliens, who were even "more aggravating" than the Strike leaders to the Citizens' Committee, were arrested, as *DYV* noted, at the Citizens' request, to lend credence to the myth of an alien conspiracy. This was a calculated attempt to appeal to fear and prejudice in order to convince the public that Jews, among other eastern Europeans, were in control of Winnipeg's government and were turning the Labor Temple into a soviet. While the three Jewish aliens had acquired some minor notoriety as radicals, and had been placed under RNWMP surveillance weeks before 15 May, they did not participate in planning or directing the Strike. Nor did they serve on any of its committees. Indeed, although they supported the Strike, they were not strikers in the sense of having walked off their jobs. Hence, it is not accurate to describe Almazoff, Blumenberg, and Charitonoff as immigrant, alien, or foreign "Strike leaders."[40]

The aliens were fortunate that the Winnipeg Trades and Labor Council's Defence Committee appointed Jewish lawyer Marcus Hyman as one of their co-counsel. Hyman believed that there was not any connection between the aliens and the Strike, claiming that their arrest was a deliberate attempt to besmirch the names of the Strike leaders. His sympathy for his clients was apparent when he identified with them by telling the special board of inquiry appointed by the Department of Colonization and Immigration that the police had several surveillance reports on him, and that he was on two lists of undesirable aliens to be deported.[41]

Born in Poland, Hyman evoked the immigrant experience, common to most Winnipeg Jews, when he stated at the Charitonoff hearing that he could not remember the name of the ship on which he had crossed the Atlantic Ocean from Great Britain, asking, "is that the material upon which a person is to be brought before a Departmental Board?" At Almazoff's hearing the inquiry chairman, Manitoba Provincial Police magistrate Robert Noble, who believed that the Strike was an attempted revolution, contended that at the sight of police an Anglo-Saxon became calm, but other "races" began to "flare up." Hyman again made reference to the situation of Jews in Russia when he asserted that Anglo-Saxon calm could not be expected from a highly strung person brought up under Russian conditions.[42]

Hyman unsuccessfully attempted before the board and Department of Immigration officials, in the courts, and in communications to Prime Minister Borden to gain his clients' release on bail. He tried also to quash the board through legal appeals. However, Hyman encountered bias and hostility at all levels. For instance, he read out loud Almazoff's articulate and eloquent plea for bail, listing legal, academic, financial, and moral justifications for it. Magistrate Noble, however, rejected the appeal, claiming that it had been made for propaganda purposes to allow people to say and write that British justice was not being done to these "poor Jews or foreigners."[43]

Hyman's defence of the aliens and ready identification with immigrant eastern European Jews made him a very popular man in the Jewish community, and certainly helped to launch and sustain his subsequent political career as a Winnipeg school trustee (1923–29) and then as a member of the Manitoba Legislative Assembly (1932–38).[44]

The emotional state of Winnipeg Jews regarding the aliens' fate was reflected in two months of front-page stories and editorials in *DYV*, publishing once again as of 20 June. The newspaper mobilized its readers for a "struggle for justice" to free the aliens: "We must have money. Every [Jewish] man and woman must contribute to the defense fund. Let every Jew undertake his duty and support according to his means. Let every Jew remember that THREE OF THE FOUR arrested foreigners are Jews. And for this reason it is even more necessary that every Jew help to free the arrested."[45]

Visceral concern about the aliens' seventy-four-hour-hunger strike because of the board's and courts' refusal to release the men on bail was mitigated by the dropping of Criminal Code charges against the aliens. Hyman also was successful in having them transferred to the Immigration Hall in Winnipeg, where relatives and friends could visit and bring them food twice daily. Nevertheless, *DYV*, reflecting the anguish of Winnipeg Jews, protested that the Dominion government was making a parody of a trial. In so doing, it was committing an "outrageous crime" not only against the arrested aliens, but against all foreign-born Canadians whose freedom was in peril and whose rights were being robbed. The leaders of the Jewish working class were praised for their spirit of freedom, while Jewish capitalists were condemned for living in fear and not protesting, thereby demonstrating that they still suffered from a "Christian ghetto psychology."[46]

Protest and strategy meetings of Jewish organizations were held at the Liberty Temple, and a Jewish Workers' Committee was formed to help free the imprisoned men. Its members canvassed the homes of Jews in the North End and made additional financial appeals, soliciting support for its Strike Relief Fund. When, on 21 June, bail was granted to the Strike leaders, but not the aliens, the Workers' Committee protested to the General Strike Committee about the different treatment. In turn, the Strike Committee passed a resolution demanding equal treatment and the granting of bail.[47]

The Jewish community was aware that all three arrested aliens self-identified as Jews at their hearings. Concern for their fate on the part of Winnipeg Jewry was enhanced when on 22 and 25 July, citing Immigration Department officials, *DYV* informed the city's Jews that "countless numbers" of "undesirable" immigrants were being deported from Canada, and protested that the country was not created for a select few, but for millions of workers.[48]

The *Winnipeg Citizen*, referring to him quite consciously by the name "Blumberg," delighted in describing Blumenberg, who symbolically wore a flaming red tie and red handkerchief to show his Marxist affinities. To the Citizens' Committee, "Agitator" Blumberg was "keenly interested in turning 'wage slaves' into automobile owners and two-hour-a-day-and-half-day-off on Saturday Socialists." However, according to the Citizens, he never worked at anything unless it was on a platform with an alien audience where he slaved for an hour "in broken English to tell them that they [were] the salt of the earth" and that the earth belonged to them.[49]

Blumenberg, more picturesque and indiscreet than the Strike leaders, was an SPC delegate to the Winnipeg Trades and Labor Council and was one of the individuals who addressed Premier T.C. Norris when prostrike returned soldiers appeared before him. Blumenberg had alluded to being a Jew when he stated that the map of Palestine was written on his face with his nose the Mount of Zion. However, he did not live or work in the Jewish North End. His home was in central Winnipeg at 318 Good Street, his cleaning business was downtown at 484 Portage Avenue, and he appears to have had little contact with the Jewish community. Hence, his deportation to the United States on a technical immigration violation did not have as severe an impact for Winnipeg Jews, especially since he had not been deported to Romania. The *Winnipeg Telegram* expressed great pleasure with Blumenberg's deportation, sarcastically commenting on its editorial page that "it takes nine tailors to make a man but one Blumberg [*sic*] makes an excellent deportee."[50]

Charitonoff, from the Russian Ukraine, was the former editor of the left-wing newspaper *Rabochii narod*, the Russian-language edition of *Robochyi narod* (*Working People*), and a former labourer in the Canadian Pacific Railway freight sheds. He was a member of the Russian Progressive Club and the Russian branch of the SDP. In 1918, his arrest on an alleged Bolshevik connection—and then his trial, conviction, and subsequent successful appeal—made him a cause célèbre in labour circles. His ties in Winnipeg appear to have been not to the Jewish, but to the Russian and Ukrainian left-wing communities. He was suspected of accepting $7,000 from the Soviet Government Information Bureau in New York to establish a Ukrainian-language "revolutionary" paper, *Nova Vic* (*New Age*), and then channelling the money to the General Strike Committee, a charge he denied. Charitonoff was ordered deported under section 41, for violation of two orders-in-council respecting his entrance to Canada, and probably for attending the Walker Theatre meeting.[51]

Charitonoff was, however, known to some Jews in Winnipeg. While in Philadelphia en route from Russia in 1914, he had contacted friends in the Manitoba capital for funds to allow him to cross the Canadian border, and while waiting in Pembina, North Dakota, had been sent the money by well-known Jewish lawyer and socialist Joseph Alter Cherniack, later Hyman's law partner.[52]

There was, moreover, empathy for Charitonoff on the part of his co-religionists when he stated at his board hearing that Jews were oppressed in Russia and he had come to Canada because Jews were not persecuted in the Dominion; and there was considerable happiness and relief among Winnipeg's Jews when Hyman's successful appeal of Charitonoff's deportation order was announced on 20 September 1919.[53]

The individual whom much of the Jewish immigrant community regarded as one of its most valued members, and whose well-being raised the greatest consternation, was Almazoff, who came to Winnipeg in March 1913. He was an orator, journalist, editor of *Die Volk Shtimme*, contributor to *DYV*, western Canadian correspondent for the American Yiddish socialist newspaper *Forverts* (*Jewish Daily Forward*), Yiddish teacher, University of Manitoba third-year student, and financial secretary for several *landsmanshaften* ("fraternal free loan," sick and mutual benefit associations composed of members from the same locality in Europe). Almazoff was a member of the Jewish branch of the SDP and one of its delegates to the Dominion Labor Party, and of Arbeiter Ring Branch 169. He had been a medical volunteer in the influenza epidemic, and had been elected by Winnipeg Jews as one of twenty delegates to the Canadian Jewish Congress founding convention in Montreal, in March 1919. Almazoff was the only one of the three Jewish aliens who could, and then problematically, be called a leader among Winnipeg Jewry.[54]

The Winnipeg Jewish community knew that Almazoff was an inveterate foe of anti-Semitism, and had offered vocal and emotional protests against pogroms in Ukraine and elsewhere in eastern Europe, even from the Immigration Hall where he was being detained. Furthermore, he had been secretary of the Western Jewish Fund for the Relief of War Sufferers before becoming publicity chairman and editor of its bulletin, *Hilf* (*Help*). The fund demanded that Almazoff be released on bail and granted a jury trial, and guaranteed his future appearance before the law. His position brought him into direct and ongoing contact not only with his future counsel, Hyman, who was the president of the fund, but also the mainstream of Winnipeg Jewry.[55]

The RNWMP, though, had another view of Almazoff. To them, he was an "agitator" and "active revolutionary plotter." An undercover agent alleged that on 28 May, when he told Jewish workers at *Die Volk Shtimme* that he knew Almazoff and wished to speak with him, he was informed that Almazoff spent little time at the office because he had to keep in touch with the Strike Committee. The agent later stated that Abraham Gutnick, who deplored Almazoff's arrest and denounced the authorities, told him Almazoff helped the committee by occasionally distributing Strike literature in Yiddish.[56]

The police view of Almazoff was shared by the Winnipeg daily press and the periodical *Saturday Night*, whose editors expressed concern that the Almazoffs and other "wretches" and "revolutionists" would escape their just deserts, deportation, for what was termed their revolutionary activities. When the allegation against Almazoff of having advocated bloodshed in a meeting at the Liberty Temple before the Strike began was refuted, counsel for the Dominion government Alfred J. Andrews claimed Almazoff had copies of a prohibited Russian newspaper at his house for which he was subject to five years' imprisonment.[57]

Only after Almazoff had made an impassioned and dramatic speech did Magistrate Noble state that his legal and judicial conscience would not allow him to concur in Almazoff's deportation. On 16 August 1919, Almazoff was freed, but his release came with the very stern admonition from Noble to "adapt to the institutions and manners" of Canada and to become a "loyal" Canadian citizen. *DYV*'s banner headline "ALMAZOFF IS FREE," reflected Winnipeg Jewry's tremendous joy and relief. The paper reported that news about the verdict spread very quickly throughout the Jewish district, many Jews congratulated Almazoff, and, as soon as he was freed, he visited *DYV* to thank its personnel for their support.[58]

For Jews and other eastern European immigrants in Winnipeg in the wake of the Strike, the threat of deportation was a very intimidating and effective governmental deterrent in controlling actions and speech. As a result, apprehension permeated much of the Jewish community. Although Winnipeg Jews did not know about it, creating trepidation among them was exactly what Winnipeg police magistrate Sir Hugh John Macdonald had in mind. In early July 1919, he advised his friend Arthur Meighen, the acting minister of justice, that "Bolsheviki ideas" were held by a large section of Russian and German Jews in Winnipeg, and that "fear" was the only method that could successfully be used to keep them within the law and "as easily controlled as sheep." Macdonald also urged the deportation of Ivens, Robert Russell, and Heaps, who had "brains and eloquence" and who had already "done enough harm."[59]

The overarching sense of alarm and reinforced feeling of isolation among Winnipeg Jews was reflected in the *DYV* editorial "Be Alert!" by Harry Wilder on Dominion Day, 1919, the same day that the RNWMP was raiding the homes of some of his readers. Distinguishing between the self-controlled Anglo-Saxon and the Jew who allegedly could not control his emotions so easily, Wilder sounded a distinct warning to Jewish workers and their sympathizers who he advised to consider the present circumstances and to be very careful in their actions and speech. When the Jewish working class declared their economic dissatisfaction, he contended, "the others" would not see them as workers, but as Jews, aliens, and foreigners.[60]

A related ramification of the Strike for the Winnipeg Jewish community was the ongoing hostility manifested to the publication of left-wing Yiddish newspapers and the surveillance of individuals by the RNWMP, and the renamed Royal Canadian Mounted Police (RCMP). Canada's chief press censor ordered *Die Volk Shtimme* to cease publication on the pretext that the necessary copies had not been forwarded to his office for examination. The fact that the newspaper was represented by the firm of Cherniack and Hyman only further incensed the censor.[61]

Shortly thereafter, Chambers corresponded with Andrews and McLean about the possible prosecution of *Die Volk Shtimme*'s new editor, Jacob Miller. Chambers attempted to eliminate the mail privileges of, and then to close down the newspaper's successor, *Die Naiye Zeit* (*The New Times*), because those associated with the paper were not individuals of "acknowledged reliability and patriotism." He relented, however, after warning editor and publisher (and school principal) Joseph Hestrin to see that the paper was "really useful" to Canada's best interests.[62]

In another development, in December 1920, a "special operative" advised Superintendent Albert Cawdron, director of criminal investigation of the RCMP, that Jews were meeting almost every second day in the North End to raise money to be sent to Russia and Poland to bring "all the poor Jews" to Canada. Cawdron forwarded the information to

Frederick Charles Blair, secretary of the Department of Immigration and Colonization, who, in a memorandum to his acting deputy minister, W.W. Cory, sounded the dire warning.[63]

Blair most likely perceived Jews as potential revolutionaries, based on governmental interpretations of the Strike. This may have been one of the reasons, along with his stereotypical view that Jews would not or could not become successful farmers, that he vehemently opposed Jewish immigration to Canada in the 1920s, and in the following two decades did his best to ensure that Canadian immigration doors closed and remained locked to European Jewry.[64]

Another result of the Strike was that many Strike leaders, in the case of Heaps and Queen with overwhelming support from North End Jews, were elected or reelected to political office in 1919 or in the years immediately thereafter. The Strike left long-lasting scars on Winnipeg's society, and generated ethnic and class divisions and a legacy of bitterness and polarization. As such, it was the fundamental determinant in the political history of Winnipeg and its Jewish community for at least the next twenty-five years, with the basic cleavage being class orientation.[65]

The majority of Jews increasingly voted along class lines not only because Jewish candidates most often were affiliated with left-wing political parties, but because of the severe impact of the General Strike, following the First World War, on the collective psyche of Winnipeg Jewry. For instance, the Strike acted as a catalyst in launching the long political career of John Blumberg. He was elected as a Labour alderman for Ward 6, again with support from Jews in the district, in the Winnipeg municipal election of November 1919.[66]

The Strike, stridently re-fought in the political arena, was also the central issue in the electoral defeat of two prominent Jewish community members in 1919. A large majority of North End Jews decided to punish them for their membership on the Citizens' Committee. In a dramatic ideological confrontation, Max Steinkopf, running under the banner of the political descendant of the Committee of 1000, the Citizens' League, sought reelection as a school trustee in Ward 5. However, he lost by almost 700 votes to Rose (Rosa) Cherniack Alcin (Elkin), a Socialist-Territorialist and member of the Jewish branch of the SDP, running as a Labour candidate and endorsed by the left-wing Jewish organizations.[67]

In a similar electoral battle, Harry Wilder, seeking an aldermanic seat in Ward 5 as a Citizens' League representative, was defeated by more than 1,100 votes by incumbent Labour candidate John Queen, whom the vast majority of Jews and the same political organizations supported. Given the popularity of Labour, social democratic, and Communist candidates in north Winnipeg among Jews in subsequent decades, *DYV* presciently forecast that the election would determine the "character and sympathy" of North End Jewish voters for many years into the future.[68]

Class, ethnicity, and socialist ideology were key determinants of Winnipeg Jews' individual and communal actions and responses before, during, and after the Strike. For the majority of North End Jewish families, both working class and of the petite bourgeoisie, who overwhelmingly supported the Strike, the legacy of the labour conflict in the short term resulted in ongoing, if not increased, economic and social distress. For instance, Casril Narvolansky returned at the same salary to his labourer's job, sixty-hours-a-week with no benefits, at Brown and Rutherford. In the longer term, however, over the course of at least another generation, as manifested in elections, a highly politicized Jewish community with an exceptional class consciousness and overtly demonstrable class loyalty developed, helping to elect left-wing candidates at every level of government in north Winnipeg.[69]

The writer wishes to thank the librarians of the Legislative Library of Manitoba, particularly Ms. Heidi Rees, during the COVID-19 pandemic, for their assistance and many research liberties granted him; his late father, Samuel, for translating *DYV* and *Mit Dem Vort Tzum Folk* from Yiddish; his son Michael, for computer assistance; and Professor Jim Mochoruk for his constructive comments and analysis.

Notes

1 Library and Archives Canada (LAC), Sir Robert Borden Papers, MG26H 1(a), vol. 113, OC564(1)-OC566, "Extract from a Report dated Winnipeg, 11th June" attached to letter, McLean to Yates, "Possible Financial Support of Winnipeg Strike by Wealthy Jews," 62036-037.

2 William Rodney, *Soldiers of the International: A History of the Communist Party of Canada 1919–1929* (Toronto: University of Toronto Press, 1968), 25–26; Reinhold

Kramer and Tom Mitchell, *When the State Trembled: How A.J. Andrews and the Citizens' Committee Broke the Winnipeg General Strike* (Toronto: University of Toronto Press, 2010), 224.

3 Stephen Speisman, "Antisemitism in Ontario: The Twentieth Century," in *Antisemitism in Canada: History and Interpretation*, ed. Alan Davies (Waterloo, ON: Wilfrid Laurier University Press, 1992), 117; Rodney, *Soldiers of the International*, 25–26.

4 Gerald Tulchinsky, *Canada's Jews: A People's Journey* (Toronto: University of Toronto Press, 2008), 124, 187–88; Wallis Lefeaux, *Winnipeg-London-Moscow: A Study of Bolshevism* (Winnipeg: Canadian Workers' Defense League, 1921), 76–77; James Jackson, *The Centennial History of Manitoba* (Toronto: McClelland and Stewart, 1970), 199.

5 Henry Trachtenberg, "The Winnipeg Jewish Community and Politics: The Inter-War Years, 1919–1939," *Historical and Scientific Society of Manitoba Transactions*, series III, no. 35, 1978–79, 115–53.

6 Trachtenberg, "Winnipeg Jewish Community and Politics"; and Arthur Chiel, *The Jews of Manitoba: A Social History* (Toronto: University of Toronto Press, 1961), 179–80.

7 Canada, *Census of the Prairie Provinces: Population and Agriculture, 1916* (Ottawa: Dept. of Trade and Commerce, 1918), 142–43, 208–09, 214–15; Harry Gutkin and Mildred Gutkin, *The Worst of Times, The Best of Times: Growing Up in Winnipeg's North End* (Markham, ON: Fitzhenry and Whiteside, 1987), 7–12.

8 Gutkin and Gutkin, *Worst of Times*, 8, 12–17; Jean Burnet with Howard Palmer, *"Coming Canadians": An Introduction to a History of Canada's Peoples* (Toronto: McClelland and Stewart, 1988), 158–59; Ian McKay, *Reasoning Otherwise: Leftists and the People's Enlightenment in Canada, 1890–1920* (Toronto: Between the Lines, 2008), 465.

9 Roz Usiskin, "The Winnipeg Jewish Community: Its Radical Elements 1905–1918," *Historical and Scientific Society of Manitoba Transactions*, series III, no. 33, 1976–1977, 10–25; Arthur Ross, *Communal Solidarity: Immigration, Settlement and Social Welfare in Winnipeg's Jewish Community, 1882–1930* (Winnipeg: University of Manitoba Press, 2019), 18–19; Tom Mitchell and James Naylor, "The Prairies: In the Eye of the Storm," in *The Workers' Revolt in Canada 1917–1925*, ed. Craig Heron (Toronto: University of Toronto Press, 1998), 179–80.

10 Joseph Kage, *With Faith and Thanksgiving: The Story of Two Hundred Years of Jewish Immigration and Immigrant Aid Effort in Canada (1760–1960)* (Montreal: Eagle Publishing Company, 1962), 60–72; *Dos Yiddishe Vort* (*DYV*), 6, 9, 13 May, 27 June 1919.

11 Orest Martynowych, *Ukrainians in Canada: The Formative Years, 1891–1924* (Edmonton: Canadian Institute of Ukrainian Studies Press, University of Alberta, 1991), 324, 326–30, 423–27; Trachtenberg, "Winnipeg Jewish Community and Politics," 118–19.

12 *DYV*, 25 July, also 6 and 16 May, 27 June, 11 July 1919; David Bercuson, *Confrontation at Winnipeg: Labor, Industrial Relations, and the General Strike*, rev. ed. (Montreal and Kingston: McGill-Queen's University Press, 1990), 163.

13 Eva Wiseman, *Healing Lives: A Century of Manitoba Jewish Physicians* (Winnipeg: Jewish Heritage Centre of Western Canada [JHCWC], 2019), 9, 11; S. Almazoff Pearl, *Mit Dem Vort Tzum Folk* (*With the Word to the Masses: Experiences of a Lecturer*) (New York: Ikuf Farlag, 1947), 11–15, 29–31.

14 Winnipeg Defence Committee, "*Saving the World from Democracy*": *The Winnipeg General Sympathetic Strike, May–June,1919* (Winnipeg: The Defence Committee, n.d.), 8–9; *Winnipeg Telegram* (*WT*), 25–30 Jan. 1919.

15 JHCWC, Jewish Historical Society of Western Canada (JHSWC) Collection, Interview of Mrs. Sarah Moscovitch, Master Tape No. 288, 1972; Randy Rostecki, ed., *Personal Recollections: The Jewish Pioneer Past on the Prairies*, Jewish Life and Times, vol. VI (Winnipeg: JHSWC, 1993), 1–2, 7–8, 28–29, 36–37, 43–46, 48–49, 64, 66, 80, 88, 91, 96.

16 Harry Gutkin, "Radical Influence in Jewish Community Organizations," and Fred Narvey, "Personal Perspective on the Leftist Theatre of the 1930s," in *Jewish Radicalism in Winnipeg, 1905–1960,* ed. Dan Stone, *Jewish Life and Times*, vol. VIII (Winnipeg: JHCWC, 2003), 34, 82.

17 *DYV*, 29 April, 2 and 13 May 1919.

18 "Winnipeg Trade Unions," in Henderson Directories, comp., *Henderson's Winnipeg City Directory 1919*, vol. 41 (Winnipeg: Henderson Directories, 1919), 190–92; Bercuson, *Confrontation at Winnipeg*, 127, 186, 197.

19 Leo Heaps, *The Rebel in the House: The Life and Times of A. A. Heaps, M.P.*, rev. ed. (Markham, ON: Fitzhenry and Whiteside, 1984), 1–28; *DYV*, 20, 26, and 27 April 1917.

20 Harry Gutkin and Mildred Gutkin, *Profiles in Dissent: The Shaping of Radical Thought in the Canadian West* (Edmonton: NeWest Press, 1997), 299–308.

21 *Winnipeg Citizen*, 16 June 1919; D.C. Masters, *The Winnipeg General Strike* (Toronto: University of Toronto Press, 1973 [1950]), 102; Gutkin and Gutkin, *Profiles in Dissent,* 309.

22 Heaps, *Rebel in the House*, 36–162.

23 Bercuson, *Confrontation at Winnipeg*, 127; Allan Levine, *Coming of Age: A History of the Jewish People of Manitoba* (Winnipeg: Heartland Associates, 2009), 164.

24 Gutkin and Gutkin, *Profiles in Dissent*, 312–15.

25 Rostecki, *Personal Recollections*, 81; Harry Gale, "The Jewish Labor Movement in Winnipeg," in JHSWC, comp., *First Annual Publication: A Selection of Papers Presented in 1968–69* (Winnipeg: JHSWC, 1970), 10; Archives of Manitoba (AM), Robert Russell Collection, MG10A 14-2, box II, Central Strike and General Strike Committee Minutes [hereafter "Minutes"], files 62–64, various pages.

26 AM, Russell Collection, Minutes, files 62–64, various pages; Henry Trachtenberg, Interviews of Sheppy Hershfield, Joseph Wilder, Winnipeg, 27 July, 7 August 1981.

27 JHCWC, JHSWC Collection, Transcript of Interview of Feivel Simkin, 1977, 18.

28 AM, Russell Collection, Minutes, files 62–64, various pages; JHCWC, JHSWC Collection, Interview of Isaac Colish, Master Tape No. 261, 1972; Rostecki, *Personal Recollections*, 59.

29 JHCWC, JHSWC Collection, Interview of Abraham Gutnick, Master Tape 192, 1972; Rostecki, *Personal Recollections*, 31, 59, 92; LAC, RG6E, Records of the Dept. of the Secretary of State, Chief Press Censor Papers [hereafter "Censor Papers"], vol. 632, file 370-Y-5, "Report re: Almazoff," 28 May 1919, in McLean to Chambers, "Almazoff and 'Die Volkstimme,'" 26 June 1919.

30 *Western Labor News*, 26 and 30 May, 14 June 1919; David Watson, "The Rosenthal Family's Strathcona Hotel" (Winnipeg: Unpublished Research Report, 2013), 9–11.

31 Narvey, "Personal Perspective," 82; Rostecki, *Personal Recollections*, 50, 59; *DYV*, 27 June, 1 and 8 July 1919.

32 *DYV*, 27 June 1919.

33 LAC, Borden Papers, McLean to Yates; Kramer and Mitchell, *When the State Trembled*, 129, 410, no. 52.

34 *DYV*, 20 June, 22 August 1919.

35 *DYV*, 22 August 1919.

36 *DYV*, 20 June, 1, 4, and 8 July, 22 August 1919; Norman Penner, ed., "Recollections of the Early Socialist Movement in Winnipeg by Jacob Penner," *Histoire sociale/ Social History* 7, no. 14 (November 1974): 377–78.

37 *DYV*, 20 June, 22 August 1919; Ben Miller, "Winnipeg History from 1905: The Writings of Ben Miller," in *Winnipeg Jewish Review*, ed. Rhonda Spivak, 20 August 2012 (Winnipeg: Spivak's Jewish Review, 2012), www.winnipegjewishreview.com.

38 Henry Trachtenberg, Interview of David Rome, Archivist, Canadian Jewish Congress Archives, Montreal, 25 July 1978; JHCWC, JHSWC Collection, Interview of Maurice Bregman, Master Tape No. 252, 1972.

39 Winnipeg Defence Committee, *"Saving the World from Democracy,"* 154, 161, 165, 180–81, 216; LAC, Records of the RCMP, RG18, vol. 3314, Winnipeg Strike File [hereafter "Strike File"], file HV-1(5), Solomon Moses Almazoff deportation hearing, 15 August 1919, 139, 142–43.

40 Kramer and Mitchell, *When the State Trembled*, 158; *DYV*, 20 June, 11 July 1919; Bercuson, *Confrontation at Winnipeg*, 126–27.

41 *DYV*, 20 June, 15 July 1919; LAC, Records of the RCMP, Strike File, Almazoff deportation hearing, 16 July, 15 August 1919, 1, 151–52.

42 LAC, Records of the RCMP, Strike File, file HV-1(6), Michael Charitonoff deportation hearing, 13 August 1919, 23–27; and Almazoff deportation hearing, 15 August 1919, 149.

43 Ibid., Charitonoff deportation hearing, 14 August 1919, 27–28, and Almazoff deportation hearing, 16 and 18 July 1919, 1–6, 28–29, 31–32; *DYV*, 1, 4, 8, 15, 18, 21, 22, 25 and 29 July, 1, 5, 12, 15, and 22 August 1919.

44 Trachtenberg, "Winnipeg Jewish Community and Politics," 125–26.

45 *DYV*, 1 August 1919; also 20 June, 1, 4, 6, 8, 11, 15, 22, 25, 29 July, 1, 5, 15, and 19 August 1919.

46 *DYV*, 1 August 1919.

47 *DYV*, 20 June, 1, 11 and 29 July, and 1 August 1919.

48 LAC, Records of the RCMP, Strike File, Almazoff deportation hearing, 16 July 1919, p. 7; LAC, Records of the RCMP, Strike File, file HV-1(4), Samuel Blumenberg deportation hearing, 15 July 1919, pp. 19, 23; *DYV*, 22 and 25 July 1919.

49 *Winnipeg Citizen*, 16 June 1919; also 11 June 1919.

50 LAC, Records of the RCMP, Strike File, Blumenberg deportation hearing, 15 July 1919, 19–24; *WT*, 12, 13, 14, 19, 20 September 1919; Henderson Directories, comp., *Henderson's Winnipeg City Directory 1919*, 528, 590, 963, 102; Masters, *Winnipeg General Strike*, 4.

51 Martynowych, *Ukrainians in Canada*, 428, 440; Henry Trachtenberg, "The 'Old Clo' Move': Anti-Semitism, Politics, and the Jews of Winnipeg, 1882–1921" (PhD thesis, York University, 1984), 660–75.

52 LAC, Records of the RCMP, Strike File, Charitonoff deportation hearing, 16 and 17 July, 13 and 14 August 1919, 2–4, 19–25, 11–15, 16–18, 20–32; Saul Cherniack, "Personal Perspective," in *Jewish Radicalism in Winnipeg*, 205.

53 LAC, Records of the RCMP, Strike File, Charitonoff deportation hearing as in note 52 above; *DYV*, 18 July, 15 August 1919; *Winnipeg Tribune*, 20 and 22 September 1919.

54 LAC, Records of the RCMP, Strike File, Almazoff deportation hearing, 16 and 18 July 1919, 7, 18; Pearl, *Mit Dem Vort Tzum Folk*, 11–20, 29–53, 58–63, 76–80.

55 Pearl, *Mit Dem Vort Tzum Folk*, 11–20, 29–53, 58–63, 76–80; *DYV*, 20 June, 18 July, 15 and 19 August 1919.

56 LAC, Records of the Dept. of the Secretary of State, Censor Papers, McLean-Chambers Correspondence; Gutnick Interview.

57 *Saturday Night*, 30 August 1919, also 7 and 28 June, 12 July, 2 and 23 August 1919; LAC, Records of the RCMP, Strike File, Almazoff deportation hearing, 18 July, n.d., 15 August 1919, 19–30, 86–135, 144, 148–55.

58 LAC, Records of the RCMP, Strike File, Almazoff deportation hearing, 15 and 16 August 1919, 139, 142–48, 156–58; *DYV*, 19 August 1919.

59 Thomas Peterson, "Manitoba: Ethnic and Class Politics," in *Canadian Provincial Politics: The Party Systems of the Ten Provinces*, ed. Martin Robin, 2nd ed. (Scarborough, ON: Prentice-Hall of Canada, 1978), 75; LAC, Arthur Meighen Papers, MG26 I, series I, vol. 5, file 30, Hugh John Macdonald to Arthur Meighen, 3 July 1919, 002537-40.

60 *DYV*, 1 July 1919.

61 LAC, Records of the Dept. of the Secretary of State, Censor Papers, Chambers to McLean, 27 June, 25 July 1919.

62 Trachtenberg, "Winnipeg Jewish Community and Politics," 120.

63 LAC, Records of the Immigration Branch, RG76, vol. 390, file 54178, pt. 2, Cawdron to Blair, Blair to Cawdron, Blair and T.B. Willans to W.W. Cory, 15, 16, and 17 December 1919, 52430, 39557.

64 Irving Abella and Harold Troper, *None Is Too Many: Canada and the Jews of Europe, 1933–1948* (Toronto: Lester and Orpen Dennys, 1982), 54–56, 70, 73.

65 J.E. Rea, "The Politics of Class: Winnipeg City Council, 1919–1945," in *The West and the Nation: Essays in Honour of W.L. Morton*, ed. Carl Berger and Ramsay Cook (Toronto: McClelland and Stewart, 1976), 232–49.

66 Trachtenberg, "Winnipeg Jewish Community and Politics," 124–25; Chiel, *Jews of Manitoba*, 179–80.

67 Trachtenberg, "'Old Clo' Move,'" 810, 824–32.

68 Trachtenberg, "'Old Clo' Move,'" 810–24; *DYV*, 27 November 1919.

69 Narvey, "Personal Perspective," 82; Trachtenberg, "Winnipeg Jewish Community and Politics," 123–41.

5

The Edmonton General Strike

Mikhail Bjorge

1919 was a year of global proletarian revolt. From Buenos Aires to Kiel, from Hungary to Glasgow, a wave of working-class militancy swept the world. In Russia, entrenchment of the revolution threatened to overthrow the entire global capitalist order. The former belligerents of the First World War, realizing that fighting communism was more important than their intra-imperial rivalries, turned their bayonets away from each other and toward the Bolsheviks. As Edmonton's the *Soviet* argued, "from the Rhine to the Yellow River, the world is in a state of unrest and revolution."[1]

In a forgivably hasty estimation, Antonio Gramsci contended that the Canadian industrial strikes "have taken on the overt character of a bid to install a soviet regime."[2] However, the workers' revolt did mean general strikes in most major western centres; a nearly complete wildcat shutdown of the coalfields; and the attempted organization of a domestic revolutionary industrial union for all workers. And the workers in and around Edmonton were deeply embroiled in these conflicts. As industrial conflict ramped up during and after the war, foreignness and radicalism were conflated and, in turn, intensely suppressed. While the leadership of most unions and the general strikes themselves were almost universally British and male, the working class in western Canada was less monolithic. English Canada's financial and industrial centre was Toronto, the metropole dotted with fifty-nine Orange halls and whose population was startlingly homogenous, clocking in at around 80 percent British and nearly as Protestant.[3] This stood in sharp juxtaposition to the Canadian West, where hundreds of thousands of barely wanted bodies, with varying (but low) status on the Anglo-supremacist pyramid, were dumped onto recently enclosed land to turn it into capital.

Winnipeg was the most populous and important city in the west, and their unions set the tone and direction for yearly bargaining. In 1919 Edmonton's workers looked towards Winnipeg for direction and closely followed negotiations by that city's machinists. In the years preceding, however, the vicious prewar depression that had forced the unemployed into the cities had slowly turned into a wartime boom for the city. While employment rose so too did the cost of living, alongside relentless inflation, state repression, and industrial unrest. As such, when the Winnipeg General Strike broke out on 15 May 1919 Edmonton was instantly abuzz. Four days later the executive of the Edmonton Trades and Labour Council (ETLC) passed a motion expressing sympathy for the Winnipeg Strikers and called for a sympathy strike vote.[4]

Yet, even holding a general strike vote was far from a preordained outcome. The relatively conservative ETLC was viewed by some labour people as "the most reactionary of all the labor councils in Western Canada," and it was clearly wary of radical contagion.[5] Less than a month before, twenty of the more conservative members of the council, generally British and skilled, had expelled nineteen members of the council. Those expelled were an assortment of radicals, socialists, and early One Big Union (OBU) supporters, all officially purged for advocating a different way forward. Socialist orator and leader of Federal Labourers Union (also known as the Federal Labour Union) Sarah Knight was voted out alongside former Industrial Workers of the World (IWW) secretary of Local 82 and fellow Labourer Carl Berg. George Perkins, a respected railway metalworker from the International Association of Machinists, was expelled. Socialist Party of Canada (SPC) member and leader of the carpenters, Joseph Knight, was ousted, as was socialist Alex Susnar, who represented mostly immigrant miners within the United Mine Workers of America's District 18.[6]

The OBU idea of splitting from the eastern craft unions had found footing earlier among an increasingly radical working class. Organizing industrially was surely the answer to the issue of conservative and ethnically exclusive unions. In their estimations, it just made sense to have one union for all workers with "no alien but the capitalist."[7] The expelled represented a more diverse crowd than did the craft unions and drew much of their membership from the more militant sectors of the working class. Their ranks contained many who lacked the franchise, had it taken from them in 1917, immigrated with revolutionary ideas, had skills that did not transfer well, or were prone to deportation. Much has been made of the prairie settler farming experience, but as historian Donald Avery pointed out, Canada's capitalists primarily "required a workforce that was both inexpensive and at their beck and call" to do the "railroad construction in the Canadian shield in the summer, harvesting in Saskatchewan in the fall, coal mining in Alberta in the winter, and lumbering in British Columbia in the spring."[8] These populations were policed by a colonial-minded paramilitary force that held British imperialism, antiradicalism, and xenophobia as official policy.[9] But wherever these workers came from, they had votes that mattered for the general strike. The newly shrunk ETLC knew that if they boycotted the vote their expelled radicals would bypass them altogether. They decided that a joint vote should be held.

Their participation notwithstanding, ETLC leaders actively agitated against the Strike by whipping votes and prodding those in their circles to vote responsibly. Despite their best efforts, the conservative and antistrike unionists were met with limited success.[10] Constable Davison from the RNWMP took to the streets to interview workers and some working-class leaders and found that the "feeling everywhere amongst all classes of workers favoured a strike in sympathy with the Winnipeg strikers." He also found, worryingly, that radical thought was most common and intense among the foreign set.[11] As the *Alberta Non-Partisan* articulated, "the general strike which a few short months since would have been thought impossible in Canada is now actually becoming a reality. The solidarity necessary for a strike of such a character only develops when the necessity arises. It could not have been built up on an abstract argument—but the actual necessity produces it speedily."[12] Needless to say, the language of respectability was mirrored by Alberta premier Charles Stewart, who said that "no responsible citizens" should support the General Strike.[13]

The ubiquitous language of "respectable" unions was a simple synecdoche for unions with acceptably British leadership and members. If they had any political orientation at all, it was an orientation toward normative electoral politics. For those excluded from specific trades over ethnicity or lacking the vote for the same reason, there were no politics to participate in. Wartime xenophobia and the threat of internment ensured that union leadership was uniform at this time and not demographically representative.[14]

Several of the more conservative craft unions were irritated with the inclusion of the unions that contained overwhelmingly lower-skilled and foreign workers in the General Strike vote. However, the ETLC executive knew that many workers in Edmonton and the surrounding area were ready to strike notwithstanding the leanings of the ETLC leadership. In the lead-up to the general strike wave, Superintendent T.A. Wroughton of the Royal North-West Mounted Police (RNWMP) noted that "all the mines in the vicinity, as far as I can make out, are now on strike or about to strike."[15] Mine owners kept close tabs on the ethnicity of their employees. Here we find a consistent pattern of a British elite in managerial and ownership positions. This contrasted to the motley assortment of predominantly southern and eastern Europeans (among others) working and dying in the mines.[16] Wroughton was further concerned by the prevalence of Austrian workers at Strike meetings.[17] Their unwanted presence, claimed Wroughton, meant that the city was "full of foreigners of all sorts"—a worrying proposition. With the possibility of a general strike now very real, and the city chock full of "dangerous foreigners" ready to "overthrow the government and start a Soviet Council," Wroughton busied himself with planning in case of "danger of life and property."[18] He was concerned that there were perhaps only thirty active military available in the city.

Wroughton may have been preparing for a violent rebellion, but Mayor Joseph Clarke foresaw no serious disorder on the horizon.[19] He explained to city council that the Strike had been called in solidarity with Winnipeg and would remain peaceful. A product of the politics of respectable labour, Clarke was a worker-friendly mayor by all accounts and made it clear that the military would neither be welcome nor needed in Edmonton.[20] Mayor Clarke's proclamation was immediately ignored by Wroughton, who liaised with the military and hastily placed their 150 rifles under guard in case the revolutionaries decided to storm the armouries. He further commanded RNWMP Constable Davison to investigate the feelings of workers regarding the proposed strike.[21] Through his interviews, Davison uncovered widespread strike support, particularly among the Europeans. He encountered a population that was disenfranchised and eking out a meagre existence, all while facing heightened wartime repression, political policing, the aura of internment, and xenophobia. Unsurprisingly, Davison found these workers to be "the most radical in their views and intentions." When confronted the next day by Superintendent Wroughton, however, a weightier symbol of the security state with the power to intern or deport, their political stance suddenly changed. While they still asked Wroughton about his thoughts on the coming revolution, this second visit from a ranking officer led to a change in stories. Now the Austrians reported that fear of the General Strike was driving them away from the city and that they were in fact heading toward safer agricultural work far afield.[22]

The General Strike vote was counted on 25 May in Edmonton's labour hall. The results were strongly in favour of a strike: 1,676 for and 506 against. Forty-nine unions were invited to vote, and thirty-eight participated. Only a very few voted against, including the Garment Workers, the Musicians, the Sheet Metal Workers, and the Federation of Postal Workers.[23] Some musicians and postal workers told the RNWMP that they were angered by the presence of Carl Berg, and demanded his removal from the Strike Committee on pains of cutting off financial assistance. According to RCMP Supt. Wroughton, "many of the union men openly charge Carl E. Berg with being a Bolshevik, an IWW, and the worst kind of agitator, the prime mover of the One Big Union scheme." Berg was no Bolshevik, but he was the former secretary of Edmonton's IWW local and a noted general strike enthusiast. Conspicuously, he was also the sole non-British member of the Strike Committee, and the attacks reflected xenophobic language.[24] Wroughton concluded that "it seems to be generally accredited that were it not for Berg the strike would quickly terminate"—a dubious proposition loaded with ideology, but one that fit rather neatly into predispositions that fused ethnicity with radicalism.[25]

Figure 5.1. Labour Council Headquarters, Purvis Block, 1920. Source: Glenbow Archives, ND-3-746.

Although it is difficult to know the exact reason why some union locals refused to even vote—the Stonecutters, the Typographical Union, the Letter Carriers' Federation, the Printing Pressmen, the ministers, and both teachers' alliances—it is notable that most of these represented the aristocracy of labour and those with some upward mobility. These were both demographics that had experienced some success in both labour and electoral politics.[26] Yet even within these unions there remained strong individual support for the Strike.[27] The railway carmen and two of Perkins's three machinist shops made up the industrial base of the Strikers. The building trades who took votes were all solidly behind the Strike, as were essentially all area miners. Municipal employees, including the streetcar drivers and utility workers, all voted in favour and joined the Strike. As nonunionized workers swelled the ranks, over 2,000 workers formed the backbone of the Edmonton General Strike.

The Strike was organized from the bottom up. Two delegates were elected from each union to a Central Strike Committee. Yet this posed its own unique set of challenges. There were many craft unions with small memberships and few industrial unions with large memberships. This meant that more conservative unions held disproportionate influence relative to their numbers. Radicals controlled only a minority of craft and industrial unions: the Laborers Union, the Brotherhood of Carpenters and Joiners, and the United Mine Workers of America District 18, and the Machinists.

The central committee oversaw the Strike executive, which handled day-to-day operations including twice-daily mass meetings in Market Square and the publication of the *Edmonton Strike Bulletin*. The executive was made up of eight delegates, including at least two radicals. C.R. Bellis, an OBU supporter, served as the chairman, while Berg from the Labourers Union served as vice chairman. Subcommittees—including those for health and safety, finance, and propaganda—were quickly organized to support the central committee.[28] There the less formal leadership included editors of Edmonton's the *Soviet,* Sarah and Joe Knight of the SPC, and Reverend F.E. Mercer of the Labour Church, among others.[29]

Instead of organizing an immediate demonstration, the Strike executive decided to wait until the morning of 26 May. The aggressively antistrike *Edmonton Bulletin* preemptively complained that "a dictator to pronounce what shall and what shall not be allowed has not yet been appointed. Whether or not Edmontonians will suffer the same results of a dictatorship as Winnipeg did could not be ascertained." Frank Oliver, former member of parliament and owner of the *Edmonton Bulletin,* chided that now that Chinese laundrymen had joined the Strike, "pestilential plutocracy can bedeck itself in negligee or go shirtless." Meanwhile, the *Edmonton Journal*, the less partisan voice of the business community, refused to believe "until the very hour of the declaration of the strike . . . that it would actually be brought into effect."[30] The world was on fire, and those who had not been paying attention were caught unaware.

Excepting the first day of the Strike, telephone service and electricity remained sporadically available. As had been done in Winnipeg, the strikers reduced water service so that only hospitals and those living on the first floor of a building could maintain water pressure. Fuses were removed from the power station, ensuring that a skeleton crew could not operate the plant at full capacity. Despite the musicians voting against the Strike, the executive granted the movie theatres "by permission of the strike committee" placards to ensure that the movies remained open, giving striking workers something to do. Overall, the Strike Committee was lenient with nonessential services so long as they displayed the signs reading "by permission of the strike committee." All of this meant that, for the first week, the city was beholden to the Strike Committee. Naturally, even this minor usurpation was resented by local aldermen, elites, and their local representatives who formed a class organization of their own, the Edmonton Citizens' Committee (ECC). Emerging out of the Edmonton Board of Trade, the committee claimed to represent "all lines of business and industry" and, rather than constituting a conspiracy against the public, they argued that such an entity was necessary to organize in "self-protection against the strike."[31]

The ECC immediately pressured Mayor Clarke to break the Strike by force and to hire strikebreakers. Clarke refused, noting that the right to strike for a decent standard of living was not up for debate. The mayor had long been involved in the labour community and the ETLC had helped elevate him to his position. Clarke was on the record predicting great hardship if the government did not stop capital from "unduly flouting labour unions" and ignoring their right to negotiate with employers. Yet during the Strike, Clarke adopted a cautiously practical approach that attempted to tame labour and appease the ECC. For example, after municipal workers joined the Strike, he ran an advertisement in the *Edmonton Bulletin* looking for "permanent employees" to replace them. As mayor, he was supportive of respectable labour and was tolerant of a progressive labour movement, but radicalism or socialism were steps too far indeed. He reassured the public that he would not have "any Bolshevik board of trade interfering" with his power or he would put the city under martial law.[32] In the end, Clarke "had the authority to run the city and meant to do it." Despite this relatively effective balancing act, the establishment newspapers continuously attacked him, calling him a "freak mayor" who had allowed the "self-elected Soviet heads" in the Strike Committee to commandeer legitimate power.[33]

Clarke's rather reasonable steps to quell the Strike were not enough for the ECC, who floated the idea of special constables and military cooperation. Concerned that the police force had declared itself ready to act at the call of the strikers, they argued that "if governmental authority . . . does not function to protect the rights of the individual by protecting its own supremacy, that constitutes in fact an abdication of authority."[34] Soon enough, disagreements and eventually clashes occurred at the yards of the Canadian Pacific Railway (CPR), Grand Trunk Pacific

(GTP), and Canadian National Railway (CNR). Meanwhile, the RNWMP started accustoming their horses to gunfire and ensuring that their heavy weaponry, including machine guns fresh from the front, were free of mud and in working order.

On 28 May, the Carpenters and both maintenance of way and shop workers from the railroads joined the Strike, prompting Berg to tell the *Strike Bulletin* that he was "much satisfied with the success of the strike so far."[35] A few days later, the newspaper announced that the teamsters, taxi drivers, carpenters, bricklayers and masons, boilermakers, plumbers, painters, railway carmen, yardmen, freight handlers, machinists, express messengers, steam shovel operators, metalworkers, stone cutters, miners, maintenance of way workers, railway clerks, and blacksmiths all remained solidly on strike.[36] At daily Strike meetings, large crowds listened to speakers who denounced misrepresentations of their cause in the media and damned the establishment press for its efforts to "beguile the public."[37]

In part, the strikers were responding to inflammatory editorials in the *Edmonton Bulletin*, which accused the strikers of being worse than wartime Germans for denying children cream or for intentionally spoiling milk. The typographers' union, which had refused to participate in the vote on the General Strike, responded by calling the editorial exaggerated and prejudiced. Their union published a public letter accusing the paper of quoting "doubtful authority designed to discredit the strikers," and asserting that such "methods of journalism" were an affront to all working people. The typographers sardonically noted that "Edmonton butter is commonly separated by agitation, as in churning... the only sort of agitation not charged against unionism by the present government."[38]

While strikes are often gendered male, the government and major newspapers are conspicuous in their complaints regarding the involvement of women in the Strike. The editors of the *Strike Bulletin* contended—and with good reason—that demands for change were not the result solely of working men, but also working women. Referring to women, the Strike Committee posed the following rhetorical question: "Who have suffered and endured for years the reign of tyranny spreading throughout the country as a result of the protection to the profiteer?" The committee continued, "We understand that the government, after its unsuccessful attempt to break the united and determined stand labor has taken, intends to take up the question of the morals of women wage-earners with unrestrained enthusiasm. Go slow, Robert," they chided the prime minister, "our working womanettes are the true soviettes."[39]

Perhaps most dramatically, strikers were incensed over ongoing attempts to demonize so-called foreign workers. The defeat of autocratic Czarism in Russia and the fleeing of that empire's deeply reactionary political elite contributed to the spread and intensification of theories of Judeo-Bolshevism all across Europe and North America. After all, their brand of targeted racial hatred was an easy answer for those who perceived the often perfunctory demands emerging from the miseries and privations of their working populations as a conspiracy and plot.[40] On the national level major newspapers whipped up xenophobia at every turn, spurred on by a government that blamed labour unrest and socialism on the foreign element alone, as in their estimation the proper British would never countenance such ideas.[41] Edmontonians were treated to a constant stream of stories in the *Edmonton Journal* and the *Edmonton Bulletin* that did their best to inflame xenophobic sentiment and laid exclusive blame for socio-economic unrest on ethnic radicals. Such news stories promoted and entrenched the conspiracy theory that the Strike was an imported plot led by "dangerous foreigners" who were "apostles of Lenine and Trotsky." To substantiate this argument, they dubiously claimed that a "highly placed union leader" informed them that Bolshevist money was behind the current labour trouble. These allegations, to which the newspapers would often return, only intensified, with mastheads denouncing the "Bolshevik Strike Committee" becoming increasingly common. The editors of the *Strike Bulletin* mused that the ruling elite's inability to conceptualize strikers as anything but Bolsheviks or dupes only proved how disconnected they really were. "Whatever man or woman thinks about Bolshevism," the *Bulletin* noted, "if he or she happens to oppose the tyranny of the Manufacturers' Association, he or she is a Bolshevik."[42]

A favoured tactic of the newspapers was to present radical Reds in stark juxtaposition with veterans, who best encapsulated imperial respectability and authority. As such, the newspapers claimed that veterans—always unnamed and rarely directly quoted—opposed the Strike's directives and were willing to wage war against dangerous foreigners: anarchists, IWWs, Bolsheviks, German sympathizers, and

Figure 5.2. *Edmonton Journal*, 20 June 1919. Reprinted from a Chicago newspaper.

the like. Yet this ran counter to the views of many returning soldiers who were far from enamoured with the employing class. While spying on the meetings at Market Square, an officer recalled a veteran who complained that the government had failed to live up to the principles that he had fought for. He was now home to "carry on the battle which was not yet won ... the battle for democracy." Perhaps more worrisome to Wroughton, the veteran noted that "soldiers who served in France would not shoot down their fellow workers."[43]

The Strike Committee responded to the charges concerning dangerous foreigners by publishing the names of its executive; all but Berg were British. In response to the xenophobic bait strikers released a rather puckish missive indicating that they would agree to certain deportations, should they be necessary. "If [an] amendment to the criminal code is justly carried out, quite a number of the members of the Senate and the Lower House will be deported," they pointed out, "together with a punishment to those who rent them their offices."[44] Responding further to the attacks, the *Strike Bulletin* turned them against their enemies, articulating that "the self-appointed [ECC] is unpopular ... and had in its composition slackers and aliens."[45] The *Strike Bulletin* later argued that the capitalist newspapers "see only Bolsheviki, anarchists, and aliens in the strikers." As a thought experiment, they shared the following:

> Suppose Robinson, Labor leader, is really a Russian or Austrian, and suppose his name is really Rubinstein; and suppose the Labor Temple, Winnipeg, is at present the Mecca

> of foreign-speaking people; and suppose there are firebrands and anarchists evident in the strikers; should it not appeal to the Free Press that it is quite impossible these elements are altogether responsible for a strike of nearly 100,000 men in different cities? Why, if these men were dominated by such classes all the troops in Winnipeg would not have preserved order, and as a matter of fact there has been no disorder.[46]

For its part, the *Soviet* responded by supporting aliens and internees, and commenting on issues of importance to immigrant populations.[47] Striker Joseph Adair argued at the daily meetings that attempts to paint foreigners as somehow treasonous was a "damnable lie." He opined that "the sweat and blood of the alien put into the railways justifies him for all time. If I have to choose between a quiet Austrian and a profiteer like Allison or Flavelle," Adair closed, "give me the Austrian."[48] The *Strike Bulletin* was similarly direct, riddling the reader "When is an alien not an alien? When he is a scab."[49]

For a while, then, the Strike held strong. Contrary to what the establishment newspapers were reporting, which was that fewer than 800 men were out on strike, as of June 9 thirty-two local unions remained on the picket line and hundreds of nonunionized workers maintained their mass refusal to go back to work.[50] While the international railway brotherhoods that represented workers in the running trades were antistrike, the "yardmen, shopmen, maintenance of way men, mechanics, machinists, baggagemen, checkers, and clerks" remained out.[51] The teamsters persisted despite the newspapers continuously reporting that they had returned, and the erstwhile miners remained steadfast. Superintendent Wroughton reported that all involved were still optimistic regarding the outcome.[52] For the strikers, the situation in Winnipeg was much the same, an encouraging sign to be sure.

Though the Strike was never as weak as the newspapers suggested, it had admittedly approached a holding pattern by the middle of June. Meetings at Market Square continued twice daily and, according to Wroughton, the crowds remained "attentive, good natured, and perfectly orderly in every way."[53] But the death knell of the Strike was being proclaimed almost daily by the newspapers since the first day, and the Strike Committee was constantly on the defensive, spending more time debunking lies than driving their own narrative.[54] Joseph Knight, for

THE ALIEN BOGEY MAN

Five minutes plain thinking will reveal to any normal mind the true nature and purpose of the alien cry now being raised so vociferously by the self-styled "Citizens' Committee of One Thousand" against the Trades Unions of this city. Consider:—

1.—That the Citizens' Committee is an offshoot of the Board of Trade.

2.—That the Board of Trade is a body of **employers**

3.—That the employing class brought the aliens to this country to provide cheap labor, against the protests of organized labor.

4.—That it is members of the Board of Trade who are employing the aliens.

5.—That the military authorities and the Alien Investigation Board can give the Board of Trade full information regarding the undesirables among the aliens.

6.—That nothing stands in the way of the employers discharging these undesirables, and replacing them with returned soldiers.

7.—That the expensive advertisements of the "Citizens' Committee" urging this change are therefore absolutely unnecessary.

8.—That the labor unrest would be with us if there was not a single alien in the country. It is a world-wide upheaval, due to economic conditions.

9.—That the employing class controls the state and all its industries, so that they and not the workers, are responsible for the present chaos.

The only conclusion to be drawn from the foregoing plain unvarnished facts, is that the anti-alien campaign of the "Citizens' Committee" is a desperate expedient, deliberately waged to confuse the issue, to disrupt the ranks of organized labor, to deceive the public and to distract attention from the misdeeds of the exploiting class.

Don't be stampeded by the bogus committee's bogey man.

Figure 5.3. *Edmonton Strike Bulletin*, 18 June 1919. This missive points toward a highly sophisticated analysis of nativism and how it was instrumentalized.

Figure 5.4. Brule Miners, 1918. "Workers of the world unite!" in Ukrainian and English. Mail from Berg to the miners in Brule was intercepted by the police. From the private collection of Larissa Stavroff.

example, was accused of being sympathetic to the Germans, Austrians, and internees. Despite her being found not guilty for speaking out against the war in 1918, Sarah Knight's Winnipeg trial for sedition was repeatedly brought up. Meanwhile, Carl Berg learned that his mail was being intercepted to gain insight on the activities of striking miners in the socialist strongholds of Brule and Drumheller.[55]

The constant insinuations of unpatriotic or anti-imperial thought caused problems for the Strike Committee. Beyond earlier demands to remove Berg from the executive, Joseph Knight was forced to resign from the Strike's press department due to outside pressure.[56] In the militant strikers' estimation such red-baiting, lies, and obfuscations from antistrike forces not only weakened working-class solidarity but were intended to humiliate and marginalize them in preparation for more mass repression. The Strike Committee warned that this was "a fair sample of what the government will do when it gets full control."[57]

The holding pattern was, in many regards, the best that could be done under the circumstances as there was little room to expand the Strike's numbers. Most workers who wanted to join had already done so. Trying to smooth over the obvious divides, the strikers tried to promote the intrinsic justness of their cause by arguing in favour of the "sympathetic strike" as it was "an expression of the growth of enlightened self-interest among the workers." With a distinctly modern rationality, they continued: "It would be as futile for one union to attempt to combat capitalistic oppression alone as it would have been for Belgium to resist Germany alone. The result in both cases would mean inevitable defeat. The workers have been educated in the hard school of experience and have learned the lesson that an injustice to one is an injustice to all. Labor men now recognize that if one body of workers is successfully denied the freedom of association, in other words the right to organize, then every existing organization is in jeopardy."[58] The timely call, however, could only do so much to sway the rest of Edmonton's toilers to join the struggle. By mid-June, any small hope that the running trades would join the sympathy strike were dashed when they decided to exercise caution, ostensibly at the behest of their international union leadership.

The decision of the running trades not to join was then coupled with a more generalized demoralization that led many municipal workers to begin drifting back to work. The Strike Committee was clear-eyed about the news. "The large part of the inhabitants of Edmonton are of the white collar, Government clerk variety," the *Edmonton Strike Bulletin* noted, "and they spread an atmosphere of frigid respectability. Having obtained their jobs by private favoritism, they are not prepared to believe that governments can be made to act by outward and visible protests."[59] Whatever their rationale, the Strike was waning.

The farmers of the province were generally only selectively supportive of organized labour, let alone the General Strike. The United Farmers of Alberta (UFA) were inclined toward moderate socialism, cooperatives, and direct democracy, with many of its members "showing the keenest interest" in turning the crisis into an electoral opportunity.[60] Some farmers were worried by more radical calls for broad nationalization, which they assumed might well include their farms.[61] As such, the *Grain Growers' Guide* printed full-page advertisements from the Winnipeg Citizens' Committee of 1000 denouncing the Strike.[62] Just east of Edmonton the Bardo section of the UFA labelled the strikers as Bolsheviks and denounced the Strike Committee. Meanwhile, farmers from the East Clover UFA local, who were struggling to transport their goods into town on the struck express trains, condemned the Strike in the "strongest possible terms." Not all UFA locals came out against the Strike, however. The majority Scandinavian UFA Local 293 at New Norway stated that they "fully endorse the action of the different labor unions in their strike for principles."[63] While progressive farmer, cooperative organizer, and prewar immigrant Heinrich Eyeben may have believed that "Leon Trotsky is God's messenger" who was sent "to free this Earth from the yoke of capitalism," this was assuredly a minority opinion.[64]

Wariness, if not outright hostility, from certain craft unions persisted. The official organ of the ETLC, the *Edmonton Free Press,* frequently either obfuscated or marginalized the radicalism among Edmonton's working class. Arguing that the current unrest was caused only by "exploitation, profiteering, and combinations of capital," the ETLC maintained that general strikes were simply particularly strident efforts to obtain collective bargaining rights and express discontent.[65] Why organized workers who already claimed these rights were on strike was never explained. As early as 31 May, the newspaper began calling on workers to return to their jobs and referred to the Strike itself as a failure.[66] In response, the *Edmonton Strike Bulletin* introduced a regular masthead reminding its readers that "The Edmonton Free Press is not the official paper of the Edmonton labor unions out on strike!"

One after another American unions started to pull the charters of locals involved in the General Strike. Irritated by the lack of respectable practices up north, the Brotherhood of Railway Carmen was the first American union to put an Edmonton local into receivership in early June for joining the Strike.[67] Although some members of the International Ladies Garment Workers' Union (ILGWU) sporadically struck in the first days, the technocratic ILGWU leadership demanded that their members cease all activity immediately. These edicts pulled some unionized workers off strike, while others, such as the machinists in locomotive maintenance, refused the demands of their union, the International Association of Machinists and Aerospace Workers (IAM). These were the same workers who Davison "got into conversation with" in the "largest garages," who he found strongly in favour of the Strike on 23 May.[68]

The *Edmonton Bulletin* contended that "the skilled crafts" had largely been against the Strike. In their estimation it was the "less responsible and more recently organized elements of labour" who chiefly supported it.[69] However xenophobic or pejorative, it was also probably accurate. Industrial discipline takes time to instill. In a similar manner, the highly skilled trades, and the unions that protected them, tended to be ethnically exclusive. Outside of the IWW, the miners, and later the OBU, there were limited opportunities for non-Anglo workers to join many unions, and internment operations continued during the postwar period. In this climate, local progressive Joseph Adair cautioned Edmonton's workers on the worrying rise in xenophobia exacerbated by the press. At a mid-June meeting of 2,500 he urged workers to be careful "lest a racial strife or struggle be started."[70]

The terminal blow to the Strike came following the news of the arrest of Winnipeg's Strike leadership and the subsequent events of Bloody Saturday. When asked for comment by the *Edmonton Bulletin,* Berg obliged, offering a warning: "Arrest the leaders of labour and you will surely have Bolshevism and have it right."[71] Railway machinist and organizer Charles Bellis began to wonder if, as chairman of the Edmonton General Strike, he would soon be arrested and deported. Word that the government planned to expel foreign leaders of the Winnipeg General Strike prompted him to somewhat facetiously quip that he had been "longing for a trip back to my old home in England for a long while now" anyway.[72] While Bellis feigned a lack of concern, Berg, perhaps more sensitive to such realities, did not rule out the possibility of Bellis's deportation. Further, Berg warned him that they could not trust that the Trades and Labour Congress of Canada (TLC) would protect them. "I, for one, cannot conceive of [the TLC] going out of their way and perhaps jeopardizing themselves in the carrying out of something that might not meet with the will of the majority of trade unions," he admitted. Instead, Berg put his faith in the power of the working class. "If anything was done in regard to the Winnipeg trouble," Berg cautioned, "the various strike committees would have to do it themselves."[73]

Soon after, the Strike Committee recalled the observers it had sent to Winnipeg.[74] Upon hearing what had transpired there, the Edmonton General Strike was officially called off.[75] This time, the obituary published by the *Edmonton Bulletin* was finally true. As soon as the Strike ended the paper went on the offensive. "For all parties concerned," the newspaper advocated, "the best result that could possibly flow from the present general strike in western cities would be that it should be the last. And it will be," the report concluded, "if organized labour puts the 'red' element where it belongs."[76]

Conclusion

With the threat of mass unrest gone, the police finally raided the SPC headquarters on 1 July in the wave of repression that followed the conclusion of the Winnipeg General Strike. As the SPC's paper described: "In the early hours of the morning the office and headquarters of the Socialist Party of Canada were raided by the R.N.W.M.P. A small amount of literature and a few letters were taken away. No Bolshevik 'bullion' was discovered." It continued that "this is a part of a Dominion-wide search party that has been launched by the Government. Labor and socialist halls have been microscopically examined, men have been shot, strikers arrested, Labor leaders and socialists imprisoned, and the homes turned upside down. From all this our 'safe' and 'sane' labour leaders, opportunists, and parsons, would have us believe that there is no 'Class War'; no fellow workers, it is indeed a love fest."[77] The paper dryly concluded that "the War to end War, the War for 'Democracy' is over, and all are clamped in a loving embrace."

The consistent strike action during the war seems to show that the upward redistribution of wealth, inflationary pressures, and the fairly naked oppression of workers were all more important than heady propaganda from business and a ruling class clinging to a teetering legitimacy. Workers involved in the general strikes did not seize the major means of production, but by the structure of their challenge they did confront the basis of the economic order: the authority of the state to protect private property and the inalienable right of the capitalist to compel the working class, as a *class*, to subordinate their time to the needs of profit or face homelessness, hunger, and poverty. The general strikes showed, perhaps lurchingly, that via strike councils workers could effectively run things for themselves.[78]

The strike wave was surely something of a victory for Canada's workers, but the *Soviet* had a different and telling line on what transpired. They argued the strike wave was "forced upon the workers of Canada by the master class deliberately." In their estimation, "the purpose was twofold: first, to justify a continuation, and, if possible, an intensification of present senseless and tyrannical legislation; second, by bringing in a clash prematurely to forestall our efforts to effect a more perfect class organization."[79] Previously, OBU delegate P. McDonneil had argued that the organized were "now ready to take their stand" and call a general strike for the six-hour day on 1 June 1919.[80] Desmond Morton's argument that the revolt was the product of "weakness" is therefore too hasty, and missed the larger project that western socialists had in mind.[81] In the *Soviet*'s estimation at least, the ruling class took the first fight they could to kneecap more significant shifts in class organization, in particular the rise and solidification of the OBU and their planned general strike for the six-hour day. The combined power of the state, capital, and some mainstream unions, many of whose members participated in the General Strike, worked together in an unholy alliance to eliminate the OBU.[82] In effect, they ensured that the leadership of Canada's unions remained out of the control of socialists and minorities, groups who were disproportionately the victims of blacklisting following 1919. So, the labour movement remained firmly in the hands of respectable, responsible actors. This group, as Carl Berg had earlier warned, did little to challenge the state's disciplinary regime cooked up in the wake of the strikes; the one that tried British agitators and summarily deported foreign ones.

It is general practice at the end of commentary regarding the workers' revolt to provide observations or reflections regarding the importance or implications of the events. Often these strikes emerge as a sort of metaphysical victory that serves as an exemplar of militancy, or perhaps a reflection of the potential horizons for organized expressions of working-class power. If there is one thing that the modern Left is adept at, it is torturing failures into victories. While there is much to be said for this approach, the wider implications of the revolt sometimes get missed in the attempt to extract triumphalism from what was, in most ways, a crushing defeat. It is too easy to forget that the workers' revolt ended not only in police and specials shooting strikers in the streets and ransacking workers' halls, but also in mass deportations, the expansion of official political repression, intensified official xenophobia, a chill to cultural pluralism, increased police powers, and grotesque distortions within the labour movement.

Perhaps the most important outcome was the reformation of the moribund RNWMP as the Royal Canadian Mounted Police, which emerged from the revolt as a national anti-red squad charged with policing foreigners and the broad Left. The RCMP proceeded to put virtually every organization left of centrist Liberals under surveillance, actively infiltrated their organizations, and disrupted them with little regard to "British fair play" or legality. The second major outcome was the politicization of local police forces. In many western cities, including Edmonton, local police had both unionized and supported the Strike Committee. This usurpation of proper authority clearly frightened the ruling class, who proceeded to fire their police forces en masse and replace or rehire them based on no-strike contracts and attestations to political belief. This political purge of the police has repercussions to the present day, as Canada's local police were reformed into instruments of direct class rule, away from the night watchman status accepted by the public earlier.[83]

But perhaps the most overlooked direct outcome of the workers' revolt was the changes made to the Dominion Elections Act in 1920—a major shift toward democracy at the time. Since well before Confederation, Canada had never been a terribly democratic place.[84] From the start, Canada's oligarchy was notoriously distrustful of the populations they imported to turn recently purloined land into private capital. Voting eligibility was unofficially proscribed in countless ways, but officially limited by high property qualifications, gender, confession, and race. Many strikers, albeit rarely their leadership, either lacked the franchise altogether or had it stripped away in 1917 under the Wartime Elections Act. The change in elections law in 1920 finally eliminated the property qualification from voting and extended the vote to some women. In doing so the Act officially extended the franchise to the majority of Canada's European population. However, it also maintained provincial rights to discriminate based on religion and race, and ensured the continued prohibitions regarding Indigenous enfranchisement. Despite these obvious limitations, it is not a stretch to say that the workers' revolt directly led to near-universal suffrage in Canada.

The Act enfranchised thousands, particularly across the Prairie West whose population made up most of the participants in the workers' revolt. People across Canada used their new voting power to elect farmer-labour and progressive governments. In the years immediately following the strikes, political formations that were far more democratic and revolutionary than is commonly assumed came to power. Edmonton's elite, or at least their representatives, managed to continue the Citizens' Committee as the city's most powerful local political formation well into the 1970s. Wary of being completely wiped out in "first past the post" elections, elites in the Liberal and Conservative parties in Canada's west gingerly allowed for changes in the very election process itself. In the wake of the strikes proportional representation was institutionalized in both Alberta and Manitoba at the provincial level. At least until they were quietly dismantled in the icy reaction against democracy that marked the Cold War.[85]

In the end, Edmonton's General Strike did not translate a revolutionary moment into a revolutionary situation. As one Calgary striker noted, "whether the general strike ends successfully for the strikers, or they are forced to call it off without having attained their immediate objects—the class war will continue."[86] In the estimation of the *Soviet* this was a setback, but "the cure for the errors of democracy is now, as always, more democracy—a more complete and more perfect democracy. And there is no real democracy to be found in anything except in immediate control by the rank and file," a dream still on the horizon.[87]

Notes

1 *Soviet*, Edmonton, 27 March 1919.

2 Antonio Gramsci, *Selections from Political Writings: 1910–1920* (New York: International Publishers, 1977), 61. Edmonton General Strike leader Joseph Knight would later argue at the founding of the Red International of Labour Unions (RILU) in Moscow that this was exactly the case. John Riddell, trans., *Protokoll des III. Weltkongresses der Kommunistischen Internationale* (Hamburg: Verlag der Kommunistischen Internationale, 1921), 850–55.

3 Cecil Houston and William Smyth, *The Sash Canada Wore: A Historical Geography of the Orange Order in Canada* (Toronto: University of Toronto Press, 1980), 49; James Lemon, *Toronto Since 1918* (Toronto: Lorimer, 1985), 13–14, 49–51; see also Cyril Levitt and William Shaffir, *The Riot at Christie Pits* (Toronto: University of Toronto Press, 2018), 12–15 and Appendix B.

4 Provincial Archives of Alberta, Edmonton District Labour Council Fonds: PR1974.0057/0002. Edmonton Trades and Labour Council Minutes, 19 May 1919; *Edmonton Bulletin*, 22 May 1919.

5 *Western Labor News*, 3 May 1919; Korbla Puplampu, "Moral Panic and Governance in Public Policy: Canadian Immigration Policy, the City of Edmonton Resolution and Blacks, 1906–1911," *Social Identities* 27, no. 2 (2021): 166–83.

6 Joseph Knight had led the fight in 1914 to launch a national general strike in response to the First World War and was rebuffed. A. Ross McCormack, *Reformers, Rebels, and Revolutionaries: The Western Canadian Radical Movement, 1899–1919* (Toronto: University of Toronto, 1991), 119. Susnar was a longtime working-class organizer who had previously worked with the South Slavic Socialist Federation, an affiliate of

the Socialist Party of America. Before the General Strike Susnar spoke out against the police for "breaking into and searching . . . homes for banned literature" and their "illegal and unwarranted prosecution" of the heavily immigrant miners. In February of 1919 Susnar advocated for the general strike to push back against police aggression and the continuation of wartime emergency powers. *Edmonton Bulletin*, 22 February 1919.

7 Report of the Proceedings from the Western Canada Labor Conference, 13–15 March 1919, 9; McCormack, *Reformers, Rebels, and Revolutionaries*, 137–64.

8 Donald Avery, *"Dangerous Foreigners": European Immigrant Workers and Labour Radicalism in Canada, 1896–1932* (Toronto: McClelland and Stewart, 1979), 17–18.

9 See, for example, the Report of the Royal Northwest Mounted Police for the year ended September 30, 1919 (Ottawa: King's Printer, 1920); and Steve Hewitt, *Riding to the Rescue: The Transformation of the RCMP in Alberta and Saskatchewan, 1914–1939* (Toronto: University of Toronto Press, 2006), 45–131; Kassandra Luciuk, "Reinserting Radicalism: Canada's First National Internment Operations, the Ukrainian Left, and the Politics of Redress," in *Civilian Internment in Canada: Histories and Legacies*, ed. Rhonda Hinther and Jim Mochoruk (Winnipeg: University of Manitoba Press, 2020), Chapter 3.

10 *Edmonton Bulletin*, 24 May 1919.

11 Library and Archives Canada [hereafter LAC], R224-76-4-E (T-2699), 153. RNWMP Report to Commissioner of G Division by H. Davison, 23 May 1919. See also RCMP G Division records R196-124-3-E.

12 *The Alberta Non-Partisan*, 5 June 1919.

13 *Edmonton Journal*, 24 May 1919.

14 Avery, *"Dangerous Foreigners,"* 67; Howard Palmer, *Patterns of Prejudice: A History of Nativism in Alberta* (Toronto: McClelland and Stewart, 1982), 17–60.

15 LAC, R224-76-4-E (T-2699), 153. RNWMP Report to Commissioner of G Division by T.A. Wroughton, 22 May 1919, Edmonton.

16 Glenbow Archives, WCC Papers, f. 174, employee lists (typescript); "Bellevue Mine, Register of Employees," c. 1910–40 quoted in Allen Seager, "Proletariat in Wild Rose Country: The Alberta Coal Miners, 1905–1945" (PhD diss., York University, 1983), 143; Karen Buckley, "Death, Dying, and Mourning in the Crowsnest Pass: An Examination of Individual and Community Response to Death and Danger in the Mines, 1902–1928" (MA thesis, University of Calgary, 2002).

17 RNWMP Report to Commissioner of G Division, 29 May 1919, Edmonton.

18 RNWMP Report to Commissioner of G Division by T.A. Wroughton, 23 May 1919.

19 "City Council Sure Labor to be Trusted," *Edmonton Bulletin*, 24 May 1919.

20 Alvin Finkel, "The Rise and Fall of the Labour Party in Alberta, 1917–42," *Labour/Le Travail* 16 (Fall 1985): 61–96.

21 RNWMP Report to Commissioner of G Division by H. Davison, 23 May 1919.

22 RNWMP Report to Commissioner of G Division by T.A. Wroughton, 24 May 1919. The only exception was German workers, however, who apparently desired to "throw up everything and act like the Bolsheviki in Russia."

23 *Edmonton Bulletin*, 27 May 1919. Postal workers had just recently won a major national victory.

24 Carl Berg's papers are in LAC and contain his IWW card, so such criticisms were

hardly unfair. However, "the worst kind of agitator" was common, if thinly coded, language for foreign.

25 RNWMP G Division, Edmonton, Alberta, "Re: General Strike of the Trades and Labour Unions, Edmonton, May 26th." Supt. T.A. Wroughton to Commissioner, 31 May 1919.

26 Elmer Roper of the printing pressmen was an example of this sort of elite "labour man." At the time of the Strike he was a foreman at the *Edmonton Bulletin* and travelled to Winnipeg to tell his co-unionists there not to join the General Strike. He was also the one-time leader of the Calgary Labor Council, secretary-treasurer of the AFL from 1922 to 1932, and later mayor of Edmonton. J.A. MacGregor, *Edmonton: A History* (Edmonton: Hurtig, 1967), 307.

27 RNWMP: Report, Edmonton, 26 May 1919. Even the police voiced their support for the Strike: fifty-seven out of fifty-nine voted in favour of supporting it although they did not join in themselves. This vote is unsurprising as they were currently embroiled in a conflict over working conditions. Their actions, coupled with those of police in Winnipeg, greatly alarmed the government. Sessional Paper No. 37 (King's Printer: Ottawa, 1920), 13–19.

28 *Edmonton Bulletin*, 26 May 1919.

29 Previous work on the Edmonton General Strike includes Warren Caragata, *Alberta Labour: A Heritage Untold* (Toronto: Lorimer, 1979); Gerald Friesen, "'Yours in Revolt': The Socialist Party of Canada and the Western Canadian Labour Movement," *Labour/Le Travail* 1 (January 1976): 139–57; William Askin, "Labour Unrest in Edmonton and District and Its Coverage by the Edmonton Press, 1918–19" (MA thesis, University of Alberta, 1973); Mikhail Bjorge, "The Edmonton General Strike of 1919: Working-Class Rebellion and Historiographical Place" (BA [Hons.] thesis, University of Alberta, 2007); Alvin Finkel, "The Great War and Labour in Alberta," in *The Frontier of Patriotism: Alberta and the First World War*, ed. Adriana Davis and Jeff Keshen (Calgary: University of Calgary Press, 2015), 307–18; and Eugene Plawiuk, "The Edmonton General Strike of 1919," Libcom.org.

30 *Edmonton Journal*, 25 May 1919; *Edmonton Bulletin*, 26 May 1919. Strikers later "unanimously" passed resolutions proscribing alcohol and reminding Strikers that free booze was a "nefarious trick" by the capitalists to "prevent the progress of the cause of labor." *Edmonton Strike Bulletin*, 11 June 1919.

31 *Edmonton Bulletin*, 28 May 1919.

32 *Edmonton Bulletin*, 23 May 1919; *Edmonton Bulletin*, 27 May 1919.

33 *Edmonton Bulletin*, 2 June 1919.

34 *Edmonton Bulletin*, 28 May 1919.

35 *Edmonton Bulletin*, 28 May 1919.

36 *Edmonton Bulletin*, 31 May 1919. Of the 111 strikes reported launched in Alberta from 1914 to 1920 fully 80 were by miners. Caragata, *Alberta Labour*, 62.

37 RNWMP Report to Commissioner of G Division, 29 May 1919, Edmonton.

38 *Edmonton Bulletin*, 30 May 1919; *Edmonton Strike Bulletin*, 10 June 1919; *Edmonton Strike Bulletin*, 13 June 1919.

39 *Edmonton Strike Bulletin*, 4 June 1919; *Edmonton Strike Bulletin*, 5 June 1919.

40 Michael Kellogg, *The Russian Roots of Nazism: White Émigrés and the Making of National Socialism, 1917–1945* (Cambridge, UK: Cambridge University Press, 2005).

41 Avery, *Dangerous Foreigners*, 65–89.

42 *Edmonton Bulletin*, 30 May 1919; *Edmonton Bulletin*, 31 May 1919; *Edmonton Strike Bulletin*, 18 June 1919.

43 RNWMP Report, [Unsigned] Edmonton, Alberta, 28 May 1919; RNWMP Report to Commissioner of G Division, T.A. Wroughton, 4 June 1919, Edmonton; *Edmonton Strike Bulletin*, 10 June 1919; *Edmonton Journal*, 11 June 1919.

44 *Edmonton Strike Bulletin*, 10 June 1919.

45 *Edmonton Strike Bulletin*, 10 June 1919; *Edmonton Bulletin*, 11 June 1919; *Edmonton Strike Bulletin*, 12 June 1919; *Edmonton Strike Bulletin*, 16 June 1919.

46 *Edmonton Strike Bulletin*, 16 June 1919.

47 *Soviet*, 27 March 1919.

48 *Edmonton Bulletin*, 6 June 1919.

49 *Edmonton Strike Bulletin*, 18 June 1919.

50 *Edmonton Journal*, 9 June 1919; *Edmonton Strike Bulletin*, 20 June 1919.

51 *Edmonton Bulletin*, 31 May 1919.

52 RNWMP Report to Commissioner of G Division, T.A. Wroughton, 4 June 1919, Edmonton.

53 RNWMP Report to Commissioner of G Division, T.A. Wroughton, 4 June 1919, Edmonton.

54 *Edmonton Journal*, 9 June 1919; *Edmonton Strike Bulletin*, 20 June 1919.

55 *Edmonton Bulletin*, 13 June 1919.

56 *Edmonton Strike Bulletin*, 20 June 1919.

57 *Edmonton Strike Bulletin*, 13 June 1919.

58 *Edmonton Strike Bulletin*, 20 June 1919.

59 *Edmonton Strike Bulletin*, 20 June 1919.

60 *Edmonton Bulletin*, 19 June 1919.

61 The UFA was not a parochial entity; in the twenties it saw large support from the urban centres and outvoted an Edmontonian labour candidate in the 1921 elections.

62 Under the masthead "Organization, Education, Cooperation." *Grain Growers Guide*, 25 June 1919.

63 *Edmonton Journal*, 31 May 1919; *Edmonton Bulletin*, 6 June 1919; *Edmonton Bulletin*, 9 June 1919; *Edmonton Strike Bulletin*, 19 June 1919.

64 Heinrich Eyeben, *Cummings Public Speech*, 3 June 1919.

65 *Edmonton Free Press*, 31 May 1919.

66 *Edmonton Journal*, 30 May 1919; *Winnipeg Telegram*, 30 May 1919.

67 *New York Times*, 8 June 1919; *Edmonton Journal*, 9 June 1919.

68 RNWMP Report to Commissioner of G Division by H. Davison, 23 May 1919. Some of these workers would have been represented by Perkins, the expelled leader of the IAM.

69 *Edmonton Bulletin*, 14 June 1919.

70 *Edmonton Bulletin*, 6 June 1919.

71 *Edmonton Bulletin*, 18 June 1919.

72 *Edmonton Journal*, 17 June 1919.

73 *Edmonton Bulletin*, 20 June 1919.

74 *Edmonton Bulletin*, 21 June 1919.

75 *Edmonton Bulletin*, 28 June 1919; *Edmonton Bulletin*, 29 June 1919.

76 *Edmonton Bulletin*, 25 June 1919.

77 *Soviet*, 5 July 1919. In the same sweep the police ransacked the home of Charles Snell, the SPC leader in Red Deer and namesake of the city library's downstairs hall.

78 Privately, Joseph Knight later referred to the Edmonton General Strike as "a tragic farce," so one should temper any overbearing importance somewhat. Quoted in David Bercuson, *Fools and Wise Men* (Toronto: McGraw-Hill Ryerson, 1978), 132.

79 *Soviet*, 19 June 1919.

80 Ninth Annual Convention of the British Columbia Federation of Labor, Calgary, 10–13 March 1919, 32.

81 Desmond Morton, *Working People* (Montreal and Kingston: McGill-Queen's University Press, 1998), 124.

82 Anne Woywitka, "The 'Unholy Alliance' Against the OBU," in *The Canadian Worker in the Twentieth Century*, ed. Irving Abella and David Millar (Toronto: Oxford University Press, 1978), 218–25; Caragata, *Alberta Labour*, 77–81.

83 Allan Greer, "The Birth of the Police in Canada," in *Colonial Leviathan: State Formation in Mid-Nineteenth-Century Canada*, ed. Allan Greer and Ian Radforth (Toronto: University of Toronto Press, 1992), 17–49; Hewitt, *Riding to the Rescue.*

84 Dennis Pilon, "Explaining Voting System Reform in Canada, 1874 to 1960," *Journal of Canadian Studies* 40, no. 3 (Fall 2006): 135–61.

85 Harold Jansen, "The Single Transferable Vote in Alberta and Manitoba" (PhD diss., University of Alberta, 1998).

86 Report of the Proceedings from the Western Canada Labor Conference, 13–15 March 1919, 31.

87 *Soviet*, 19 June 1919.

6

The Winnipeg General Strike in the Crowsnest Pass

Tom Langford

The Crowsnest Pass is the southernmost pass through the Canadian Rocky Mountains. It is located 1,250 kilometres from Winnipeg, almost due west. Yet despite their geographical separation, Winnipeg and the Crowsnest Pass were intertwined with one another at the time of the 1919 Winnipeg General Strike. There are three main reasons for the bond. First, in early 1919 a secret report prepared for the Royal North-West Mounted Police (RNWMP) identified Winnipeg, Vancouver, and the Crowsnest Pass as the main locations of "Bolshevik" activity in western Canada. As a consequence, throughout 1919 the Canadian state treated working-class struggles in each of these locales as necessitating close surveillance and antidemocratic repression.[1] Second, a strike by 7,000 unionized coalminers in Alberta and southeastern British Columbia, almost half of whom worked in mines in the Crowsnest Pass, overlapped with all but the first nine days of the Winnipeg General Strike. There is ample evidence that the miners and their union leaders actively followed developments in Winnipeg in May and June of 1919. At the same time, how these two simultaneous mass strikes were coupled is still a matter of historiographic dispute given that the miners' strike was never straightforwardly portrayed as a sympathy strike with Winnipeg. And third, key leaders of the workers' movement in the

Crowsnest Pass, like key leaders of the Winnipeg General Strike, were enthusiastic backers of the movement to build one big union for all workers "irrespective of nationality, sex, or craft."[2]

The goal of this chapter is to reconsider the nature of the connections between Winnipeg and the Crowsnest Pass during the heady days of working-class struggle in 1919. While this period in the Pass's labour history has been well explored in classic studies by Allen Seager and David Bercuson, and a recent book by Wayne Norton, the linkages with the events in Winnipeg have not been adequately developed—linkages that help to make developments in the region explicable.[3] My main objectives are to divine how the events in Winnipeg figured in the consciousness and strategic thinking of rank-and-file coalminers in the Crowsnest Pass as well as their union leaders, and identify parallels between what transpired in each locale. I conclude with a brief overview of two important developments following the 1919 strike in the Pass: a concerted campaign to repress the One Big Union (OBU) and the election of labour representatives to the British Columbia and Alberta legislatures.

Connecting the Winnipeg General Strike to the Crowsnest Pass

The only unambiguous direct connection between the Winnipeg General Strike and the Crowsnest Pass was a sympathy strike by local power plant workers that plunged Fernie, the largest municipality in the Pass, into darkness for two nights starting on 28 May 1919. This strike involved three members of the International Union of Steam and Operating Engineers who were attached to this craft union's branch in Vancouver. These workers went on strike when instructed to do so by their Vancouver-based union leaders.[4] This directive was issued just as the Vancouver Trades and Labour Council was making final preparations for a general strike in sympathy with the strikers in Winnipeg—it began on 3 June and was joined by 11,000 Vancouver workers represented by forty-five unions.[5]

The total blackout of Fernie only lasted two days with electricity restored at 5 p.m. on 30 May. However, under a compromise negotiated by Thomas Uphill, Fernie's labour mayor, a sympathy strike by the stationary engineers occurred between 7:00 a.m. and 5:00 p.m. every day between 31 May and 23 June, during which time Fernie residents and businesses had a ten-hour daily reminder of the ongoing struggle in Winnipeg.[6] This sympathy protest is of particular note because it involved so few workers and yet was highly unsettling to everyday life in Fernie.

The 28 May sympathy strike by stationary engineers in Fernie began just four days after 7,000 coalminers in District 18 of the United Mine Workers of America (UMWA) had gone on strike. This included approximately 3,000 miners working at mines stretching from Hillcrest, Alberta, to Coal Creek, British Columbia, in the Crowsnest Pass. The timing of the District 18 strike—nine days after the beginning of the Winnipeg General Strike and a mere two days before the initiation of sympathy strikes in Calgary and Edmonton—demonstrates that events in Winnipeg influenced the initiation of a walkout across District 18. So does the fact that the strike by coalminers was not the logical culmination of a drawn-out, failed attempt to negotiate a new collective agreement. Indeed, at the request of District 18 in late February of 1919, the existing collective agreement had been extended by the government-appointed wartime director of coal operations for western Canada beyond its ordinary expiration on 1 April "until the declaration of peace."[7] Consequently the walkout by the 7,000 coalminers that started on 24 May was organized "on the fly" by the District 18 leadership. It had been pitched to the membership as being necessary to reverse a ruling of coal director W.H. Armstrong that reduced the daily wages of a small number of the surface workers at the three mines in the British Columbia section of the Crowsnest Pass (but not anyone in the underground workforce). Therefore, workers at the thirty-eight UMWA locals in Alberta (including the five locals in the Alberta section of the Pass) were asked to go on strike against a ruling that not only did not apply to their mines but affected only a tiny minority of the memberships of the three UMWA locals in southeastern British Columbia.[8]

Marshalling 7,000 workers out on strike over a relatively small pay reduction affecting as few as twenty-five workers is puzzling and indicates that there was more to this strike than meets the eye. On this exact point Allen Seager has commented, "This protest is not easily explained; the official pretext was weak indeed."[9] Even the membership of the Fernie local of the UMWA, which included in its ranks a few members who would experience a pay reduction as a result of coal director Armstrong's ruling, questioned the logic of strike action on this issue—the union local initially refused to vote on whether to go on strike when so requested by the District 18 leadership. In response, the president of District 18, Phillip Christophers, journeyed to Fernie for a special meeting to try to convince the miners at the Coal Creek mine to get on board with the strike. "According to street talk after the meeting," Christophers "had assured the men that 'a strike would bring the Company to its knees in a few days.'" Even with this brazen (and ultimately inaccurate) promise, the District 18 president only managed to get two-thirds of the 572 voters from the Fernie local to approve strike action.[10]

Phillip Christophers's intervention in Fernie indicated he was strongly committed to orchestrating a district-wide walkout. Allen Seager has suggested that he arrived at this position after travelling to Ottawa in late March of 1919 to meet with Prime Minister Borden and other federal government officials. When these meetings did not yield any benefits for miners, "apparently, Christophers resolved that what the government needed was a good dose of industrial war—at the very least."[11] That President Christophers's commitment to orchestrating "a good dose of industrial war" preceded the Winnipeg General Strike is confirmed by how he responded to a pithead strike at the Blue Diamond mine in Brule. It began on 1 May. Around 10 May (five days before the commencement of the Winnipeg General Strike), the office of coal director Armstrong as well as two senior District 18 officials worked out a plan for addressing the miners' grievance that included a return to work. However, when the union officials telephoned Christophers in the Crowsnest Pass to explain what had transpired and to request that he instruct Brule miners to end their strike, he refused, saying, "Let them stay out."[12]

The last steps in organizing the district-wide walkout of coalminers occurred against the backdrop of the first days of the Winnipeg General Strike. From its base in Fernie, District 18's weekly newspaper reported sympathetically on the Winnipeg Strike and the subsequent organization of solidarity strikes across Western Canada.[13] The keen interest among Fernie miners in what was happening in Winnipeg is shown by the Fernie local's decision to post its own "News Bulletin" on the Winnipeg strike.[14] Furthermore, evidence of the strong support for the cause of the Winnipeg strikers among coalminers in the Crowsnest Pass was revealed by a decision taken at a mass membership meeting of the UMWA's Bellevue, Alberta, local on 23 June 1919 in response to the arrests of Winnipeg Strike leaders on 17 June.[15] The perspective of the membership was recorded in a letter to the *District Ledger* from the union local's secretary, John Brooks:

> We wish, through the medium of your paper, to convey by the most effective means (Labor Press) to the workers of Winnipeg our admiration for the splendid fight they are making on Labor's behalf throughout the Dominion of Canada.
>
> ...Also through the Labor Press we call on our fellow workers to protest in the most effective manner (by laying down tools) until a constitutional trial is granted our Comrades now languishing in jail for daring to raise their voices, and direct the course of labor along any path that leads to a greater portion of the wealth we produce.[16]

In passing this resolution, the Bellevue miners intimated that if they had not already been on strike they would have gone on strike to push for justice for the arrested Winnipeg strike leaders. Hence it is conceivable that, had the District 18 leadership not found a homegrown issue on which to launch a district-wide strike in late May, many union locals across District 18 would have launched sympathy strikes with Winnipeg at different points in May and June. Phillip Christophers and associates might well have reasoned that an uncoordinated series of sympathy strikes would have created more difficulties for District 18 than a unified job action. Furthermore, the fact that the Winnipeg General Strike had already begun on 15 May undoubtedly made it easier for coalminers to accept the necessity of going on strike on 24 May despite District 18's weak rationale for a mass job action. In addition, the fact that the Winnipeg strike remained strong well into June undeniably made it easier for coalminers to rationalize carrying on with their own strike even though the promise of a rapid capitulation by coal director Armstrong and the coal operators proved to be false, and coalmining families were struggling to find ways to make ends meet in the absence of any strike pay.

My conclusion is that the Winnipeg General Strike played a crucial role in powering the collective struggle of coalminers in the Crowsnest Pass (and elsewhere in District 18). After the Winnipeg General Strike was initiated on 15 May, and soon thereafter was recognized as a working-class struggle of historic importance, it figured prominently in the calculations of both the coalminers and their union leaders. Therefore, while it is true that the strike by miners was never portrayed as a sympathy action with the Winnipeg strikers, the events in Winnipeg were the essential backdrop to understanding how a coalminers' strike on a flimsy pretext demonstrated such broad support and staying power.

The strike by coalminers in Alberta and southeastern British Columbia was a parallel front in the Workers' Revolt of 1919. Phillip Christophers saw it as the dose of "industrial war" that would bring the federal government and the coal companies to their senses prior to the imminent contract negotiations. Furthermore, many miners would have seen the strike as an effective way to build momentum toward the OBU's establishment. Without the Winnipeg General Strike already being in motion, however, it is hard to imagine that the strike by coalminers would have lasted very long, assuming it had even managed to get off the ground. Across those 1,250 kilometres, the spirit of the Winnipeg General Strike breathed life into the strike by three thousand coalminers in the Crowsnest Pass.

In looking back at the factors driving coalminers in the Crowsnest Pass toward going on strike in May 1919, it is difficult to analytically separate the spirit of the Winnipeg General Strike from enthusiasm for the OBU. More than thirty coal-community delegates (out of a total of 237 delegates) had participated in the Western Labour Conference in Calgary in March of that year. Ross McCormack asserts that militant industrial unionism triumphed at the Calgary conference. The delegates strongly supported a resolution calling for a referendum on the proposition that unions in western Canada leave their international unions and form "an industrial organization of all workers." They also unanimously endorsed a resolution "urging the workers to abandon the practice of 'lobbying parliament for palliatives which do not palliate' and to enforce their demands 'by virtue of their industrial strength.'"[17]

The debate about whether to jettison the UMWA for the OBU was waged vigorously throughout District 18 during April and the first part of May in 1919. At the outset of the debate, Phillip Christophers himself criticized the lack of details about the OBU's organizational structure.[18] Despite this initial dose of hesitation, however, Christophers soon warmed toward the OBU, influenced by the unambiguous enthusiasm of coalminers for this alternative conception of unionism. That enthusiasm was demonstrated in "two rousing meetings" held on back-to-back nights in early April at Fernie's Grand Theatre. Both meetings discussed the advisability of severing connection to the UMWA in favour of helping to found the OBU, with Christophers himself being a featured speaker at the second meeting. It is noteworthy that, according to the *District Ledger*, "ninety per cent of those in the crowded theatre were hearts and souls with the ONE BIG UNION." Given the dearth of details about the One Big Union at that point, this enthusiasm reflected the fact that the miners were, as Drumheller mine owner Jesse Gouge put it later in 1919, "in revolt against their organization [the UMWA] . . . on the plea that it supports the present system." The UMWA's stock among western Canadian coalminers had fallen precipitously during the First World War because of its failure to back workers' strikes in 1916, 1917, and 1918. Indeed, the reputation of the U.S.-based leadership of the UMWA was so bad that the editor of the *District Ledger*, Peter Lawson, referred to them in print as "the corrupt Indianapolis outfit," and the District 18 convention of February 1919 voted in favour of a motion put forward by the Blairmore, Alberta, local to stop the distribution throughout District 18 of the U.S.-produced *United Mine Workers Journal*. When the votes on coalminers' organizational preference were tallied across the Crowsnest Pass in the middle of May, the result was an astonishing 2,276 in favour and only 70 opposed to severing ties with the UMWA and "becom[ing] part of the One Big Industrial Organization of all workers."[19]

Given that the district-wide strike began just days after the conclusion of the strong vote in favour of joining the OBU, it is reasonable to consider whether the strike had been called to somehow facilitate the transition from UMWA to OBU in District 18. David Bercuson has answered this question in the affirmative, making the following claim: "But in fact, the leaders of District 18 . . . supported the OBU and were about to lead a break-away of the district into OBU ranks. [By organizing the strike] they were trying to manoeuvre the operators into concluding an agreement directly with them, completely bypassing UMWA headquarters in the United States."[20]

This claim is implausible for two reasons. First, there was no attempt by Christophers and associates to initiate talks for a new collective agreement during the early weeks of the strike. Rather the strike and the planned transition from UMWA to OBU were treated as separate organizational processes even as the strike was portrayed as following the logic of the OBU principle, "an injury to one is the concern to all." Second, if Christophers's team had initiated new contract talks early on in the strike, they would have had to do so as the UMWA's District 18 rather than as the OBU because it took time to bring the OBU into existence (which included holding a founding convention in early June followed by votes in subsequent weeks by union locals on the proposed OBU constitution). In this counterfactual scenario, concluding a new collective agreement on behalf of District 18 might well have worked against the establishment of the OBU as the union representing coalminers.

The preceding arguments lead to the conclusion that the timing of the beginning of the district-wide strike of coalminers in Western Canada was driven more by the events in Winnipeg rather than the campaign to shift affiliation from UMWA to OBU. Nevertheless, enthusiasm for the OBU and faith in the industrial strike as the best way to advance the workers' cause were supplementary reasons for why both union leaders and rank-and-file miners threw caution to the wind and went all-in on the district-wide strike. That enthusiasm was contagious at the strike's outset, as demonstrated by salaried firebosses (or safety officials) throughout the Crowsnest Pass refusing to do the work of the striking miners, instead going on strike themselves and coordinating their stance through a Firebosses Association. In recognition of the solidarity demonstrated by many firebosses at coal mines throughout Alberta and southeastern British Columbia, the District 18 board pledged on 3 June "unwavering support to the firebosses who have gone out on strike," declaring "that the firebosses will be backed to the limit and that no workers in District 18 will return to work until the firebosses are re-instated."[21]

The swagger behind the pledge to back the firebosses "to the limit" belied the fact that the District 18 leadership had already come to the realization that the miners' strike was at an impasse—neither coal director Armstrong nor the coal companies had made a move to settle the dispute. The union's first attempt to break the impasse involved a two-pronged strategy. On 6 June, a long article appeared in District 18's weekly newspaper that not only blamed Crow's Nest Pass Coal Company (CNPCC) and its general manager, W.R. Wilson, for the ongoing strike but claimed that the company (termed "an alien corporation" because it was controlled by the Great Northern Railway of the United States) was planning to close its Coal Creek operations, thereby imperilling Fernie's future. Under an ominous title in one-inch, bolded and capped letters (**"IS IT FERNIE'S FINISH?"**), the article called upon other coal operators in western Canada to put pressure on CNPCC to unilaterally restore the weekly pay of the handful of surface workers in British Columbia who had experienced a pay cut as a result of the coal director's recent ruling. It also called upon "every business man and every property owner" in Fernie to take steps to protect their investments by demanding that the provincial government appoint a commission to investigate what CNPCC was up to. The complementary second prong of the strategy involved telegrams sent from Christophers and District 18 secretary-treasurer Ed Browne to British Columbia premier John Oliver on 5 and 9 June asking for a provincial investigation because "there is every reason to believe that the present shut down of the coal miners [*sic*] in South Eastern British Columbia is part of a scheme of the Crow's Nest Pass Coal Co. to secure a pretext for the abandonment of the Coal Creek mines." The premier also received a telegram from Samuel Whitehouse, president of the Fernie local of the UMWA, which expressed concern about the "loss of hundreds of homes and business[es]" if CNPCC were to close its Coal Creek operations.[22]

District 18's new strategy tried to mobilize unlikely allies—coal operators, Fernie's small business class, and the provincial government—to help break the impasse in the strike. If Premier Oliver had been sympathetic to the union's quandary, perhaps he would have commissioned some sort of provincial investigation that would have allowed the District 18 leadership to end the strike while claiming a victory of sorts. The premier, however, was inclined to be sympathetic with CNPCC rather than District 18 and took his cues from W.R. Wilson. After Wilson assured the premier that CNPCC had no plans to close its Coal Creek operation (and indeed would keep mining coal there until 1958), there was no possibility of a face-saving provincial investigation coming to the union's rescue. Furthermore, the implausible attempt to shift the blame for the work stoppage to CNPCC had the unintended consequence of hardening W.R. Wilson's negative views of the current leadership of District 18. Wilson had already been perturbed that on 25 May the UMWA local at Fernie had ordered out on strike those "[union] men who ordinarily under the present agreement and under all past agreements would have remained at work for the protection and preservation of the mines." By 12 June he was of the opinion that Christophers, "rather than admit that his determination to bring out the men was an ill-considered one ... would like to prolong the controversy by any methods that occur, or may be suggested, to him" and "that it is not the desire of the present executive of District 18 to see these mines work steadily." Furthermore, CNPCC's Wilson informed Premier Oliver "that the action of Mr. Christophers and his executive associates is, in my opinion, more due to the desire on his part to advance the aims and objects of the One Big Union than to any grievance on the part of the men."[23]

While the attempt to secure a provincial investigation fizzled, the strike by firebosses started to collapse. At a "stormy" meeting of the Firebosses Association at Blairmore on 9 June, "quite a number" of the striking firebosses in attendance took "the position that they should be at work," and the president of the association resigned. Three days later, some of the firebosses at Coal Creek returned to work. Furthermore, there was "restlessness" among the rank-and-file coalminers and "the evident desire on the part of a great many of them to return to work."[24] It was starting to look as if the spirit of the Winnipeg General Strike and enthusiasm for the One Big Union would not be enough to win this labour confrontation.

Nevertheless, in the middle of June there was still an opportunity for the District 18 leadership to unilaterally call off the strike and promise to revisit the issue of pay for surface workers in the British Columbia mines in upcoming contract negotiations. At that point, the federal government was preoccupied with events in Winnipeg and the International UMWA leadership was still on the sidelines. Christophers and Browne had an opportunity to act before their opponents could fashion a coordinated anti-OBU strategy. Furthermore, by offering to end the miners' strike within twenty-four hours of the promise of some sort of government investigation, they had already come to terms with delinking their struggle from what was happening in Winnipeg.[25] Yet the District 18 executive failed to realize how quickly the opportunity for a strategic retreat would close, holding out hope for far too many days that a face-saving government investigation would be ordered.

The Winnipeg General Strike ended on 26 June. The next day the leaders of District 18 initiated a second strategy to try and break the impasse—they proposed entering into negotiations for a contract "under which the membership of this district might resume work." What they didn't know, however, was that coal director Armstrong had already exchanged telegrams with John L. Lewis, the acting UMWA international president, who indicated that the District 18 leaders had proceeded with the current strike without consulting the International Office.[26] Shortly after receiving this information, W.R. Wilson concluded, "Th[e District 18 officers] are not receiving the support of the International Union ... and it seems to me that it would be unwise for the Operators to even attempt to make an agreement with men who have so deliberately defied the Government and so unnecessarily overridden all honorable precedents of Union organization that have commanded the respect of invested rights for the last thirty years." Armstrong, the coal director, was of the same opinion. In the first week of July, while Christophers and Browne were still getting the runaround on their proposal for negotiations, a plan was concocted to try to force the OBU and its leaders out of the western Canadian coal industry. The parties to the scheme were the commissioner of the WCOA, a representative from the coal director's office, and Dave Irwin, UMWA international organizer. The plan involved the International Union taking charge of District 18, replacing all of the current officers, and determining whether a critical mass of miners would be willing to go back to work under the terms of the old contract. In the meantime, the coal operators committed to maintaining a lockout until the International had cleaned house and let them know that miners were ready to resume employment.[27]

It did not take the Christophers/Browne group of District 18 leaders long to figure out what was happening. By the second week of July they had recognized that the original economic issue in dispute (whether some surface workers should experience a pay cut) had been superseded by a political issue, succinctly identified in the 11 July edition of the *District Ledger*: "The chief concern of the Director of Coal Operations and of the Western Coal Operators Association is regarding the organization with whom the agreement is to be made, the UMWA or the One Big Union. The government and the operators are determined that the One Big Union will not be recognized." Furthermore, the pro-OBU leaders had come to an understanding of what they were up against, as expressed by a member of the Fernie local at a union meeting in early July: "The triple alliance of the governments, the operators and the international labor organizations is a heavy force to buck."[28]

Backed into a corner, on 14 July District 18's policy committee offered to end the strike and accept coal director Armstrong's ruling on the pay of surface workers in British Columbia, as long as none of the strikers would face discriminatory treatment during the return to work. This offer was rejected by Armstrong on the grounds he would only deal with union officials vouched for by the International UMWA. The miners now had incontrovertible evidence that the strike had become a lockout, and their elected, pro-OBU union officials would soon be purged.[29]

Through this difficult stretch in the miners' strike, the situation in Winnipeg was not forgotten. The 11 July edition of the *District Ledger* ran a front-page appeal for donations to the Defence Committee set up to pay for the Winnipeg Strike leaders' legal defence against the charge of seditious conspiracy. Under the headline "Help!" the appeal listed some of the mining unions across Canada that had already contributed to the Defence Committee but noted, "District 18 is not in a position to donate." Therefore, the appeal was for coalminers to follow the lead of "several individuals who have already pulled their belts up a notch tighter and sent a few dollars." At this point, the main influence of the concluded Winnipeg General Strike on the ongoing struggle in the Crowsnest Pass was as a forewarning of the repressive intent of the triple alliance of strike opponents.

In the Crowsnest Pass, the wave of repression began on 27 July 1919 when John L. Lewis revoked the charter of District 18, thereby forcing Phillip Christophers, Ed Browne, and their allies to reorganize themselves as District 1, Mining Department, One Big Union, provisionally constituted at the end of July. In doing so they remained defiant, immediately informing coal director Armstrong that the OBU was willing to negotiate a settlement to the ongoing labour dispute in the coalfields (even though they knew that Armstrong had already proclaimed he would have nothing to do with them). Furthermore, on 2 August the new OBU district "sent letters to mine owners in the Drumheller Valley seeking meetings 'to make the necessary arrangements for a resumption of work.'"[30] The main strength of District 1, Mining Department, OBU was the allegiance of the overwhelming majority of coalminers in Alberta and southeastern British Columbia. Many of the UMWA union locals immediately declared "their fidelity to the OBU," and the new district's membership stood at over 7,000 within days of its inception.[31] However, in the face of the machinations of the triple alliance of opponents over the next fifteen months, this would not prove to be enough to save the OBU in the coalfields.

Parallels Between the Two Struggles

Clearly, the Winnipeg General Strike had loomed very large in the consciousness of coalminers and their union leaders in the Crowsnest Pass, both as a struggle to cheer for and support, and as containing important lessons about the strength of the opposition to militant industrial unionism in Canadian society in 1919. It is also important to recognize that there were parallels between the labour struggles in the two locales that constitute another layer of connection between Winnipeg and the Pass in 1919.

First, in both struggles the federal government decided that the OBU and its challenge to established authority was the underlying issue. As a consequence, the government prolonged the strikes by blocking the negotiation processes that could have led to orderly and timely settlements. In Winnipeg on 25 May, labour minister Gideon Robertson refused to support the principle of collective bargaining on the grounds that it would be interpreted as a sign of the potency of the sympathetic strike. Similarly on 9 June, justice minister Arthur Meighen vetoed the terms of a settlement proposed by metal employers on the basis that it "would be a triumph for the strike leaders."[32] Meanwhile, in the Crowsnest Pass, the federal government—through the office of the coal director, Armstrong—stonewalled attempts by the OBU leaders in District 18 to negotiate the coalminers' return to work in the days immediately after the conclusion of the Winnipeg General Strike on 26 June, turning the strike into a lockout. Only after the International UMWA had removed the OBU leaders from their elected leadership roles would Armstrong approve a return to work facilitated by the UMWA.[33]

Second, both struggles unintentionally undermined efforts to build the OBU. On this point, D.C. Masters has argued: "Before the O.B.U. was well started, the movement was jeopardized by the Winnipeg strike, which diverted the attention of many radical leaders, eventually landing some of them in jail, and which largely discredited the general policy they advocated."[34] The process worked somewhat differently in the Crowsnest Pass and throughout District 18 where support for the OBU was almost unanimous prior to the strike that began on 24 May: the strike interrupted the sequence of events that was required to democratically shift coalminers' organizational affiliation from the UMWA to the OBU, and left OBU sympathizers vulnerable to counterattacks by the triple alliance. If the transition to the OBU had been orchestrated while the mines were working and labour relations were stable, the coal operators and federal government might have stayed on the sidelines and let the OBU versus UMWA conflict play out as merely another internal union dispute. In this scenario, the OBU would have had a better chance to prevail.

Third, in the latter part of 1918 and the early part of 1919, some war veterans in both Winnipeg and the Crowsnest Pass campaigned against "alien enemies." In January 1919 in Winnipeg, bands of returned soldiers threatened and harassed suspected "aliens" on the streets; vandalized the Socialist Party of Canada hall and the shop of prominent socialist leader Sam Blumenberg; and demonstrated in front of the Swift meat-packing plant, demanding that "alien" workers be fired.[35] In the same month, the Fernie branch of the Great War Veterans' Association (GWVA) lobbied CNPCC to support the deportation of all "enemy aliens." The following month the same organization demanded that the Fernie city council support a resolution circulated by the Vancouver city council calling for "the deportation of all undesirable aliens, regardless of whether they had been interned during the war." Mayor Thomas Uphill skillfully sidelined this reactionary demand by convincing his council to support the idea that "only those who 'by action or speech had proven themselves undesirable' should be deported."[36]

By the start of the strike by coalminers on 24 May, however, attacks on the rights of those with German or Austro-Hungarian ancestry had largely petered out in the Crowsnest Pass. One reason for this change was that many returned soldiers had been hired by the coal companies in the Pass, partly because many miners had voluntarily quit their jobs in order to return to their European home countries now that transoceanic transportation routes were reopened.[37] In addition, labour activists promoting the OBU successfully countered attacks on "alien enemies" with arguments such as, "Since the interests of all members of the working class were identical, there could be no 'alien' but the capitalist." Finally, the soaring popularity of the OBU in the Pass might well have caused those with entrenched xenophobic worldviews to keep their mouths shut rather than risk the opprobrium of their fellow workers. It is particularly noteworthy that, when the editor of the *Fernie Free Press* publicly urged members of the GWVA to use force to break the strike by stationary engineers at the city's power plant, there were no takers. The wave of chauvinistic sentiment in this coalfield society had subsided.[38]

In Winnipeg there was also a noticeable decline in reactionary activism by returned soldiers. For instance, at a mass meeting of the GWVA held on 3 June, two-thirds of a crowd of 2,000 voted to back the strike. Nevertheless, a relatively large number of returned soldiers in Winnipeg continued to see "alien enemy" workers as unwelcome outsiders and were available and willing to scab during the strike (including signing on as special constables after Winnipeg's regular police force was recklessly locked out). Hence the situation in Winnipeg was considerably more volatile than in the Crowsnest Pass.[39]

The fourth parallel also involves xenophobia. "Foreign" agitators were frequently blamed for the militant labour activism in each locale. The *Fernie Free Press* (a conservative newspaper) dismissed this claim in the fall of 1918. "The alien enemies who are employed here are almost as tame as any old cow," stated the editor, who pointed to "six old country Englishmen" as "the real trouble-makers." Along the length of the Crowsnest Pass, none of the secretaries for the eight UMWA locals had a name which was not obviously Anglo-Saxon or Irish. And of the thirteen names associated with the District 18 office in June 1919, only one was not obviously Anglo-Saxon or Irish. Therefore, while the District 18 delegation at the Western Labour Conference in March 1919 had been quite diverse (with seven out of about thirty delegates having names that were not obviously Anglo-Saxon or Irish) compared to other delegations, there was next to no ethno-cultural diversity at the senior levels of leadership in District 18. Along the same line, D.C. Masters noted that, with the exception of Canadian-born George Armstrong, the labour leaders in Winnipeg in 1919 had been "born and educated in the British Isles." Furthermore, the delegation from Winnipeg at the Western Labour Conference, representing twenty-six different unions, was solidly Anglo-Saxon. Hence "foreign agitation" was a theory of labour unrest without demonstrable support in either locale. In 1919, immigrant miners from different points in continental Europe were solid trade unionists, but few as yet had attained senior leadership responsibilities in the labour movement.[40]

The fifth parallel concerns the successes of the labour movements in both Winnipeg and the Crowsnest Pass leading up to the coterminous strikes in 1919. In Winnipeg in 1918, three major strikes had been victorious, including a strike by civic employees that had been resolved by the "conciliatory and decisive" intervention of labour minister Gideon Robertson, who had supported the right of public utilities workers to strike. In the Crowsnest Pass, labour's victories were real although more modest: miners' purchasing power was protected by quarterly cost-of-living increases authorized by the coal director, and a wildcat strike over the buildup of methane and other gasses in one of the mines at Coal Creek convinced coal director Armstrong to order a sixty-day trial of whether working a single shift (rather than back-to-back shifts) at that mine would help to dissipate the gasses. Furthermore, the sense of accomplishment stemming from labour victories in local struggles was amplified by the victories of postal workers and railway freight handlers in regional disputes in 1918, plus the success of the Western Labour Conference in March 1919.[41]

These victories may have created a counterproductive level of overconfidence. Reinhold Kramer and Tom Mitchell note that, at the beginning of the Winnipeg General Strike, "workers . . . expect[ed] overwhelmed employers to cave in within two or three days." Quoting a labour man, D.C. Masters argued that a consequence of victory in the civic workers' strike in Winnipeg of 1918 was that Winnipeg labour leaders came to believe "that if they said 'Boo' the boss would run." A similar outlook had developed in District 18 given President Christophers's claim in May 1919 (see above) that a strike at that juncture would "bring the Company to its knees in a few days."[42]

Conclusion

As in Winnipeg, the aftermath of the 1919 strike in the Crowsnest Pass was a mix of repression and renewed labour resistance. Between the summer of 1919 and the fall of 1920, the triple alliance used a carrot-and-stick approach to get miners to abandon the OBU and grudgingly accept the UMWA. OBU leaders and "agitators" were fired and blacklisted. Furthermore, coal director Armstrong, following the directive of labour minister Gideon Robertson, in early 1920 ordered West Canadian Collieries to lock out its Bellevue labour force in order to force the workers to accept membership in the UMWA and the dues checkoff as a condition of employment. In short order, all of the workers at mines on the Alberta side of the Pass were either on a sympathy strike or locked out. Within a few weeks, however, they had all chosen to return to work on the triple alliance's terms rather than commit their families to a stretch of hardship that would rival that endured during the May through August strike/lockout in 1919. The "carrots" brokered by the federal government were substantial wage increases in both 1919 and 1920 in order to make UMWA membership economically rewarding. In a last-ditch effort to remain relevant, the OBU leaders called a strike in October 1920 against compulsory UMWA membership and dues checkoff; it was quickly abandoned because of patchy initial support and an injunction that spurred many strikers to return to work. Although pockets of organized support for the OBU persisted in the Crowsnest Pass up until 1922, this militant industrial union would never again become a rallying point for miners' struggles in the western Canadian coal industry.[43]

Nevertheless, as noted by Allen Seager, "Destruction of the O.B.U.... had not dampened the radical zeal of many of its members, exactly the opposite in many cases." That zeal was demonstrated in the provincial elections that immediately followed the defeat of the OBU. Thomas Uphill, one-time secretary of the Fernie local of the UMWA and Fernie's mayor in 1919, was elected to the British Columbia legislature as the representative for Fernie district in December 1920; he ran on behalf of the Federated Labour Party. Meanwhile Phillip Christophers, who more than anyone else had come to epitomize the OBU movement in the Pass, was elected to the Alberta legislature as the representative for the constituency of Rocky Mountain (which included the coalmining areas of Canmore and the Crowsnest Pass) in July 1921; he ran on behalf of the Rocky Mountain Labour Party.[44]

Notes

1 David Bercuson, *Fools and Wise Men: The Rise and Fall of the One Big Union* (Toronto: McGraw-Hill Ryerson, 1978), 92–93; J.M. Bumsted, *The Winnipeg General Strike of 1919: An Illustrated History* (Winnipeg: Watson and Dwyer, 1994), 25. The RNWMP established a new detachment in Fernie, BC, at the western edge of the Crowsnest Pass in April 1919, with two officers stationed in the hamlet next to the nearby Coal Creek mine—see Wayne Norton, *Fernie at War: 1914–1919* (Halfmoon Bay, BC: Caitlin Press, 2017), 167–68. It almost goes without saying that the RNWMP's secret report was incorrect and no evidence of preparations to mount a Bolshevik-style armed insurrection was ever uncovered (Bercuson, *Fools and Wise Men*, 103).

2 "The Constitution of the One Big Union," *District Ledger*, 20 June 1919.

3 Charles Allen Seager, "A Proletariat in Wild Rose Country: The Alberta Coal Miners, 1905–1945" (PhD diss., York University, 1982); Bercuson, *Fools and Wise Men*; Norton, *Fernie at War*.

4 Norton, *Fernie at War*, 174–76. Background information on the coal-fired power plant at Fernie and the union representing the three stationary engineers is found in *Fernie Free Press*, 28 March and 26 December 1919.

5 Bercuson, *Fools and Wise Men*, 130–31. Allen Seager and David Roth, "British Columbia and the Mining West: A Ghost of a Chance," in *The Workers' Revolt in Canada, 1917–1925*, ed. Craig Heron (Toronto: University of Toronto Press, 1998), 254–58.

6 Norton, *Fernie at War*, 174–76.

7 Bercuson, *Fools and Wise Men*, 131–33, 137; David Bright, *The Limits of Labour: Class Formation and the Labour Movement in Calgary, 1883–1929* (Vancouver: UBC Press, 1998), 155–56; Letter from W.R. Wilson (the general manager of Crow's Nest Pass Coal Company [CNPCC], operator of coal mines at Coal Creek and Michel, BC) to British Columbia premier John Oliver, 12 June 1919 (Glenbow Archives [GA], located at the Glenbow Western Research Centre, University of Calgary, F0617 [Crowsnest Resources Ltd. fonds], file 183). In 1919, W.R. Wilson was also the president of the Western Coal Operators Union (WCOA), which, he informed the premier, "comprises over twenty-five mines." Peace negotiations had commenced in Versailles in mid-January 1919 and the formal treaty ending the war with Germany would not be signed until the end of June.

8 The forty-one union locals in District 18 were listed in *District Ledger*, 13 June 1919; *District Ledger*, 23 May 1919; Wilson letter to Oliver, 12 June 1919.

9 Seager, "Proletariat in Wild Rose Country," 336. The estimate of twenty-five affected workers was made by W.R. Wilson (Norton, *Fernie at War*, 172n266).

10 Wilson letter to Oliver, 12 June 1919; Norton, *Fernie at War*, 172n265.

11 Seager, "Proletariat in Wild Rose Country," 331.

12 Seager, "Proletariat in Wild Rose Country," 330, 336; David Jay Bercuson, ed., *Alberta's Coal Industry, 1919* (Calgary: Historical Society of Alberta, 1978), 142.

13 Examples are found in front-page stories on the Winnipeg strike in the *District Ledger* issues of 23 May and 6 June 1919.

14 Gladstone Local Union News Bulletin, undated (GA, F0617, file 183).

15 Bumsted, *Winnipeg General Strike of 1919*, 54–55; Reinhold Kramer and Tom Mitchell, *When the State Trembled: How A.J. Andrews and the Citizens' Committee*

Broke the Winnipeg General Strike (Toronto: University of Toronto Press, 2010), 163–65.

16 *District Ledger*, 27 June 1919.

17 Seager, "Proletariat in Wild Rose Country," 326. A. Ross McCormack, *Reformers, Rebels, and Revolutionaries: The Western Canadian Radical Movement, 1899–1919* (Toronto: University of Toronto Press, 1977), 158.

18 *District Ledger*, 4 April 1919; Seager, "Proletariat in Wild Rose Country," 330–31. Seager portrays Phillip Christophers as a moderate voice in the District 18 leadership whose eventual decision to wholeheartedly support the OBU cause helped to legitimize it. In 1919 Christophers, who would turn forty-eight that year, already had a long history of union activism in the Crowsnest Pass. Indeed, prior to the UMWA moving into the Pass in 1903, he had been the president of the Western Federation of Miners local union during a strike that year at CNPCC's Morrissey, BC, coal mine (*District Ledger*, 20 June 1919).

19 *District Ledger*, 4 April 1919; Seager, "Proletariat in Wild Rose Country," 320, 335, 337; Norton, *Fernie at War*, 162, 170. Bercuson, *Fools and Wise Men*, 79.

20 Bercuson, *Alberta's Coal Industry, 1919*, xiii.

21 *District Ledger*, 6 June 1919. Norton, *Fernie at War*, 173.

22 *District Ledger*, 6 June 1919. Oliver telegram to Wilson, 12 June 1919, reported on two telegrams he had received from Christophers and Browne; Whitehouse telegram to Oliver, 5 June 1919 (GA, F0617, file 183).

23 Oliver telegram to Wilson, 5 June 1919 (GA, F0617, file 183); Wilson letter to Oliver, 12 June 1919.

24 W.F. McNeill, WCOA commissioner, letter to Wilson, 10 June 1919; Wilson letter to McNeill, 13 June 1919 (GA, F0617, file 183); Wilson letter to Oliver, 12 June 1919.

25 *District Ledger*, 20 June 1919.

26 The telegrams involving John L. Lewis are attached to a letter from McNeill to Wilson, 8 July 1919 (GA, F0617, file 183). A report on the communications between District 18 and the coal director's office, 27 June–17 July 1919, is found in *District Ledger*, 25 July 1919. The request for a new agreement was publicly reported in *District Ledger*, 6 July 1919.

27 Wilson letter to S.G. Blaylock, Consolidated Mining & Smelting Company, 2 July 1919; McNeill letters to Wilson, 2 and 5 July 1919 (GA, F0617, file 183).

28 *District Ledger*, 11 July 1919. This analysis is also apparent in Browne's commentary on the correspondence reproduced in *District Ledger*, 25 July 1919.

29 Bercuson, *Fools and Wise Men*, 142. See the union's correspondence with Armstrong in *District Ledger*, 25 July 1919. The p. 1 headline in the 18 July 1919 edition of the *District Ledger* reads: "Strike Becomes Lockout."

30 *District Ledger*, 11 July 1919. OBU Book (GA, F1844 [UMWA District 18 fonds], box 203, files 1516-1517); *Calgary Daily Herald*, 28 July and 5 August 1919; Bercuson, *Fools and Wise Men*, 197.

31 OBU Book; *Albertan*, 1 and 5 August 1919; Bercuson, *Fools and Wise Men*, 143.

32 D.C. Masters, *The Winnipeg General Strike* (Toronto: University of Toronto Press, 1950), 78, 104. Kramer and Mitchell have shown that the federal government's policy of non-negotiation emanated from A.J. Andrews and the Citizens' Committee of 1000 (*When the State Trembled*, 44, 51, 147–49).

33 McNeill letters to Wilson, 2 and 5 July 1919.

34 Masters, *Winnipeg General Strike*, 43.

35 Bumsted, *Winnipeg General Strike of 1919*, 21–23, 29–30.

36 Norton, *Fernie at War*, 160–61.

37 Wayne Norton reports that as many as 100 Russian workers left Fernie in February 1919 to return to their home country and Austrian-born Ukrainians were also leaving the region at that time (*Fernie at War*, 165).

38 Norton, *Fernie at War*, 175. Unlike in the Crowsnest Pass, in the Drumheller Valley some returned soldiers worked against the miners' cause in the summer of 1919, both as strikebreakers and as vigilantes who illegally kidnapped and then ran OBU leaders like Phillip Christophers out of the area (Bercuson, *Fools and Wise Men*, 198–200).

39 Bumsted, *Winnipeg General Strike of 1919*, 29, 43–8. Kramer and Mitchell point out the Citizens' Committee ran antialien advertisements in daily newspapers in early June that "were direct incitements to soldiers to attack foreigners, as the soldiers had done in January" (*When the State Trembled*, 125–26).

40 Norton, *Fernie at War*, 149; *District Ledger*, 13 June 1919; Masters, *Winnipeg General Strike*, 8, 19, 36.

41 Masters, *Winnipeg General Strike*, 13–17; Norton, *Fernie at War*, 147–49, 158–59; Tom Mitchell and James Naylor, "The Prairies: In the Eye of the Storm," in *The Workers' Revolt in Canada*, 193.

42 Kramer and Mitchell, *When the State Trembled*, 18; Masters, *Winnipeg General Strike*, 14.

43 Bercuson, *Fools and Wise Men*, 197, 201–6, 208–14; Seager, "Proletariat in Wild Rose Country," 341–45, 351–53, 371–74.

44 Seager, "Proletariat in Wild Rose Country," 353–54, 371; Robert McDonald, "'Simply A Working Man': Tom Uphill of Fernie," in *A World Apart: The Crowsnest Communities of Alberta and British Columbia*, ed. Wayne Norton and Tom Langford (Kamloops, BC: Plateau Press, 2002), 100.

7

Montreal's Civil War: The Municipal Workers' Strike of 1918

Geoffrey Ewen

In Montreal in December 1918, over 1,600 police, firefighters, sanitation workers, and waterworks mechanics organized unions, formed a common front, and launched a two-day strike. The years 1918 to 1921 witnessed a surge of organization and strike activity by civic workers across Canada, the United States, and the United Kingdom for the right to bargain collectively, to join the labour movement, and to negotiate improvements in wages and working conditions. They provoked quick responses from business and government, particularly if they involved unionized police. Public sector unions were considered illegitimate as they sometimes provided essential services but more seriously because authorities felt that they challenged the sovereignty of the state. What I want to emphasize about the Montreal dispute is the remarkable degree of working-class support and spontaneous direct action by sympathetic crowds in support of the strikers. It is not surprising that antiunion forces frequently maligned walkouts by law enforcement workers, claiming they were characterized by rioting and looting. The immediate working-class uprising against the antiunion actions of the municipal authorities and business and professional classes made sharp class divisions in Canada's largest industrial and commercial city so clear that one journalist likened the conflict to civil war.[1] In this case crowds were forceful and sometimes pugnacious, but rarely engaged in random acts of violence or pillaging. These were not the peaceful and respectable strike methods sanctioned by international union leaders represented in the leadership of the Montreal Trades and Labour Council (MTLC), the Trades and Labour Congress of Canada (TLC), or the American Federation of Labor (AFL). The crowds, though, were mostly quite disciplined despite the absence of recognized leadership. They directed their ire almost exclusively at specific targets, at actions by municipal authorities and the business community that were considered illegitimate and unacceptable.

The formation of unions among civic employees and their willingness to strike during these years is well documented, as is the hostility of the business community and governments. They also often paved the way for larger confrontations. As Gregory Kealey has noted, walkouts by municipal workers often preceded general strikes or the threat of a general strike.[2] Often opponents of police strikes characterize them as periods of unrestrained rioting and looting. This was the case for the Boston Police Strike of September 1919 even though the nine people known to have died were all killed by militia or in one case by an antistrike vigilante.[3] One labour historian claimed long ago that the Montreal civic strike of 1918 involved extensive robbing of stores.[4] I suggest that the desire to join the labour movement and the support that police, firefighters, and other municipal employees received from follow workers during these years requires reexamination. In Montreal, the characterization of working-class actions as needless or as manifestations of willful damage and lawlessness seriously distorts our understanding of this event.

The importance of public sector organizing is evident when placed in the context of the Workers' Revolt. The labour movement massively expanded from 1916 to 1920 to include new groups of workers, who often resorted to fresh tactics. One of its most notable features was the unionization of government employees. In this "international workers insurgency," there was a transnational public sector uprising.[5] While there were organizing efforts in a few parts of federal public service, as among Canadian postal workers who went on strike in 1918, it was at the municipal level that there was a first major wave of public sector organization. Workers, unions, and employers were all conscious of this breakthrough by the labour movement.

In 1918, the Montreal labour movement was a bastion of international craft unionism. MTLC leaders were strong supporters of AFL policies and organizing practices, and they were firmly entrenched. Labourists for the most part, they left political activities to the Labour Party. Socialists were a weak presence in the labour council, and neither the Socialist Party of Canada nor the Social Democratic Party had much influence among francophone workers, probably because of the Catholic Church's hostility to socialism. This meant that challenges from the left were far weaker in Montreal than in cities such as Winnipeg or Seattle. Indeed, international unionism in Quebec faced a far stronger threat from a growing Catholic labour movement that had the moral and financial backing of the church, even if through the war years Catholic unionism had not reached Montreal in any significant manner.

Montreal workers may have had more recent experiences of taking to the streets than those in other urban centres.[6] The combination of deep unemployment and the election of a more labour-sympathetic mayor in Médéric Martin in 1914 led to the daily appearance at city hall of hundreds and sometimes thousands of men and women from various nationalities demanding work.[7] There were demonstrations by workers and members of other classes every evening over the summer of 1917 after the government announced conscription.[8] Nor were francophones alone in opposing the Military Service Act, as 2,000 Irish nationalists from working-class Griffintown also rallied against the measure.[9] There were more protests against the search for draft evaders by military units and federal police in 1918. Some demonstrations were organized; others were spontaneous, evidenced little leadership, or may have had more informal leadership. Montreal workers were practised at crowd actions that went beyond the well-organized orderly Labour Day parades, religious processions, or ethnic displays as on St. Patrick's Day. They had learned that spontaneous mass gatherings were sometimes the only way to express their positions.

Almost all details on crowd actions during this strike come from the daily press, particularly from the popular and pro-civic worker union *La Patrie*, the high-brow Nationalist and Catholic *Le Devoir*, and the business-friendly anglophone *Montreal Gazette*. There are few other sources for these actions. Files in the Montreal City Archives direct readers to the daily press. There is no mention or discussion of crowd actions in the labour press. Montreal was poorly served by having only a single labour newspaper in French and English, the bilingual weekly *Le Monde ouvrier/The Labor World*, published by MTLC Corresponding-Secretary Gustave Francq, a solid supporter of AFL policies. Descriptions of crowd actions in daily newspapers are similar, and all lack interviews with participants or spectators. There are no quotes from people in the streets. Descriptions of the composition of the street gatherings are laconic. We are not told what the crowds yelled at volunteer replacements or scabs or what songs they sang. On occasion, journalists remarked on strikers' and strikebreakers' mood. As Ian Radforth comments in an article on crowd actions, such newspaper articles are frustrating for historians. In this case, the views of working-class strike supporters, as opposed to union officials, must be ascertained primarily from their actions.[10]

Recent experience taught Montreal civic workers to fear reprisals, demotion, or dismissal for union activities, so they organized secretly with lightning speed in September 1918. The TLCC chartered a Policeman's Federal Labour Union, as the AFL refused to accept police unions until June 1919. The next day, firefighters formed an AFL-affiliated International Association of Fire Fighters local, while AFL organizers signed up garbage collectors into a Teamsters local, and mechanics at the waterworks formed two locals of the International Union of Operating Engineers. Police accounted for the largest group with over 850 members. There were about 550 firefighters, over 250 garbage collectors, and 15 to 25 waterworks engineers. If union leadership is any indication, most of these new unionists were francophone, except possibly for waterworks engineers who joined separate francophone and anglophone locals.[11] Police will receive the largest share of attention in this chapter for a number of reasons: first, they were the largest of the four unions; second, police union president Albert Carle played a leading role in the negotiations; third, police were the key focus of both government and employers; and finally, the problematic relationship of the members of police unions with other union members demands attention.[12]

Many of the civic workers' grievances had accumulated during the First World War. Wage increases were withheld and, with substantial inflation, this meant declining real wages and a relative decline compared to many workers' in other occupations or those who worked for different employers. Mechanics at the waterworks earned far less than their peers in the railway shops. Police, firefighters, and waterworks employees were not supplied with the customary boots and uniforms, important because decent uniforms commanded public respect. All groups faced long working hours. Most worked seven days a week and had to do unpaid overtime. Police had twelve-hour shifts. If they made arrests, they went to court on their own time. Firefighters remained in their stations around the clock, sleeping in their clothes, with only a half day home each week. Unions charged that hiring, firing, and promotion was rife with favouritism, prejudice, and bribery. Firefighters and police had recently been combined in a new Department of Public Safety under fresh management and with a director hired from outside the force, angering those wanting access to channels of promotion. In addition, the Department of Public Safety cut the workforce by about 150 and demoted union activists, while middle-class reform groups accused the three heads of the department of corruption for tolerating and profiting from the sex trade. The deputy director of Public Safety, Arthur Mann, did not speak French. In a context where anglophones outside Quebec had been suppressing public school instruction in French, and when Montreal francophones were demanding that private utilities provide services in French, such an appointment was unacceptable.[13]

The new unions had to negotiate with a city under trusteeship. In February 1918, the Quebec Liberal government of Lomer Gouin had placed most of Montreal's affairs under the authority of an appointed Administrative Commission whose purpose was to impose fiscal retrenchment. Heavily indebted by rapid industrial and demographic expansion, Montreal's financial situation was exacerbated by the forced annexation of smaller, deeply indebted working-class municipalities, such as Maisonneuve, whose development had enriched developers and capitalists but left a heavy tax burden on residents.[14] As a result, the power of Mayor Médéric Martin and of the elected city council had been greatly reduced.

Mayor Martin was an interesting character, as he also served as a Liberal member of Parliament for working-class Sainte-Marie and was an industrialist claiming to represent the working class. The MTLC rejected this assertion, while Martin boasted about maintaining his membership in the Cigarmakers' Union. His election in 1914 broke the long-standing practice of alternating francophone and anglophone mayors and represented the growing strength of francophone voters.

For its part, the Administrative Commission was headed by Ernest Décary, an autocratic notary who had founded a firm that specialized in working for banking and railway companies.[15] Louis Dupire, a journalist at *Le Devoir*, described Montreal's governance under the commission as "le régime du dictature."[16] Still, it is significant that the civic workers had some political support. Mayor Martin and most elected city councillors voted to support unionization and many of the workers' demands, giving the unions a degree of legitimacy.[17]

The Administrative Commission hired an American firm specializing in Taylorism to reorganize municipal services, close police stations, and fire numerous constables and firefighters. When union leaders tried to negotiate, Décary refused to meet them. To allay fears of a police strike, the union stated that in principle it was opposed to striking. Only the prospect of a work stoppage by waterworks mechanics forced Décary to accept conciliation under the Industrial Dispute Investigation Act (IDIA). In the case of municipal workers, this legislation established a process for voluntary conciliation if employers and workers both agreed to it. This tripartite commission issued majority and minority reports. The majority report recommended overtime pay and a two-week holiday but no wage increase. Recommendations could be rejected by either side, but the city tried to coerce workers into accepting the majority report. The small concessions and employer's pressure tactics ensured that civic unions were deeply suspicious of conciliation and arbitration. Décary urged the unions to wait until he announced new wage scales in the city budget, imploring them to help place Montreal on a "business footing." When he issued his financial plan, it rejected most of the workers' demands and offered paltry wage increases.[18]

On Saturday, 7 December, the four unions formed a common front, a move characteristic of private sector labour organizations seeking solidarity across occupational lines when confronted with a single employer or working with multiple employers in the same industry. In this coalition, police and firefighters carried the most weight because of their numbers. Parading arm in arm from their headquarters to their meeting hall behind a marching band, they were cheered by onlookers who thought the strike had begun, an early indication of public support. At the meeting, union members added the dismissal of the three heads of the Department of Public Safety recently accused by reformers of corruption to their list of demands, and they voted to strike the following Wednesday, 11 December, if their demands were not met.[19]

The possibility that civic employees would cease work rapidly drew many elements of Montreal society into the dispute, including business and professional organizations, municipal and provincial politicians, the Catholic archbishop, and the MTLC. On Monday, 9 December, Mayor Martin requested a twenty-four-hour postponement, enough time to convince Quebec premier Gouin to personally intervene. The next evening, Gouin met union leaders who rejected his offer of arbitration. The premier promised to talk to Administrative Commission president Décary the following morning, 11 December, offering some hope. Gouin convinced Décary to accept two twelve-hour shifts each day for firefighters, but Décary refused to make any other concessions. The Administrative Commission was a creature of the Quebec government, so we can conclude that Premier Gouin supported this position. Décary then declared: "Maintenant que vous connaissez nos conditions, faites ce que vous voudrez."[20]

Union leaders were then summoned to meet Montreal's Catholic archbishop Paul Bruchési that afternoon. As most unionists were Catholics, they listened respectfully but declined his offer to arbitrate, unwilling to put their fate in the archbishop's hands. It was not unusual for religious leaders to offer to mediate or arbitrate, and not surprising that the unions declined. In 1903 after a long and painful lockout, Quebec City shoe workers had accepted their archbishop's offer to arbitrate and were taken aback when his decision dealt with far more than the issues under dispute. It included the removal of provisions in their constitutions and forced them to accept chaplains, appointed by the archbishop, at their meetings.[21] Bruchési's views on public sector unions and strikes resembled those of employers. He opposed unions and strikes among workers who served the public rather than private employers.[22] Bruchési, however, played a role as intermediary between Décary and the unions.[23]

To the ire of union members who feared losing momentum, Décary used the twenty-four-hour delay to ensure he had the support of the business community, securing the services of the union-busting Thiel and Burns Detective Agencies, calling for volunteers, and hiring strikebreakers.[24] He announced that "notre projet de défense et de protection de la ville a été soumis à plusieurs institutions financières, commerciales et d'assurances et il a été approuvé." Décary hired men and signed up volunteers on 11 and 12 December. To have at least one officer on duty at each police station, he tried to promote twenty-one unionized police captains to the rank of inspector. Most, if not all, declined. The union announced that if the city hoped to rely on members of the Office of Provincial Detectives in Montreal, it would be disappointed because police at this agency promised to answer calls of theft or assault but not to deal with social unrest. At the same time drivers in the city's road department refused to drive fire engines and formed their own union. Décary asked Major-General Wilson, commander of the Montreal military district, for assistance and was assured that soldiers would be available to help put out fires or provide other aid to the civil authorities if the mayor read the Riot Act and the city was placed under martial law. When soldiers were ordered to return to their barracks to be available, a firefighters' union leader warned that if the army intervened "c'est là qu'apparaîtra le trouble." *La Patrie* reported that the Thiel Detective Agency had sworn in more than 1,000 men the night of 11 December. The director of Public Safety engaged another 200 on the afternoon of 12 December. The Administrative Commission counted on businesses, merchants, and industrialists to protect their own property. The Canadian Pacific Railway assigned large numbers of its own private railway police agents to serve as temporary city police. The Board of Trade organized a corps of volunteers. Insurance companies supplied firefighters. Bell Telephone provided operators to answer police switchboards. The City of Westmount, home to many anglophone capitalists, promised aid. Décary claimed that he had enough help to maintain services throughout the city.[25]

In response, the city's working class showed a remarkable degree of solidarity with the strikers. At noon Thursday 12 December, a signal was sent to each station to begin the walkout—a phone call of two rings. The walkout started with great enthusiasm. As the strike began, Director of Public Safety Joseph Tremblay declared that in case of fire, one should pull the nearest fire alarm and phone the central alarm bureau. Taken as a challenge, the first false alarm was raised at 12:35. By the end of the day, 304 alarms had been set off; only six were for genuine fires. About 100 street fire alarm boxes were destroyed. There were running battles between strike supporters and Décary's forces at several major intersections on St. Denis Street. In working-class districts sympathizers assembled at fire stations to prevent volunteers from emerging. In other cases, they booed when volunteers rushed to answer calls. At Station #14, corner of Rachel and St-Dominique, a residential district on the Plateau Mont-Royal, a large crowd refused to allow the replacements to go on duty and prevented the fire captain, who had remained at his post with his two daughters, from leaving until a late hour. At Station #16, on Rachel Street near Lafontaine Park, the strikebreakers were forcibly ejected.[26]

Crowds could be cheerful and celebratory or angry.[27] At Station #4 at Chaboillez Square, today the intersection of St. Jacques and Peel Streets, in front of the Intercolonial Railway freight offices and just north of working-class Griffintown, a wagon driven by the district fire chief and a volunteer tried to answer a false alarm. Attacked by strikers or sympathizers, the strikebreaker fled with a bloodied face. Crowds and strikers had a clear idea of who had a right to touch fire equipment; only district chiefs could drive the fire trucks. At five in the evening this scene was repeated, though this time the volunteer was not harmed, only stripped of equipment. In the evening, the crowd forced the remaining volunteers to flee. At Station #23, at Place Saint-Henri, a police captain who remained on duty was severely beaten and two volunteers quickly retreated. At Station #5, on Ontario Street at the corner of St-Dominique in Ville-Marie, volunteers and two special constables were chased away.[28]

Ernest Décary set up his antistrike headquarters at Station #20 at the corner of Craig and Chenneville, now Saint-Antoine between Saint-Jacques and Notre-Dame Streets. This was the location where replacement police and firefighters were asked to present themselves. Here on the first evening of the strike, the crowd was most forceful, and there was a lot of fighting. The crowd set the doors on fire; once inside they fought their way up the stairs, forcing volunteer firefighters to flee. Three Thiel detectives hired to protect volunteers were beaten and sent to hospital.[29] Newspaper reports indicate that this was done either by strikers or sympathizers.

Far from the extensive looting of stores, most of the violence was aimed at the volunteer firefighters, the rare policeman who remained on the job, and agents from the strikebreaking Thiel Detective Agency. There even appeared to be a logic to the retribution: usually volunteers were chased away, working members of the police force were beaten, and

Thiel operatives sent to hospital. In addition, many observers claimed that sympathizers, rather than strikers, were responsible for most such incidents, as most strikers were reportedly assembled in their meeting hall. For a city without police on duty, relatively few other crimes were reported in the press. Amid the extensive newspaper coverage of these events, papers such as the anglophone *Montreal Gazette* and Henri Bourassa's *Le Devoir* each assigned a single line to a few store robberies and noted that pickpockets were active. Most violence was directed at specific targets. On two occasions, crowds took actions that went beyond what strikers would accept.

In front of Station #4, Chaboillez Square, a truck was run into the street to block the streetcar. The entire contents of the firehouse, including machinery, hoses, tires, and even the firefighters' personal belongings were smashed and thrown onto the street. This was done in "high good spirits" with singing and shouting, creating a festival-like atmosphere that allowed those involved to let off steam. Five to six hundred neighbourhood residents looked on and some made off with booty that fell to the street. The only record of a voice raised by a spectator occurred here when a man warned participants not to hurt the horses. While they showed no respect for civic property, or in this case for the property of striking firefighters, there were limits, and no harm was ever done to working horses during this strike or in any other in 1919. The scene ended late in the evening when a striking firefighter arrived to ask the crowd to stop, arguing that they were doing the strikers' cause more harm than good.[30] This suggests that strikers were not among this crowd and that they did not want to lose wider support. Mayor Martin claimed he was unaware of these events and would have asked striking police to intervene had he known. He suspected the director of Public Safety of conspiring to allow the destruction to continue in order to force him to read the Riot Act.[31]

There was only one report of serious looting and damage that extended beyond a fire or police station. At Station #13, on Sherbrooke Street in the former municipality of Maisonneuve, close to Dominion Textile Factories and near the Vickers Shipyards, a streetcar was attacked, its windows broken, and it was left to stop traffic. Stones were then thrown through a store window and an estimated 100 men, women, and youths rushed in to loot. The entire contents of Mendel Mallek's clothing store were either destroyed or stolen.[32] Did anti-Semitism play a role? Possibly, although this was not the only target of this crowd,[33] which also severely damaged the neighbouring Laurier Palace movie theatre. Why did the only incident that targeted more than civic property happen in Maisonneuve? Were other issues at play? Working-class Maisonneuve was the most recent municipality annexed to Montreal in 1918. It had one of the most active labour clubs in Montreal, and workers expected to exert influence over local affairs. This was a riding that had elected a federal Parti ouvrier member of Parliament in 1906, and it would elect a Parti ouvrier candidate in the 1919 Quebec elections. Maisonneuve's firefighters were dismissed in 1918 because they had been hired by the annexed town and not by the City of Montreal. It was near the Vickers Shipyards where workers were being laid off and replaced with returning veterans. Thus, it is very likely that multiple factors influenced those involved in the havoc.

What is most striking about this incident is that on hearing of what was happening, police union president Albert Carle and several police union members rushed to the scene, fired their revolvers in the air, and made arrests. At a strikers' meeting that night Mayor Martin entered the hall to a round of applause. He boasted that when asked to read the Riot Act, he had refused, saying that he would not do so for a few black eyes, then he urged the strikers to organize their own patrols to prevent disorder. The mayor appeared to tolerate beating scabs and volunteers, but there were limits to what elected politicians and union leaders would accept. Carle asked his members to protect anyone in danger.[34] Striking firefighters helped volunteers put out fires. There was a recognition among the striking police and firefighters that their services were essential, and they had little desire to see this kind of mayhem and did not want to lose public support. They would not tolerate theft or the destruction of private property.

So, where were these incidents? Of the seven stations that were the sites of confrontations described in newspapers, one was in Saint-Henri, another on the north edge of Griffintown, two were in Ville-Marie, two were on the Plateau Mont-Royal, and one in Maisonneuve. Disorder was described as widespread, but all the dailies covering these scenes focused on the same incidents, suggesting that these were the most serious. Most were in heavily francophone working-class areas. The Plateau, and especially the area near Station #14, had a mixed French-Canadian and Jewish immigrant population who were usually strong union supporters. Griffintown, where Station #4 at Chaboillez Square was located, had been a mostly Irish enclave but was changing, becoming increasingly Catholic as Protestants moved out, while more francophones and Jewish and Italian immigrants moved in.[35] Unfortunately, the press is silent on who was among the crowds of supporters and spectators.

In front of Station #14, some 500 strike supporters listened to speeches delivered from an impromptu stage. Presided over by George Remington, the assembly cheered two police constables, Aristide Lefebvre and Télesphore Rondré, who explained their grievances and demands. J.A. Brosseau, described as a well-known baker, offered support for police and firefighters, suggesting that support came not just from wage earners but from small business owners. The crowd actions make a strong case for working-class solidarity with firefighters, and these speeches and their reception indicate that their support extended to police as well. Next J.A. Thibault and M. Thérien addressed the crowd, but they are not further identified, and their comments were not reported. Nonetheless, all who took the stage were francophone. The final speaker was well known. This was Gédéon Martel, who had been the president of the Fédération des clubs ouvriers municipaux de Montréal, a breakaway group from the Parti ouvrier, and an independent labour candidate in the 1917 federal elections. Martel attacked Premier Lomer Gouin and Administrative Commission President Ernest Décary.[36] This emphasizes that popular resentment was directed not just against the Administrative Commission but against the Quebec government that had imposed it.

There are a few references to women or youths in these accounts. Women telephone workers walked off the job in solidarity during the strike.[37] Women were present in crowds as witnesses and to offer encouragement. When Station #4 Chaboillez Square was sacked, the participants were described in the press as boys aged ten to eighteen.[38] Men, women, and youth are reported looting the store in Maisonneuve. This is the only mention of women taking any crowd action. This may tell us something about the views of a journalist and about the image they wanted to project about the male strikers, but little about the strike supporters. Certainly, these actions were not those expected of respectable union members or more mature male workers. While there is no mention of women engaging in actions to confront scabs or volunteers, we should not discount the possibility. In other wartime

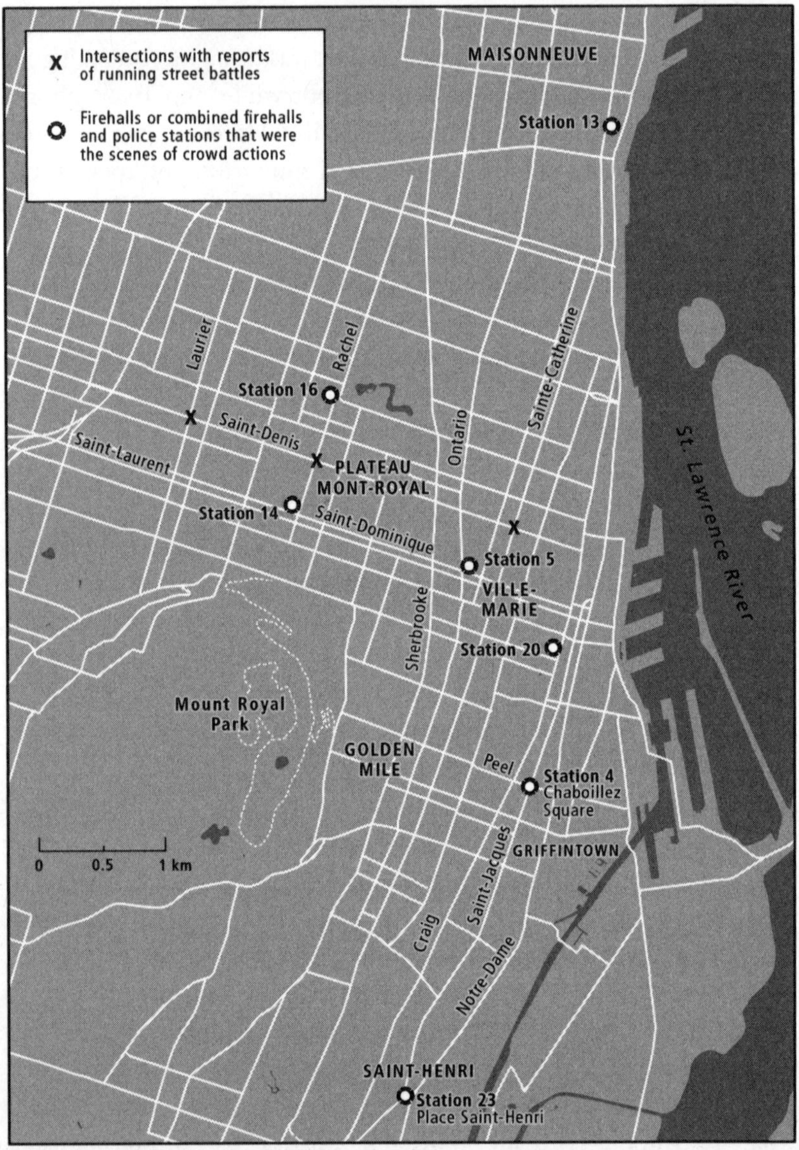

Figure 7.1. The locations of crowd actions during the 1918 Montreal civic workers' strike. Source: Erin Greb Cartography.

and postwar labour disputes in Montreal, women, as picketers or strike supporters, were vocal and assertive, just as many were during the Winnipeg General Strike.[39]

Employers were clearly alarmed that striking police were patrolling the streets armed, deciding on their own what and who to protect.[40] Police, along with the militia and the army, were the ultimate recourse for employers who expected them to suppress strikes, protect scabs, attack picket lines, and squash demonstrations and protests.[41] There was a fear that police might show support for other striking workers or might even be obliged to do so by the labour council.[42] A few months later, some Montreal police showed a marked sympathy for striking teamsters. When 4,000 carters walked off the job and prevented fellow haulers from working, often unloading their goods onto the road, some working carters sought police protection. Police responded by asking to see the carters' union badges, refusing to defend strikebreakers.[43] A frequent refrain from employers and organizations such as the Association des Propriétaires, which represented landlords in a city of tenants, was that police should protect all classes, not just one group. Couched in the language of neutrality, in fact they were primarily concerned about the rights of property owners and employers.

In the early hours of Friday, 13 December, Ernest Décary again met with military authorities to ensure that 200 soldiers would be provided that day. One hundred soldiers chased away the crowd at Décary's headquarters and remained to guard the building. Militiamen with clubs protected some fire stations, and armed soldiers were stationed at the waterworks, while others were kept in reserve or sent to put out fires.[44] Since Martin refused to read the Riot Act, the *Gazette* claimed that the soldiers "were simply lent to civic authorities" and acted "simply as good citizens." This view was not shared by the soldiers. Many were clearly not happy. The *Gazette* reporter observed that it was an "experience, which they did not seem to relish."[45] Indeed, they may well have resented how they were used.

Numerous efforts were made to end the conflict. The striking unions had asked the MTLC for help as soon as the strike commenced. The next day, labour council leaders, including President John Thomas Foster and Gustave Francq, met Administrative Commission president Décary, who accepted their offer to mediate.[46]

At the same time, the business community organized. A Citizens Protective Association (CPA) was formed on the morning of 13 December by business, service, and civic organizations from the English, French, and Jewish communities. It included representatives of the Montreal branch of the Canadian Manufacturers Association, the Chamber of Commerce, and the Young Men's Hebrew Association. Overwhelmingly hostile to the strikers, most advocated a fight to the finish and wanted the army to crush the strike.[47]

Few at this meeting advocated negotiations. One who did was Adélard Fortier, president of the Montréal Dairy Company and former president of the Chamber of Commerce, who was considered in 1916 as a candidate for mayor by the Fédération des clubs ouvriers municipaux de Montréal.[48] Fortier, who had already expressed sympathy for municipal employees, asserted that strikers were more interested in justice than money. He proposed forming a delegation to negotiate a settlement with strike leaders. Fortier met with such hostility that the chair had to intervene to get him a hearing. However, it would seem that his proposal was acted upon. The meeting formed the aforementioned CPA, which immediately established a fifty-member Committee of Public Safety (CPS) that was tasked with resolving the conflict. Representative of the Montreal ruling class, the CPS was chaired by William Allan Black, president of the Montreal Board of Trade. The vice-chairs were Frederick William Stewart, director of the City Improvement League and managing director of Cluett, Peabody, and Company of Canada, a manufacturer of men's shirts, and Alfred Lambert, a shoe manufacturer and member of the Chamber of Commerce.

The CPS arranged to meet union leaders and presented a position that combined threats with an offer to resolve the conflict. It proposed that a five-member board of arbitration composed of CPS members chosen by both the CPA and the unions would address the disputed issues. The CPS promised a "fair, square deal," but if rejected, the CPS would "take such legal and military steps as might seem necessary to cope with the situation." Montreal workers faced resistance from employers in the form of a united front like the one created later in Winnipeg during the General Strike. Police union president Carle feared that the city would plead poverty and refuse higher wages. When the CPS pledged to find the necessary funds for wage increases, the leaders of the striking unions agreed to present the offer to the membership; according to the *Montreal Gazette*, these leaders stated that "the committee of fifty guarantees that the necessary funds for higher wages expected to be awarded would be forthcoming even if not provided for in the city budget [and they understood] that these citizens will support increased taxation for this purpose." For his part, Décary agreed on condition that the strike was called off. At the urging of Premier Gouin and Archbishop Bruchési, he made another concession, removing the three discredited heads of the Department of Public Safety. Refusing direct communication with strikers, Décary agreed to the CPS proposal in a letter to Archbishop Bruchési. The unions initially rejected his undertaking because it did not include the twelve-hour shift to firefighters. Once inserted, the unions accepted the CPS offer, ending the strike.[49]

The outcome was greeted enthusiastically by the strikers. This was viewed as a victory as the unions had shown their power by winning two major concessions, dismissal of the directors of Public Safety and acceptance of two separate daily shifts for firefighters. Police detectives were "d'un enthousiasme délirant," and firemen celebrated by singing, shouting, and blowing the horns on their fire trucks.[50] Union leaders were confident that arbitration on these terms would meet their demands. They placed their faith in the CPS guarantee.

The settlement came as a major surprise and embarrassment to MTLC leaders who were still attempting to get their mediation efforts under way. The civic unions had agreed to an arbitration board chosen entirely from the employer-based CPA, two to be nominated by the association, two nominated by the unions, and the fifth to be named by agreement among these four. This outcome revealed a spectacular degree of deference among civic union leaders who placed more confidence in the CPA than in the MTLC. Little thought was given to the efforts of labour council leaders who were not even informed of negotiations with the employer's group. Stunned, council leaders downplayed the incident, attributing it to new union recruits who had not yet developed the required skills in union-management negotiating.[51] The MTLC would not have agreed to arbitration without labour representation. It also raises questions about the ability of labour council leaders to keep in touch with newly organized workers and their leaders during important strikes.

The MTLC was wary of being associated with any broader mobilization that they could not control. In both the 1914 unemployed movement and in response to conscription in 1917, the MTLC appears to have organized only a single event in each instance. In the case of the unemployed, the labour council leadership feared that their efforts would be hijacked by socialists, with whom most of them did not want to be associated. In general, the council did not like to organize beyond its own membership. For example, although most MTLC leaders were anticonscriptionist,[52] the council preferred to leave political issues to the Parti ouvrier, prohibiting signs on conscription during the 1917 Labour Day parade to avoid fostering divisions among workers.

For their part, many socialists eschewed spontaneous and forceful worker engagements, preferring to place an emphasis on education, disciplined restraint, and use of peaceful measures such as general strikes. They considered the latter tactic a better way to secure worker demands and a much more serious threat to employers and governments.[53] While socialists were present at unemployed demonstrations and anticonscriptionist events, neither the Socialist Party of Canada nor the Social Democratic Party had much influence among francophone workers. Socialism was strongest among immigrants, sometimes in labour organizations not represented in the MTLC, or who were not organized in unions at all.

One of the key features of the Workers' Revolt was the central role of labour councils where militant and radical workers were flexing their muscles. This was the case not only in Winnipeg and Seattle but in Toronto and Vancouver as well, to take a few examples.[54] In contrast, Montreal workers sent fewer socialists to their labour councils, and socialism had less influence in the working class. Certainly, Montreal and the MTLC appears to have been an AFL stronghold, in contrast to numerous other industrial cities. The spontaneous crowd actions in Montreal may well have stemmed from this absence of leadership. Indeed, in 1919, and particularly during the Winnipeg General Strike, the MTLC executive would do all it could to undermine the Workers' Revolt.[55] Crowd actions then, employed since 1914, may have been a strategic choice for Montreal workers. Tellingly, the crowds aimed their anger almost exclusively at the strikebreaking activities of the Administrative Commission.

The social unrest witnessed during this strike was the result of deep systemic divisions and inequalities. Certainly, Quebec workers were angry with the imposition and enforcement of the Military Service Act. In 1918, convinced that Quebec francophones were not doing their share for the war effort, army patrols and the Dominion Police searched for draft evaders throughout Quebec. These actions were deeply resented. When a working-class crowd demonstrated against these searches in Quebec City around Easter 1918, anglophone military units from Toronto fired on the gathering, killing four protesters. The raids also hastened the spread of influenza infections. Young Quebec men, even those with exemptions, were rounded up and confined overnight at close quarters in military camps. Once released many returned to their families with the infection, spreading it further. The flu pandemic revealed economic disparities. The working class was hardest hit because of crowded, unhealthy living conditions, the lack of ventilation or running water in many homes, and the limited access to health care. Historian Esyllt Jones has argued that the handling of the flu epidemic added to the grievances of workers; she maintains persuasively that it did not lead directly to the Winnipeg General Strike, but it deepened the determination of workers to resist social injustices.[56] Similar conclusions can be drawn about crowd actions during the Montreal strike. In addition, the armistice abruptly ended most munitions production, sharply increasing unemployment in the winter of 1918–19.

For most Montreal workers, governments at all levels had little legitimacy. The federal Union government held only three seats from Quebec—all anglophone. It owed its overwhelming victory in the 1917 elections in the rest of Canada to a combination of massive voter suppression and anti-francophone and anti-immigrant sentiment. Resentment against the provincially appointed Administrative Commission may account for the ferocity of working-class support for the strike. To be sure, elected municipal politicians could be unsympathetic to unions, and many cities across North America were reorganizing and centralizing their workforce, and in the case of the police imposing bureaucratic hierarchies based on military lines. Elected governments were not necessarily more representative of workers elsewhere, but government policies were clearly perceived as contrary to the interests of Montreal workers and of French Canadians.

An absence of even the appearance of political legitimacy needs to be considered to explain the vehemence and speed of crowd action.

Despite the massive outpouring of working-class support and the strikers' elation at the end of the strike, it was risky placing the outcome in the hands of an arbitration board composed entirely of employers. The CPA chose Grant Hall, a vice-president of the Canadian Pacific Railway, and Alfred Lambert as representatives. The unions chose F.W. Stewart and Adélard Fortier, the latter a choice that firefighters union Secretary J.B. Dalphond said would assure them "entière justice." William Allan Black was chosen to preside over the board.[57] The civic unions rejected arbitration by the archbishop, refused pleas from Premier Gouin, ignored MTLC efforts, and acceded to a group of employers. Perhaps civic union leaders believed that the business community alone had the influence to guarantee the funds for wage increases.[58] Still, this must have made some workers wonder about the loyalties of the civic workers, and especially the police. Members of the force might be of working-class origins and part of the working class because of the nature of their work, but they revealed a remarkable confidence in employers.

The final settlement, in February 1919, was met with astonishment and disappointment. Police and firefighters got less than one-third of their wage demands, nor were the waterworks mechanics happy with the result. Worse, it conceded the right to form independent societies or associations; that is, the civic workers were to sever ties with each other and with the labour movement. They could not affiliate with any other organization, whether a union, a federation of municipal bodies, a labour council, or the TLCC. Employers were alarmed at the solidarity between different groups of civic workers. Both employers and the unions understood that uniting support among workers in different city departments, and belonging to the labour movement, offered more influence and a greater likelihood of achieving their aims. They all realized that there was strength in numbers. The CPA arbitration report stated specifically that "those who are named for the maintenance of public security should not be bound by obligations, to societies of organizations, which would in any way restrain them or embarrass them in the exercise and performance of their functions and duties—primarily the protection of all classes of society without distinction, and at all times and under all circumstances."[59] This concern was aimed particularly at police who should not, in their view, show solidarity toward other workers; there was a particular fear of sympathy strikes, and a fear that the police would show favour to strikers and fail to defend strikebreakers.[60] The order to withdraw from the labour movement was ignored by the unions. Police, for example, made every effort to maintain affiliations to the MTLC at least into the 1930s. For years, they battled through the courts to maintain this relationship. Continued membership in the TLCC and MTLC was the pretext that the city used to refuse to recognize the Montreal police union or to negotiate with it in the 1920s. While all the civic unions were attacked, the most intense antiunion campaign targeted police.

The discussions at the meeting to form the CPA and the arbitration board report revealed the two principal strategies used by employers and the state when faced with public sector unionism, and particularly by the organization of the police. Some members of the ruling class wanted to destroy the new civic labour organizations. This would be the approach taken during the Winnipeg General Strike when all police who did not sign a renunciation of the union were fired and replaced. Striking police in Boston and England faced the same fate in 1919. The other option was to tolerate an association or society on condition that it severed all ties with the labour movement. This might apply, as well, to a mutual benefit society. This was the approach adopted in Montreal. If employers were divided on whether to tolerate any organization for police, firefighters, or waterworks employees, all were opposed to any link to the labour movement. Either way, they hoped to isolate government workers' organizations, to ensure that they were too weak to flex their muscles and were firmly under the control of the state and employers.

Membership in the MTLC revealed the internal contradictions of including police within the labour movement. Organized workers hoped unionized police would act differently during labour disputes. Frequently, other unions complained about police actions during strikes. Delegates objected to police guarding construction sites during a building trades dispute later in 1919. One argued that police were intentionally intimidating strikers at the Canadian Rubber Company. During the 1920s, the labour council heard complaints that the police were enforcing injunctions intended to hinder any kind of picketing, the distribution of literature during strikes, and even speaking to a scab—hardly the sorts of actions once expected from comrades in the labour movement.

Labour council president John Thomas Foster had to defend the police on several occasions. His argument rested on two grounds. Like employers and governments, labour leaders believed that public sector unions would increase the power of the labour movement. Foster argued that the police union was a good labour council member, participating proudly in the Labour Day parade. In the Montreal parades in 1919 and the early 1920s, the municipal workers unions were given pride of place leading the procession, highlighting the symbolic importance attached to the expansion of organized labour into the municipal public sphere. After a return to elected government in 1921, civic unions continued to be attacked. Police formed the largest of these bodies, and successfully separating them from the MTLC would have been a blow to all public sector organization.[61] In 1922, other civic unions wanted to see how the police would fare before embarking on their own negotiations.

The second basis of Foster's argument was more serious and problematic. Police work obligations included enforcing federal and Quebec antiunion legislation and antiunion municipal bylaws. It entailed enforcing injunctions issued by unsympathetic judges.[62] Foster and other MTLC leaders argued that police were just doing their duty.[63] Labour council leaders found themselves defending police when they were ordered to take antiunion action by the judiciary, to apply legislation that clearly favoured employers. The relationship between police unions and organized labour was fraught from the beginning despite sometimes widespread support from working-class sympathizers.

Conclusion

Class divisions were every bit as acute in Montreal as in many other North American cities. The difference was in how they were manifested. There were numerous similarities with class conflict elsewhere. This civic workers' strike reflected the trend toward larger labour-capital confrontations. These unions formed a united front, akin to the joint councils in the metal, shipbuilding, and building trades, even though unity might be informal and temporary. Public sector workers wanted unions and saw the advantages of solidarity with private sector workers—hence the decision to join the labour movement. The strikers received a remarkable degree of support from other members of the community, including both organized and unorganized wage earners.

As in other cities such as Winnipeg, Montreal's capitalists quickly established their own ad hoc association. They wanted police to be subject to a kind of semi-military hierarchical structure and discipline, and they wanted their loyalty during labour disputes. Employers were divided in their response. Many wanted to eliminate the new unions, others were willing to accept independent organizations without links to organized labour. For the police, the settlement in Montreal was in marked contrast to the outcome during the Winnipeg General Strike where the city fired all union police. These two options were debated in numerous cities, including Boston during its police strike. What all employer reactions had in common was a determination to ensure that public sector workers and especially police would not be part of the larger organized labour movement.

Alongside these similarities, local circumstances led to differences. The active exception sympathetic workers took to the strikebreaking policies of the unelected Administrative Commission provoked a broad uprising. Indeed, the rapidity of the sympathizers' reaction, their vehemence, as well as the targeted violence, cannot be fully explained by their support for unionization and the strikers' specific demands. Rather, these were the product of a multitude of grievances: the conduct of the war effort, which was more widely and acutely resented in Quebec than elsewhere, the class-based inequities of the influenza pandemic, and the effects of immediate postwar unemployment. Governments at all levels were considered illegitimate. Montreal workers had numerous reasons to seethe.

As was the case with recent movements when Montreal workers took to the streets, the strike provoked the spontaneous mobilization of working-class support. Properly considered, crowd actions were far from the havoc-wreaking events described by many unsympathetic observers. In most cases, what is striking is the discipline of crowds whose targets appear to have been well chosen to communicate their objections; crowds rarely overstepped what was considered legitimate. In 1919, the AFL-aligned leadership of the Montreal labour movement was reluctant to engage in radical or militant action, to act or even to pass motions to defend Winnipeg workers during their General Strike. This does not mean that the Montreal working class was not militant. It does lead us to another difference, and that is the weakness of socialism among francophones. In cities such as Winnipeg, socialists had won leadership roles in local labour councils and sought allies beyond union membership. This was not the case in Montreal. In Montreal, if workers took to the streets, it was in part because they did not have a leadership that could or would direct rage and resistance along other paths. Indeed, the MTLC leadership rarely acted contrary to AFL policies which, in turn, exposed their insignificance during this strike and uprising. Socialists in Montreal were unable and MTLC leaders were unwilling to harness working-class militancy.

This active working-class support for municipal workers came from both organized and unorganized workers who were willing to erupt in a spur-of-the-moment defence of the right to collective bargaining and to decent working conditions, and to express resentment at numerous inequities and injustices. This was a widespread burst of outrage against the ruling class. It was in conspicuous divergence with the Winnipeg General Strike, where workers engaged in a well-organized, well-planned, and peaceful strike, at least until the specials, defended by the North-West Mounted Police, rioted against strike-supporting veterans on Bloody Saturday.

Notes

1 *La Patrie*, 13 December 1918.

2 For a few examples of civic workers strikes, see David Bercuson, *Confrontation at Winnipeg: Labour, Industrial Relations, and the General Strike,* rev. ed. (Montreal and Kingston: McGill-Queen's University Press, 1990); Clive Emsley, *The English Police: A Political and Social History*, 2nd ed. (London, UK: Longman, 1996); Ron Bean, "Police Unrest, Unionization, and the 1919 Strike in Liverpool," *Journal of Contemporary History* 15 (1980): 633–53; Gregory Kealey, "State Repression and the Left in Canada, 1914–1920: The Impact of the First World War," *Canadian Historical Review* 73, no. 3 (September 1992): 306–12.

3 Francis Russell, *A City in Terror: 1919, The Boston Police Strike* (New York: Viking, 1975); Richard L. Lyons, "The Boston Police Strike of 1919," *New England Quarterly* 20, no. 2 (June 1947): 147–68; Joseph Slater, "Public Workers: Labor and the Boston Police Strike of 1919," *Labor History* 38, no. 1 (Winter 1996/97): 7–27.

4 Terry Copp, *The Anatomy of Poverty* (Toronto: McClelland and Stewart, 1974), 133.

5 The quote is from Douglas Cruikshank and Gregory S. Kealey, "Canadian Strike Statistics, 1891–1950," *Labour/Le Travail* 20 (1987): 109.

6 For earlier crowd actions in Montreal, see Dan Horner, "Solemn Processions and Terrifying Violence: Spectacle, Authority, and Citizenship during the Lachine Canada Strike of 1843," *Urban History Review* 38, no. 2 (Spring 2010): 36–47; Dan

Horner, "'Shame upon you as men!': Contesting Authority in the Aftermath of Montréal's Gavazzi Riot," *Histoire sociale/Social History* 44, no. 87 (May 2011): 29–52.

7 Claude Larivière, *Albert Saint-Martin, militant d'avant-garde (1865–1947)* (Laval, QC: Éditions coopératives Albert Saint-Martin, 1979).

8 Bernard Dansereau, "Le mouvement ouvrier montréalais et la crise de la conscription, 1916–1918" (MA thesis, Université du Québec à Montréal, 1994).

9 Matthew Barlow, *Griffintown: Identity and Memory in an Irish Diaspora Neighbourhood* (Vancouver: UBC Press, 2017), 67.

10 Ian Radforth, "Playful Crowds and the 1886 Toronto Street Railway Strikes," *Labour/Le travail* 76 (2015): 134–39. For a biography of Gustave Francq, see Éric Leroux, *Gustave Francq: Figure marquante du syndicalisme et précurseur de la FTQ* (Montreal: VLB Éditeur, 2001).

11 *La Patrie*, 9, 11 September 1918; *Le monde ouvrier/The Labor World*, 14 September 1918 ; *Le Devoir*, 9 December 1918. For literature on the formation of firefighters' unions in the United States and United Kingdom, see Michael G. Matejka, *Fiery Struggle: Illinois Fire Fighters Build a Union, 1901–1985* (Chicago: Illinois Labor History Society, 2002); Sian Moore, Tessa Wright, and Philip Taylor, *Fighting Fire: One Hundred Years of the Fire Brigades Union* (Oxford, UK: New Internationalist, 2018).

12 For an authorized institutional history of the police union in Montreal, see Jacques Rouillard and Henri Goulet, *Solidarité et determination: Histoire de la Fraternité des policiers et policières de la Communauté urbaine de Montréal* (Montreal: Boréal, 1999).

13 *La Patrie*, 29 June, 26 August, 31 July, 9 November 1918; *Le Devoir*, 8, 9 November 1918; *Montreal Gazette*, 6 December 1918.

14 On Maisonneuve, see Paul-André Linteau, *Maisonneuve: Comment des promoteurs fabriquent une ville* (Montreal: Boréal Express, 1981).

15 Ernest-Rémi Décary (baptized Joseph-Rémi-Ernest) in *Dictionary of Canadian Biography*, vol. 16, http://www.biographi.ca/en/bio/decary_ernest_remi_16E.html.

16 *Le Devoir*, 13 December 1918.

17 Archive de la Ville de Montréal (AVM), Fonds du Conseil de Ville, Procès-Verbaux de l'assemblé spécial du Conseil municipal de Montréal, 8 October 1918.

18 *Le Devoir*, 29 November, 9, 10 December 1918; *La Patrie*, 6, 9 December 1918; *Montreal Gazette*, 10 December 1918.

19 *Le Devoir*, 9 December 1918; *La Patrie*, 9 December 1918; *Montreal Gazette*, 9 December 1918.

20 *La Patrie*, 11 December 1918.

21 Jacques Rouillard, *Les syndicats nationaux au Québec de 1900 à 1930* (Quebec: Presses de l'Université Laval, 1979).

22 *Semaine sociale du Canada* (Montreal: École sociale populaire, 1920), 8–9, 206.

23 *Montreal Gazette*, 12 December 1918.

24 AVM, Fond de la Commission Administrative, VM 001-3-2 0058 88. The chief of the Department of Public Safety, J.A.A. Belanger, also hired Arthur Leblanc as a member of Montreal's "secret service" for a month leading up to the Strike. Indeed, the City of Montreal had spies who reported on union meetings. AVM, Fond de la Commission Administrative, VM 001-3-2 0058 88. Note by Arthur Leblanc dated 13 December 1918; Médéric Martin to the President and Members of the Administrative Commission, 16 December 1918.

25 *La Patrie*, 11, 12, 13 December 1918; *Le Devoir*, 9, 10, 11, 12 December 1918; *Montreal Gazette*, 11, 12, 13 December 1918; In the late nineteenth century, the federal government had given railway constables powers like those of police, see Greg Marquis, *Policing Canada's Century: A History of the Canadian Association of Chiefs of Police* (Toronto: University of Toronto Press, 1993).

26 *Le Devoir*, 12, 13 December 1918; *Montreal Gazette*, 13 December 1918.

27 On the changing moods of crowds, see Radforth, "Playful Crowds," 133–64.

28 *Le Devoir*, 13 December 1918; *Montreal Gazette*, 13 December 1918.

29 *Le Devoir*, 13 December 1918; *La Patrie*, 13, 14 December 1918.

30 *Montreal Gazette*, 13 December 1918.

31 *Montreal Gazette*, 19 December 1918.

32 *Le Devoir*, 13 December 1918; *La Patrie*, 13 December 1918.

33 Magda Fahrni has examined the letters sent to the municipal government and Montreal Board of Health during the influenza pandemic. She found some evidence of anti-Semitism, usually from a few rival shopkeepers, but concluded that what is surprising is that there was not more ethnic scapegoating. Magda Fahrni, "'Respectfully Submitted': Citizens and Public Health Letter Writing during Montreal Influenza Epidemic, 1918–20," in *Epidemic Encounters: Influenza, Society, and Culture in Canada, 1918–20*, ed. Esyllt W. Jones and Magda Fahrni (Vancouver: UBC Press, 2012), 78.

34 *Montreal Gazette*, 13 December 1918 ; *Le Devoir*, 13 December 1918.

35 David B. Hanna, "Griffintown: Son Histoire et Son Cadre Bati. Ville de Montréal" (Service de la mise en valeur du territoire du patrimoine, 2007).

36 *La Patrie*, 13 December 1918 ; *Le Devoir*, 13 December 1918.

37 *Le Devoir*, 13 December 1918.

38 *Montreal Gazette*, 13 December 1918.

39 For women confronting scabs during the 1917 Montreal general garment workers strike, and on their refusal to disperse on the orders of police, see *Montreal Gazette*, 2 February 1917; on women strikers and strike supporters in Winnipeg, see Mary Horodyski, "Women and the Winnipeg General Strike," *Manitoba History* 11 (Spring 1986): 28–37.

40 *La Patrie*, 13 December 1918.

41 This had long been the case. See, for instance, Thomas Lineman, *Scabs and Traitors: Taboo, Violence, and Punishment in Labour Disputes in Britain, 1760–1871* (New York: Routledge, 2018).

42 *La Patrie*, 3 February 1919.

43 *Montreal Gazette*, 23, 24 April 1919.

44 *Le Devoir*, 13 December 1918.

45 *Montreal Gazette*, 14 December 1918.

46 *Montreal Gazette*, 14 December 1918.

47 *La Patrie*, 13 December 1918; *Montreal Gazette*, 14 December 1918.

48 He was also the author of a pamphlet against conscription. See Adélard Fortier, *The Economics of War* (Montréal: Le Devoir, 1917).

49 *Montreal Gazette*, 14 December 1918; *La Patrie*, 14 December 1918.

50 *Montreal Gazette*, 14 December 1918; *La Patrie*, 14 December 1918.

51 *La Patrie*, 20 December 1918; *Montreal Gazette*, 14 December 1918; *Le monde ouvrier/The Labor World*, 21 December 1918.

52 One prominent francophone exception was Gustave Francq.

53 For a good discussion on the emphasis on education, see Peter Campbell, *Canadian Marxists and the Search for a Third Way* (Montreal and Kingston: McGill-Queen's University Press, 2000).

54 See Craig Heron, ed., *The Workers' Revolt in Canada* (Toronto: University of Toronto Press, 1998); and Cal Winslow, *Radical Seattle: The General Strike of 1919* (New York: Monthly Review Press, 2020).

55 Geoffrey Ewen, "Quebec: Class and Ethnicity," in *Workers' Revolt in Canada*, 110–13.

56 Mark Osborne Humphries, "The Limits of Necessity: Public Health, Dissent, and the War Effort during the 1918 Influenza Pandemic," in *Epidemic Encounters*, 21–47; D. Ann Herring and Ellen Korol, "The North-South Divide: Social Inequality and Mortality from the 1918 Influenza Pandemic in Hamilton, Ontario," in *Epidemic Encounters*, 70–96; Esyllt W. Jones, *Influenza 1918: Disease, Death, and Struggle in Winnipeg* (Toronto: University of Toronto Press, 2007), 91–94.

57 *La Patrie*, 18 December 1918.

58 *La Patrie*, 20 December 1918; *Le monde ouvrier/The Labor World*, 21 December 1918.

59 *Award of the Board Appointed to Arbitrate as to Wages and Working Conditions with Respect to Employees of Montréal Police Department and Corporation of the City of Montreal* (Montreal: City of Montreal, 1919), 5.

60 See the exchanges between police union executive member Lieutenant Lanteigne and Montréal municipal councillors in AVM, Fond de la Commission Administrative, VM 001-3-2 0058 88, Résumé des questions et réponses posées et données lors de la séance de la Commission re: Département de Police, 20 December 1923, 17, 18, 24.

61 Slater, "Public Workers," 8. The argument resembles ones voiced today. See Matthew Cunningham-Cook, "The AFL-CIO's Police Union Problem Is Bigger Than You Think," *Intercept*, 18 June 2020.

62 *Justice*, 21 July 1921; Trades and Labour Congress of Canada, *Proceedings*, 1922, 58–60, 146; 1923, 44–45, 100; 1924, 48; 1925, 112; 1926, 49, 125; International Ladies Garment Workers Union, *Report*, 1924, 153.

63 *La Patrie*, 3 October 1919.

8

"Justice and Not Charity Should Be Your Demand!": Montreal's Unemployed and the Workers' Revolt

Benoit Marsan

At the end of the First World War working-class militancy increased across Canada, signalling a Workers' Revolt of which the Winnipeg General Strike was one emblematic moment. Riding this wave of protests, jobless people responded to massive unemployment by taking to the streets in the main industrial centres of the country.[1] According to the report of the 1919 Royal Commission on Industrial Relations (RCIR), "Unemployment and the fear of unemployment" was one of "the chief causes of unrest."[2] The postwar depression marked by the collapse of war-related production and soldiers' reentry into the labour market heralded a new era for jobless movements and marked a turning point in the politicization of male unemployment. By denouncing charity as a stopgap measure to combat unemployment and demanding work or full maintenance, the unemployed asked for jobs at a living wage or access to free goods and services. In doing so, they claimed access to some form of social citizenship that was denied to the Canadian working class.[3] Albeit not radical at first sight, the unemployed of the Workers' Revolt, not unlike the strikers in Winnipeg in 1919, challenged the uneven distribution of wealth and democracy among Canadian society.

After the armistice, as elsewhere in Canada, unemployed workers in Montreal organized and sought solutions to this employment crisis. As a result, the city was the scene of seasonal unemployment protests. Even if they fall outside the scope of labour relations, these actions were fundamental to the Workers' Revolt in both Quebec and Canada.

While the Labour Revolt in Quebec has been largely marginalized in Canadian and Québécois historiography, the postwar history of unemployment and of the unemployed has been almost completely ignored.[4] Through the example of Montreal, this chapter aims to demonstrate how the fight against unemployment is an integral part of the Workers' Revolt. It also claims that the postwar mobilization of the unemployed was the genesis of unemployed protests in Quebec and in Canada during the Great Depression.

Unemployment: A Social Problem Difficult to Politicize

Since the onset of industrialization, unemployment has been an important phenomenon. It is closely linked to the spread of wage labour and the overall working-class experience.[5] However, the "discovery" of unemployment occurred late in the history of capitalist development. In classical nineteenth-century liberal thought, poverty was understood as the result of the moral or personal failure of individuals.[6] From this perspective, the unemployed were not seen as working poor, victims of the capitalist economy, but as outcasts. Social recognition of unemployment is thus achieved when it is acknowledged as being a systemic issue linked to the structure of capitalism, rather than a merely individual problem. Consequently, discovering unemployment was a long, complex, and contested historical process. Even today, the definition of unemployment and who counts as unemployed are still subject to debate. As historian Matt Perry points out, this knowledge was "brought into the realm of public recognition and policy through two obviously connected factors: a critique of industrial capitalism and the protest of those threatened by unemployment,"[7] thus linking the problem of unemployment to the political organization of society.[8]

Today, historians such as Matt Perry and Matthias Reiss believe that the actual perception of unemployment evolved in four stages. The first stage culminated with the emerging predominance of free wage labour in contemporary society. The second stage brought about the bridging of the cultural gap linking unemployment's inception and its social recognition. Thirdly, the unemployed claimed recognition as being the focal actors in the process through their protests. Finally, after the initial recognition of unemployment, contention surrounding the phenomenon endured.[9] Of course, this process of appreciation was not homogeneous due to the uneven development of industrial capitalism, as well as the ideological contexts and the institutional frameworks that vary from one national environment to another. Such elements were also conditioned by the dynamics of gender, class, ethnicity, and citizenship. To various degrees, this relates to many factors such as the political programs of social, political, and economic actors, public policies administered by the state, social representations of unemployment and the unemployed, as well as the demands brought by their own struggles. There is, therefore, a dissonance between the materiality of unemployment and its perception.[10] As such, the definition of who is unemployed and who is entitled to receive relief or unemployment benefits fluctuates in time and space. On the other hand, wherever unemployment is socially recognized, it always factors "in the balance of power between capital and labour, a threat to those in work and a determinant of wages through the operation of labour markets."[11]

In Canada, the seasonal character of the economy and the large territory open to colonization blurred the true nature of unemployment well into the twentieth century. Also, the long process leading to the generalization of wage labour, especially with agricultural work as an important source of subsistence, tends to obscure unemployment until the interwar period.[12] From the fin de siècle until after the First World War, some municipalities across Canada offered temporary and discretionary measures to deal with major job market collapse such as public works, soup kitchens, shelters, or food vouchers. Until the Great Depression, these municipal policies were the main means of regulating joblessness during economic slumps. Following massive unemployed protests for work or bread across Canada in the first half of the 1930s, unemployment emerged more clearly from within the broader issue of poverty. In a context of an unprecedented level of joblessness, coupled with working-class movements to establish social citizenship, unemployment no longer appeared as an issue generated by moral deficiency or the destitution of individuals, but as a social issue linked to the political organization of society. These conjunctions of events led to permanent state-sponsored policies, such as unemployment insurance in 1940.[13]

In Quebec, the importance of the Catholic Church in the regulation of poverty further mystified the problem of unemployment. Historians Matt Perry and Matthias Reiss point out that "in Catholic countries, the construction of the poor as the dependent object of compassion and charity obstructed the social recognition of unemployment."[14] Within Catholic polities, the social condition of indigence was very hard to politicize. Unlike other Canadian provinces, the Poor Laws were never established in Quebec. Thus, houses of industry were a marginal phenomenon. Since the middle of the nineteenth century, the gigantic Catholic charity network showed little interest in workers who were able to work.[15] Based on a rigid understanding of the patriarchal family, the Québécois assistance was mainly offered to indigent persons unable to work and who could not rely on the support of a male breadwinner. In times of job scarcity, the unemployed thus had few alternatives. If they were heads of families with irreproachable Catholic morality, they were considered "deserving" of minimal material assistance from the Société Saint-Vincent-de-Paul and may even have qualified for occasional work on public work sites during economic crises. If they were single and homeless, the options were limited to a bed in the few shelters or in the common prison. Relocation was another alternative available to the poor as many left for the industrial cities of the northeastern United States or colonized areas in northern Quebec. This was a particularly rigorous liberal model of the governance of poverty.[16]

At the beginning of the twentieth century in Quebec and in Canada, the elites, the state, and a segment of organized labour perceived unemployment as a normal seasonal phenomenon. Also, nonemployment among able-bodied men was largely seen by the same demographic as the result of a bad work ethic and a lack of foresightedness, thus a matter of individual responsibility. Many feared that assistance to these workers would encourage laziness. As a result, no large-scale measure to counter unemployment was in place in 1918. With the descent of the postwar depression, thousands of jobless Canadian and Québécois had few options for survival. Responding to this dire perspective, the unemployed in Montreal, as elsewhere in the country, would challenge the state and claim their rights.

The Workers' Revolt in Quebec

Apart from historian Geoffrey Ewen, no scholar has specifically studied the Workers' Revolt in Quebec.[17] However, some labour historians allude to the era as a catalyst of workers' militancy. This is notably the case with Bernard Dansereau's research on the Montreal workers' movement in the 1920s, Mathieu Houle-Courcelles' One Big Union (OBU) history in Quebec, and Jacques Rouillard's work devoted to the history of unionism in the province.[18]

The historiography generally situates the Québécois Labour Revolt as occurring between 1919 and 1921 and suggests that, although it reflected similar causes and aspirations as elsewhere in Canada, it did not gain the strength and momentum observed in other areas.[19] Dansereau notes that this event "illustre une volonté d'affirmation ouvrière" was underlined by unemployment, the high cost of living, and the returning soldiers, all of which undermined living and working conditions for many workers, who consequently turned to union organizing as a mean to improve their plight. If at the beginning the "mouvement ouvrier présente des aspects défensifs, il se transforme en un gigantesque mouvement de contestation sociale qui fait trembler bien des élites bourgeoises."[20] Although Quebec's trade union historiography recognizes that during this period workers expressed a desire for profound social change, the focus has been primarily on the record number of strikes, and, apart from Ewen, labour historians have mostly overlooked revolts that occurred outside of the workplace.[21]

The historiography also asserts that the agitation remained largely confined to Montreal. The working class of the metropolis benefited from a diverse ethnic base, less direct manipulation from the Catholic Church, and an established labour movement that thwarted the rise of clergy-controlled unions formed to undermine the propagation of international unionism in the province—conditions that were largely absent from the more homogeneous, conservative, Catholic strongholds outside of the city. However, in the end, the ideological, political, gender, religious, and linguistic divisions would also play a major role in curbing the Workers' Revolt in Montreal.[22]

Finally, although the agitation in the province was channelled primarily through the established international unions, Quebec's workers in the postwar era, like those elsewhere, widened their purview to include electoral politics and public protests.[23] The expanded tactics and sites of struggle of a new wave of socialist activists fuelled political and ideological clashes with traditional trade union leaders. Supporting the Winnipeg Strike, expressing sympathy with revolutionary moments in Europe, adopting industrial unionism and the general strike as a tactic, and even the value of organizing the unemployed were among the issues debated by traditional trade unionists and those inspired by the postwar revolutionary moment.[24]

Unemployment, Social Order, and the Royal Commission on Industrial Relations

Although the historians of the period state that unemployment was one of the main causes of the Workers' Revolt in Canada, few have specifically examined the unemployed in the postwar era.[25] According to historian David A. Thompson, apart from the Winnipeg General Strike and the Cape Breton strikes, unemployment protests constituted the main threat to the post-1918 liberal order.[26] With the end of the war, the job shortage was exacerbated by the closure of ammunition factories and the returning soldiers. Montreal, the country's metropolis, was particularly affected. Estimates are that the city's wintertime joblessness grew from 20,000 in 1918–19, to 25,000 the following year, and to 40,000 in 1921–22.[27]

In Montreal, on the morning of 7 January 1919, a crowd of 900 jobless workers gathered in front of the Vickers factory. They chanted, "'Nous voulons du travail. Nous voulons du pain !'"[28] These scenes were not uncommon in the city during that month; hundreds of unemployed congregated every day in front of the city's main mills.[29] The situation was particularly tense and many dreaded further troubles. These fears were widely reported in Montreal major daily papers and in the trade union press.[30]

Moreover, for many political and labour leaders and commentators of the period, the spread of unemployment was directly related to the rise of postwar workers' radicalism. The revolutionary sympathies among the militant unemployed in Montreal were considered by many as a harbinger of political upheaval. For Charles Marcil, a Quebec federal Liberal member of Parliament, "the need to take prompt measures to deal with this problem is imminent and the federal, provincial and municipal authorities should give this matter serious consideration, with a view to providing work for the unemployed so that they may have food for themselves and their families. Idleness breeds mischiefs, and Bolshevism is very likely to flourish under such conditions."[31] Those views were also shared by the leaders of the Montreal Trades and Labour Council (MTLC). According to T.J. Foster, the council's president, "Le manque d'emploi amène la pauvreté et la pauvreté amène le mécontentement et le mécontentement amène les révolutions."[32] For Joseph Gauthier, the MTLC vice-president, "Si l'on veut empêcher que les événements qui se sont produits dans la vieille Europe, notamment en Russie, se répètent ici, on doit donner du travail à ceux qui en demandent."[33]

Those fears must be understood in the context of the Red Scare that took shape in Quebec and Canada at the end of the war and that was linked to the ongoing worldwide working-class unrest.[34] It is true that European revolutions were gaining sympathizers in some workers' circles in Montreal, especially among immigrants.[35] However, this radical political imaginary was not confined to close-knit ethnic groups. The unemployed movement itself facilitated a revolutionary class consciousness that was multiethnic and diverse, and that included Canadian and British-born workers. This can be seen in the major jobless assemblies and protests, among which there was a high proportion of unemployed Anglo-Canadians and French Canadians. The leadership of the unemployed movement also indicates these upheavals were not an "immigrant" problem, but rather reflected the cultural, religious, and linguistic diversity of Montreal's working class. Some of these activists also constituted the nucleus of the OBU in Montreal.[36] Albert Saint-Martin[37] and Gaston Pilon[38] were main figures advocating socialism in almost every unemployed French-Canadian movement in Montreal until the middle of the 1930s.[39]

From 26 April to 13 June, the members of the RCIR toured industrial Canada, visiting twenty-eight cities from Victoria to Sydney and examining a total of 486 witnesses.[40] According to their report published in July 1919, unemployment was the first cause of the revolt. The commissioners explained: "We have placed unemployment first because we found that there was the greatest unrest where there were the most unemployed."[41]

During the Montreal hearings, from 29 to 31 May 1919, the issue of unemployment was indeed an important feature of several testimonies. To illustrate the huge number of unemployed in Montreal and in the country, James Arthur Woodward, the president of the Montreal branch of the Brotherhood of Railroad Trainman, reported: "This time last year I don't believe there was any unemployment in the city of Montreal, or any other city of Canada. There was a law on the statute book, made by Order-in-Council that if a man was unemployed he was liable to be arrested and put in jail. That Order-in-Council has since been done away with, and perhaps it is just as well, because if it had been, we would have to build more jails with the thousands and thousands of men out of work at the present time."[42] Harry Olive, the representative of the International Brick Layers Union, told the commissioners that "we are of the opinion that the unemployment question has got to do with the labor unrest."[43] As for the MTLC, it was of the opinion that "the continuous depreciation of the purchasing power of the dollar and the ever present bogey of unemployment can be designated as among the fundamental causes of unrest."[44]

Taking seriously that unemployment posed a threat to public order, the RCIR report recommended a series of measures to alleviate it, including the establishment of unemployment insurance.[45] Along with the ongoing protests of unemployed workers in the first half of the 1920s, the debate surrounding unemployment insurance became a political issue as never before across Canada. Many actors, ranging from left and labour organizations to government authorities, studied and debated the matter throughout the decade.[46] In the end, the state opted for repression over protection, and it took over twenty years and massive unemployed protests during the 1930s for the state to provide welfare relief for those without work.

"L'heure des pétitions est passée, il faut des actes": Unemployed Protests in Montreal, 1919–1922

The first stage of unemployed revolt in Montreal occurred between December 1918 and April 1919 and was characterized by the organization of mass meetings as well as representations to the authorities. Those actions were undertaken primarily by construction trade unions, the MTLC, the Labour Party of Canada (LPC), labour clubs, and socialist groups. Some assemblies were attended by up to 2,000 people. Compared to the following winters, newspapers reported that there were many working-class women in attendance, though few spoke out, and one senses the movement was dominated by men.[47] At these events,

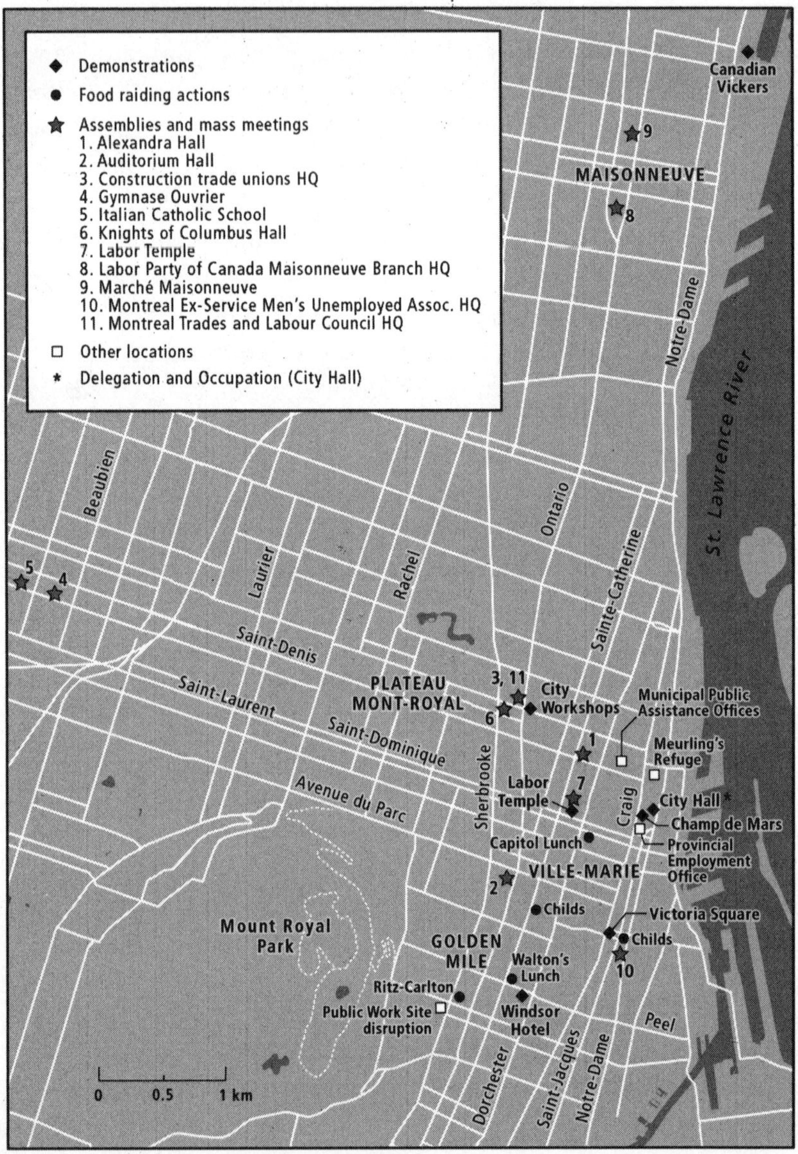

Figure 8.1. Sites of unemployed mobilizations in Montreal. Source: Erin Greb Cartography.

the unemployed denounced the use of charity to counter unemployment and instead asked for the reduction of working hours and massive work projects sponsored by municipal, provincial, and federal governments. The gatherings were also marked by disagreements between socialists and trade unionists about the nature of their demands, the organization of the unemployed, and the means of action.

As a sign that radicalism was gaining ground among the working class, many speakers held capitalism responsible for unemployment and decried the inherent injustice of the economic system. For example, *La Presse* reported on the speech of Mrs. S. Larocque[48] at an unemployed meeting held in the premises of the construction unions on 19 January 1919: "Elle dit qu'il y a actuellement 25.000 hommes sans emploi, et, par conséquent, sans salaire, à Montréal. Elle fit de violentes sorties contre le système social actuel."[49]

Sympathies expressed toward the Russian and German revolutions were also a common feature of these assemblies. At an eventful mass meeting convened by the MTLC on 23 January at the Knights of Columbus Hall on Sherbrooke Street, the meeting evinced its solidarity with the global upheaval: "Les auditeurs se sont dispersés en chantant l'Internationale. D'autres criaient : Vive Trotzky . . . Vive Lénine . . . Vive le bolchevisme. . . ."[50] The day after, at an assembly at the Alexandra Hall, Edmond Simard[51] declared: "'Dans le monde entier . . . les ouvriers s'organisent et montrent au grand jour la puissance dont ils disposent. Faisons comme les ouvriers russes, secouons le joug des capitalistes, et faisons valoir nos droits.'"[52] On 26 January, at yet another public gathering, this time at the labour temple, Albert Saint-Martin and other speakers expressed their sympathies toward Lenin, Bolshevism, and the Russian Revolution. For Saint-Martin, there were few alternatives beyond starvation or rebellion for the unemployed of Quebec: "'Notre province de Québec est l'un des pays les plus riches au monde . . . et cependant, on y laisse des malheureux mourir de faim, parce qu'on a pas de travail à faire. . . . Le sans-travail . . . doit choisir entre ces quatre alternatives: ou se trouver de l'ouvrage; ou aller mendier; ou se faire voleur; ou bien se servir de la torche ou de la baïonnette!'"[53]

During the winter of 1919, Montreal's socialists, most of them active members of the local branch of the LPC, encouraged the unemployed to form their own committees and to resort to direct action. They also warned the unemployed not to trust the leadership of the MTLC. To fulfill these objectives, the Montreal Unemployed Committee (MUC) was founded on 24 January during a mass meeting. Elected onto the central committee were Étienne, Gaston Pilon, Edmond Simard, Thibodeau, Hart, Rosenbaum, and Isidore Boltuck.[54] The program of the organization appeared in their pamphlet entitled *To the Unemployed*, which was printed in both French and English and distributed in unemployed mass meetings during the month of January. It was also reprinted by the Social Democratic Party of Canada and circulated at rallies of the unemployed elsewhere in the country.[55]

The MUC declaration called on Montreal's unemployed to organize and take matters into their own hands: "All who don't work should make one big organization. Then if your landlord wants to put you out, because you have not paid your rent, your Union will stand by you and keep out the bailiff of whoever wants to evict you. If you have no food, your organization should find a way of getting food for you. . . . A man may be unemployed, but his stomach does not know it, and every man who is willing to work and cannot get a job, must get food and shelter, or our present economic system has no reason to exist."[56] For the MUC and its partisans, the only immediate solution to alleviate unemployment was the establishment of the six-hour day and the five-day week. To achieve this goal, they called upon sincere trade unionists to demonstrate their solidarity with the unemployed through concrete actions and by calling a general strike. The document concluded with the following slogans: "Justice and not charity should be your demand! Do not petition or beg as [a] slave, but organize and state your demand as men!"[57]

For Montreal's mainstream press, the involvement of socialists in unemployed meetings was concrete proof that Bolshevism was spreading in the city. The main leaders of the MTLC also felt the presence of socialists undermined their authority. They called for restraint, denounced the speeches of socialists, and asked the unemployed to trust them as their representatives lobbying the authorities.[58] MTLC president T.J. Foster was greeted with heckles by the unemployed at a mass meeting on 23 January, when he declared that "we are here not to inflame, and if I thought that anyone else was here for that purpose, I would call the meeting off. . . . We want simply and coolly to analyze the situation. . . . I am not an extremist, and I hope there is not anyone here who is."[59] Four days later at another assembly, replying to those who advocated direct action, Foster cautioned: "While it is an easy thing to advise men to go into a restaurant and eat without paying the bill, or to jump on a street car without taking a ticket, yet that sort of thing will not get you far: usually you get the other end of the stick. We prefer to try some sane and constructive methods by taking collective action which will bring pressure to bear on the Government, and which, though it may not completely solve the problem, will at least help to alleviate the distress."[60] During the winter of 1919, the MTLC lobbied all levels of governments to undertake immediate large public work projects and to establish the eight-hour day.[61]

With spring on the horizon, like every year, the unemployment situation improved somewhat, and the issue of unemployment gave way to sectorial strike actions as well as the debates about organizing the new OBU and whether to strike in support of the Winnipeg General Strike.[62] Even though the unemployment protests did not resume until December 1920, the questions and clashes of 1919 within Montreal's workers' movement set the tone and the framework for the upcoming years.

Agitation among the jobless workers reemerged in December 1920. This time the unemployed Anglo-Canadian veterans were at the forefront of the movement through the Montreal Ex-Service Men's Unemployed Association (MEMUA), at least until the organization ousted its "Red" elements following threats of reprisal by the Montreal authorities.[63] Subsequently, the OBU created a rival organization of the unemployed which broadened and reinvigorated the movement beyond the ex-soldiers by creating French and English sections.[64] Compared to the 1919 organization of jobless workers, the 1920 and 1921 mobilization was not confined to mass meetings and delegations. Patrick-J. Reid, a leader of the unemployed ex-servicemen and a member of the One Big Union, argued that "the time for delegations and talk was ended, and that the only way in which the unemployed could get a square deal was by relying upon themselves and not upon some Moses to lead them out of the wilderness."[65]

From December 1920 to February 1921, direct actions by the unemployed included the occupation of city hall,[66] the disruption of public work sites,[67] and food raiding in Montreal restaurants.[68] The unemployed thus denounced not only the city's condescending measures in general terms, but also highlighted the poor conditions at the

Meurling Municipal Refuge and the inadequate municipal relief projects. They also decried that they were required to register at the police stations and submit themselves to investigation. They demanded cash relief for male unemployed and the elimination of relief investigations. Besides targeting municipal government, they called for intervention from Ottawa, arguing that the province was ignoring the plight of Montreal's unemployed. On 19 January 1921, a delegation of the MEMUA met in Ottawa with the federal minister of labour, Senator Gideon Robertson. A delegate, J.T. Thompson, "complained that the civic authorities of Montreal were shelving the problem of caring for the needy unemployed to the shoulders of religious and benevolent organizations... Returned men were not looking for charity, but they felt, if it was impossible to get work, they should be given relief as a right."[69] Although city authorities did not provide cash relief, they conceded some ground to the unemployed after the first food raids. They offered to hire all unemployed veterans on public work, promised a change in the registration process, and agreed to provide more direct relief and also to serve three meals a day instead of two at the Meurling shelter.[70]

But for the more radical elements of the MEMUA, those concessions were far from enough. In solidarity with recently discharged municipal employees, they refused the work offered.[71] They also invoked for the first time in Montreal the notion of work or full maintenance. Aware that Winnipeg's unemployed had just gained $7.00 per week for a single man, $12.00 a week for a married man, as well as $2.00 for every child, and rent payment for all, MEMUA demanded equivalent treatment.[72] The city representatives refused these modest requests outright. In February, following a second wave of food raiding in restaurants and the expression of sympathies toward the Russian Revolution in meetings and demonstrations, the municipal authorities opted for repression. They argued that public order and private property were being threatened by unemployed protests. Activists were arrested after the 22 February raid on Child's restaurant; all were released except for P.J. Reid who was incarcerated for three months on vagrancy charges. Despite the efforts of the OBU unemployed committee, Reid was deported to Ireland after serving his sentence.[73]

The MTLC proved even more cautious during the 1920 and 1921 unrest. Refusing to be associated with the rowdiness of the unemployed, the council dissociated itself from the movement at the first street demonstration.[74] Although it condemned direct action and food raiding, the council newspaper, *The Labor World*, conceded that "sacred property being threatened, the city officials acted. . . . It began to give work and relief. Men wanting work were given an opportunity and were paid every night. And the red tape concerning unemployed relief was abolished. . . . [This] would not have been brought about had not the hunger-smitten committed the illegal acts of food raiding."[75]

The deportation of Reid and the repression that followed the food raid undermined later attempts by the OBU to organize the unemployed. In the third and final revival of unemployment activism in Montreal during the period of the Workers' Revolt, the fledgling Communist Party of Canada (CPC) entered the fray. Supporters of the CPC founded the Montreal Unemployed Workers' Association (MUWA), which subsequently affiliated with the National Committee of Unemployed Workers, a mass organization of the party.[76] The MUWA held its first mass meeting on 15 January 1922 at Marché Maisonneuve. Charity measures were once again denounced by speakers. The assembly declared itself in favour of work, a weekly unemployment allowance, and rental subsidies. With massive unemployment in the city, a structural condition caused by no fault of their own, the unemployed attending the meeting considered their demands as a legitimate right, not a form of charity. However, despite calls for demonstrations and the convening of a subsequent meeting on the Champ de Mars, there was no repeat of the direct actions of the winter of 1920 and 1921.[77] In line with the CPC's strategy of "boring from within" the existing trade unions, MUWA, unlike its MUC and OBU predecessors, joined forces with the MTLC. By doing so, the communist activists allowed the conservative elements within the MTLC to dictate a policy of delegations and hierarchical leadership that neutralized the power of disruption by the unemployed. Until 1924, MUWA's political activities were limited to composing reports on unemployment in the city and lobbying authorities for relief and public work.[78]

Not everyone was content with MUWA's conservative turn. Opposed to the CPC strategy of organizing the unemployed in collaboration with the MTLC, Albert Saint-Martin and a few trade union organizers called for the formation of a new organization in March 1922. This would lead to the founding of la Ligue des sans-travail (LST) by Albert Saint-Martin and a group of French-Canadian unemployed, in the very next month.[79] This organization mustered a few rallies and demonstrations that mobilized hundreds of unemployed on the Champ de Mars at the end of the winter.[80] A Red Army of the unemployed was also symbolically formed and paraded a few times in front of city hall.[81] The LST, like its predecessors, continued to denounce the increase in municipal funding to charitable organizations that help the unemployed, instead of increases in work and cash relief.[82] In the organizers' speeches, the unemployment crisis was blamed on the capitalist system. They also encouraged the unemployed to follow the example of Russian workers and take control of industries in order to remedy the situation.[83] However, with the arrival of summer, the protests faded and the LST disappeared. In the following years, sporadic demonstrations against unemployment could be seen here and there in the city, mostly during wintertime, but nothing of the magnitude of the years of the Workers' Revolt. One must wait for the 1930s to see unemployed protests return to the forefront of Montreal's political landscape.

Conclusion

Like other large cities in Canada, Montreal was the scene of unemployed demonstrations during the Workers' Revolt. Although these demonstrations were not a new phenomenon in the city,[84] they represented a new era for unemployed protests. First, compared to the previous uprisings of Montreal's workless, the postwar mobilization of the unemployed relied on what historian Matt Perry has called the three repertoires of protest available to the workless: "transgressive" (food raiding and occupations), "intermediary" (disruptions of public work and demonstrations), and "non-transgressive" (public meetings, petitioning, representations and cooperative/self-help activity) means.[85] Second, in contrast to the prewar outbursts of the unemployed, these actions were increasingly organized. Third, the commitment to organization meant the unemployed protests in Montreal during the Workers' Revolt cannot be dismissed as mere riots; their organizations, albeit short-lived, helped to build solidarities and provide a collective meaning to unemployment that countered the individualizing prescriptions and the blame levelled against them by the state. Fourth, although their actions were still local in nature, they targeted not just the local authorities, but also demanded that provincial and federal governments assume responsibility for the problem of unemployment. These developments prefigured the unemployed protests of the 1930s.

Regardless of these evolutions, the protests also had their limits. Although socialist activists played a key role in their configuration, as the case of Montreal exemplifies, the movement was structured, for the most part, around modest economic demands for "Bread or Work." Despite a revolutionary imaginary inspired by the Russian Revolution of 1917, it failed to articulate a coherent and consistent social critique of work and unemployment within capitalist society. For example, the movement did not question the foundations of the wage system, nor did it conceive of unemployment as anything other than a male problem. Finally, notwithstanding the creation of new solidarities at a small-scale level within Montreal's working class, the important ethnic, religious, linguistic, and gender divisions that existed within Quebec society were still too strong to allow for a greater extension of the revolt of the unemployed in Quebec.

Even so, by denouncing the economic insecurity of joblessness and claiming the right to have access to decent jobs or to proper unemployment relief, jobless workers shared the global working-class aspirations of the Workers' Revolt, including a more equitable distribution of wealth and further democratic rights. Their actions on the streets echoed the workers on the picket line in Winnipeg and elsewhere in the country by offering a challenge to the political and economic organization of Canadian society. In occupying public spaces through demonstrations, mass meetings, and direct actions, the unemployed in Montreal showed that unemployment was not an individual problem, but a structural one. By rejecting charity and putting forward the concept of "Work or Full Maintenance," they outlined the contradictions of a social and economic system based on profit. They also anticipated the 1930s demand for state-sponsored, noncontributory unemployment insurance. The collective agency of the workless contributed to making unemployment an increasingly political issue in the context of the interwar years.

Even if Montreal's unemployed only managed to obtain a few immediate gains during the winter of 1920 and 1921, they nonetheless contributed to addressing the male unemployment problem at the local level. It was the spectre of their unrest that compelled the city to offer winter public works or an unemployment relief fund, distributed by faith-based charitable organizations, until the end of the economic crisis in 1925. Of course, the state's measures were wholly inadequate in tackling the recurring unemployment problem in Montreal during the 1920s. Coupled with other protests taking place elsewhere in Canada, the Montreal unemployed movement of the period allowed the discussion surrounding unemployment to make its way past the local level. After the RCIR recommended the introduction of a federal unemployment insurance scheme in 1919, the proposal became a matter of heated debate in Ottawa in the first half of the 1920s.[86] In the context of the economic crisis taking place between 1921 and 1925 and in response to the mounting demands of the unemployed, the municipal and provincial authorities pressured the federal government to finance temporary relief measures and public work schemes to alleviate unemployment. Indeed, although the poor had to wait until 1940 for the adoption of the Unemployment Insurance Act, the debate surrounding state responsibility for unemployment began with the growing agency of the workless during the Workers' Revolt.

Notes

1 David A. Thompson, "Working-Class Anguish and Revolutionary Indignation: The Making of Radical and Socialist Unemployment Movements in Canada, 1875–1928" (PhD diss., Queen's University, 2014).

2 Royal Commission on Industrial Relations, *Report of Commission*, 1919: 6, http://publications.gc.ca/collections/collection_2016/bcp-pco/Z1-1919-2-eng.pdf.

3 Benoit Marsan, "Des droits et non la charité: les sans-emploi, les secours et la citoyenneté à Montréal pendant la Grande Dépression," in *Question sociale et citoyenneté: Perspectives internationales*, ed. Martin Petitclerc, et al. [forthcoming].

4 The important exception is Geoffrey Ewen, "The International Unions and the Workers' Revolt in Quebec, 1914–1925" (PhD diss., York University, 1998); Geoffrey Ewen, "Quebec: Class and Ethnicity," in *The Worker's Revolt in Canada, 1917–1925*, ed. Craig Heron (Toronto: University of Toronto Press, 1998), 87–143.

5 Peter Baskerville and Eric W. Sager, *Unwilling Idlers: The Urban Unemployed and Their Families in Late Victorian Canada* (Toronto: University of Toronto Press, 1998); Richard Croucher, "The History of Unemployed Movements," *Labour History Review* 73, no. 1 (2008): 1–17; Mike Davis, *Planet of Slums* (New York: Verso, 2007); Michael Denning, "Wageless Life," *New Left Review* 66 (2010): 19–79; Alexander Keyssar, *Out of Work: The First Century of Unemployment in Massachusetts* (New York: Cambridge University Press, 1986); Bryan D. Palmer and Gaétan Héroux, *Toronto's Poor, A Rebellious History* (Toronto: Between the Lines, 2016), Matthias Reiss and

Matt Perry, ed., *Unemployment and Protest: New Perspectives on Two Centuries of Contention* (New York: Oxford University Press, 2011).

6 Mitchell Dean, *The Constitution of Poverty: Toward a Genealogy of Liberal Governance* (1991; repr., New York: Routledge, 2011).

7 Matt Perry, *Bread and Work: Social Policy and the Experience of Unemployment, 1918–1939* (London: Pluto Press, 2000), 23.

8 Matt Perry, *Prisoners of Want: The Experience and Protest of the Unemployed in France, 1921–45* (Aldershot, UK: Ashgate, 2007), 5.

9 Matt Perry and Matthias Reiss, "Beyond Marienthal: Understanding Movements of the Unemployed," in *Unemployment and Protest: New Perspectives on Two Centuries of Contention*, ed. Matthias Reiss and Matt Perry (Oxford: Oxford University Press, 2011), 13–14. See also John A. Garraty, *Unemployment in History: Economic Thought and Public Policy* (New York: Harper and Row, 1978).

10 Perry and Reiss, "Beyond Marienthal," 10–18; Florence Loriaux, ed., *Le chômeur suspect: histoire d'une stigmatisation* (Brussels: CARHOP-CRISP, 2015).

11 Perry and Reiss, "Beyond Marienthal," 14.

12 Baskerville and Sager, *Unwilling Idlers*; François Bisson, "L'État et le placement des chômeurs au Québec, les premiers bureaux d'emploi publics, 1909–1932" (PhD diss., Université du Québec à Montréal, 2007), 13; Lara Campbell, *Respectable Citizens: Gender, Family, and Unemployment in Ontario's Great Depression* (Toronto: University of Toronto Press, 2009); Michael Ekers, "'The Dirty Stuff': Relief and the Production of the Unemployed in Depression-Era British Columbia," *Antipode* 44, no. 4 (2012): 1119–42; Alvin Finkel, *Social Policy and Practice in Canada: A History* (Waterloo, ON: Wilfrid Laurier University Press, 2006); James Struthers, *No Fault of Their Own: Unemployment and the Canadian Welfare State, 1914–1941* (Toronto: University of Toronto Press, 1983); Eric Strikwerda, *The Wages of Relief: Cities and the Unemployed in Prairie Canada, 1929–39* (Edmonton: Athabasca University Press, 2013).

13 Campbell, *Respectable Citizens*; Marsan, "Des droits et non la charité"; Bryan D. Palmer, *Canada's 1960s: The Ironies of Identity in a Rebellious Era* (Toronto: University of Toronto Press, 2009): 212–13; Struthers, *No Fault of Their Own*.

14 Perry and Reiss, "Beyond Marienthal," 14.

15 Janice Harvey, "Dealing with 'the Destitute and the Wretched': The Protestant House of Industry and Refuge in Nineteenth-Century Montreal," *Journal of the Canadian Historical Association* 12, no. 1 (2001): 73–94.

16 Jean-Marie Fecteau, *La liberté du pauvre: Crime et pauvreté au XIXe siècle québécois* (Montreal: VLB éditeur, 2004); Martin Petitclerc, "À propos de 'ceux qui sont en dehors de la société': L'indigent et l'assistance publique au Québec dans la première moitié du XXe siècle," *Revue d'histoire de l'Amérique française* 65, no. 2–3 (2011/2012): 227–56.

17 Ewen, "International Unions and the Workers' Revolt"; Ewen, "Quebec: Class and Ethnicity."

18 Bernard Dansereau, "Le mouvement ouvrier montréalais, 1918–1929: structure et conjoncture" (PhD diss., Université de Montréal, 2000); Mathieu Houle-Courcelles, "'Une Grande Union pour tous les travailleurs': la One Big Union au Québec (1919–1929)" (MA thesis, Université Laval, 2013); Jacques Rouillard, *Histoire du syndicalisme québécois* (Montreal: Boréal, 1989); Jacques Rouillard, *Le syndicalisme québécois: deux siècles d'histoire* (Montreal: Boréal, 2004).

19 Craig Heron, ed., *The Workers' Revolt in Canada, 1917–1925* (Toronto: University of Toronto Press, 1998).

20 Dansereau, "Le mouvement ouvrier montréalais," 4.

21 Ewen, "International Unions and the Workers' Revolt"; Rouillard, *Histoire du syndicalisme Québécois*, 147–50.

22 Ewen, "Quebec: Class and Ethnicity," 131–33.

23 Ewen, "International Unions and the Workers' Revolt."

24 Dansereau, "Le mouvement ouvrier montréalais"; Ewen, " International Unions and the Workers' Revolt"; Houle-Courcelles, "Une Grande Union pour tous les travailleurs"; Rouillard, *Histoire du syndicalisme québécois*; Rouillard, *Le syndicalisme québécois*.

25 In his work on the Workers' Revolt, Ewen addresses the unemployed mobilizations in Montreal at the beginning of the war. As for Houle-Courcelles, he underlines the involvement of the One Big Union among the unemployed in Montreal during the winter of 1921. Only Thompson provides a detailed history of unemployed protests in Canada in that era and analyzes this issue in the aftermath of the Royal Commission on Industrial Relations. Ewen, "Quebec: Class and Ethnicity"; Houle-Courcelles, "Une Grande Union pour tous les travailleurs"; Thompson, "Working-Class Anguish and Revolutionary Indignation."

26 Thompson, "Working-Class Anguish and Revolutionary Indignation," 311.

27 "La crise du chômage," *Presse*, 12 December 1920, 4; "Le problème des ouvriers sans travail," *Presse*, 28 January 1919, 7; "Sees Unemployed Problem Serious," *Gazette*, 28 January 1919, 3; "Une nouvelle crise est-elle possible l'hiver prochain à Montréal ?," *Presse*, 18 September 1922, 6.

28 "900 ouvriers demandent du travail," *Patrie*, 7 January 1919, 2.

29 "100,000 sans-travail dans la Métropole," *Patrie*, 17 January 1919, 3.

30 "Chroniques municipales," *Devoir*, 18 January 1919, 1; "Le problème des ouvriers sans travail"; "Sees Unemployed Problem Serious"; "La crise du travail," *Presse*, 27 January 1919, 4; "Les ouvriers font de nombreuses demandes," *Devoir*, 31 January 1919, 3; "Le mouvement ouvrier," *Le monde ouvrier/The Labor World*, 8 March 1919, 1; Julien Saint-Michel [Eva Circé-Côté], "Les sans-travail," *Monde ouvrier/Labor World*, 22 February 1919, 1.

31 "Sees Unemployed Problem Serious."

32 "L'heure des pétitions est passée, il faut des actes," *Canada*, 24 January 1919, 8 and 3.

33 Ibid.

34 Daniel Francis, *Seeing Reds: The Red Scare of 1918–1919, Canada's First War on Terror* (Vancouver: Arsenal Pulp Press, 2010); Mathieu Houle-Courcelles, "Censure et surveillance de la presse socialiste au Québec (1918–1920): le cas du journal Labor et de son éditeur Isidore Boltuck," *Bulletin d'histoire politique* 24, no. 3 (2016): 34–50; Ian McKay, *Reasoning Otherwise: Leftists and the People's Enlightenment in Canada, 1890–1920* (Toronto: Between the Lines, 2008); Dennis G. Molinaro, *An Exceptional Law: Section 98 and the Emergency State, 1919–1936* (Toronto: University of Toronto Press, 2017); Reg Whitaker and Gregory S. Kealey, *Secret Service: Political Policing in Canada from the Fenians to Fortress America* (Toronto: University of Toronto Press, 2012); Barry Wright, Eric Tucker, and Susan Binnie, eds., *Security, Dissent, and the Limits of Toleration in War and Peace, 1914–1939* (Toronto: Toronto University Press, 2015).

35 Donald Avery, *"Dangerous foreigners": European Immigrant Workers and Labour Radicalism in Canada: 1896–1932* (Toronto: McClelland and Stewart, 1979); Dansereau, "Le mouvement ouvrier montréalais"; Ewen, "International Unions and the Workers' Revolt"; McKay, *Reasoning Otherwise.*

36 Houle-Courcelles, "Une Grande Union pour tous les travailleurs."

37 Albert Saint-Martin (1865–1947), stenographer, translator, and clerk at Montreal's municipal courthouse, is arguably the most well-known French-Canadian socialist activist figure of his period. He joined the Socialist Party of Canada in 1907 and the Social Democratic Party of Canada (SDPC) after 1911. He was an active member of the OBU in Montreal between 1919 and 1921. From 1920 to 1922, he taught political economy to French-Canadian workers at Montreal Labor College. He refused to join the Communist Party of Canada and tried in vain to have an independent francophone organization affiliated to the Third International in 1923. In 1925, he founded l'Université Ouvrière (l'UO), an essential institution among radical French-Canadian workers until 1935. Through organizations such as the Labour Party of Canada (LPC), SDPC, OBU, la Ligue des sans-travail, l'UO, le mouvement Spartacus, and l'Association humanitaire, Albert Saint-Martin advocated on the behalf of the unemployed from 1914 until the mid-1930s. Fiercely anticlerical, he was harassed by the Catholic Church and prosecuted by provincial authorities for blasphemous libel in the 1930s. In 1933, he was beaten by a fascist mob in the streets of Montreal. He wrote two controversial pamphlets entitled *T'as Menti* (1920) and *Sandwiches à la « shouashe »* (1933). Claude Larivière, *Albert St-Martin, militant d'avant-garde (1865–1947)* (Laval, QC: Éditions coopératives Albert St-Martin, 1979).

38 Gaston Pilon was a freethinker and a socialist activist. He was active in the Montreal branch of the LPC before joining the ranks of the OBU in 1919. Alongside Albert Saint-Martin, he played an essential role in the unemployed movement in Montreal until the 1930s. One of the well-known figures of l'UO, in the 1930s he attracted many French-Canadian workers to his conferences where he made violently colourful anticlerical speeches. In 1934, he was condemned for blasphemous libel against the Catholic Church. In a surprising twist while in jail for this charge, he converted to Catholicism and afterward began propaganda campaigns against communism and his former comrades. Andrée Lévesque, "Red Scares and Repression in Quebec, 1919–39," in *Security, Dissent, and the Limits of Toleration in War and Peace, 1914–1939*, 305.

39 Dansereau, "Le mouvement ouvrier montréalais"; Ewen, "International Unions and the Workers' Revolt"; Larivière, *Albert St-Martin*; Andrée Lévesque, *Virage à gauche interdit: les communistes, les socialistes et leurs ennemis au Québec 1929–1939* (Montreal: Boréal Express, 1984); Lévesque, "Red Scares and Repression."

40 Gregory S. Kealey, "1919: The Canadian Labour Revolt," *Labour/Le Travail*, no. 13 (1984): 11.

41 Royal Commission on Industrial Relations, *Report of Commission*, 6.

42 Commission to Inquire into and Report upon Industrial Relations in Canada fonds, Evidence, Montreal, Quebec, 29 May 1919, Library and Archives Canada [LAC], RG33-95, 246–47.

43 Ibid., 30 May 1919, 468.

44 Ibid., 29 May 1919, 216.

45 Royal Commission on Industrial Relations, *Report of Commission.*

46 Thompson, "Working-Class Anguish and Revolutionary Indignation."

47 "On recommande du calme, de l'ordre et du sang-froid," *Presse*, 20 January 1919, 9; "La journée de six heures et cinq jours de travail," *Presse*, 24 January 1919, 11.

48 Mrs. S. Larocque was a socialist and the secretary of the club ouvrier Saint-Édouard. She was also a leader of the Montreal branch of the LPC. Joining in 1919, she was among the first partisans of the OBU in Montreal. Dansereau, "Le mouvement ouvrier montréalais," 147 and 172.

49 "On recommande du calme, de l'ordre et du sang-froid."

50 "Le bolchevick montre le nez," *Devoir*, 24 January 1919, 7. See also: "Bolchevists Capture the Labor Meeting," *Montreal Daily Star*, 24 January 1919, 14; "La journée de six heures et cinq jours de travail"; "'L'heure des pétitions est passées, il faut des actes,'" *Canada*, 24 January 1919, 8 and 3.

51 Edmond Simard was a blacksmith and a socialist activist active among the unemployed in 1919. In the following years, he attended the Montreal Labor College. He was among the first group of French Canadians to join the Communist Party of Canada in the 1920s. He ran in Maisonneuve as the party candidate during the federal elections of 1930. He was also an organizer for the Workers Unity League at the Canadian Pacific Railway plant at the Angus Shops in Montreal in the 1930s as well as during the strike led by the organization in the textile industry in Cowansville, Quebec, in 1931. Bernard Dansereau, "La présence communiste au Québec (1929–1939) ou la présence de 'l'homme au couteau entre les dents,'" *Bulletin d'histoire politique* 9, no. 2 (2001): 24–25; Marcel Fournier, *Communisme et anticommunisme au Québec (1920–1950)* (Laval, QC: Éditions coopératives Albert St-Martin, 1979), 16; Lévesque, *Virage à gauche interdit*, 50; 56–57.

52 "Le chef du 'comité des sans-travail' est arrêté," *Patrie*, 25 January 1919, 12.

53 "'Cherchez du travail, mendier ensuite et puis se livrer au vol ou recourir aux torches,'" *Presse*, 27 January 1919, 7.

54 Isidore Boltuck was born in a Jewish family in Poland in 1894. With his parents, he immigrated from Russia in 1903. He was secretary-treasurer of the Worker's Cooperative Press for the province of Quebec, which printed and distributed radical literature and pamphlets. In 1918, he began publishing *Labor*, a bilingual journal in English and in French. Suspected as an enemy alien, he was arrested during an unemployed meeting in January 1919. Having been a naturalized Canadian citizen through his father, he was released one day later. After his organizational role in the unemployed movement in 1919, he joined the group of supporters of the OBU in Montreal. From 1918 to 1920, he was under surveillance by federal authorities. Houle-Courcelles, "Censure et surveillance de la presse socialiste au Québec (1918–1920): le cas du journal Labor et de son éditeur Isidore Boltuck"; "Boltuck venait de donner de forts étranges conseils à ses auditeurs quand on l'a arrêté," *Presse*, 25 January 1919, 9.

55 A.T. Willgress, Letter to E.J. Chambers, 25 March 1919, LAC, RG6, E, volume 614, file 292, part 3.

56 *To The Unemployed*, LAC, RG6, E, volume 614, file 292, part 3.

57 Ibid.

58 "Bolchevist Talk to Unemployed Heard by 1,500," *Gazette*, 24 January 1919, 4; "Labor Chairman Called Autocrat," *Gazette*, 28 January 1919, 4; "Établir la journée de six heures," *Presse*, 28 January 1919, 9; "Nous voulons du travail, nous voulons du pain," *Le monde ouvrier/The Labor World*, 19 January 1919, 1; "On recommande du calme, de l'ordre et du sang-froid."

59 "Bolchevist Talk to Unemployed Heard by 1,500."

60 "Machinists Are for Sane Policy of Reconstruction," *Montreal Daily Star*, 28 January 1919, 14.

61 "Bolchevists Capture the Labor Meeting"; "La journée de six heures et cinq jours de travail"; "Le bolchevick montre le nez"; "L'heure des pétitions est passées, il faut des actes."

62 Dansereau, "Le mouvement ouvrier montréalais"; Ewen, "International Unions and the Workers' Revolt"; Houle-Courcelles, "Une Grande Union pour tous les travailleurs."

63 Thompson, "Working-Class Anguish and Revolutionary Indignation."

64 "Réunion de sans-travail," *Presse*, 14 February 1921, 17.

65 "Montreal O.B.U. Hold Mass Meetings for Unemployed," *One Big Union Bulletin*, 12 February 1921, 1.

66 "Des chômeurs affamés prennent d'assaut, un restaurant, rue Mcgill," *Patrie*, 21 January 1921, 14; "Offre de la ville à ses sans-travail," *Presse*, 21 January 1921, 13.

67 "Nous ne permettrons aucun désordre," *Patrie*, 22 January 1921, 9; "Trois hommes détenus par la police," *Presse*, 22 January 1921, 27.

68 "La police a arrêté douze sans-travail," *Presse*, 23 February 1921, 12; "Les vétérans continuent leur jeu," *Devoir*, 21 January 1921, 3; "Nouveau raid des chômeurs," *Patrie*, 21 January 1921, 1; "Nouveau raid," *Patrie*, 23 February 1921, 12; "Unemployed Ask for a Free Meal and They Get It," *Montreal Daily Star*, 20 January 1921, 1; "Unemployed Flock into Restaurant and Demand Food," *Gazette*, 21 January 1921, 4; "Unemployed Raid; Twelve Arrested," *Gazette*, 23 February 1921, 4.

69 "Civic Authorities Must Initiate Plan for Relief," *Gazette*, 20 January 1921, 2.

70 "Supplément de secours pour les chômeurs," *Presse*, 31 January 1921, 19; "To Alter Rules at Meurling Refuge," *Montreal Daily Star*, 17 January 1921, 3.

71 Chas. B. Hoby, "More 'Free' Meals," *OBU Bulletin*, 5 March 1921, 1; "Three Men Held After Unemployed Made Disturbance," *Gazette*, 22 January 1921, 4; "Trois meneurs des vétérans sont sous arrêts," *Devoir*, 22 January 1921, 3.

72 "No Cash Dole for Unemployed," *Montreal Daily Star*, 22 February 1921, 8.

73 "Les sans-travail," *Presse*, 29 December 1921, 16; "Une rebufade aux socialistes," *Presse*, 8 April 1921, 17; "Workers Urged to Protest," *OBU Bulletin*, 28 May 1921, 1.

74 "Parade de vétérans sans-travail," *Patrie*, 21 December 1920, 3.

75 "Food Raiding in Montreal," *Le monde ouvrier/The Labor World*, 29 January 1921, 5.

76 "Au Conseil des métiers et du travail," *Le monde ouvrier/The Labor World*, 18 March, 1922, 3; "Un conseil national des associations de sans-travail," *Presse*, 22 January 1922, 18; "Une nouvelle crise du chômage est-elle possible l'hiver prochain à Montréal?," *Presse*, 18 September 1922, 1; "Unemployed Get Busy," *The Worker*, 15 February 1922, 1.

77 "Chômeurs en assemblée à Maisonneuve," *Presse*, 16 January 1922, 9; "Exigence des sans-travail," *Devoir*, 16 January 1922, 4; "Moratorium relativement aux loyers," *Patrie*, 16 January 1922, 7.

78 "Assemblée mouvementée au Conseil des Métiers," *Le monde ouvrier/The Labor World*, 4 March 1922, 1; "Au Conseil des métiers et du travail," *Le monde ouvrier/The Labor World*, 18 March 1922, 4, "Une nouvelle crise du chômage est-elle possible l'hiver prochain à Montréal ?"; "Une résolution," *Presse*, 10 March 1922, 7; "Meeting

of Protest," *Le monde ouvrier/The Labor World*, 18 March 1922, 4; "Une assemblée paisible," *Le monde ouvrier/The Labor World*, 19 August 1922, 1.

79 "Une assemblée," *Devoir*, 15 March 1922, 2.

80 "Assemblée de sans-travail sur le champ de Mars," *Presse*, 7 April 1922, 1; "L'assemblée des sans-travail sur le champ de Mars," *Presse*, 7 April 1922, 23; "On invoque la révolte guérisseuse", *Soleil*, 25 April 1922, 1; "Une manifestation de sans-travail," *Presse*, 5 April 1922, 13.

81 "Montréal possède depuis jeudi son armée rouge," *Patrie*, 15 April 1922, 12; "Une assemblée de sans-travail sur le champ de Mars," *Presse*, 15 April 1922, 13.

82 "Au sans-travail," *Devoir*, 20 March 1922, 2; "Un crédit de $15,000 pour venir en aide aux pauvres," *Presse*, 21 March 1922, 20.

83 "Le capitaliste devrait se reposer, et les ouvriers conduire les industries," *Patrie*, 7 April 1922, 12.

84 Peter C. Bischoff, " 'Un chaînon incontournable au Québec': les Chevaliers du travail, 1882–1902," *Labour/Le Travail* 70 (2012): 13–59; Ewen, "Quebec: Class and Ethnicity"; Larivière, *Albert St-Martin*; Ross A. McCormack, "'Wobblies' et 'blanketstiffs': la composition et le contexte de l'IWW dans l'Ouest canadien," in *Travail et syndicalisme: Origines, évolution et défis d'une action nationale*, ed. James D. Thwaits (1996; repr., Ste-Foy, QC: Presses de l'Université Laval, 2002), 136–51; Thompson, "Working-Class Anguish and Revolutionary Indignation."

85 Matt Perry, "The British and French Hunger Marches of the 1930s: An Exclusive Mode of Protest, a Cultural Transfer, and a Fulcrum of Success," in *Economic and Political Change in Asia and Europe Social Movement Analyses*, ed. Bernadette Andreosso-O'Callaghan and Frédéric Royall (New York: Springer, 2013), 145–61. See also Thompson, "Working-Class Anguish and Revolutionary Indignation," 534–37.

86 Struthers, *No Fault of Their Own*, 12–43; Thompson, "Working-Class Anguish and Revolutionary Indignation," 276–80.

9

The Kansas City General Strike: Wartime Solidarity in the American Midwest

Jeff Stilley

The Winnipeg and Seattle General Strikes of 1919 illustrated the militancy of Canadian and American workers following the First World War. But a week-long general strike in Kansas City in March 1918, dubbed "the most important general strike which occurred during the war itself," has received scant scholarly attention.[1] Rank-and-file workers called the general strike in sympathy with commercial laundry workers—mostly low-wage white and Black women. The sympathy strike represented the culmination of a wartime labour movement that resisted divisions across wage levels, gender, and race, and enjoyed the support of middle- and upper-class clubwomen.

The Kansas City General Strike was unique because breaking contracts to take part in a sympathy strike demonstrated a level of solidarity and class-based action that was unattainable—in fact virtually unthinkable—for most workers during the war. The forces of the courts, the new Department of Labor, the American Federation of Labor (AFL, the conservative federation of trade unions), and the Council of National Defense (an agency made up of army and cabinet officials who coordinated the war economy with the help of an advisory commission) were lined up behind maintaining war production levels and honouring contracts. Union leaders and friendly elites did support walkouts for union recognition under certain conditions, but there was no appetite for sympathy actions or striking while under contract. Individual workers struggling to eat could be sympathized with; workers acting as a class in the midst of war were not. Six days after the General Strike ended, Samuel Gompers (AFL president and a member of the Council of National Defense), communicated with union leaders around the country summarizing his feelings: "No strike ought to be inaugurated that cannot be justified to the men facing momentary death. A strike during the war is not justified unless principles are involved equally fundamental as those for which fellow citizens have offered their lives—their all."[2]

The United States did not enter the Great War until 6 April 1917, but for the nineteen months it participated, worker combativeness escalated across the country. Over 1.2 million people (more than 6 percent of the workforce) participated in work stoppages in both 1917 and 1918. U.S. strike activity during the First World War has been explained as "a response to the wartime pressures for personal sacrifice, patriotism, and productivity." War contracts brought massive profits to capital and a dramatic loss of purchasing power for workers. From 1916 to 1919, the dollar inflated 16.7 percent each year, and consumer prices increased 58.7 percent.[3]

Additionally, the Woodrow Wilson administration signalled that it believed workers had rights to maintain their standard of living and to organize without interference from employers, lending unprecedented legitimacy to unionization. Since the Civil War, the Republican and Democratic parties both embraced "right to work" language, which framed labour contracts as agreements between bosses and individual workers.[4] Wilson's vague pro-union overtures (along with a series of "New Freedom" labour law reforms passed in his first term) felt like a dramatic shift to union activists. Employers around the country, however, continued using company spies to fire militant workers, as they pressured employees to speed up production.

Influenced by the idea of "industrial democracy" from Kansas City labour lawyer Frank P. Walsh, workers simply could not see how their sacrifices were "making the world safe for democracy."[5] What was the point of fighting the German kaiser abroad if the working masses were immiserated at home? Conservative trade union leaders, however, discouraged wartime militancy, meaning wartime collective action usually took the forms of walkouts and wildcat strikes. Before narrating the lead-up to the General Strike, a few words to contextualize Kansas City's economy, people, and political landscape are in order.

Kansas City

The construction of a railroad bridge over the Missouri River in 1869 transformed Kansas City into the second largest railroad and meat-packing centre in the country. The city straddles the Missouri-Kansas state line, where railroad company warehouses, food manufacturing plants, granaries, petroleum refineries, lumber processing factories, stockyards, and meat-packing plants drove economic development.[6] Modern industrial capitalism dominated the scene, with meat-packing acting as the vanguard of continuous (dis)assembly lines, and railroads as the vanguard of large bureaucratic organizations.[7]

The Kansas City area held an unusually large proportion of African American residents for an industrial area. Whereas most industrial cities in the United States lacked significant shares of African American residents until at least the First World War, Black Kansas City remained at over 10 percent from 1880 to 1920.[8] Voting rights for Black men in Missouri and Kansas (unlike in the South) meant African Americans could form a uniquely consequential political bloc. On the Kansas side, this resulted in a rare political coalition between working-class Irish, Germans, and African Americans gaining municipal control through the Republican ticket in the early 1880s, facilitated by the Knights of Labor.[9] In Missouri, Democratic ward boss Jim Pendergast gained respect from Black people by posting bond for Black prisoners. By the 1890s, Kansas City was among the first cities where significant numbers of African American voters had left the Republican Party.[10]

A handful of strikes around the turn of the century featured interracial solidarity by workers.[11] While these instances were relatively ephemeral, they are revealing when we consider that the late 1890s was the time when the AFL leadership shed its overtures to interracial solidarity, allowed whites-only unions for the first time, and embraced imperialist "scientific" racism.[12] However, many local unions continued to exclude Black workers, and the labour market forced most Black men into low-wage and intermittent jobs, and Black women into domestic labour. Throughout the 1910s, African American residents suffered far higher death rates from disease and arrest rates by the police than whites, illustrating the fact that Kansas City was no oasis of racial harmony.[13] In sum, although conditions were relatively favourable for interracial alliances at work and at the polls, neither was automatic.

Several producerist and leftist organizations flourished during the Gilded Age and Progressive Era. The Kansas City Syndicalist League, for example, organized a massive AFL-funded unionization drive in the spring of 1914. These revolutionary syndicalists eschewed separatist unions like the Industrial Workers of the World, preferring to "bore from within" trade unions. Thus, alongside conservative trade unionism stood radical syndicalism within the labour movement.[14]

Kansas City also hosted a militant branch of the Women's Trade Union League (KCWTUL), which forged strong networks with the labour movement and middle-class clubwomen. A tax on male union members funded the branch, illustrating a much closer relationship with male unionists than had branches in other American cities.[15] The KCWTUL also collaborated with clubwomen on female suffrage, unionizing teachers, aiding the unemployed, and passing legislative reforms for women and children.[16] The national clubwomen movement grew out of literary groups and the desire of well-connected women to expand women's political influence beyond religious reforms like alcohol prohibition. In Kansas City, twenty-one organizations founded the local chapter of the General Federation of Women's Clubs in 1896, and worked on prison, child labour, and education reforms.[17]

A waitress named Sarah Green served as KCWTUL president. Already a fixture of the labour movement in 1917, by the end of the war Green had become one of the most effective—and therefore feared—organizers in the city, renowned for both her confrontational tenacity and her skill in turning clubwomen against business owners. Additionally, the most involved upper-class KCWTUL member, Peake Faxon, believed passionately in worker militancy, and was herself beaten by police on a picket line in 1913 in New York City.[18]

The 1918 General Strike constituted a showdown between organized labour and the Employers' Association (EA), which became determined to break the labour movement in 1918. Capitalists originally formed the EA in 1903 to fight city laws requiring union labour for contract work, and to organize business boycotts against unionized closed shops.[19] The reason for the EA's determination in 1918 was simple: a series of successful strikes and an explosion of interest in unionization swept across the city in the last half of 1917, to which we now turn.

Fall 1917 Rebellion

An August streetcar strike catalyzed working-class insurgency. When the Kansas City Railways Company fired twenty-five employees who were secretly organizing a transit union, their fellow workers walked off the job on 8 August 1917, tying up transit service for a week. The company hired Berghoff Brothers and Waddell, the most notorious and effective strikebreaking agency in the country.[20] On the fourth day of the strike, however, thousands of citizens spent hours battling the incoming "finks" before they could operate a single trolley. Several hundred starving strikebreakers from New York City were forced onto a train and unceremoniously dumped on a farm outside of city limits. Undeterred, the streetcar owners allegedly gave Berghoff Brothers and Waddell a new budget of $1 million and secured a court injunction against the strike.[21]

As the strikers prepared for a second violent confrontation—and almost certain defeat—a federal mediator named Fred Feick arrived from the Department of Labor. Within thirty-six hours, the company gave in to every demand, and all 2,600 workers were unionized. How did this turn of events come about? Federal mediators had no real power over employers, but a group of clubwomen with preexisting ties to the KCWTUL sent two frantic telegrams to the Department of Labor requesting assistance for the strikers anyway. Speaking for the strikers and their wives, the women requested federal intervention to prevent the "body of armed thugs" from breaking the strike. After the scabs were deported, the clubwomen sent another telegram to Washington when it was rumored the Kansas City Railways Company's president Philip Kealy, then on leave from the company and serving in the military as a colonel, would be called upon to personally break the strike using national guardsmen. They wrote that his presence would be "absolutely incompatible" with a peaceful strike as it meant a business owner would be "placed in charge" by the government "to oppress his workers." On the same morning that the injunction was issued, one of the clubwomen, Phoebe Ess, told a mass meeting of strikers, "Thousands of good citizens are behind you. We want you to win."[22] The clubwomen's public agitation pushed the transit company into an impossible position.

The committee included three of the most active clubwomen in Kansas City and an investigative journalist. Mary Harmon Weeks, Carolyn Fuller, and Ess were all named as leading members of the Athenaeum by historian K. David Hanzlick in his detailed study of women's activism in Kansas City. The Athenaeum, a consolidation of several women's groups, promoted public kindergartens, free swimming pools, public playgrounds, safe milk, health care for children, suffrage, citizenship education for immigrants, and "moral" entertainment for working-class women. All three women were former schoolteachers who had married wealthy men. The KCWTUL and the Industrial Council of the Labor Temple collaborated throughout the 1910s with these clubwomen on public education to advocate for free textbooks and higher wages for teachers.[23] Ess previously worked with the labour movement on prison reform in Missouri (the infamous state penitentiary contracted its inmates to private companies that competed with union-made goods), and later ran for an elected position on the school board in 1918 on a third-party ticket that joined clubwomen and unionists. Thus, the labour movement, the KCWTUL, and these clubwomen had collaborated on several projects. The journalist was Alice Mary Kimball, who soon thereafter became a nationally recognized suffrage activist on the east coast.[24]

With Kansas City, Missouri, officials, citizenry, clubwomen, and a representative of the federal government pressuring the company to accede to the workers' demands, the employers gave in. The acting president of Kansas City Railways Company told Feick that "the Company desired to do what was right in the matter, and if it was the wish of the Government, and if the men accepted it, he would not stand in the way, but would sign the agreement in good faith."[25] Between the symbolic weight of federal mediators, and a labour movement coalition forged by the KCWTUL, the company felt it could not withstand the public pressure.

The success and broad support for the streetcar strike had an incendiary impact upon the Kansas City working class. Through September and October of 1917, thousands of workers walked off the job for the right to unionize and for better wages and working conditions, on both sides of the state line. For example, a meat-packing strike completely shut down operations in the 14,000-person industry for two days. The strikers were a diverse group composed of white butchers, African

American labourers, Croatian and other ethnic low-wage workers, and white and Black women canners. The strikers elected a Black labourer to the strike committee, and women presented demands specific to their working conditions. The strike won a modest wage increase, protections from discrimination against union members, the establishment of grievance committees, and reforms in labourer hiring practices.[26] Again, a Department of Labor mediator, the KCWTUL, and Kansas City, Kansas, municipal officials pressured the companies to recognize workers' rights to organize and maintain living standards.

Dozens of other walkouts followed with mixed results. Thousands of women struck soap and food plants, and thousands of white and Black male freight handlers and clerks took strike action against a dozen railroad companies. In every case, the KCWTUL helped organize strikers, and government mediators cajoled employers to meet with their workers. Large parades of diverse working-class people marching through industrial sections and downtown, coupled with a steady stream of workers at the Labor Temple asking for assistance in forming unions, sent the Employers' Association into a panic. It placed seventeen large ads in the three major daily newspapers through the fall of 1917, claiming that the workers' revolt was the result of highly paid outside agitators whose efforts aided the German kaiser against American troops. As strike action waned in the face of the historically cold winter of 1917–18, the EA put together a $1 million fund to smash whatever strike might break out next—by any means necessary.[27] It is worthwhile noting that while employer obstinacy and federal mediation were common features in most industrial disputes in America during this period, what made the situation in Kansas City so remarkable was this: the KCWTUL and its clubwomen supporters helped to tip the scales in some key strikes that built solidarity and momentum, leading to a larger showdown with the city's Employers' Association.

Commercial Laundry Strike

The laundry strike that precipitated the late March 1918 General Strike began in mid-February. Even before transit workers commenced the strike wave described above, laundry delivery drivers began the process of forming a union in July of 1917. The drivers were primarily teamsters who used horses to pull their wagons and had to pay helpers out of their own wages. Designated as "salesmen," they received a flat wage plus a commission. They had not received a wage increase in fifteen years, although their commissions had increased with sales prices. With inflation, however, the drivers did not feel this was enough to cover paying their helpers and asked for a guaranteed minimum of $18 per week in take-home pay.[28]

The union was presented with a strategic opening when nine of the largest laundries of the city combined in September to form the Kansas City Laundry Service Company. The consolidation of management provided a single target to establish higher prevailing wages, and the drivers demanded a wage increase in December. The Kansas City Laundry Service Company spearheaded the formation of an industry-wide trade association—the Laundry Owners Association (LOA)—in order to deal with the drivers' demands. This body turned down the union's demands on 11 January 1918, and had the audacity to use the low wages its members paid to the female workers inside the laundries in order to portray the men's wage demands as being illegitimate from the "standpoint of humanity and justice." Striking a particularly sanctimonious tone, the LOA wrote, "let us all get together with our respective employers and employees and work harmoniously for our country and for ourselves."[29]

The white and Black women workers inside the dozens of commercial laundries were indeed some of the lowest paid in the city. In 1914, half of these workers received less than $7 per week, with some making as little as $4. Until Missouri passed a nine-hour workday for women in 1912, it was not unusual for workers to be forced to work twelve- or sixteen-hour shifts (though the law was repeatedly broken throughout the 1910s). Most working women in the city were in their teens or early twenties and unmarried, but 34 percent of laundry workers were over thirty, and close to half were married, widowed, separated, or divorced. These numbers likely reflect the presence of African American women in many of the lower-paid positions. The best local jobs for Black women were in the meat-packing plants on the Kansas side. But for those who could not get work there, employment at a commercial laundry meant escaping domestic work—a demeaning and abusive job that paid no better, and where long hours fluctuated from day to day.[30]

Laundry work involved standing for hours on end and repetitive motions in dangerous environments. The women breathed in carbon monoxide gas and handled bleaching chemicals. Relatively fortunate workers could be in rooms with temperatures around 35 degrees Celsius, while low-wage workers operating steam-powered mangle machines dealt with temperatures around 50 degrees. Many laundries had no break rooms or separate bathrooms. Workers fainted often, and suffered from stomach ulcers, joint swelling, anemia, loss of feeling in fingers, kidney disease, and skin and respiratory problems. One industrial inspector was bedridden for a week after spending a brief time observing commercial laundries.[31]

It is unclear from documentary evidence what delivery drivers decided to do when the LOA rejected their demands in January. Newspaper reports suggest that their strike may have begun with an unplanned walkout in one plant. Nonetheless, when all the drivers struck on 15 February 1918, it is no surprise that over 1,000 women in the industry had joined them by the 18th. Wages and working conditions had not improved since 1914, and wartime inflation took its toll on the women's budgets. What made it unusual is that the labour movement turned it into a general strike. Sympathy strikes were very rare during either world war, and the fact that it was in sympathy with mostly low-wage women workers is even more surprising. This was not lost on local organizers. A KCWTUL report noted, "Never in the history of the labor movement in Kansas City, has organized labor stood more loyally behind any group of unorganized, under-paid employees, than it did in this strike." The laundry owners framed the situation very differently. Signalling how they would condescendingly speak about women employees throughout the Strike, Frank Porter, spokesperson for the LOA, said, "We feel like we have treated our employees fairly and if there is any consideration to be shown any workers it will be the inside help. The women are being made 'goats' by the men, who are merely using them."[32]

The support of clubwomen and working-class solidarity played important roles in the laundry strike, just as they had in so many of the strikes of 1917. After the first several days of the Strike, the laundries, with EA financial support, reopened with scabs and highly paid armed guards, placed in the laundries and on delivery wagons. The women strikers and armed guards battled on the picket lines and in residential areas. Several instances of assault, which were sometimes initiated by guards and sometimes by strikers, caused deep concern among clubwomen. A 27 February hearing to get testimony from owners and strikers, hosted by the women members of the Jackson County, Missouri, branch of the Council of Defense, provides a window into both clubwomen's support of the strike, and tentative interracial solidarities among the strikers. Clubwomen had already held one public meeting in support of the laundry workers at the Labor Temple and pressured Mayor Edwards to get the LOA to recognize the laundry union as arrests and violent confrontations multiplied. The hearing on the 27th was to be conducted at Hotel Muehlebach, a downtown "whites-only" hotel. When African American strikers were denied entry, all the white strikers walked out in protest at the behest of Sarah Green of the KCWTUL. Multiple instances of white and Black strikers being arrested together on the picket line suggest this was not an isolated incident of interracial solidarity.[33]

However, racial tension among workers remained evident in other contexts, demonstrating that class solidarity had to be organized. When laundry owners raised women's wages to a minimum of $9 per week soon after the strike began, many of the replacement workers were African American women, and some African American men took jobs as delivery drivers. Three white union members violently accosted one such driver outside the Labor Temple after he allegedly pulled a knife on women strikers. In a separate strike that was occurring at the same time, white waiters at the Baltimore Hotel were replaced with a Black staff. The strikers were unable to convince the Black replacement workers to join them, as they had previously denied them entry to their union. In a report addressed to the Department of Labor, the clubwomen on the local Council of Defense noted, "The use of negro strikebreakers in several laundries and in the Baltimore Hotel where a strike is in progress has added a sinister element of race antagonism to the strike situation. A negro investigator reported to our committee that negro strikebreakers are permitted by the police to carry guns and knives, and that street fights between negro and white workers occur frequently."[34] Despite such racially fraught challenges, the laundry strike continued.

Clubwomen's support was crucial for pressuring local and federal officials. The violence of the strike, in which women strikers enthusiastically took part, could have easily turned government and public opinion against the strike, but clubwomen placed 100 percent of the blame on the owners. This was important because the strikers were unable to prevent the laundries from operating for more than a few days, so extending the Strike required public pressure.

By early March, the Missouri state-controlled police department had approved 300 weapons permits for private laundry guards, who were paid by the EA. The clubwomen on the local Council of National Defense wrote to the Department of Labor, "Several [guards] are known to have police records. Their behavior is such as to provoke violence and to add immeasurably to unrest. Girl strikers have been beaten, waylaid on dark streets and assaulted, and otherwise brutally treated. A member of this committee stopped a strikebreaking policeman who was firing shots directly into a crowd containing girls and women." As newspapers focused on the actions of picketers and arrest reports, clubwomen bore witnesses to the EA-sponsored violence. Even after unknown assailants murdered a laundry wagon guard, the clubwomen refused to turn against arrested picketers: "Until the strikebreaking police appeared, the workers were peaceful, and kindly, orderly spirit pervaded the striking body. The character of the special police is so notorious that a municipal judge discharged all strikers brought to his court, declaring that the special officers were provocateurs, and that their appointment was illegal."[35]

For its part, the Kansas City Common Council (the municipal legislative body) put together a committee to investigate the Strike and followed the clubwomen in placing the blame for the violent strike situation on the owners. "All of the laundries were guarded on the inside by persons who were armed, some of whom were under age and most of them apparently iresponsible [*sic*] and lacking in intelligence and judgment." After recommending that the police commissioners revisit their decision to arm private guards, representatives of the Common Council wrote that the LOA was, "in our judgment, solely responsible for [the strike's] continuation."[36] In other words, the LOA's outright refusal to talk to strikers or mediators was defined as the underlying cause of the situation.

Thus, the actions of the strikers, the KCWTUL, clubwomen, and elected municipal legislators helped extend this strike of low-wage workers, who were steadily being replaced. Referring to the laundry union, the KCWTUL wrote, "All the women's civic organizations in Kansas City were behind this organization. The club women of Kansas City fought . . . the Employers' Association a battle of wits against capital."[37] Without the support of allied clubwomen, the strike may have fizzled out before the General Strike could occur.

The General Strike Call

The "moral and financial support" that the Employers' Association supplied to laundry owners felt like an existential crisis to labour organizers and rank-and-file workers alike. Rank-and-file outrage led to the formation of a twelve-member board of business agents on 4 March 1918, to discuss strategies to win the laundry strike. Business agents were full-time organizers, paid by union locals' membership dues. They functioned "as a job dispenser, organizer, protector of his trade's jurisdiction, and [as] the local union's chief executive."[38] Business agents spent most of their time with rank-and-file workers and confronting management, rather than meeting with politicians or international union executives. The board immediately recommended a general strike and scheduled a mass meeting of business agents at the Labor Temple on 14th March to discuss the proposal. They extended an invitation to 120 union locals to send a total of 840 representatives. After almost five hours of speeches from labour leaders attempting to prevent a general strike (who were hissed from the gallery), the general "cessation of work" was approved by a vote of 476 to 16.[39]

The only unions to oppose the General Strike were the musicians and printing trades. The conservatism of the printing trades was particularly significant because the weekly labour newspaper did not release extra General Strike issues, and very little information or promotion of the sympathy strike was included before or after the Strike. After noting the obstinacy of the LOA, and the EA funding of violent guards, as well as their own patriotic loyalty to President Wilson, the strike resolution set the date for 25 March, "exempting only hospitals; [and] exempting the city water works [for] a period of forty-eight hours."[40] As it turned out, the clause to call out city waterworks personnel would sow confusion and panic across the city in the days leading up to, and including, the General Strike.

How do we explain the widespread enthusiasm for the general strike as a tactic among rank-and-file workers? There had only been one general strike in the United States since the early 1890s. The massive Philadelphia General Strike of March 1910, in sympathy with transit workers, collapsed without achieving its goals.[41] The general strike was neither a common nor a particularly successful tactic. Locally, sympathy strikes among the building trades were apparently a regular tactic around the turn of the century. The Building Trades Council called a strike in solidarity with the African American Hod Carriers Union in 1899, for example. By 1905, at least one influential carpenter argued that sympathy strikes had not proved themselves effective, advocating a shift in strategy toward arbitration instead.[42] While experienced construction workers certainly had memories of this sort of working-class solidarity, a building trades tradition with mixed results cannot fully explain the enthusiasm for the general strike tactic demonstrated by the rank and file.

With no dramatic precipitating event, like a striker being killed on a picket line, the most convincing explanation is that revolutionary syndicalists had sold the general strike tactic to a critical mass of rank-and-file activists. A particular brand of syndicalism, as elucidated by William Z. Foster, had an outsized influence on the Kansas City labour movement. Inspired by French syndicalism, Foster established the Syndicalist League of North America in 1912 as a loose collection of a few branches around the country. The Kansas City branch was the most successful, due to the efforts of former Wobbly Max Dezettel, and the former Socialist Earl Browder.[43] Joined for a brief time by Wobbly James P. Cannon, they published a syndicalist paper between October 1913 and January 1915, and led an AFL-sponsored unionization push among the "unskilled" workers of Kansas City in the spring of 1914. According to Browder and Foster, the syndicalists were dominant among the local Cooks, Barbers, and Office Workers unions, and had gained significant power within the Industrial Council. The syndicalist-led Labor Forward Movement expanded unionization levels by 28.2 percent between January of 1914 and January 1915, including a 63.6 percent increase in women membership. The new recruits, including Sarah Green and a new Waitresses' local that she presided over, helped stabilize unionization levels through the economic downturn of 1914–16.[44]

Syndicalists favoured the general strike tactic. In Foster's words: "By the term 'general strike,' used in a revolutionary sense, is meant the period of more or less *general cessation of labor* by the workers, during which period, the workers, by disorganizing the mechanism of capitalist society, will expose its weakness and their own strength" (emphasis added). Note that the Kansas City General Strike authorization also used the language of "general cessation," rather than general strike. According to Foster's logic, "The general strike will be so devastating in its effects that it can last only a few days, during which period, if need be, the workers, accustomed as they are to starvation, and sustained by the enthusiasm of the revolution, could live on the most meager rations."[45] Archival evidence does not allow for strong conclusions regarding the extent of syndicalist influence in 1918, but Foster's ideas would certainly have been familiar.

For their part, federal mediators Luther Steward and Patrick Gill blamed the employers for the general strike decision. Gill told the press, "The Laundry owners of Kansas City, with two exceptions, believe themselves above the United States government and have refused to meet with its representatives in an effort to prevent the strike Monday." Steward wrote to the Department of Labor just after the general strike authorization that "Mr. Porter's attitude toward organized labor in general is characterized by such extreme bitterness that almost his entire conversation consists of charges of violence, anarchy, dishonesty, bad faith, etc. directed at all persons in any way connected with organized labor."[46] Such intransigence assisted general strike enthusiasts, since a more conciliatory posture toward the laundry strikers may have derailed the general confrontation between the EA and the working class. It is possible that the EA was aware of this but hoped that decisively defeating a general strike would break the labour movement.

The board of business agents did not waver either. On 13 March, laundry guard William Weaver was ambushed and murdered in cold blood. While the killers were never caught, it certainly appeared at the time that the assailants' motive must have been to support the Strike. The meeting to vote on a general strike was already scheduled for the night of the 14th, which the business agents went ahead with. In response to the killing of Weaver, the spokesperson for the business agents said, "Organized labor meets the killing of a laundry wagon guard and strike violence with the charge [that replacement] drivers and guards on laundry wagons are men with criminal records, disreputable and irresponsible for their acts to the detriment and danger of peace loving and law abiding citizens of the community. The hiring of these men is charged jointly to the laundry owners and the Kansas City Employers' Association." The board of business agents doubled down on the eve of the General Strike, arguing, "No violence on the part of laundry workers, incited and provoked by corporation gunmen, can equal this larger violence on the part of employers. It is as violent to starve a girl slowly and to shorten her life by unwholesome working conditions as to kill her quickly with a club. It is as violent to strike her down with the power of a million dollars as to deal her a physical blow. It is as violent to put her in the hospital by vicious surroundings as to make a direct assault upon her person."[47] The workers thus felt the violence of exploitation itself to be justification enough for a general strike.

By the time of the general strike authorization, hundreds of the women strikers had already returned to work or found other jobs. Around 700 of 1,500 plus women, and 200 of 300 male drivers, stayed on strike through mid-March. But some conservative labour figures viewed the General Strike primarily as a defence of the drivers. William D. Mahon of the international streetcar union, who helped broker the end of the General Strike, erroneously told Gompers that "there was only left, practically, these ten laundry drivers, and it was over them that the sympathetic strike was called, demanding their reinstatement and the right of the laundry workers to organize."[48] Mahon's use of LOA framing to downplay the extent of participation in the laundry strike laid in stark contrast to the emphasis on the exploitation of women workers displayed in the above quote from the business agents.

Following the general strike vote, the secretariat of the Industrial Council at the Labor Temple appealed to every authority they could think of to pressure the LOA and EA to meet with laundry strikers, in order to prevent the sympathy strike. They wrote letters to President Wilson, the Department of Labor, Gompers, and met with the Kansas City Chamber of Commerce to plead their case, but to no avail. The Department of Labor appealed directly to the laundry owners for their cooperation with mediators, but they had no power to force them. Behind closed doors, the Chamber of Commerce felt that the EA and LOA were behaving unreasonably, but put forth a united class front in public. After a forty-eight-hour delay brokered by a prominent pastor, the Kansas City General Strike began on 27 March 1918.[49]

While support from clubwomen, religious figures, city officials, and newspapers during earlier strikes had been crucial for building the momentum and collective confidence necessary for the general strike call, many liberal figures across the city were horrified by the call for a sympathy strike in the context of anti-German feelings and growing anti-Bolshevik sentiment. The *Star* wrote, "This campaign, carrying a menace to every man, woman and child in Kansas City, is to be used against employers with whom their employees have no quarrel." The Rev. O. P. Bishop, who helped investigate working conditions of commercial laundries, "said that in the face of the war and in considerations of the tremendous demands now laid on the Nation for self-sacrifice, any attempt to cripple the city by closing the waterworks plant or taking other such radical steps by union men could not be countenanced by their friends and would be nothing short of treason." Once the General Strike began, the *Post* editorialized, "That among the first arrests for participation in strike riots were German aliens, without union cards, should make every union man in this city stop and think again before he participates in a strike which has no parallel in the history of craft unionism."[50] Even the clubwomen who were writing to the government and the AFL in support of the laundry strikers throughout mid-March apparently went silent once the General Strike began. The participants would have to fight the EA based on working-class solidarity alone.

The General Strike

Labour leaders did their best to symbolically assert that the sympathetic strike did not contradict patriotism or cooperation with the war effort. Even rank-and-file strikers marched with American flags as they destroyed laundries with bricks on the first day, likely hoping to prevent the public from thinking they were anti-American or pro-German. The General Strike Committee, composed of Frank Peterson, E.L. Keeran, and G.C. Skaggs (two building tradesmen and one barber), worked around the clock to prevent the federal government from intervening against the Strike, or martial law being declared by the Missouri governor. In practice, this meant the leaders spent most of their time in meetings with city officials, pleading with strikers to stop destroying property, and exempting various categories of workers from the General Strike.

Yet the business agents understood the tactic in terms of general class struggle: "From the inception of this controversy the laundry owners have been upheld and supported both morally and financially by the Employers' Association of Kansas City, which latter organization we are informed represents the greater part of the business interests of this vicinity. . . . The issue thus broadened out from one between laundry workers and laundry owners to one between capital and labor." They also framed class struggle, however, in national terms. "Organized labor has not attempted to go against the wishes or ideas of the National Council of Defense, and is not attempting to change present conditions, and is simply asking for the right of the American citizen to maintain an organization."[51] It is unclear to what extent patriotic sentiments were genuinely held, or professed strategically. In early 1914, the Industrial Council declared itself opposed to all wars except for class war, and the same body opposed war "preparedness" measures in 1916.[52] However, once the United States entered, many Americans who were previously antiwar rallied around Wilson and the war effort.

The opening day of the sympathy strike, 27 March, was the most dramatic, with violence and widespread property destruction at laundries and downtown restaurants. The first trades to join were building trades, bartenders, barbers, cooks, waiters, waitresses, brewers, porters, and film and theatre workers. Several construction projects were halted, and downtown buildings lost elevator, electricity, and heat services. The board of business agents exempted all workers on war contracts, including the large contingent of meat-packing workers, who voted not to participate anyway (meat-packing workers across the nation were participating in federal arbitration of labour disputes). But they remained indecisive with respect to whether they would call out waterworks employees on the third day. Prior to the General Strike, some labour leaders had told reporters that the clause to include water workers would be removed, but the board of business agents reconfirmed they would *not* alter the original plan on the 22nd.[53]

Throughout the afternoon and evening, Labor Temple officials attempted to keep a crowd of 3,000 strikers at an open-air rally at a public park. But as one striker put it, "We don't want to hear any stump speeches now. What we want is action in wrecking [laundries]." Several laundries and delivery wagons were subsequently destroyed with bricks. Participants overwhelmed police forces at multiple sites, where strikers freed detained strikers and set fire to paddy wagons. A private guard shot striker Lon Amos Millsap in the stomach, and he died two days later. The General Strike Committee pleaded with workers at the Labor Temple in the evening to stop wrecking private property. Nonetheless, several hundred marched downtown at 10:00 p.m. and destroyed a few restaurants, including one with Mayor Edwards inside. By 2:00 a.m., the National Guard had machine guns posted downtown, and city officials weighed in, requesting martial law.[54]

Kansas Citians woke up the second day to newspapers showing several drawings of destroyed buildings and a full-page ad, placed by the employers, asking, "How long shall Kansas City continue to be a victim of Ruin, Riot and Vandalism?" City officials decided not to declare martial law, but 500 national guardsmen, mostly comprised of businessmen, augmented the police with fixed bayonet rifles and machine guns. The streetcar union joined the General Strike in the afternoon, causing a panic downtown as office workers and clerks suddenly had to figure out how to get home. The announcement that trolley workers were breaking their new contract for a sympathy strike also induced dread at the streetcar international union headquarters in Detroit, where Mahon and vice-president Frank O'Shea immediately boarded trains to Kansas City. Tailors and more cooks, waiters, and barbers officially joined the General Strike, bringing the total to between 13,000 and 15,000 staying off the job. The General Strike Committee finally declared in the evening they would not shut down water service, but the waffling led to weeks of rumors and hysteria among the public.[55]

Police violence marked the third day of the Strike. The streetcar company decided to operate a couple of dozen cars with National Guard protection. About 5,000 people showed up to block the tracks and throw rocks at trolleys. The streetcars knocked down strikers on the tracks. In contrast to police behavior during the August 1917 streetcar strike, the police fired guns into the crowd and swung their clubs indiscriminately. Although the Strike Committee initially exempted chauffeurs and jitney taxi drivers to help with transportation issues, they were called out on strike after the police melee.[56]

Mahon arrived from Detroit on 30th March, the same day Missouri governor Frederick Gardner vowed, "Law and order will prevail." The police also declared that property would be defended with no mercy shown to strikers. Limited streetcar service returned without incident, and national guardsmen were posted outside the laundries. Strikers and organizers feared Mahon would order streetcar workers to return to the job and honour their contracts. However, when Mahon arrived he discovered an EA and LOA that were so unreasonable, and a rank and file so determined, that he felt ordering the streetcar workers back to work before resolving the General Strike would do more harm than good. As Mahon later wrote, "I took the position that the men had violated their agreements and did wrong, but two wrongs did not make a right. I said the Employers had taken advantage of it, and in my opinion had checkered the men to some extent, into this position, and that the only way to settle it would be to restore the Organizations and to have a distinct understanding that no such strike should occur again, and especially during the war period."[57] Thus, Mahon joined mediators Gill and Steward in harassing employers to enter talks to end the General Strike. To this end they created a committee of businessmen, headed by Henry Faxon and George Fuller, to act as a go-between for the labour movement and the Employers' Association, since the employers still refused to meet with government mediators. Faxon and Fuller were both friendly to the labour movement, as Faxon's wife, Peake, was the most active and radical ally in the KCWTUL, while Fuller's wife, Carolyn, had been intimately involved with assisting strikes.

Easter Sunday fell on the fifth day of the Strike, and limited streetcar service continued to operate with minimal interference from strikers. Bakers joined the Strike, almost completely eliminating the availability of bread in the city. Members of the Missouri Council of Defense made clear that they considered an adequate bread supply to be a critical component of the war effort, so the walkout by the militant bakers was likely not preapproved by the Strike Committee. However, federal food administrator Herbert Hoover said he had no power to force the workers back. Several of the large churches lambasted the General Strike in sermons, as anti-Bolshevik sentiments spread. A mass meeting of 1,500 streetcar workers (out of about 2,600) affirmed the decision to stick with the General Strike. In the final days of the sympathy strike, roughly 25,000 workers stayed home, although there was little activity in terms of mass meetings or pickets in the face of police and National Guard repression.[58]

Negotiations to end the General Strike began on Monday, between the businessmen's committee (headed by Faxon and Fuller), Mayor Edwards, and the EA. The businessmen's committee spent extensive time with Gill and Steward, as well as with Mahon and O'Shea, so they could properly represent the unions' and Department of Labor positions. As talks dragged on throughout the day and into the next morning, the streets remained quiet.[59]

The second of April, the seventh and final day of the General Strike, was a municipal election day. Labour and clubwomen fielded a joint third-party ticket, but lost at the ballot box. The Democrats carried the day, partially through police intimidation and ballot clerks switching the votes of Black Republicans and independent ticket voters.[60] By sunrise, the EA proposed a truce. Employers would reinstate contracts that were broken for the General Strikc, and laundry strikers would be rehired without discriminating against union members. Mayor Edwards delivered the details to a meeting of business agents at the Labor Temple in the morning. The business agents debated the proposal for several hours, with the general mood against accepting the offer. Mahon threatened that if they did not accept the deal, he would order streetcar workers back to work to save their contract. Mediator Gill also applied as much pressure as he could, writing to Steward, "You have no idea how much fun you missed when you were not with me at the Labor Temple."[61] On the night of 2 April 1918, the board of business agents reluctantly voted to end the General Strike.

After the week-long General Strike, most unionized workers returned to work under their old contracts. The laundry strike was over, and while the male drivers did not achieve any wage victories, the women workers had sufficiently embarrassed their employers to improve wages and working conditions. The verbal promise to raise their minimum wage to $9 a week meant many women's wages, particularly African Americans', nearly doubled. It also meant the EA's antiunion offensive had failed, and that labour could hold on to the gains they made during the war. The biggest losers were cooks, waiters, and waitresses. Over 1,000 of them were locked out after the General Strike and were never able to regain their unionized jobs. Mayor Edwards and the federal mediators put pressure on restaurateurs to abide by the same deal agreed to by the EA (restaurant owners had their own trade association and did not feel bound by EA negotiations). Nevertheless, restaurant owners weathered lengthy pickets and boycotts after the General Strike to become a nonunion sector of the local economy.[62]

With the KCWTUL's help, about 300 women maintained membership in the laundry union throughout 1918, calling mass meetings on 18 April and 6 June to strategize how to hold the laundry owners to their promises. After the KCWTUL helped establish an industrial union of drivers and women laundry workers in Leavenworth, Kansas, local drivers expressed interest in merging with the women. However, neither union could prevent the owners from dropping wages, and by September 1919, there were no laundry union members left.[63]

Conclusion

The Kansas City General Strike ended in a truce, but it put a stop to the Employers' Association well-funded campaign to destroy the labour movement. Business owners did not forget the solidarity on display any time soon, as the Strike had reduced bank clearings by $10 million per day. While many of the wartime unions did not make it to 1920, overall union membership in Kansas City still showed an increase of 47.5 percent from January 1917, to September 1919, with women's membership increasing 86.7 percent. No wonder, then, that a late 1919 profile of Kansas City in the *New York Times* made it clear that Sarah Green of the Kansas City Women's Trade Union League remained a much-feared figure among employers.[64]

The General Strike's effectiveness was constrained by a number of factors, however. The absence of a strike newspaper limited the ability of leaders and business agents to communicate effectively with the rank and file. In order to prevent the federal government from taking a more repressive line of action, many workers stayed on the job. The emerging red scare among political moderates complicated the strikers' attempts to neutralize the symbolic linkage of prowar attitudes with antistrike sentiment. Finally, the business agents did not put Sarah Green on the General Strike Committee. While there is no evidence this was even discussed as a possibility, having Green on the Strike Committee may have induced stronger support for the General Strike from sympathetic clubwomen.

Nonetheless, the only major predecessors to the Kansas City General Strike in U.S. history were St. Louis in 1877, New Orleans in 1892, and Philadelphia in 1910.[65] The Kansas City labour movement helped pioneer the general strike tactic, and under unlikely circumstances. That they did so by building historically unique levels of class solidarity across gender and race, plus political support from clubwomen, is a testament to the organizing work that the KCWTUL and radical syndicalists engaged in throughout the 1910s.

Notes

1 Alexander M. Bing, *War-Time Strikes and Their Adjustment* (New York: E.P. Dutton and Company, 1921), 30.

2 Quoted in Phillip S. Foner, *History of the Labor Movement in the United States, Volume VII: Labor and World War I, 1914–1918* (New York: International Publishers, 1987), 168.

3 Strike data are from the U.S. Bureau of Labor Statistics. Quote from Maurine Weiner Greenwald, *Women, War, and Work: The Impact of World War I on Women Workers in the United States* (Ithaca, NY: Cornell University Press, 1990), 32; also see Foner, *History of the Labor Movement, Vol. 7*, 150; Joseph A. McCartin, *Labor's Great War: The Struggle for Industrial Democracy and the Origins of Modern American Labor Relations, 1912–1921* (Chapel Hill, NC: University of North Carolina Press, 1997), 38–63; CPI Inflation Calculator, U.S. BLS data, http://www.in2013dollars.com/.

4 Cedric de Leon, *The Origins of Right to Work: Antilabor Democracy in Nineteenth-Century Chicago* (Ithaca: Cornell University Press, 2015).

5 McCartin, *Labor's Great War*, 12–37.

6 Philip Neff and Robert M. Williams, *The Industrial Development of Kansas City* (Federal Reserve Bank of Kansas City, 1954); A. Theodore Brown and Lyle W. Dorsett, *KC: A History of Kansas City, Missouri* (Boulder, CO: Pruett Publishing, 1978); Darryn Snell, "Meat-packing, Race, and Unionization in Kansas City, Kansas, 1880–1904," in *Global Humanization: Studies in the Manufacture of Labor*, ed. M. Neary (London: Mansell, 1999), 127–63.

7 James R. Barrett, *Work and Community in the Jungle: Chicago's Packinghouse Workers, 1894–1922* (Champaign: University of Illinois Press, 1987); Charles Perrow, *Organizing America: Wealth, Power, and the Origins of Corporate Capitalism* (Princeton, NJ: Princeton University Press, 2002).

8 U.S. census data were used to combine both cities in Missouri and Kansas. If we average the African American populations of the five most populous cities (in 1900) by region, then the Northeast remained below 3 percent until after 1910, the Midwest under 4 percent, and the West below 2 percent. U.S. Census, "Historical Census Statistics on Population Totals by Race, 1790 to 1990," https://www.census.gov/content/dam/Census/library/working-papers/2005/demo/POP-twps0076.pdf.

9 Leon Fink, *Workingmen's Democracy: The Knights of Labor and American Politics* (Champaign: University of Illinois Press, 1983), 112–48.

10 Lyle W. Dorsett, *The Pendergast Machine* (1968; repr., Lincoln: University of Nebraska Press, 1980), 3–21; Manning Marable, *How Capitalism Underdeveloped Black America: Problems in Race, Political Economy, and Society* (1983; repr., Chicago: Haymarket Books, 2015), 167.

11 Snell, "Meat-packing, Race and Unionization"; Sherry Lamb Schirmer, *A City Divided: The Racial Landscape of Kansas City, 1900–1960* (Columbia: University of Missouri Press, 2002), 58–60.

12 Melvyn Dubofsky, *We Shall Be All: A History of the Industrial Workers of the World* (1969; repr., Urbana: University of Illinois Press, 2000), 12; David Montgomery, *The Fall of the House of Labor: The Workplace, the State, and American Labor Activism, 1865–1925* (Cambridge, UK: Cambridge University Press, 1987), 199; Daniel Rosenberg, *New Orleans Dockworkers: Race, Labor, and Unionism, 1892–1923* (Albany: State University of New York Press, 1988),12–16, 36, 99–110.

13 Asa E. Martin, *Our Negro Population: A Sociological Study of the Negroes of Kansas City, Missouri* (MA thesis, William Jewell College, 1913), 51–57, 110–20, 134–36; Schirmer, *City Divided,* 49–55; Charles E. Coulter, *"Take Up the Black Man's Burden": Kansas City's African American Communities, 1865–1939* (Columbia: University of Missouri Press, 2006).

14 Edward P. Johanningsmeier, *Forging American Communism: The Life of William Z. Foster* (Princeton, NJ: Princeton University Press, 1994), 60, 71–72; James R. Barrett, *William Z. Foster and the Tragedy of American Radicalism* (Champaign: University of Illinois Press, 1999), 63; Bryan D. Palmer, *James P. Cannon and the Origins of the American Revolutionary Left, 1890–1928* (Champaign: University of Illinois Press, 2007), 52–57.

15 While WTUL rules gave formal majorities to trade union members, branches were typically funded by wealthy members, who also determined branch activities. Nancy Schrom Dye, *As Equals and as Sisters: Feminism, the Labor Movement, and the Women's Trade Union League of New York* (Columbia: University of Missouri Press, 1980); Colette A. Hyman, "Labor Organizing and Female Institution-Building: The Chicago Women's Trade Union League, 1904–24," in *Women, Work, and Protest: A Century of U.S. Women's Labor History,* ed. R. Milkman (Boston: Routledge and Kegan Paul, 1985), 22–41; Sarah Deutsch, *Women and the City: Gender, Space, and Power in Boston, 1870–1940* (Oxford, UK: Oxford University Press, 2000), 196–228.

16 U.S. Library of Congress [LOC], National Women's Trade Union League Papers, reel 20, frames 126–36, KWTUL Report 1910–11; r21, frames 430–35, KWTUL Report 1913–15; LOC, Cornelia Bryce Pinchot Papers, I/9, KCWTUL Report 1917–19.

17 K. David Hanzlick, *Benevolence, Moral Reform, Equality: Women's Activism in Kansas City, 1870 to 1940* (Columbia: University of Missouri Press, 2018), 141, 172–73; Alixandra B. Yanus, "Learning to 'Play the Game as Men Do,'" *PS: Political Science and Politics* (October 2019): 659–62.

18 Correspondence written by Faxon and her husband Henry throughout the mid-1910s can be found in LOC, Leonora O'Reilly Papers, reels 6, 7, 12.

19 ProQuest Historical Newspapers, *The New York Times,* 14 May, 27 June 1903.

20 Stephen H. Norwood, *Strike-Breaking and Intimidation: Mercenaries and Masculinity in Twentieth-Century America* (Chapel Hill: University of North Carolina Press, 2002), 51–70, which mistakenly dates the strike in 1918.

21 *Labor Herald,* 17 August 1917; Kansas City daily newspapers, 8–15 August 1917: *Star, Journal, Post.* All local papers available at the State Historical Society of Missouri [SHSMO].

22 U.S. National Archives [NA], 280 33/621, Telegrams from Woman's Committee on Peaceful Settlement to William B. Wilson 11, 13 August 1917; *Post,* 14 August 1917.

23 *Labor Herald,* 1 March, 29 March 1912, 11 July, 29 August 1913; 3 April 1914.

24 Emily Acker, "Biography of Alice Mary Kimball, 1887–1982," *Alexander Street,* https://documents.alexanderstreet.com/d/1009995309.

25 NA, 280 33/621, Feick's Final Report, 28 November 1917.

26 Wisconsin Historical Society [WHS], AFL Papers, series 117A, file 11A, Samuel Gompers Papers, reel 88, frame 216; NA, 280 33/673, Gill's Final Report, Dec. 10 1917; LOC, Pinchot Papers, KCWTUL 1917–19 Report; *Post,* 7, 9, 12 September 1917.

27 NA, 280 33/690, Gill's Final Report, 10 January 1917; Gill's Report, 5 April 1917; NA, 280 33/673, Gill's Report 2 October 1917; Dailies and *Labor Herald*, September and October 1917.

28 NA, 280 33/993, Porter letter to Department of Labor, 16 March 1918; *Labor Herald*, 22 February 1918.

29 *Star*, 4, 5 March; SHSMO, Kansas City Chamber of Commerce Papers, Executive Committee minutes, 20 March 1918; LOC, Pinchot Papers, KCWTUL Report, 1917–19; *Journal*, 15 March 1918.

30 Black domestics averaged about $3.77/week over a year, including idle weeks, in 1912. Martin, *Our Negro Population*, 56.

31 SHSMO, Annual Report of the Board of Public Welfare (1912–16), 172–74, 206–09, 212–15.

32 LOC, Pinchot Papers, KCWTUL Report, 1917–19; NA, 280 33/993, Industrial Relations Committee, Jackson County Council of National Defense, Report, 13 March 1918; *Star*, 18 February 1918.

33 *Star*, 18, 24, 26, 27 February 1918; *Post*, 16, 20, 27 February 1918; *Journal*, 28 February 1918.

34 NA, 280 33/993, Report of Industrial Relations Committee Report; *Journal*, 4 March 1918; *Star*, 6, 9 March 1918.

35 *Post*, 6 March 1918; NA, 280 33/993, Industrial Relations Committee Report.

36 NA, 280 33/993, Upper House Common Council Committee Report, undated.

37 LOC, Pinchot Papers, KCWTUL Report, 1917–19.

38 Wilford R. Sears, "The Kansas City Building Trades and Trade Unionism" (MA thesis, University of Missouri, 1947), 83.

39 *Star*, 4, 5 March 1918; SHSMO, Kansas City Chamber of Commerce Papers, Executive Committee minutes, 20 March 1918; LOC, Pinchot Papers, KCWTUL Report, 1917–19; *Journal*, 15 March 1918.

40 NA, 280 33/993, Resolution attached to letter from James Anderson to President Wilson, 15 March 1918.

41 James Wolfinger, *Running the Rails: Capital and Labor in the Philadelphia Transit Industry* (Ithaca, NY: Cornell University Press, 2016), 75–88.

42 Sears, "Kansas City Building Trades," 40; Schirmer, *City Divided*, 58–60.

43 Johanningsmeier, *Forging American Communism*, 71–72.

44 Missouri Bureau of Labor Statistics [MBOLS], *Missouri Red Book* (Jefferson City, 1917), 112; *Labor Herald*, 17 May 1912, January–May 1914; WHS, *The Toiler, Kansas City, MO, 1913–15*, microfilm.

45 Earl C. Ford and William Z. Foster, *Syndicalism* (1912; repr., Chicago: Charles H. Kerr Publishing, 1990), 9–10, 12. The book was primarily written by Foster, based on his time spent in Europe.

46 *Star*, 24 March 1918; NA, 280 33/933, Steward Preliminary Report to Department of Labor, 16 March 1918; Steward letter to Kerwin, 16 March 1918.

47 *Star*, 13–15, 24 March 1918; *Journal*, 14 March 1918.

48 NA, 280 33/993, Steward letter to Kerwin, 16 March 1918; WHS, Gompers Papers, reel 93, frame 252–64, Mahon letter to Gompers, 8 April 1918.

49 NA, 280 33/993, Kerwin letter to Porter, 22 March 1918; SHSMO, Kansas City Chamber of Commerce Papers, Executive Committee Minutes, 20, 22 March 1918; daily newspapers, 25 March 1918.

50 *Star*, 24 March; *Post*, 30 March 1918.

51 Keeran quoted in *Star*, 27 March 1918.

52 *Labor Herald*, 8 May 1914; Gary M. Fink, *Labor's Search for Political Order: The Political Behavior of the Missouri Labor Movement, 1890–1940* (Columbia: University of Missouri Press, 1973), 61.

53 Newspapers, 27–28 March 1918; *Star*, 17, 22 March 1918.

54 *Journal*, 28 March 1918; Janet Raye, "Lon Amos Millsap Who Lost His Life in Freedom's Cause," *We Never Forget: The Labor Martyrs Project*, 2018, http://www.weneverforget.org/we-never-forget-lon-amos-millsap-who-lost-his-life-in-freedoms-cause-kansas-city-general-strike-of-1918/; newspapers, 27, 28 March 1918.

55 Newspapers, 28, 29 March 1918.

56 Newspapers, 29, 30 March 1918.

57 WHS, Gompers Papers, Mahon letter to Gompers, 8 April 1918; newspapers, 30, 31 March 1918.

58 Newspapers, 31 March, 1 April 1918.

59 Newspapers, 1, 2 April 1918.

60 *Journal* and *Post*, 3 April 1918. Also see the *Sun* (6 April 1918), a weekly African American newspaper, available at the LOC *Chronicling America* online database.

61 WHS, Gompers Papers, Mahon letter to Gompers, 8 April 1918; NA, 280 33/993, Gill letter to Steward, 6 April 1918.

62 NA, 280 33/993, Gill to W. B. Wilson, 5 April 1918.

63 LOC, Pinchot Papers, KCWTUL Report, 1917–19; MOBLS, *Missouri Redbook 1918–20*, 905.

64 *Post*, 30 March 1918; MOBLS, *Missouri Red Book 1917*, 112; *Missouri Red Book 1918–20*, 905; *New York Times*, 28 December 1919.

65 See Victoria Johnson, *How Many Machine Guns Does It Take to Cook One Meal?: The Seattle and San Francisco General Strikes* (Seattle: University of Washington Press, 2008), 5.

10

The Seattle General Strike: Five Days That Matter

Cal Winslow

On 6 February 1919, at 10:00 a.m., Seattle's workers struck. All of them. The strike was in support of 35,000 shipyard workers, then in conflict with the city's shipyard owners and the federal government's U.S. Shipping Board, the latter still enforcing wartime wage agreements. Silence settled on the city. "Nothing moved but the tide," recalled the young African American Earl George, just demobilized at nearby Camp Lewis.[1]

The strike's origin was in the war years, but stretched as well to the tumultuous decade before that in which Seattle's workers became a class, a class made by themselves. In what was to be the culmination of this decade of free speech fights, bloody waterfront battles, class war in the woods, and the development of an extraordinary trade union movement, workers took control of a modern industrial city and ran it for five remarkable days, five days that matter.

11 November 1918, the war in Europe ended. There were wild celebrations everywhere. Millions took to the streets of Paris, London, and New York. The *Seattle Star* pronounced, "War is Over!" The people learned of the armistice on Sunday night, the tenth; at once, they took to the streets. In the morning, the mayor was awakened to find the streets

filled, his projected proclamation of a "holiday" irrelevant; his plan for a great, patriotic manifestation had been superseded.

Makeshift bands appeared, people banging garbage can lids and lunch buckets, and car horns blasting. The shipyards were abandoned; the city centre was in gridlock. The city's health authorities too were taken aback; there were no masks, the city still staggering back from the great pandemic of 1918. Sailors, carriers of the influenza, also its first victims in Seattle, were ordered into the crowds to ensure that the celebration would be controlled and properly official.

"The war to end all wars," the patriotic papers repeated without a blush. Ten million lost in the slaughter on the Western Front; 36 million casualties. In central and eastern Europe, millions more dead, vast swathes of devastation, the heart of the continent in ruins, new armies, this time of scavengers, of homeless, creatures without hope—the *Star* featured a half-page, triumphant Jesus, "Peace on Earth." Then the mindless boastings of victory, of "sacred unions," "homes for heroes, "democracy at full tilt." "We won the war!" The workers of Seattle, however, had never really supported this war, unless, of course, one reduces "support" to mean "supporting the troops," the mantra in all wars. Still, they celebrated; especially if it meant an end to long hours, short pay, conscription, to "sedition" charges and "criminal syndicalism" laws, to the red squads, raids, prison sentences.

Seattle can be grim in November, more so perhaps in December. In the winter of 1918, much of the city—the schools, most public places—was still reopening. It remained unclear if the epidemic was in fact finished, and indeed there was a second spike just before Christmas. The heavy rains had begun. The first loggers were drifting back; they joined others—wandering, homeless men on the city's mean streets, waiting for spring and work to resume. This was ordinary in Seattle in winter. Now, however, newcomers appeared, some still in uniform, wanting work. Some sick. The *Union Record,* the city's union-owned daily newspaper, reported that "peace" abroad was bringing hunger at home. One man, a union representative from the Metal Trades Council (MTC), told reporters that he had been approached "by 15 soldiers in one night, all for bed and board."[2]

Seattle's shipyard workers believed they had sacrificed for the sake of the war. Their hours had been long, the work gruelling. Hulet Wells, the one-time socialist president of the Central Labor Council (CLC), also president of the state's Socialist Party, then awaiting sentencing for opposing conscription, sought temporary employment at Skinner and Eddy, the largest of the yards. There he found a "howling bedlam . . . a wilderness of strange machines, whirling belts and belching fires . . . The human ant heap boiled with all the specialists that fit into the modern shipyard. Everywhere there was deafening noise, boilers rang, planers screamed, long white-hot rods were smashed into bolt machines. Here was the angle-bending floor where Black men beat a tattoo with heavy sledges, and here a steam hammer thumped its measured blows." Add to this "the wrenching scenes of the injured, the sirens of the ambulances, and the dying or dead being carted off into the chaos of the waterfront roadways."[3]

The shipyard workers had worked with standards set nationally, even when believing themselves punished by these standards. It was indisputable that prices were higher on the West Coast, above all in Seattle, than in the East. In 1917 and 1918, the city's unions increasingly felt pressure from the federal government and its shipping board to abide by wartime restrictions. So in 1919 the unions were especially intent on raising the wages of the unskilled and semiskilled, an immediate necessity in breaking down divisions in the shops. However, wage demands were repeatedly rejected, and by the war's end, the workers felt betrayed by the government. They had been lied to, they believed—by the president, the Shipping Board, by the city's health officials. They were bitter, angry, and itching for a fight. They voted to strike in December. The shipyard strike was inevitable.

The men walked out the morning of 21 January 1919. There were women scattered through their ranks, also Black workers, though they were few and their union status is unclear. Virtually all the American Federation of Labor's (AFL's) national unions in these trades barred women and Blacks, but Seattle's metal trades had won the closed shop and controlled hiring. A.E. Miller, the chairman of the MTC, announced the strike "absolutely clean," that is 35,000 struck en masse, and none came to take their places. They showed "splendid solidarity and great enthusiasm," undaunted by the winter rain.[4] Tacoma, then Aberdeen, quickly followed. Speaking on behalf of the workers, John McKelvey confronted the owners. The "shipyard millionaires have been getting all the credit for the ships we have built."[5]

The *Union Record* brought news of the strikers' fight to its 50,000 subscribers, supporting the Strike without qualification. Next to its front-page lead on 21 January, "45,000 Men Out in Sound Cities," it ran an article titled, "Tremendous Profits Made by Seattle Shipbuilding Firms," revealing the businesses' costs, sales, and profits. The day's editorial, "A Great Strike," explained: "The whole question of wages is bound up in the tremendous increase in the cost of living in Seattle."[6]

This was true enough in itself—but also an indication of deeper frustrations and dissatisfactions. The strike wave of the war years—"an epidemic of strikes" was local, national, and international, inspired in part by syndicalism—workplace and trade union–based socialism and a wave of radicalism. And Seattle was both a strike centre and a radical centre, a stronghold of working-class socialism; its unions' commitment to workers' control ran deep and support for the Russian Revolution was widespread.

Meanwhile, Seattle was filling up with unemployed, homeless, demobilized young men and still not entirely free from the flu. The *Union Record* foresaw unemployment and "bread lines coming."[7] "It looks as if that move for the six-hour day or even the four-hour day, in order to pass the jobs around, may be needed in a hurry, right here in Seattle."[8] The machinists of Hope Lodge proposed "a shortening of the work day policy as palliative to unemployment, for civilians and discharged service men alike, as a result of the large number of men suddenly thrown on the labor market." The response of the MTC was a packed Hippodrome with thousands to announce the formation of a "Soldiers, Sailors and Workers Council."[9] The meeting went forward despite the authorities who surrounded the hall with military police. Thousands gathered in Tacoma as well, including Camp Lewis soldiers, no longer under quarantine. At the same time, it became clear that unions did not know with whom they were to negotiate, the national board, or the local employers. In either case, the employers, passing the buck back and forth, refused to budge, as did the eastern board members, the shippers, and their allies in the national AFL unions.

The MTC turned to Seattle's CLC, representative of 120 local unions—the organization that in defiance of the national AFL was built from the bottom up, that championed industrial unions, supported sympathy strikes, cooperated with the Industrial Workers of the

World (IWW), and was led by socialists—with a request for support for a general strike.

"The idea of a general strike swept through the ranks of organized labor like a gale," wrote Harvey O'Conner, the author of the marvellous memoir *Revolution in Seattle*.[10] On 22 January, in an assembly of the CLC, in the Labor Temple, the metal workers made their case, requesting that Seattle's workers join them in a general strike. The aim would be not only to win their demands but also to present a show of force in the face of the employers' renewed open-shop campaign. They believed that the fate of the organized labour movement itself was at stake. Representatives of the city's local trade unions and rank-and-file militants packed the Labor Temple. According to O'Conner, "Every reference to the general strike was cheered to the echo; the cautions of the conservatives . . . were hooted down," or interrupted by shouting, clapping, and singing. The CLC proposed a referendum on the strike, which passed unanimously. The enthusiasm that evening brought with it high rhetoric, emotion, even tears. Then came a cornucopia of demands; appetites grew, delegates revealing their own grievances and aspirations, hopeful that these too might be addressed. The metal workers, however, insisted that the strike's demands be limited to those of the shipyard workers already out—what they wanted was a "clean-cut demonstration of the economic power of organized labor."[11]

On the morning of 6 February, then, Seattle's workers simply put down their tools. It was, however, no ordinary strike. There had been nothing like this in the United States before, nor has there been since. In doing so, they virtually took control of the city. Anna Louise Strong, a young reporter writing in the *Union Record*, announced the movement's intentions: "Labor will feed the People. . . . Labor will care for the babies and the sick. . . . Labor will preserve order. . . ." And indeed it did.[12] Seattle's CLC, craft unions, all affiliated with the AFL, sanctioned the General Strike. The *Union Record* reported 65,000 union members on strike. Perhaps as many as 100,000 working people participated; the strikers were joined by unorganized workers, unemployed workers, and family members. The Strike rendered the authorities virtually powerless. There were soldiers in the city, and many more at nearby Camp Lewis, not to mention thousands of newly enlisted, armed deputies—but to unleash these on a peaceful city? The regular police were reduced to onlookers; the generals hesitated.

Seattle in 1919 was a city of 300,000. A prosperous and progressive city, it had won women's suffrage, prohibition, and planning. Its prosperity was built largely on its port. Its municipal piers were state of the art, pride of the city's reformers. Seattle was terminus of the northern railroads, gateway to Alaska, and it was two days closer to China than its rival, San Francisco.

Seattle had long been a working-class destination, for the adventurous as well as for the victims of the squalid East. Freethinkers and utopians had encamped in utopian "colonies" nearby in the 1890s, intent on founding an industrial democracy in their own time. Eugene Debs, the old railroad man and socialist icon, encouraged socialists to settle in Washington, at one point even suggesting 300,000 resettle from Chicago. He considered it "the most advanced state" and admired its 1900 Socialist Party platform: "We are fighting for no half-way measures."[13]

Seattle's unions supported the reforms of the era's Progressives. They endorsed women's suffrage and public ownership, but were divided on prohibition. Nevertheless, labour steadily shifted to the left in the 1910s, driven by widening conflict with employers and in keeping with the new syndicalism and the national strike wave that began with and intensified during the First World War. When the U.S. Commission on Industrial Relations met in the city in 1914, Wisconsin labour specialist John R. Commons attended, observing that in Seattle he "found more bitter feeling between employers and employees than in any other U.S. city."[14] The economic recovery that began in 1914, spurred on by the war in Europe, would last into the summer of 1920. It gave millions of workers both the confidence to switch jobs when it was to their advantage, and the willingness to strike on a scale that "dwarfed all previously recorded turnover and strike activity." In the years 1919 to 1922 there were more than 10,000 strikes involving 8 million workers, 4 million in 1919 alone.[15]

Then, too, the international revolt—culminating in 1919 with rebellion in Germany, Hungary, Egypt, the Irish war of independence, the fate of the revolution in Russia still unknown. The Seattle General Strike was a precursor of what was to come that year, a succession of spectacular battles. Some have seen the Winnipeg General Strike, for example, as an extension of what happened in Seattle. Indeed, the Canadian strikers, to the alarm of authorities on both sides of the border, feted James Duncan, CLC secretary, and a delegation from Seattle as a gesture of international solidarity. Then came further strikes in diverse sectors—garments, steel, coal, the Boston police, and the New York longshoremen. All historic, even in defeat.

Seattle's socialists, and nearly all Socialist Party members, were advocates of industrial unionism. They sat at the helm of the city's unions, where they had their own version of it, "Duncanism," after James "Jimmy" Duncan, president of the CLC. The craft unions were united in "councils" with joint common bargaining, common expiration dates, and common contracts. The Metal Trades Council was the most powerful of these. Seattle was also home to the *Industrial Worker*, the western paper of the IWW. Its crusades for direct action and industrial democracy were influential far beyond its numbers, perhaps no place more so than in the Northwest. Seattle, then, became the base camp for radical workers throughout Washington, but also in Alaska, Oregon, and the mining towns of Idaho and Montana.

Western Washington timber continued to dominate the regional economy, and in few industries was conflict more intense. IWW organizer James Thompson, testifying before the Industrial Relations Commission, reported the loggers "breathe bad air in the camps. That ruins their lungs. They eat bad food. That ruins their stomachs. The foul conditions shorten their lives and make their short lives miserable."[16]

When winter rains made work in the woods impossible, loggers settled in Seattle, sleeping in Skid Road's flophouses, seeking relief in its brothels and cheap saloons. There they were joined by migrant agriculturalists, redundant railroad workers, and blacklisted miners. They also mingled with Seattle's radicals, including the rapidly increasing ranks of shipyard workers. It was an explosive mix.

Seattle's organized labour movement grew in these years, though not evenly. A bitter waterfront strike in 1916 was defeated. A strike that same year by shingle weavers in nearby Everett was broken, brutally and in the end only after six workers were murdered. The strikers had appealed for support, and in early November 1916, 250 unarmed IWW members boarded the steamships *Verona* and *Calista* in Seattle, setting sail to support their embattled fellow workers in Everett. When the *Verona* entered Port Gardner Bay, its passengers were singing the English transport workers' song:

We meet today in freedom's cause, And raise our voices high;
We'll join our hands in union strong, To battle or to die.

Hold the fort for we are coming, Union men be strong,
Side by side we battle onward, Victory will come!

The dock was silent as the *Verona* approached, though a cheer rose from the hillside beyond, where thousands of Everett workers and their families assembled to welcome the Wobblies. Those on board did not know that a small army awaited them, nor suspect what was in store. Certainly no one expected a warm welcome from the authorities. Neither did they foresee murder. On the dock they were met and surrounded by gun-packing deputies and vigilantes who opened fire from both sides on the *Verona* as it docked. Six Wobblies were killed, as were two deputies in the crossfire. Seventy-four IWW survivors were charged with murder.

The massacre was seen as an assault on free speech, fair play, and the very notion of "rights." Disbelief, then anger, coursed through Seattle's working-class districts. In an act of collaboration increasingly common among the city's competing unions, Seattle's CLC joined in the defence of the victims.

The IWW made the Everett catastrophe its cause célèbre. When the Wobblies were acquitted, it was cause for celebration. Wobbly membership soared, setting the stage for the general strike in the woods which followed that June. Some 50,000 loggers struck; the strike would stretch into the next year. Ultimately, in part due to federal intervention, it was won—the eight-hour day, dramatically better conditions in the camps, child labour banned. But not without cost; the authorities and the lumbermen, humiliated in the woods, responded with savage repression. For the loggers, the Red Scare (and the Palmer Raids) began in Washington's woods, culminating in Centralia in November 1919, where Wesley Everest, veteran, logger, and IWW member, was lynched.

Working-class Seattle's great forum was the Labor Temple, the auditorium where the council met. Strong recalled it "filled with unionists, radicals, and Wobblies, listening to the dramatic debates and the speeches by visiting luminaries . . . and where "every Wednesday night the Central Labor Council sat till midnight listening to emissaries of suppressed and rebelling peoples. . . . We were stirred by the seizure of factories in Germany, by the mutiny of French troops in Odessa, by the rising of soviets in Hungary and Bavaria."[17] And there, free speech was the order of the day. "The suppression anywhere of ordinary rights of free speech added zest and exhilaration to the scene as people struggled, in guarded and Aesopian terms, to express the ideas that burned within them."[18]

In these years, the IWW, the Socialists, and the CLC's rank and file increasingly found themselves on the same stages, in the same demonstrations, and on the same street corners—collaborating on issues such as Everett, preparedness, May Day, and repression. The IWW remained relentless in condemning craft unions; the Socialists would not retreat on the need for a party; the Duncanites insisted on staying within the mainstream. Yet the IWW was gracious in accepting support from the CLC on Everett, and the CLC and the *Union Record* joined in celebrating the Everett trial victory. Further, it was no secret that Seattle's working people admired the courage and direct action of the loggers and the mill workers, supporting them regardless of their nominal allegiance to Samuel Gompers, president of the AFL, and his acolytes. In 1917 and 1918 there existed a modus vivendi on the ground. More, there was a division of labour; the IWW working in the woods and fields, the CLC in the cities and in the shops. On the waterfront, cooperation was complex, but it took the form of a common front against the shippers and the national officers of the International Longshoremen's Association (ILA).

"I belong to the IWW for a principle and to the AFL for a job": this was the "two-card man." O'Connor suggests there may have been several thousand workers holding both AFL and IWW cards.[19] This allowed the logger to work on the docks, the harvest hand to work in construction, and IWW members to have steady jobs in occupations and workplaces represented by AFL local unions. The national AFL leaders were scandalized; they demanded the expulsion of the two-card men. The CLC, typically, refused. Some of these workers may have been boring from within, in practice "dual unionists." The majority, however, were simply good union workers living with the reality of two working-class movements. The IWWs, the two-card men, and the CLC's rank and file rubbed shoulders, fraternized, and fused into a still provisional but radicalized militant majority in Seattle's labour movement.

The IWW's vision certainly pulled the others, but the IWW adapted as well, becoming ever more like the unions it still denounced—with its "on the job" strategy in the woods, its members on the city's waterfront, in AFL shops and local unions, and above all in the shipyard's wild multitude. Seattle's working class, then, was unparalleled.

Of course, there were radicals elsewhere, but they tended to be a fringe. In Seattle, however, there was a radical consensus. Seattle workers welcomed radical ideas as well as radical visitors, and political lines were fluid. Margaret Sanger and Emma Goldman each visited in turn during the summer of 1916. Goldman spoke on "Anarchism and Human Nature" at the Tivoli Theater, Sanger on "The Right of the Child not to Be Born" at the longshoremen's hall.[20] In the aftermath of the Russia Revolutions, Louise Bryant, Albert Rhys Williams, Raymond Robbins, Robert Minor, and Wilfred Humphries came to speak. Strong remembers when Louise Bryant returned from the revolution in Russia to dazzle the smoke-laden air of the close-packed longshoremen's hall: "We heard voices of women's freedom, of the equality of backward [*sic*] races, of children rationed first when supplies were scant. . . . I spent hours, sometimes days, with each of these lecturers, and wrote whole series of articles from what they told me." Strong admired "these messengers" yet "not once in those years did it occur to me to leave Seattle . . . The reason is simple . . . the revolution had begun in Moscow [*sic*], but not in Moscow alone. It was world revolution that took us in. Its messengers crossed all seas, from India, Ireland, Germany, and Hungary. It had begun in Moscow, but it was coming to Seattle; and Seattle was our battle post. We also were part of this new world."[21]

In the city's shops and factories and offices, the CLC's Duncan declared 1917 "a red-letter year in the history of organized labor. A dozen new unions have been organized and all of Seattle unions are flourishing."[22] These included large numbers of women workers, 1,100 "telephone girls," hundreds of laundresses, and hotel maids. The Seattle CLC, unlike many counterparts, understood and endorsed the "vital importance of the [AFL] Pacific Coast movement's campaign to organize women workers in all industries."[23] The *Union Record* championed the women's unions and their strikes. It also covered an array of women's issues—Mary Heaton Vorse, one of labour's most celebrated journalists, was a regular contributor, frequently reporting on the conditions of women workers. Readers debated whether married women ought or ought not to work. Organized labour in Seattle grew by 300 percent in 1917, and the closed shop became the rule.

In 1919, then, with the war behind them, Seattle's workers were well-organized and experienced fighters. It was a city, wrote Anna Louise Strong, who had become a mainstay at the *Union Record* by the time of the strike, "divided into two hostile camps."[24] Class lines had hardened.

It was in this context that shipyard workers went out on strike, on 21 January 1919. It had been expected, indeed long postponed. The 35,000 strikers celebrated; cheering throngs left the yards in the winter rains and swarmed into the city's streets. According to Miller, "the men walked out en masse, none remained in the plants."[25] Tacoma followed suit with 15,000 more, then Aberdeen. Again, none came to take their places.

The shipyard strike was about wages, pure and simple. Yet the city was on edge. Just three nights earlier, thousands of Seattle's workers had packed the Hippodrome, where the Metal Trades, fearful of the discharged soldiers as strikebreakers, had announced formation of their "Soldiers, Sailors and Workers' Council." The meeting was held despite the authorities; the hall was surrounded by military police.[26]

The shipyard workers were defiant. John McKelvey, speaking for the metal workers, made this clear. The "shipyard millionaires," he reminded readers, "have been getting all the credit for the ships we have built. Oh yes, they're the ship builders. If they think they can build ships, let 'em go ahead and build them! They've got the yards. Can they build ships?" Dan McKillop, a Boilermakers' official, responding to ship builders' threats to close: "If they think they can build ships, let them go ahead and build them."[27]

The solidarity of Seattle's workers in the Strike was, by any standard, staggering; workers from barbers to boilermakers would cease work. There would be no pickets—as there were no strikebreakers. Still, qualifications need be made. Seattle and the Puget Sound country were not immune to the anti-Chinese movements of the 1880s and 1890s. Thus, by 1919, the Chinese in Seattle were few, and the experience of the Japanese, then the city's largest minority, was likewise one of discrimination and exclusion.

The historian Katsutoshi Kurokawa, however, has documented instances of solidarity with Japanese workers. In his study of Japanese immigrants in Seattle, Kurokawa wrote, "The IWW's appeal for unity of workers of all countries, and its opposition to racial discrimination was genuine. The Japanese community in Seattle understood this fact."[28] Moreover, "In the late 1910s," he wrote, "progressive and radical activists who had no racial prejudice increased their influence in the Seattle labor movement." Kurokawa pointed to Duncan's inauguration as a "milestone."[29]

There were others. Kate Sadler was a fierce opponent of Asian exclusion. Sadler took to the streets to oppose it, from the skid road up and down. Socialist journalist, and chronicler of the General Strike, Anna Louise Strong had travelled widely—including to Japan—before settling in Seattle.

On the eve of the Strike, the Japanese unions approached Duncan, offering support. Duncan accepted and Japanese unions joined, contributing conspicuously to the euphoric solidarity of the day. In the great meeting convened to sanction the Strike, "A Woman Who Was There" reflected on the "high rhetoric, great emotion, even tears . . ." In the Strike itself, she recalled, "The Japanese and American restaurant workers went out side by side. The Japanese barbers struck when the American barbers struck and were given seats of honor at the barbers' union meeting that occurred immediately thereafter."[30]

The *Union Record*, in its first strike edition, concurred: "Even in the midst of strike excitement, let us stop for a moment to recognize the action of the Japanese barbers and restaurant workers who, through their own unions, voted to take part in the general strike. The strike here in Seattle is proving the biggest demonstration of internationalism that has yet occurred in this country."[31] The Japanese, it concluded, "deserve the greater credit because they have been denied admission and affiliation with the rest of the labor movement and have joined the strike of their own Initiative. We hope that this evidence of labor's solidarity will have an influence on the relations between the two races in the future." Kurokawa reported that these events resonated widely throughout the Japanese population.[32]

The general strike as a tactic was widely identified with the IWW. Yet the CLC had used the threat of a general strike half a dozen times as a bargaining chip in fights for wages and benefits, as well as in its insistence that the closed shop prevail. But for Sadler, the general strike was about far more—the power of workers to transform society: "We will progress to the full knowledge that no man is good enough to be another man's master. That the private ownership of things used in common must go, and social ownership take its place."[33]

Sadler, now a "hard-core North westerner," flourished in Seattle. She was born in poverty in Scotland, where she "learned socialism at her father's knee." In the United States, she came first to Philadelphia, where she worked as a domestic. There she met Sam Sadler, the longshoremen's future leader, and in 1909 they moved west, settling in Seattle. In the decade that followed, Sadler worked tirelessly to build the Socialist Party. O'Connor considered her "a peerless socialist orator," on the level with Kate Richards O'Hare and Elizabeth Gurley Flynn.[34] Sadler was Seattle's representative to the Socialist Party's National Committee, but she rarely returned east; her commitment was to the workers of Seattle and its hinterland. Here, she supported workers whenever called, as long as someone could pay expenses. Sadler was as well known in the mining camps and mill towns as in the Puget Sound cities. She was also the featured guest at Colville's 1916 socialist "encampment," a weekend educational event in the tiny mining and timber town in Washington's far northeast corner. "Kate Sadler," they announced, welcoming her, "is one of the great socialist women of the nation. . . . She is known throughout the length and breadth of Washington as a fearless champion of the working class. A veritable reincarnation of Joan of Arc, Kate Sadler's splendidly fiery eloquence inspires hope, kindles courage, and arouses enthusiasm among the workers wherever she is heard." Organizers promoted her as "full to overflowing with what Debs so aptly calls 'the fine spirit of revolt.' We especially invite the women and the young people to hear her. You will never regret it."[35]

A 1917 report from Everett recounts her giving an "inspiring lecture," speaking on the "War Crisis" to a large outdoor crowd. Other accounts find her in Sumas on the Canadian border; in Liberty, a mining camp in the Cascades; and in Pierce County's coal camps. At Butte's metal mine workers' June picnic in 1919, "the event of the day [was] an address by Kate Sadler of Seattle, labor's gifted woman orator, who [talked about] world happenings and their relation to the working class."[36] O'Connor wrote that "when workers called for help, in strikes, jailings, free speech struggles, Kate came. Kate the fearless one. . . . The police, of course, knew her, [but] always hesitated to drag her off the soapbox, for the workers formed an iron ring, daring them to touch *our* Kate."[37]

When the shipyard workers, on strike since 21 January, appealed to the CLC for support, there was no opposition to speak of. The workers, union by union, elected the Strike's leadership, a strike committee comprised largely of rank-and-file workers. The Strike Committee elected an executive committee. These bodies, meeting virtually nonstop, ensured the health, welfare, and safety of the city. Garbage was collected, the hospitals were supplied, babies got milk, and the people were fed, including some 30,000 a day at the strikers' kitchens. There may have been no other time, before or since, when no one went hungry in the city. The streets were safe—rarely safer—patrolled by an unarmed labour guard. It was reported that crime abated. Off the streets, Seattle was a festival—in the union halls, the co-op markets, "feeding stations," and neighbourhood centres where workers and their families gathered. On Saturday night there was a dance. A massive Monday night strike rally in Georgetown attracted a crowd so large, the building had to be evacuated. The meeting reconvened, and with "great enthusiasm . . . it was decided to make the meetings a regular weekly event . . . it was unanimous that the strike should continue until a living wage had been obtained by the shipyard workers. . . . Many of those present expressed the opinion that the scope of the meetings should be enlarged to include the wives and daughters of the workers, and to make them real community gatherings."[38] In all these places the Strike was the topic—it was analyzed, criticized, extolled, and debated, and thus when these workers representatives packed the rowdy, emotion-filled Strike Committee meetings they came prepared. They were making history and they knew it.

Local historian Kathleen O'Connell called it "a calm sort of strike, the tensions all submerged," pointing out that workers walked out "quietly and amiably" into empty streets.[39] This was true in the sense that there was no storming of the Winter Palace and almost no violence. This high level of discipline was the work of the Labor Guards—union officers and veterans who belonged to unions—who carried no weapons and wore only white armbands to identify themselves.[40] The New York *Tribune*'s reporter wrote, "The normal police docket fell to about 30."[41] The IWW had long insisted that workers' power came with "arms folded," and this image of a pacific but assertive worker gets us closer to the truth, for there was no shortage of activity in the Strike, nor was enthusiasm in any way absent. Joe Pass, a young New Yorker, resident in Seattle, writing in the New York *Call*,[42] exclaimed that only "an immortal" could have "lived through the five days of the strike in Seattle and emerged impartial.... Men whose temperature in the past remained around the frigid zone suddenly awakened from their cold atmosphere in passionate ecstasy ... Professors from the University of Washington, keen students who are studying the labor movement at close range, lose their pedagogical dignity and cheer loudly and wildly the enthusiastic assembly ... and a woman next to me sheds tears from the pure joy of living." Pass also learned of a union official "dispatched to the city in an effort to halt the streetcar men from 'breaking' their agreement with the company who, "after 24 hours . . . was so affected by the spirit of the hour that he advised the car men to join their striking fellow workers, and so defeated this original purpose of coming. Miracles were the order of the day."[43]

There was indeed virtually no violence, and that is what the strikers wanted, which is perplexing only if radicalism is associated with violence. Certainly, the employers and the press clamoured for blood, and the authorities prepared for a confrontation. The workers whose paths home that first morning took them through downtown streets discovered machine guns in place and sandbag barricades. Those who passed by the armoury met munitions wagons clogging the streets on all sides and soldiers everywhere. Armed vigilantes gathered on city street corners. The *Union Record* stated the union's position: "Sane men there are, some, who believe that in the end all peaceful means to abolish the profit system will fail, and the age-long struggle between the suppressors and the oppressed will close with violence. But no sane man believes that time is now."[44] The *Star*, the *Record* explained, "pretends to believe that the unarmed and defenseless workers mean to capture City Hall and run up the red flag in spite of the fact ... that the workers know that there are thousands of soldiers in Camp Lewis and Fort Lawton.... [No] revolution of violence will be started during this strike be the strike long or short."[45] This was the consensus; the Strike was in support of the shipyard workers. It was to be the trade unions' show of strength.

It was not a revolution, nor a conspiracy, yet its roots were deep.

It was planned, but its outcome could not have been predicted. Few, for example, expected the utter intransigence of the shipyard owners and the government. The Strike was, then, a radical departure for U.S. labour: planned, but open-ended, the future not known. How could it have been anything else? Surely all wanted to see the shipyard workers victorious. And all wanted to see the labour movement strengthened in the process. Beyond this, clarity did indeed fade. "Truth was," wrote O'Connor, "a revolutionary spark did exist in Seattle in February 1919. The strike leaders knew that as well as the government."[46] There was indeed a far left of dissenters, of revolutionaries, though it was not clear how many. O'Connor himself wrote the text for "Russia Did It," a flyer showing a brawny worker (drawn by Morris Pass) shoving a fat little capitalist into a coffin. There were 20,000 copies of this flyer, which was aimed at shipyard workers, arguing that the workers should take over the yards. "Take over the management of the shipyards yourselves," it proposed, "make the shipyards your own, make the jobs your own, decide the working conditions yourselves, decide your wages yourselves." There is no doubt that there were workers who responded favourably to the flyer's argument. The ideas were in the air. For example, socialist unionists in the CLC demanded that if the Strike were prolonged the strikers should "take over the shipbuilding industry, eliminate the bosses, and operate in the interests of the workers," while Sam Sadler advocated confiscating food supplies and declaring a rent moratorium.[47] Seattle, however, was not Gdansk. The yards remained in the owners' hands, defended by soldiers and armed company guards.

"The exhilaration from the marvelous display of solidarity experienced Thursday and Friday began to give way to apprehension," wrote O'Connor. "By the third day of the strike they realized that the Seattle labor movement stood all alone."[48] The Strike had not spread down the coast to California, nor was there support from around the nation. There was little, O'Connor observed, "to give aid and comfort, even verbally, to the labor movements of Seattle and Tacoma. Seattle, unfortunately, was all too unique in its militancy."[49] And, against them, the response of the authorities was unrelenting, especially the fearmongers. They frantically forecast a terrible future at hand, Bolshevism, anarchy. Ole Hanson, a real estate agent elected mayor, egged on by the papers, denounced the Strike as "un-American" and refused to negotiate. The *Post-Intelligencer* observed, "The big fact that stands out from the temporary confusion of business is that Seattle, given a brief time for readjustment, would be well off, if not better than before, if the whole of its striking population [were] suddenly withdrawn from the city."[50] The Seattle *Star* in a jingoist editorial titled "Under Which Flag!" declared, "There can be no compromise on Americanism."[51] Hanson threatened martial law, if the Strike were not ended by 10:00 a.m. on Saturday. The "Interests" in New York and Washington, DC, joined the chorus. The Teamsters' Joint Council ordered strikers back to work. There were telephone calls and telegrams, a deluge of intimidation, threats, vilification from the international offices. The AFL censored the CLC and would later take credit for defeating its "strike." Then the international officers arrived in person, threatening to rescind charters, seize union properties, and fire staff. Meanwhile, the shipyards in the East and California carried on as usual. The risk of the owners shutting down the Seattle yards now seemed only too real.

On Saturday, 8 February, several unions returned, though this was by no means a stampede. The executive committee took advantage and voted 11 to 2 to end the Strike. They chose Duncan, not a delegate, to speak to the Strike Committee for them. He tried to convince those in attendance that continuing the Strike was futile. He failed. The Strike Committee, infuriated by Hanson's threats and still committed to staying out, overwhelmingly voted to continue the Strike. The longshoremen and the metal trades led the movement to carry on with the Strike; the divide increasingly became one between the rank and file, on the one hand, and the executive committee, on the other. Then on Monday, with more unions yielding, Duncan returned to the Strike Committee. He recommended ending the Strike on Tuesday at noon. He requested that those unions that had returned to their jobs come back out so that the strikers could return united; as they had left on Thursday they would return on Tuesday. The shipyard strikers remained out one month more.

The Strike lasted through the weekend, five working days. Then, unions began returning to work, first individually, then in small batches. On Tuesday, the Strike was pronounced off. Duncan, sensibly, would have preferred all to go back together. But just as some unions wanted to go back, many favoured staying out. Still, the authorities had stubbornly resisted negotiation, solidarity strikes failed to materialize, and the majority felt they had made their point.

"We did something in this strike which has never been done before," explained Ben Neuman of the Hoisting Engineers, a leader of the Strike Committee.[52] "Most of the men went back to work in good spirits" (observed "the woman who was there"), "realizing, not indeed that they had won the recognition of the shipyard workers which they had asked for, but that perhaps they had done something bigger."[53] The *History of the General Strike*, produced by the CLC, written by Strong, reported,

> The workers of Seattle did not go back to work with the feeling that they had been beaten. They went smiling, like men who had gained something worth gaining, like men who had done a big job and done it well. The men went back, feeling that they had won the strike. . . . They went back proud of themselves for the way they had come out; proud of themselves for the way they had kept order under provocation; glad to have gained so much education with so little comparative suffering; glad to have worked shoulder to shoulder with their fellow unionists on a lot of big problems; and a bit relieved, to tell the truth, that no one had been raided, no one shot and that the labor movement of Seattle was still "going strong." For they were quite aware that they had held in their hands a weapon which might have exploded in any one of a dozen different directions. They were glad to find themselves able to use it, to examine it and to lay it down without any premature explosions.[54]

Today, this Strike is largely forgotten, or worse, when remembered, dismissed as a lost cause. The dailies had pronounced, "The Revolution is Over." Hanson took personal responsibility for breaking the Strike and embarked on a nationwide speaking tour to boast of this. Gompers at the AFL joined in, extolling the defeat of the "revolution" and pledging to rid the unions of the radicals. One historian of the Strike, Robert Friedheim, denigrated it as a "disaster"—that is, "a near fatal setback for Seattle's working people."[55]

It was neither. It was a not a revolution nor had it been intended to be one. It was a strike to support the shipyard workers, though it did contain a "revolutionary spark." Seattle's workers returned to work "proud" of their strike, "cheerfully" believing they "had made their point," wrote the *Union Record*. With their unions intact, they would live to fight another day.[56] In the meantime, the IWW commended Seattle as having shown the general strike to be a useful weapon in labour's "arsenal." The New York *Call,* congratulating the strikers, explained the Strike as an indication that capital's days were numbered.

Seattle's workers had formed themselves as a class in conflict—in their experience in a decade of struggle. They forged this class identity in the long, hard fight for industrial unions and the closed shop, and in the fight for workers' power. At an early moment, the utopians—the colonies and the Co-operative Commonwealth—had preached workers' power. Later, the IWW and the Socialists fought for it, with the CLC, one step at a time, aspiring to implement it. The 1910s had been a decade of organizing, cooperating, and striking, the most basic weapons of working people in battles that were sometimes won and sometimes lost. Consciousness arose in the utopian colonies; in logging camps and mills; in free speech fights; in the Everett catastrophe; and on the waterfront; in war and in dissent; in strikes of the "telephone girls," waitresses, hotel maids, "lady barbers," and laundry workers; in co-ops; and in working-class neighbourhoods. Seattle's workers transformed a world of war, of sickness, death and grief into a great celebration of the living, if only for five days. The General Strike was for Seattle's workers a giant step toward a future that might be theirs. These aspirations were valid in terms of their own experience.

Max Eastman, the Greenwich Village intellectual, in Seattle, spoke for many when he judged that Seattle "filled with hope and happiness the hearts of millions of people in all places of the earth . . . [it] demonstrated the possibility of that loyal solidarity of the working class which is the sole remaining hope of liberty for mankind."[57] Hardly a "disaster," far from quashed, the Seattle General Strike remains, borrowing from Rosa Luxemburg, a link in the great chain of historic events that is the pride and strength of international socialism.

Notes

1 This phrase is from Earl George, interviewed in Rob Rosenthal, "After the Deluge, the Seattle General Strike and Its Aftermath" (MA thesis, University of California, Santa Barbara, 1980).

2 *Union Record* [Seattle], 4 January 1919.

3 Hulet Wells, "I Wanted to Work," Wells Papers, University of Washington Special Collections, n.d., box 1, folder 5, 182.

4 *Union Record,* 21 January 1919.
5 Harvey O'Connor, *Revolution in Seattle* (New York: Monthly Review Press, 1963), 128.
6 *Union Record,* 21 January 1919.
7 O'Connor, *Revolution in Seattle,* 128.
8 *Union Record,* 4 January 1919.
9 Ibid.
10 O'Connor, *Revolution in Seattle,* 128–29.
11 O'Connor, 129.
12 *Union Record,* 6 February 1919.
13 Cal Winslow, *Radical Seattle: The General Strike of 1919* (Monthly Review Press: New York, 2020), 12.
14 *Municipal News* [Seattle], 22 August 1914.
15 Priscilla Murolo and A.B. Chitty, *From the Folks Who Brought You the Weekend: An Illustrated History of Labor in the United States* (New York: New Press, 2018), 137.
16 Final Report of the United States Commission on Industrial Relations (Washington, DC: 1915) V, 4236–37.
17 Anna Louise Strong, *I Change Worlds: The Remaking if an American* (Seattle: Seal Press, 1979), 68.
18 O'Connor, *Revolution in Seattle,* 90.
19 O'Connor, 90.
20 *Industrial Worker,* 19 August 1916.
21 Strong, *I Change Worlds,* 68, 69; *Industrial Worker,* 17 June 1916, 19 August 1916.
22 Seattle *Daily Call,* 3 September 1917.
23 *Union Record,* 24 July 1917.
24 Anna Louis Strong Papers, University of Washington Library, Special Collections, box 10, folder (file) 30.
25 *Union Record,* 21 January 1919.
26 *Union Record,* 4 January 1919.
27 Ibid; O'Connor, *Revolution in Seattle,* 128.
28 Katsutoshi Kurokawa, *The Labor Movement and Japanese Immigrants in Seattle* (Seattle: University Education Press, 2006), 36.
29 Kurokawa, 36.
30 "When Is a Revolution Not a Revolution: Reflections on the Seattle General Strike by a Woman Who Was There," *Liberator,* April 1919.
31 *Union Record,* 8 February 1919.
32 Kurokawa, *Labor Movement and Japanese Immigrants,* 5.
33 *International Socialist Review* 15, no. 1 (July 1914): 30.
34 O'Connor, *Revolution in Seattle,* 98.
35 *Examiner* [Colville, WA], 17 January 1916.
36 *Daily Bulletin* [Butte, MT], 28 June 1919.
37 O'Connor, *Revolution in Seattle,* 98 [italics in original].
38 *Union Record,* 10 February 1919.
39 Mary Joan O'Connell, "The Seattle Union Record, 1918–1928: A Pioneer Labor Daily" (MA thesis, University of Washington, 1964), 76.

40 Robert Friedheim, *The Seattle General Strike* (Seattle: University of Washington Press, 1964), 29.

41 Friedheim, 29.

42 Joseph Pass, "The Seattle Class Rebellion," *Call Magazine*, 2 March 1919.

43 Pass, "Seattle Class Rebellion."

44 *The History of the Seattle General Strike* (Seattle: History Committee of the General Strike Committee, Seattle Union Record Publishing, 1919), 47.

45 *Union Record*, 6 February 1919.

46 O'Connor, *Revolution*, 145.

47 O'Connor, 145.

48 O'Connor, 145.

49 O'Connor, 145.

50 Seattle *Post-Intelligencer*, 6 February 1919.

51 Seattle *Star*, 4 February and 6 February 1919.

52 *Union Record*, 14 February 1919.

53 "When Is a Revolution Not a Revolution," *Liberator*, April 1919.

54 *History of the Seattle General Strike*, 42.

55 Friedheim, *Seattle General Strike*, 146.

56 *Call* [New York], 14 February 1919.

57 *Union Record*, 11 February 1919.

11

The Storm before the Calm: Social and Political Upheaval in the Western Hemisphere

Joel Wolfe

On 15 January 1919, Boston, Massachusetts, was rocked by a massive explosion that brought death and destruction to a wide swath of the city's North End. Neither striking workers nor anarchist militants bombed the area. It was an industrial accident at Purity Distilling, where a massive molasses tank exploded. While a giant, slow-moving flood of molasses may at first sound comical, the scene around the plant seemed like a war zone to the local reporters. Both the *Boston Globe* and the *Boston Post* printed photographs on their front pages of the devastation caused by the 2.3 million–gallon, 50-feet-high wave of molasses.[1] The molasses killed eleven and injured fifty. The initial estimate was that the explosion caused $500,000 ($7.4 million in 2020) in damages.

The explosion and giant wave of molasses was an isolated, bizarre, and sad tragedy. And yet, it resonated beyond Boston. It was yet another way that so many promises of the modern, highly interconnected world seemed to bring more dangers and problems than promise and prosperity. The Western Hemisphere, Europe, and much of the rest of the world had become more integrated economically and even socially during the great spurt of globalized trade that had begun in the mid-1870s. Factories produced new and exciting machinery and consumer goods. New and expanded commodity chains transformed both production and consumption throughout the globe. Mass migrations from eastern and southern Europe as well as from Asia transformed much of the Western Hemisphere, as did the movement of people from Mexico and Canada to the United States. And, new technologies provided a vague sense of progress with the promise of more affluent and peaceful lives. The hopefulness and even hubris of that era came crashing down with the advent and then ongoing slog of the Great War.[2] Despite the fact that the Western Hemisphere in the 1920s witnessed economic growth, the spread of new consumer goods, and a general sense of macro-level peace and prosperity, the years between the end of the war and the beginning of the 1920s were challenging for the liberal economic and political order. Winnipeg's 1919 General Strike, like other upheavals in the hemisphere at this time, was both local and global. It was yet another example of the tumult the postwar hemisphere faced. The ways the hemisphere's nations reacted to this period of upheaval set the stage for the 1920s, a decade of great, albeit uneven, economic growth and innovation in the region that was bracketed by a short but severe depression at the start of the decade and a long and even more severe depression at its end. Many of the social, political, and economic issues affecting the hemisphere in the years right after the end of the Great War remained throughout the 1920s and would not be addressed until the crisis of the Great Depression.

The war far away in Europe was closer to the Canadians than to any other people in the hemisphere. And so, no country in the hemisphere had more reason to celebrate the 1918 armistice. Joy over the victorious end to hostilities masked all the tensions over conscription during the war and questions about Canada's place in the British empire at its end.[3] The United States, although late to combat, had mobilized for extended hostilities. Like Canada, the United States faced important questions raised by the Great War. Canadians felt more independent, while Americans worried about their increased role in European politics. Throughout Latin America, the war had altered many nations' economies in unexpected ways. It had expanded commodity production, and at the same time unleashed new industrial capacity. It was not only the relief and joy brought on by the armistice that left the hemisphere inexorably changed; there were also domestic changes and challenges. The Mexican Revolution had transformed Latin America's second most populous nation, and along the way challenged long-held ideas about commodity production and trade. Mexico's revolutionary 1917 constitution sought to alter just about every aspect of traditional Latin American liberalism's focus on free trade and exclusion of political rights for the majority of the region's citizens. In the hemisphere, the years immediately after the end of the Great War were marked by the emergence of seemingly new, even catastrophic problems.

Even before the end of hostilities in Europe, events in the hemisphere revealed new tensions and problems, many of which were reactions against the established liberal economic order; others simply reflected the complexities engendered by new levels of regional interconnectedness. In May 1917, women weavers in São Paulo's Cotonifício Crespi approached their bosses with a series of complaints.[4] They were exhausted by work speedups and low wages. The war was increasing demand for domestically made goods, and so the factories buzzed day and night. These women, many of whom were the children of Italian immigrants who had been brought to Brazil to work in the coffee sector, were also tired of having to pay high prices for adulterated and poor-quality food, which was often all that was available in working-class neighbourhoods. São Paulo's textile workers also wanted a system of factory fines ended, and concluded by demanding "more respect." They said that "in everything there should be reason and justice." When the Crespi mill's managers refused these demands, the women struck. Women throughout the city's burgeoning textile sector followed with strikes of their own. Soon, men and women throughout São Paulo entered into a General Strike that became a turning point in Brazilian labour history.

São Paulo's 1917 General Strike was just the first of many popular reactions to the hardships brought on by the Great War in the hemisphere. As early as 1914, São Paulo's working people had rejected attempts by anarchist and socialist leaders to organize protests against the war in Europe. Workers rejected blanket condemnations of capitalism and war as beside the point. They were already worried about increasing food prices and deteriorating conditions at work. The demands for higher wages and better conditions articulated by women textile workers in 1917 focused on the war's local impact rather than its origins and meaning. São Paulo's workers gained wage increases once the Strike became widespread in June and July 1917. The city even established a new system of local street markets in working-class neighbourhoods to provide less expensive and higher-quality food. When women textile workers' protests expanded into a general strike, workers who had either had no contact with or had rejected anarchist activists increasingly adopted their ideas. Anarchist leaders embraced rank-and-file perspectives, and so began to pay closer attention to workers' needs rather than macro-level political issues.[5]

At about the same time, the victorious Constitutionalists began the process of consolidating their power after the Mexican Revolution. They, too, embraced an interesting mix of ideas ranging from the demands of the landless peasants in Mexico's central valley who had fought for Emiliano Zapata, and rural proletarians in the North who had followed Francisco "Pancho" Villa, to the demands of anarchist unions that had provided some 10,000 troops who fought as the "Red Battalions."[6] The northern elites who won wrote the 1917 constitution, which clearly signalled that Mexico would not return to its pre-1910 place in the liberal world order. It was a careful mix of ideas that promoted national economic development with social planks that protected workers' rights and provided for an agrarian reform.[7] The new constitution also forbade foreign ownership of subsoil rights, which in theory ended foreign—particularly American—participation in the Mexican oil industry.[8] Both the 1917 General Strike in São Paulo and the Mexican Revolution and the constitution it produced signalled important changes in the hemisphere. Cities were growing and industrializing. Although commodity production and export would continue to dominate the region's economies, factory production and workers began to change Latin American politics and economics. The Mexican Revolution not only demonstrated the failure of that nation's liberal economic model, it also revealed a latent nationalism that would shape domestic politics and trade relations, especially with the United States.

At the same time, the 1917 Russian Revolution created a new sense of danger and urgency to social and political upheaval among the hemisphere's elites. Bolshevism also gave a new set of vocabularies and strategies to the region's labour leaders and radicals. Although the Mexican Revolution and labour uprisings in Brazil revealed cracks in the old order, the Russian Revolution made social protest in the hemisphere feel much more dangerous and connected. 1917, the year the Bolsheviks seized power in Russia, witnessed the highest number of strikes in U.S. history: 4,450. Conditions at work and at home for many Americans did not improve with the war's end.[9] In the immediate aftermath of the Great War, returning soldiers—along with workers who had been pushed to do more, often with fewer resources during the war—appeared to the hemisphere's political and business leaders to be capable of fomenting revolution in the region. As we shall see, those fears would soon manifest themselves in the United States as the so-called Red Scare.

Canadian politicians quickly devised a rural resettlement program for returning soldiers to reward them for their service, and to keep them from joining forces with increasingly restless urban workers.[10] In the United States, there was not the same initial sense of urgency in dealing with the potential social consequences of soldiers returning from Europe, but events on the ground changed that. Chicago's July 1919 race riots had a wide variety of causes, but racial and ethnic tensions had been increasing with the ongoing migration of African Americans from the South during the Great War.[11] The racial upheaval had long-term consequences that included accelerating racial and ethnic segregation in housing. The bloody Chicago riots, in which thirty-eight people died, only ended after more than 6,000 National Guard troops intervened. Chicago's race riots were yet another manifestation of upheaval and uncertainty in the aftermath of the war.[12]

The war and its end did not bring about Chicago's 1919 race riots, but the era's economic and social changes created some of preconditions for the uprising. Like São Paulo's labour mobilizations and aspects of the Mexican Revolution, the Great War had altered the economic, political, and even social calculus of life in the hemisphere. And, in the immediate postwar years, those changes all seemed to be quite bad. Even baseball, America's great pastime, was tarred by greed and contentious labour relations. When the heavily favoured Chicago White Sox lost the 1919 World Series to the Cincinnati Reds five games to three (the 1903 and 1919–21 World Series were a best of nine games), the pre-series rumours about a possible fix took on new levels of credibility. Even though they were found not guilty by a jury in 1921, most people understood that eight Chicago players had been paid by a group of gamblers to lose the series. Despite being cleared by a Chicago jury, the so-called Black Sox received lifetime bans from the newly installed commissioner of major league baseball, Kenesaw Mountain Landis.[13] Gambling and various forms of cheating had long been part of baseball, but deliberately losing the World Series was a new low for the sport. No other annual event could equal the World Series in the American psyche at this time. The Black Sox scandal, although much less significant than race riots and strikes, was yet another way in which the years immediately after the armistice felt increasingly bleak in the United States and throughout the hemisphere.

A baseball scandal, although culturally powerful, was the least of 1919's challenges to the status quo ante. War's end brought labour upheaval throughout the hemisphere. In February, 60,000 workers in Seattle initiated a general strike that paralyzed the city. Dockworkers on the American Pacific Coast and Great Lakes struck against their increasing workloads and stagnant pay. Steelworkers in the United States and Canada, and American coalminers, launched effective strikes that shut down their industries and brought violent police and military interventions. Workers in Rio de Janeiro, São Paulo, and other Brazilian cities organized to demand higher wages.[14] In the aftermath of the Russian Revolution, these strikes felt more dangerous to elites throughout the hemisphere. Increasing numbers of socialists, anarchists, and others declared themselves to be communists. In Moscow in early March 1919, the Soviet Communist Party even organized the First Congress of the Comintern (also known as the Third Communist International) to coordinate foreign revolutionary efforts and defend the Soviet Union during the Russian Civil War. Although the Comintern was initially focused on Europe and so had little immediate impact on the hemisphere, the existence of an organized, international communist movement unnerved political and business leaders who faced increasingly mobilized and radicalized workers.[15]

As unnerving as the strikes throughout the hemisphere seemed, industrial conflicts in Winnipeg and Buenos Aires were somehow worse. They seemed to portend revolutionary movements that might actually upend the capitalist order. The postwar period left Winnipeg and Buenos Aires ripe for industrial conflict. Both before and during the war, Winnipeg had boomed economically, but the economy contracted soon after the armistice. Moreover, labour groups in the West were often at odds with what they considered more conservative or at least cautious unions in Ontario and Quebec, many of which were affiliated with the U.S.-based American Federation of Labor.[16] And, workers in a variety of Winnipeg's industries had been organizing for improved wages and safer conditions for months. The return of troops from the war, along with the sudden drop in commodity prices, increased tensions throughout the region. Those conditions combined with a broad sense of national unease not only about conscription and Canada's role in the European war, but also about domestic politics in the wake of the Conservative/Unionist victory in the 1917 elections and the ongoing tension between French- and English-speaking Canada.

In Calgary in March, western labour leaders had formed "One Big Union" to confront employers. In Winnipeg itself, smaller labour groups congregated into a larger and larger movement during April and May until they could shut down the entire city. On 15 May 1919, Winnipeg was on strike, with more than 30,000 in the streets demanding change.[17] Business elites formed their own organization, the "Citizens' Committee of 1000," to work with the authorities in suppressing the daily protests and street demonstrations. Business and political leaders panicked as life in Winnipeg ground to a halt. City services stopped as did commerce. Then, on 9 June, Winnipeg's unionized police force—which had remained on the job and had been perceived by many of Winnipeg's elite as being too sympathetic to the strikers—was fired for refusing to sign a new contract that precluded taking part in sympathetic strikes. With the regular police on the sidelines, city leaders employed vigilantes and called in the Royal North-West Mounted Police. Ongoing clashes culminated on 21 June, which quickly became known as "Bloody Saturday," when Mounties dispersed strikers by charging into crowds on horseback. Two men were shot dead, and between thirty-five and forty others were seriously wounded. Strike leaders finally called off the movement on 26 June, but Winnipeg loomed large in the national and regional consciousness. U.S. officials had worked with their Canadian counterparts to deport eastern European immigrants involved in the Strike, and distant press accounts recounted the precariousness of the capitalist order in western Canada. Just one day after "Bloody Saturday," the *New York Times* headlined its account of events "Bolshevism in Winnipeg." The story began, "Winnipeg, Canada has emerged from Bolshevist rule. The dictatorship of the proletariat was broken by the counterorganization [*sic*] of a Committee of One Thousand, so called, actually numbers many thousands of that class the Bolsheviki are fond of calling the bourgeoisie."[18]

Earlier in 1919, Buenos Aires had its own experience with labour strife, accusations of foreign infiltration, and manipulation, followed by a business-backed, violent backlash. The clashes were so violent and destabilizing that they quickly became known simply as *la Semana Trágica* or the Tragic Week.[19] Over the course of the first week of January, strikes in foreign-owned businesses spread to dockworkers, and then became a general strike. As they would do in Winnipeg, Buenos Aires's city leaders and business elites worked closely with the police and military to violently suppress the strikes. Working-class neighbourhoods became combat zones as residents dug up paving stones to create barricades, and the military moved in with heavy machine guns and other weapons. Foreign intelligence services reported to the Argentine government that communists, led by Russian Jews, planned to topple the government. To this day, it is not clear how many people were killed during the military crackdown. Some of the worst fighting took place once Argentina's president, Hipólito Yrigoyen, placed the city under martial law. In addition to police and military, vigilantes calling themselves the Argentine Patriotic League targeted Jewish immigrant neighbourhoods where they attempted to begin a pogrom. Argentines and foreigners viewed events in and around Buenos Aires through the lens of the Russian Revolution. The *New York Times* reported in its headline that the vast majority of the 2,000 protesters arrested were "Nearly All of Them Revolutionists from Russia."[20]

The ways elites in both Argentina and Canada focused on the role of Jews in the upheavals speaks to another significant way the hemisphere was increasingly connected. There were Jewish communities in both Buenos Aires and Winnipeg, and some Jews played prominent roles in the strikes.[21] In Argentina, the Jews were demonized as leading actors in the strikes even though they played a small role. In Canada, Jews were lumped together with other eastern European immigrants as dangerous outsiders. No matter, the focus on Jewish radicals and the near automatic association of Jewishness with Bolshevism reveals how an older sense of transnationalism elided into a new one. Jewishness has often been read as a transnational ethnicity. Jewish immigrants were not typically seen as tied to a particular nation in Europe or the Middle East; their ethnicity is Jewish. After the Russian Revolution, international communism and the Comintern were seen in the

Western Hemisphere as being Jewish, and so any Jews involved in any aspect of these upheavals were read as communists.

Foreign and domestic press reports of attempted communist takeovers of Buenos Aires, Winnipeg, and other cities experiencing large-scale labour mobilizations were part paranoid fantasy and part cynical manipulation of public opinion. Despite the presence of anarchists, syndicalists, and communists, the vast majority of working people in the hemisphere struck for better wages and working conditions. They did not look to overturn the capitalist system; they simply wanted better treatment in it. One anarchist group in the United States did, however, specifically target individual capitalists in a widespread bombing campaign in 1919. Beginning in April, anarchists sent out some thirty-six bombs through the U.S. mail to a variety of prominent American business and political leaders, including John D. Rockefeller and a number of members of the U.S. Congress. On 2 June, anarchists set off eight larger bombs in eight cities on the same day, around the same time. The American attorney general A. Mitchell Palmer turned the full power of the federal government against all suspected left and radical elements in the United States. The so-called Palmer Raids took place from November 1919 to January 1920, and targeted both radical and moderate labour groups. Thousands of activists and intellectuals were arrested, and more than 550 foreign-born "resident aliens" were deported. All levels of government followed Palmer's lead. William B. Wilson, the Secretary of Labor, blamed recent strikes on Russians intent on fomenting revolution in the United States, and the mayor of Cleveland even proposed deporting large numbers of immigrants who had not yet been naturalized as citizens.[22] As in Buenos Aires and Winnipeg, immigrants and foreign ideologies were blamed for the upheaval and violence.[23]

The 1919 bombings were clearly aimed at the political and business elite in the United States. On 16 September 1920, though, the target was Wall Street itself, a key institution in the world economic order. A wagon packed with explosives stopped in front of the J.P. Morgan bank at noon. The explosion immediately killed thirty people; another eight died soon after. The blast also injured 143. An anarchist group took credit for the terrorism, which was aimed squarely at the heart of American finance.[24] Unlike the general strikes that had convulsed the hemisphere throughout 1919, the anarchist bombings—particularly of Wall Street itself—were direct assaults on capitalism as a system. And members of the same anarchist group would later attack U.S. interests in Latin America, even attempting to assassinate then president-elect Herbert Hoover while he was visiting Argentina almost a decade later.[25] Race riots, strikes, and terrorist attacks, along with the Russian Civil War and the revolutionary uprising in Germany, created an atmosphere of disorder and apprehension that not only questioned the very structure of the economy, but also the political system itself. And, the press increasingly tied the questioning of that system to the presence of foreign radicals inspired by the Russian Revolution and perhaps in the service of the newly formed Comintern. The nations of the hemisphere had long sought foreign immigrant labour from Europe and Asia, and so had also grappled with the social, religious, and political complexities that multiethnic communities brought with them. In the years immediately after the end of the Great War, those dangers seemed even more real and precipitous.

Throughout the hemisphere, there was a growing sense of dread about life in an increasingly interconnected world. The outbreak of the Spanish influenza in 1918 only made things worse. The first outbreak may have been among troops stationed in Kansas in 1918. It then quickly spread through the U.S. military. The first outbreak in Europe followed the landing of U.S. troops in Brest in early April. By late May, it had spread to Bombay (present-day Mumbai); African nations reported cases in August. The pandemic moved into Latin America at about the same time.[26] The disease moved along rail and other shipping routes, revealing the ways trade had connected the hemisphere's nations. Fully 10 percent of the Chiapas, Mexico, population was reported to have died from the influenza. The once isolated state had only recently expanded its connections to foreign trade by exporting coffee. The estimated mortality rate for Mexico was from 2.3 to 4 percent of the entire population, and 5 to 9 percent of young adults.[27] The infection rate in South America's largest port cities was also high, but the mortality rate was lower than in rural areas. In Buenos Aires, the flu infected 55 percent of the population; in Rio de Janeiro it affected 35 percent. The flu devastated urban and rural populations in Costa Rica, Cuba, Chile, Peru, and Venezuela.[28] Given its ties to the United States and increasing trade during the war, Canada also suffered high mortality rates. Throughout October 1918, influenza spread along the path of the Canadian Pacific Railway. Soldiers travelling from Quebec City to Vancouver brought the flu with them. Panic had already struck Montreal, and Ottawa city hall served as an emergency hospital.[29] Estimates of total Canadian deaths from the influenza range from 30,000 to 55,000. About 1,200 people died in Winnipeg itself (out of a population of 180,000).[30] The United States had 545,452 reported killed by the flu; Mexico about 300,000, and Brazil 180,000. Guatemala, Mexico, and Chile had the highest reported death rates from influenza in the hemisphere.[31] Like the much less destructive Boston molasses explosion, the flu pandemic became yet another example of how an increasingly interconnected world with the rapidly increasing exchange of people, goods, and ideas brought unimaginable dangers more often than did peace and prosperity.

The chaotic atmosphere in the hemisphere from 1917 through the 1919 general strikes obscured the fact that the region was more integrated economically and politically than it had ever been before, and that there were new institutions and mechanisms in place that would facilitate even greater exchanges of goods, money, and people among the nations. And, when that integration brought the hemisphere's nations closer through increased trade and economic growth throughout much of the 1920s, the horrors of the late 1910s seemed to recede. Two events in 1914 initiated the dramatic increase in hemispheric economic consolidation and growth: the onset of the First World War, with the concomitant ways the U.S. government took advantage of the financial and trade opportunities it created in the hemisphere, and the opening of the Panama Canal. The opening of the Panama Canal is often associated with the era of its building.[32] Theodore Roosevelt's separation of Panama from Colombia, as well as the success of American engineering in the aftermath of French failure, dominate thinking about the canal's early days, but it in fact opened to cross-isthmus traffic on 15 August 1914, which was less than a month after the onset of the First World War. The first ship through the canal, the *Ancon*, carried passengers and freight, and made the trip in only nine hours, but it was a ceremonial voyage. By September, regular shipping had begun the process of moving freight, including fresh fruit, from the hemisphere's Pacific ports to those on the East Coast. But, trade from South America to Europe had ground to a halt because of the onset of the war.[33] Indeed, soon after its opening, Europeans noted that the United States was in a perfect position to take over the bulk of Latin America's trade that it had not already controlled.[34] Europeans were also put off by the lower rates that American flag ships paid to use the canal.[35]

In 1915, the canal's first full year in operation, 1,075 vessels crossed the isthmus with 4,888,000 tons of cargo. In 1916, those numbers dropped to 758 vessels carrying 3,094,000 tons. Shipping recovered in 1917 but did not take off until after the armistice. From 1919 through the onset of the Great Depression, the total number of vessels grew from 2,024 in 1919 to 6,413 in 1929, and gross tonnage of cargo from 6,124,990 to 29,838,000.[36] Canal traffic was hardly the only measure of increasing trade within or from the hemisphere, but it does demonstrate a key difference from the prewar era. As well, the canal quickly affected Canadian trade. Winnipeg was the nation's third largest city, behind on Montreal and Toronto, and it played a central role shipping wheat from Alberta and Saskatchewan to eastern Canada and Europe. The canal allowed Vancouver exporters to erode Winnipeg's dominance in the export trade, thus hastening Vancouver's rise at Winnipeg's expense.[37]

The entire hemisphere had changed in ways that facilitated increased flows of goods, money, and people. Some of those changes involved modern infrastructure, while others were more institutional. There were even important cultural changes that tied the region together more in the 1920s than it had ever been before.[38] By the time of the 1919 general strikes in the hemisphere, the geography of trade and concomitant movement of people, goods, and money began to foster new cultural, political, and institutional mechanisms that increased integration in ways that benefited the United States, often at the expense of the region's other nations.

Those changes highlighted America's uneasy relationship with a powerful, central government; an uneasiness that was put aside during times of war. The Civil War had brought the first paper currency and a dramatic increase in the federal government's size and scope. Woodrow Wilson, again, expanded the national government's reach during the Great War. He built on some institutional innovations from previous administrations, particularly that of Theodore Roosevelt (1901–9), but the exigencies of war led Wilson to push the government even further into the management of the American economy. And many of those changes in the U.S. government's scope further facilitated trade in the hemisphere, often at the expense of the European nations. The resulting integration brought Canada and Latin America more firmly into the U.S. orbit.

The first substantive change was a product of financial panic in 1907, rather than the war.[39] The 1913 Federal Reserve Act created a permanent central bank for the United States that could combat the sorts of panics that had plagued the nation in the nineteenth century. J.P. Morgan and other private bankers had bailed out the nation in 1907, which forced policy-makers to create a central bank similar to the Bank of England, which had been founded in 1694, or even the Banco do Brasil, which dates from 1808.[40] The Federal Reserve system did not, at first, affect foreign trade because the United States remained on the gold standard even during the war. It was the system's support for the creation of foreign branch banking that revolutionized finance and trade at this time. Domestic American banks had been technically prohibited from establishing foreign branches, although a small number of institutions had skirted the rules with a modest presence abroad. The Continental Banking and Trust Company of Panama, which had been incorporated in West Virginia in 1913, operated in Latin America. Its limited role only highlighted the failure of U.S.-based financial institutions to conduct business abroad. All told, there were only four American domestic banks and two American foreign banking corporations with a foreign presence. Those institutions maintained only twenty-six total branches throughout the world.[41] With the Federal Reserve Act, however, they were now free to expand overseas, and the focus became Latin America.[42]

While the United States dominated trade and finance in the hemisphere, changes in Canadian policy also affected the region. Throughout the nineteenth and early twentieth centuries, Canada sought to balance its ties to Great Britain and its proximity to the United States. From the establishment of the Canadian Dominion in 1867 through the onset of the Great Depression, trade between the neighbouring nations grew from $45 million per year in goods to more than $1.4 billion. The greatest change in that trade was the imbalance between the two. In 1867, Canada sent $25 million in exports to the U.S., while bringing in $20 million of imports. By 1929, Canada was importing $900 million and exporting only $500 million.[43] Canadian and American leaders attempted on several occasions to remove barriers to increased trade, but often faced Canadian fears of American economic dominance. A

1910 reciprocal trade pact signed by Republican president William Howard Taft and Liberal prime minister Wilfrid Laurier failed when Canadian Conservatives characterized it as yet another example of U.S. control over their economy. They argued instead for ongoing fealty to the British and rode the controversy to victory in the 1911 elections.[44]

American economic might and the rise of a new Canadian nationalism altered attitudes and ushered in a period of robust, if uneven, cross-border exchange in the 1920s. Over 1 million Canadians emigrated to the United States during the decade, and a new form of "booze tourism" brought throngs of Americans to Canada looking to drink legally during U.S. Prohibition.[45] Indeed, Canadian distillers and brewers became one of America's primary suppliers of alcohol during the decade, and Canadian producers earned huge profits on this illicit export trade.[46] But the 1920s also witnessed the entry of U.S. capital in everything from paper pulp and automobiles to alcohol production itself. The expanding ethos and reach of U.S.-style capitalism and capital itself engendered a series of nationalist backlashes. Conservative Catholic priests in Quebec even made common cause with conservative Mexicans involved in that country's Cristero Rebellion (1924–27), demonstrating a new type of hemispheric integration and solidarity.[47]

Several Latin American countries' industrial sectors expanded rapidly in response to the cut-off in trade during the war. While Canadian armaments industries also grew dramatically, and the U.S. economy boomed as well, new industrial production in Latin America presented a real change for the region. Strikes in São Paulo's textile factories and Argentina's "Tragic Week" were the most obvious expressions of that growth. Commodity production and exports still defined Latin American economies, but cities such as Santiago, Buenos Aires, São Paulo, Rio de Janeiro, Lima, Medellín, and elsewhere saw steadily growing numbers of textile and other factories during the war. In addition to new factories, and the labour unrest that came with them, Latin American nations experienced another important shift that was felt throughout the hemisphere: when trade resumed in the aftermath of the war, American markets and businesses increasingly dominated the region.

Although the increases in trade and interconnectedness coloured how people throughout the hemisphere interpreted everything from massive general strikes to industrial accidents, the flu pandemic and even a sports scandal, they also set the stage for close to a decade of economic growth in the 1920s. And a lot of that growth was tied to increased trade in the hemisphere. Strikes in Argentina, Brazil, Canada, and the United States in 1919 revealed real problems created by the liberal economic order, but the ways that they were suppressed or settled set the stage for a decade of relative macro-level political peace in the hemisphere.[48] The Winnipeg General Strike, like the *Semana Trágica* in Buenos Aires and strikes in Brazil and the United States, turned out to be the storm before the calm of a decade of economic growth. But, many of the issues raised in those strikes had not been fixed or settled, and they would reappear throughout the hemisphere during the Great Depression.

Notes

1 *Boston Globe*, 16 January 1919; and *Boston Post*, 16 January 1919. All of the details here are from those initial news reports. A highly destructive explosion rocked Halifax harbour on 6 December 1917, but it was different from the Boston molasses tragedy in that one of the ships that collided in the harbour was laden with explosives and other munitions. The Boston tragedy reflected trade relations, while Halifax was a product of the Great War. On Halifax, see Jacob A.C. Remes, *Disaster Citizenship: Survivors, Solidarity, and Power in the Progressive Era* (Urbana: University of Illinois Press, 2016), 21–53.

2 On the postwar reevaluation of notions of progress related to Western technology, see Micahel Adas, *Machines as the Measure of Men: Science, Technology, and Ideologies of Western Dominance* (Ithaca, NY: Cornell University Press, 1989). Paul Fussell's classic *The Great War and Modern Memory* (New York: Oxford University Press, 1975) analyzes the cultural shock of the war. An excellent study of the international reordering of colonialism and global politics after the war is Adam Tooze, *The Deluge: The Great War, America, and the Remaking of the Global Order, 1916–1931* (London: Allen Lane, 2014).

3 Brian Douglas Tennyson, *Canada's Great War, 1914–1918: How Canada Helped Save the British Empire and Became a North American Nation* (New York: Rowman and Littlefield, 2015).

4 The following discussion is based on Joel Wolfe, "Anarchist Ideology, Worker Practice: The 1917 General Strike and the Formation of São Paulo's Working Class," *Hispanic American Historical Review* 71, no. 4 (November 1991): 809–46. On the General Strike's role in the ongoing development of São Paulo's and Brazil's history, see Wolfe, *Working Women, Working Men: São Paulo and the Rise of Brazil's Industrial Working Class, 1900–1955* (Durham, NC: Duke University Press, 1993).

5 On the creation of this variant of Anarcho-Syndicalism and how it operated in São Paulo in the aftermath of the General Strike, see Wolfe, *Working Women, Working Men*, 23–39.

6 The single best source on the Revolution is Alan Knight, *The Mexican Revolution,* 2 vols. (Cambridge, UK: Cambridge University Press, 1986). Excellent analytical portraits of these revolutionary participants are John Womack, *Zapata and the Mexican Revolution* (New York: Knopf, 1969); Friedrich Katz, *The Life and Times of Pancho Villa* (Stanford, CT: Stanford University Press, 1998); and John Lear, *Workers, Neighbors, and Citizens: The Revolution in Mexico City* (Lincoln: University of Nebraska Press, 2001).

7 The classic work on the developmentalist orientation of the Revolution's victors is Hector Aguilar Camin, *La frontera nómada: Sonora y la Revolución Mexicana* (México: D.F.L Colegio de México, 1977). For how the victors codified their politics in the 1917 constitution, see Marcelo Blidstein, "Política y caudillismo en el Congreso Constituyente mexicano de 1917," *Mexican Studies/Estudios Mexicanos* 16, no. 1 (Winter 2000): 39–78.

8 Lorenzo Meyer, *México y los Estados Unidos en el conflicto petrolero, 1917–1942* (México; D.F.: Colegio de Mexico, 1988).

9 On the record number of strikes in the United States in 1917, see David M. Kennedy, *Over Here: The First World War and American Society* (New York: Oxford University Press, 2004), 262.

10 Desmond Morton and Glenn T. Wright, *Winning the Second Battle: Canadian Veterans and the Return to Civilian Life, 1915–1930* (Toronto: University of Toronto Press, 1987).

11 On the Great Migration, see Isabel Wilkerson, *The Warmth of Other Suns: The Epic Story of America's Great Migration* (New York: Vintage, 2010).

12 For an excellent analysis of the general sense of dislocation and crisis in Chicago at this time, see Gary Krist, *City of Scoundrels: The Twelve Days of Disaster that Gave Birth to Modern Chicago* (New York: Random House, 2013).

13 An excellent study of the scandal that places the players' actions within a labour relations framework is Robin F. Bachin, "At the Nexus of Labor and Leisure: Baseball, Nativism, and the 1919 Black Sox Scandal," *The Journal of Social History* (Summer 2003): 941–62. On the ways the scandal has been reported and remembered, see Daniel A. Nathan, *Saying It's So: A Cultural History of the Black Sox Scandal* (Urbana: University of Illinois Press, 2003).

14 Kennedy, *Over Here*, 277–79; Bruce Nelson, *Workers on the Waterfront: Seamen, Longshoremen, and Unions in the 1930s* (Urbana: University of Illinois Press, 1988), 7–10; Andrew Parnaby, *Citizen Docker: Making a New Deal on the Vancouver Waterfront, 1919–1939* (Toronto: University of Toronto Press, 2008), 18–19; Craig Heron, *Working in Steel: The Early Years in Canada, 1883–1935* (Toronto: University of Toronto Press, 1991), 138–59; Wolfe, *Working Women, Working Men,* 30–33.

15 Manuel Caballero, *Latin America and the Comintern, 1919–1943* (Cambridge, UK: Cambridge University Press, 1986).

16 This volume's introductory essay provides an excellent overview of the background and outbreak of the General Strike.

17 *New York Times,* 22 June 1919. The *Times* closely covered the Canadian and Argentine upheavals. As is detailed below, the so-called paper of record in the United States facilely employed distinct themes and vocabularies to describe both sets of events.

18 *New York Times,* 22 June 1919.

19 A classic analysis of the upheaval is David Rock, "Lucha Civil en la Argentina: La Semana Trágica de Enero de 1919," *Desarrollo Econômico* 11, no. 42–44 (July/March 1971): 165–215.

20 *New York Times*, 14 January 1919.

21 Victor Mirelman, "The *Semana Trágica* of 1919 and the Jews in Argentina," *Jewish Social Studies* 37, no. 1 (Winter 1975): 61–73. The ongoing issue of separating Jews from the rest of Argentine society is detailed in Federico Pablo Feldstein, "Argentine Jews as Scapegoat: A Textual Analysis of the Bombing of AMIA," *Journal of Communication Inquiry* 27, no. 2 (April 2003): 152–70. Reinhold Kramer and Tom Mitchell's *When the State Trembled: How A.J. Andrews and the Citizens' Committee Broke the Winnipeg General Strike* (Toronto: University of Toronto Press, 2010) details the presence of Jews in the city and the Strike, and the ways Andrews and his allies exaggerated and demonized those Jews as foreigners and as Bolsheviks and in their work to quell the Strike. See pp. 22, 32, 93–94, 215–17, 221–22, and 232–34.

22 Harlan Grant Cohen, "The (Un)Favorable Judgement of History: Deportation Hearings, the Palmer Raids, and the Meaning of History," *New York University Law Review* 78, no. 4 (October 2003): 1456.

23 Cohen, "(Un)Favorable Judgement of History," 1456–58.

24 Beverly Gage, *The Day Wall Street Exploded: A Story of America in Its First Age of Terror* (New York: Oxford University Press, 2010).

25 An Argentine official found bombs on the train tracks hours before Hoover was to travel over them. See *La Nación*, 12 December 1928; *Chicago Tribune*, 12 December 1928; and the *New York Times*, 12 December 1928.

26 John M. Barry, *The Great Influenza: The Epic Story of the Deadliest Plague in History* (New York: Penguin, 2005), 92, 170–92.

27 Barry, *Great Influenza*, 225, 310–13; on Chiapas see 363; for all of Mexico, 398. On the transformation of Chiapas at this time, see Casey Lurtz, *From the Grounds Up: Building an Export Economy in Southern Mexico* (Stanford, CA: Stanford University Press, 2019).

28 Barry, *Great Influenza*, 363, 398; Richard Collier, *The Plague of the Spanish Lady: The Influenza Pandemic of 1918–1919* (London: Allison and Busby, 1996), 7.

29 Mark Osborne Humphries, *The Last Plague: Spanish Influenza and the Politics of Health in Canada* (Toronto: University of Toronto Press, 2013); and Collier, *Plague of the Spanish Lady*, 81–82, 89.

30 Esyllt W. Jones, *Influenza 1918: Disease, Death, and Struggle in Winnipeg* (Toronto: University of Toronto Press, 2007), 14. Jones argues convincingly that struggling with the devastation wrought by the flu in winter 1918–19 increased the bonds of solidarity among the city's workers and contributed to social cohesion during the General Strike.

31 Collier, *Plague of the Spanish Lady*, 305–06; *Toronto Star*, 19 September 2008.

32 David G. McCullough, *The Path Between the Seas: The Creation of the Panama Canal* (New York: Simon and Schuster, 1977). On the Caribbean migrants who built the canal, see Marixa Lasso, *Erased: The Untold Story of the Panama Canal* (Cambridge, MA: Harvard University Press, 2019).

33 *New York Times*, 16 August 1914; 28 August 1914; "Opening of the Panama Canal," *Economist*, 12 September 1914; and "War Crisis in Chili and Peru," *Economist*, 19 September 1914.

34 "Capturing German Trade," *Economist*, 29 August 1914; and "Peru and the Panama Canal," and "The Canal and British Trade," *Economist*, 5 December 1914. The latter articles make the point that the canal was expected eventually to help develop deeper trade ties between both the U.S. and Canadian west coasts and Great Britain.

35 George H. Nash, *The Life of Herbert Hoover: The Engineer, 1874–1914* (New York: W.W. Norton, 1983), 544–45.

36 *Annual Report of the Governor of the Panama Canal for the Fiscal Year Ended June 30, 1921* (Washington, DC: Government Printing Office, 1921), 109–17; United States Department of Commerce, *Statistical Abstract of the United States, 1926* (Washington, DC: Government Printing Office, 1927), 421; United States Department of Commerce, *Statistical Abstract of the United States, 1935* (Washington, DC: Government Printing Office, 1936), 400.

37 A glut in shipping capacity at the end of the war and its associated lowering of freight costs accelerated this shift toward Vancouver at this time. See Ruben Bellan, *Winnipeg's First Century: An Economic History* (Winnipeg: Queenston House, 1978), 144–46, 154–55.

38 A new, pan-Latin American identity developed in the 1920s. See, among others, Iñigo García-Bryce, *Haya de la Torre and the Pursuit of Power in Twentieth-Century Peru and Latin America* (Chapel Hill: University of North Carolina Press, 2018), especially Chapter 2; and Alan McPherson, *The Invaded: How Latin Americans and Their Allies Fought and Ended U.S. Occupations* (New York: Oxford University Press, 2014).

39 For a succinct history of the how the panic led to the creation of the U.S. Federal Reserve system, see Liaquat Ahamed, *Lords of Finance: The Bankers Who Broke the World* (New York: Penguin, 2009), 54–57.

40 On early U.S. opposition to central banks, see Daniel Walker Howe, *What Hath God Wrought: The Transformation of America, 1815–1848* (New York: Oxford University Press, 2007), 142–47. An excellent comparative analysis is John H. Wood, *A History of Central Banking in Great Britain and the United States* (Cambridge, UK: Cambridge University Press, 2005). The Banco do Brasil lost its central banking role in 1967 with the creation of the Banco Central do Brasil.

41 Clyde Williams Phelps, *The Foreign Expansion of American Banks: American Branch Banking Abroad* (New York: The Ronald Press Company, 1927), 85–86.

42 On international financial competition and its pressure on U.S. policy-makers to create the Federal Reserve, see J. Lawrence Broz, *The International Origins of the Federal Reserve System* (Ithaca, NY: Cornell University Press, 1997).

43 Vera Reynolds Kilduff, "Economic Factors in the Development of Canadian-American Trade," *Southern Economic Journal* 8, no. 2 (October 1941): 201. The Canadian export figure may understate trade because it does not include the illicit export from Canadian distilleries of alcoholic beverages during American Prohibition.

44 Michael Hart, *A Trading Nation: Canadian Trade Policy from Colonization to Globalization* (Vancouver: UBC Press, 2002), 78–84. See also Peter H. Russell, *Canada's Odyssey: A Country Based on Incomplete Conquests* (Toronto: University of Toronto Press, 2017), 233–35.

45 Daniel Okrent, *Last Call: The Rise and Fall of Prohibition* (New York: Scribner, 2010), 216–17; Nicole Neatby, *From Old Quebec to La Belle Province: Tourism Promotion, Travel Writing, and National Identities, 1920–1967* (Montreal and Kingston: McGill-Queen's University Press, 2018), 21, 250n29.

46 Matthew J. Bellamy, *Brewed in the North: A History of Labatt's* (Montreal and Kingston: McGill-Queen's University Press, 2019), 144–45.

47 Maurice Demers, *Connected Struggles: Catholics, Nationalists, and Transnational Relations between Mexico and Quebec, 1917–1945* (Montreal and Kingston: McGill-Queen's University Press, 2014), 57–87.

48 There were plenty of conflicts in the 1920s, but labour relations in most countries in the hemisphere were more peaceful than they had been during the 1917 to 1919 period. A great deal of that "social peace" was due to police repression of union activity throughout the hemisphere.

12

The "Rural Nothing Worth Monkey Police," or the Winnipeg Origins of 100 Years of Canadian State Spying on Labour and the Left[1]

Gregory S. Kealey

The seething cauldron of the First World War boiled over on the domestic home front in two significant parallel but yet contradictory streams.[2] The first torrent, represented by the rebellious participants in the General Strike and its national, indeed international, analogues across Canada and the world, fed into the socialist struggles against capitalism of the twentieth century.[3] The second river, represented by the eponymous "Citizens" Committee of 1000 and its state-sanctioned instruments of repression, the Canadian military, and the Royal North-West—soon to be Canadian—Mounted Police, flowed into new forms of state surveillance intended to support and protect capitalism in the long Cold War.[4] This second, underground tributary, far less studied in the Canadian context, is the subject of this chapter. While we know much about the judicial proceedings that occurred in the aftermath of the Winnipeg General Strike, thanks to the work of Tom Mitchell and others, we know relatively little about the murky waters of the secret agents, informants, and underground detectives of both the mounted police and Canadian military intelligence.[5]

Indeed, the activities of the latter have received little attention in the literature of rebellion and repression in Canada.[6] As Mark Humphries has argued, this lacuna in the historical record stems from the fact that the records of the Military Intelligence Branch of the Department of Militia and Defence are "curiously absent from the official files in Ottawa."[7] Fortunately for our examination of the Winnipeg situation, some of the local files survived and provide periodic day-to-day accounts of the activities of Military Intelligence (MI) in Military District 10 (MD10) with responsibility for Winnipeg, rural Manitoba, and northwestern Ontario. The militia officers running intelligence in Winnipeg were drawn from the youth of the ambitious local elite, primarily professionals such as engineers, surveyors, and contractors, and were all of English or Anglo-Canadian origin. Literature on the Canadian militia in this period depicts these part-time soldiers in terms of their loyalty to empire, their focus on masculinity, and their fascination with ritual, patriotism, and pageantry.[8] Mark Humphries has pithily described the militia in this period as "more of an elite social club than an active military force—a site where dominant notions of citizenship and masculinity were reified and reinforced."[9]

With the outbreak of war their initial focus was on alien registration and internment, and private detectives from the American-based Thiel Agency were hired to investigate the immigrant communities, especially in Winnipeg's North End. When fears of enemy fifth-column activities declined, MD10's MI focus shifted quickly to labour and the Left. As early as late spring and early summer of 1915, for example, undercover agents, probably private detectives, concentrated their efforts on the unemployed organizing of the "Ruthenian" Social Democratic Party (SDP), which led crowds in marches on city hall and the legislature demanding credit and jobs on public works.[10] In addition to MI's agents' information, the Winnipeg chief of police also warned the officer commanding (OC) MD10 of threatened violence and claimed that members of the crowd bore arms based on an informant's allegations. On occasion, the MI agent struck a surprisingly supportive note after visiting several North End boarding houses, sympathizing with the immigrants' suffering and describing how they were "loyal to the country and only hunger and a lack of work compel them to agitate for work to avoid starvation." Such empathy had little influence on the OC, however, who reassured the chief of police that the militia was ready to provide support if called on. The MI agent reported daily on public meetings in the week leading to the SDP's May Day march and meetings, which culminated in crowds estimated by the agent as 25,000-strong with some twenty-five speakers in English, Yiddish, Russian, Ruthenian, and Swedish. The demonstration remained peaceful even when threatened with disruption by local militia men. Agitation for work continued in May, and the MI agent remained busy supplying reports to his employer. The agents, both military and police, appeared to know at least some of the SDP leaders as they reported on conversations and provided copies of its paper *Robochi Narod (Working People)*. The ongoing emphasis in these reports was to blame the SDP for its allegedly opportunistic leadership of the unemployed movement.[11] In June 1915, Chief of the General Staff Gwatkin refused the district intelligence officer (DIO) MD10's request to hire more secret service agents and ordered him to use local police resources instead.[12]

In response to Ottawa's strictures the DIO of MD10 turned to using his own men from the newly expanded Corps of Guides (the quaint alternative name for Military Intelligence) as undercover agents. The primary operative from summer 1917 forward was Sergeant Major Francis Edward Langdale, who in 1919 would be a major witness for the prosecution in a number of the state's trials and immigration hearings against labour and socialist leaders in Winnipeg.[13] Langdale was deployed initially against Anti-Conscription League forces, which not surprisingly overlapped with labour and the Left. On the basis of Langdale's reports, Lieutenant D.A. Campbell, MD10's DIO, composed for General H.N. Ruttan, his OC, a remarkable inflammatory summation of his view of the "Alien Enemy Situation in MD No. 10." Commencing with his fears of a potential general strike, he described the strikes of "alien enemy" labourers on infrastructure projects in the Winnipeg area. He amplified his concerns with descriptions of foreign workers "congregating in groups of 20–100 to talk over the labour situation." His recommendation to Ruttan: lobby Colonel Sir Percy Sherwood, the commissioner of the Dominion Police, to amend the order-in-council to allow the internment of the "Ring Leaders," because to date his efforts to have the local registrar of alien enemies intern "agitators" had been "absolutely unsuccessful." He closed his jeremiad by reminding his OC that in 1914, when internment was frequent, the alien enemies "were very impressed, and as a rule always made their reports and always had a certain amount of respect for men in uniform," whereas now "men of this Department have often a hand to hand fight with an Alien Enemy on the streets of Winnipeg before he can be brought into detention."[14] Ruttan dutifully passed on his subordinate's recommendations to Sherwood, who responded that the minister of justice was not interested in such amendments and reminded the military that even enemy aliens had the right to "agitate for better terms in the way of pay, shorter hours or more congenial work." Moreover, he added, the country badly needed workers and therefore "it is a positive detriment that many of them should be locked up, whereby the country is not only deprived of their labour but has the expense of maintaining them."[15] Perhaps to soften his harsh response Sherwood noted in a P.S. to his letter that convictions under the Vagrancy Act in other parts of the country had led to "very satisfactory results."

By far our best archival record of MI agent reports comes from 1918. Between 20 August and 25 October, no fewer than sixty-seven reports were filed by operative Z-14 to the DIO of MD10, possibly Langdale but more likely one of the translators in the corps.[16] The agent focused his efforts on the North End and primarily on the Ukrainian SDP and its new labour temple at the corner of Pritchard and MacGregor. Among his preferred haunts were the Budiuk[17] fruit store, the Cirka Fruit and Confectionery Store, and the Harris Restaurant and Boarding House, all places where Ukrainian socialists and nationalists congregated daily. His intent clearly was to infiltrate the party, but its careful recruitment strategies made that difficult. He noted on more than one occasion the need for caution as he "did not want to arouse their suspicion for they are on the alert and very watchful of strangers." In his nightly wanderings in the socialist gathering spots and in attendance at socialist meetings (before they were banned under Order-in-Council PC2384), he gathered names, information, and literature, which were all dutifully reported to his MI handler. His interest in literature, the press, and the bookstores through which they circulated noticeably increased in late September after the passage of PC2381, which banned all publications in an "enemy language," including Finnish, Russian, and Ukrainian.

Campbell crowed in early October that the "recent raid on the foreign papers in this City by the Police and Intelligence Dept. has had a wonderful effect on the different labor leaders." A separate undercover operative "No. 8" from the Corps of Guides also reported on the raids against the left Ukrainian press from the perspective of his observations on a meeting of the Winnipeg Trades and Labor Council. He reported in detail on a debate concerning warnings delivered to the council regarding the *Western Labor News*, edited by the Rev. William Ivens, by Chief Press Censor Colonel Ernest J. Chambers. In light of the raids in the North End the delegates decided not to send Ivens's "very strong and sarcastic" rejoinder to Chambers. Their choice of a diplomatic response led the agent to enthuse that "the recent raids and arrests had great impression on the labor leaders" and "all seemed to agree . . . that the authorities had the club and enough weight behind it, and would not hesitate if necessary."[18]

Z-14 continued his observation of the usual socialist haunts in October but also started to surveil the Labor Temple and Liberty Hall, both used as meeting places before PC2384. He sought socialist literature at the various shops and bookstores but found that the material had been removed to avoid further prosecution. Meetings, of course, became illegal because of the flu epidemic that reached its peak that fall, leading public health authorities to forbid all public meetings including religious services.[19] The operative's initial enthusiasm for the suppression of the Ukrainian press turned as the month passed into warnings to his handler that the Ukrainian Nationalists were becoming increasingly critical as they had never thought that their press would be banned, and that some were now accepting the socialist criticism of state repression.[20] Such information gleaned from an operative in Winnipeg may have provided support for the slow retreat away from a total ban on the enemy language press that occurred over the fall and winter of 1918–19.[21]

In early 1919, as fears of labour and the Left dramatically rose in Ottawa, fed by MI reports from across the country, Major General Willoughby Gwatkin, chief of staff, summarized his perspective on resources available to suppress the threat of revolution:

> We, in the Militia Department, through our Intelligence Division, have a pretty good idea of what is going on; we do not act, but turn any information we obtain over to the two Federal Police Agencies. There are Dominion Police, which is being strengthened, and will look after Federal police work in Eastern Canada, and the Royal North West Mounted, which has been increased and had its area of operations expanded to cover the territory from Port Arthur to the Pacific Coast. In

> addition, the more direct responsibility for the enforcement of law and order rests upon the Attorney General of the several provinces. As regards means of dealing with overt disorder, steps are being taken to reconstitute the Permanent Force; its establishment will be about 5,000 and it is hoped to keep it up to strength.[22]

When the Winnipeg Strike leaders faced trials and immigration hearings Sergeant Major Francis Langdale served as a major witness for the prosecution.[23] The military under OC MD10 General Ketchen had played a major role in the events of 1919 that went far beyond their infamous role on Bloody Saturday, and also well beyond the passive depiction quoted above by Gwatkin to his British colleague. Two years later Ketchen, in a self-congratulatory reminiscence for Ottawa headquarters, took considerable credit for his role in organizing the Citizens' Committee and using them to mobilize "loyal citizens" to join the militia and to organize volunteer committees that provided critical services such as fire protection and transportation, the latter of which allegedly facilitated access from four to 5,000 motor cars. Strikingly, he placed huge emphasis on the necessity of "a really effective Intelligence Department." He noted, based on his experience in 1919, that "whilst the RCMP are doing all they can, most of their people are quite well known to all the Red element, and many secret meetings are held to which there is no doubt the RCMP Operators do not obtain access."[24] Again, dutifully noting his warm relationship with his "old friend" Colonel Cortland Starnes, the RCMP OC, he nevertheless advised "really efficient intelligence men of our own . . . as it is always somewhat dangerous to rely on others for information." These reflections and recommendations derived from direct experience: "I put down success at the Winnipeg Strike in 1919 simply to the fact that I was able to procure advance information in practically all the plans of the radical element, and was thus able to check-mate them on every occasion. This was only possible because I had a fairly good intelligence Department of my own at that time, as well as having engaged one or two special men at my own expense."[25] One suspects that Colonel Starnes and Commissioner Perry of the RWNMP might not share Ketchen's version of the 1919 events. The RNWMP had first used secret agents in 1914 to fulfill its new wartime mandate in Saskatchewan and Alberta to enforce enemy alien registration.[26] Its initial experience with hired agents from private detective agencies left Perry committed to using his own agents whenever possible. Unfortunately, the demographics of his force made that difficult to achieve. Anglo-Canadians and British immigrants filled the ranks and lacked the language skills necessary for undercover work in the multicultural Canadian working class.[27] When the force's geographic mandate was extended at the beginning of 1919 to include all of Canada west of the Lakehead, Perry expanded the total force to 1,200 and started to recruit additional secret agents.[28] His initial request in early January 1919 was for twenty secret agents at a cost of $87,500 per annum, further broken down as $32,500 for salaries, $30,000 for expenses, and an additional $25,000 for informants.[29] In mid-January he noted that he currently only had two secret agents in place but had charged Starnes in Winnipeg to hire more and Horrigan in Vancouver to investigate what the departing Dominion Police might have had in place and subsequently to hire secret agents.[30] Demonstrating the significant lack of cooperation among the myriad state repressive agencies, Perry also noted that "it is possible that the Intelligence Branch of the Department of Militia have Secret Agents in their employ, but I do not know."[31]

Starnes and other OCs experienced difficulties recruiting secret agents with the requisite backgrounds and language skills. In the months preceding the General Strike there appear to have been at least four SAs in place in Winnipeg as well as undercover detectives.[32] The agents who can be identified are SA21 (Harry Daskaluk), SA32, SA50 (F.E. Riethdorf aka Frederick Edwards), and Julius Chmielewski; the detectives included D/S Albert E. Reames and D/C W.H. McLaughlin.[33] From the still heavily redacted records currently available the agents appear to have filed about 100 reports in 1919, with SA50 responsible for almost sixty. Therefore, for the purposes of this chapter, we shall focus on SA50, whose major achievement in these months was winning the confidence of Jacob Penner, a leader in the Social Democratic Party of Canada (SDP) and member of the Bakers and Confectionery Workers Union, which he represented on the General Strike Committee.[34]

F.E. Riethdorf first appears as Secret Agent 50 in November 1916 in Earl Grey, Saskatchewan, where his intention to spy on a Lutheran minister was thwarted by the close-knit community's immediate identification of him as a police agent in their midst.[35] In 1917 he played a key role in attempting to entrap socialist Joseph Clarke of Edmonton for sedition for his antiwar beliefs. The efforts failed despite significant RNWMP effort. Clarke was soon after elected mayor and, unsurprisingly, made no effort to hide his antagonism to the mounted police in 1919.[36] SA50 either continued in his role as a RNWMP secret agent or was rehired as he surfaces again in early 1919 as a key informant of Commissioner Perry, reporting on the revolutionary threat of the Socialist Party of Canada in Edmonton and its ties to "the Bolsheviki element among the aliens."[37] SA50 must have moved from Edmonton to Winnipeg shortly after the exchange with Perry because he commenced to report from there in early March 1919. It should be noted here that the RNWMP initially used a convoluted process for its SAs' reports. The agent initially sent the report directly to the commissioner in Regina, who would then forward it to the comptroller in Ottawa with appropriate instructions for further distribution, which almost always included the officer commanding the implicated division. While demonstrating the import Perry placed on his SAs' reports, this routing proved too cumbersome as the number of agents increased. Hence this was changed sometime after the creation of a separate Criminal Investigation Branch (CIB) structure at headquarters and in each district.[38] Thereafter the reports moved from the secret agent to the RNWMP local handler, usually a detective, to the OC and then to the commissioner.

Riethdorf's German-language skills plus his Calgary socialist experience allowed him to befriend Jacob Penner in early March. He became a frequent visitor to the Penner household and filed detailed reports on his conversations with Jacob and his wife Rose as well with as Rose's sister and her husband who also lived there. In addition, he attended and reported on numerous labour and left-wing public meetings and rallies before, during, and after the General Strike. He remained undercover in Winnipeg for at least a year, since his available reports on Penner continued until the end of February 1920.[39] Uncharacteristically, on two occasions Commissioner Perry directly reached out to SA50, addressing letters to his pseudonym, Frederick Edwards.[40] In his second missive Perry instructed SA50 to endeavour "to secure documentary evidence of the activities of Penner with a view to further action at a later date." Perry suggested to his agent that engaging him in correspondence might succeed. As a result, SA50 decamped for Kenora and the Lakehead not only to check on labour and the Left in those locations but also to correspond with Penner back in Winnipeg. After a lengthy pause that caused the agent some anxiety, Penner did respond and that letter accompanied the agent's next report to Perry.[41] Although the spying continued, no "further action" ensued.

SA50's March reports provided copious details on socialist plans for 1919 culled from lengthy conversations with Penner and from his attendance at intimate meetings of the Winnipeg socialist leadership, described by him as "the inner council." These plans, based on earlier convention discussions and the Calgary Western Labour Conference, combined the traditional SPC focus on working-class education with a more activist industrial strategy based on revolutionary syndicalism, embracing general strikes and in the Canadian case the One Big Union.[42] All of this brought the SPC and the SDP closer together and allowed them to collaborate during the General Strike.

Another recurring theme in these reports was Penner's view of spies, spying, and the RNWMP. Ironically, in July he observed that "I know a spy when I see one, and none will ever cross our threshold for the purpose of getting information." While conceding that "the Government ought to have a good deal of information collected by its 'spies,'" he argued that "it would nevertheless be hard for the authorities to 'put one over' on 'the workers.'"[43] Earlier that month he also described the RNWMP raid on his home on 2 July at 2:00 a.m. "He was not much surprised but that his wife felt quite threatened," while he also credited the three "Mounties" with "doing their duty in a gentlemanly manner." The raid did not garner much literature as he had burned "the worst stuff long ago" and "had placed other books with 'harmless friends' for safe-keeping."[44] Penner's views of the RNWMP worsened as he put most of his considerable energy into organizing the strike leaders' defence activities through summer and fall 1919. In late October he predicted a Borden electoral defeat and the disappearance of "the Red Coats."[45] He returned to the same theme more vehemently in early November, angered by a RNWMP interview with his father, an apolitical Mennonite. "The abolition of the RNWMP or its reduction to impotence" must be the aim of any Farmer-Labour political alliance. SA50 described his criticism of the RNWMP as "quite hot" and "indignant."[46] But Penner outdid himself in February 1920 when he provided a sobriquet for the old RNWMP, namely the "Rural Nothing Worth Monkey Police."[47]

In the aftermath of the arrests of the strike leaders, "Bloody Saturday," and the Immigration Board hearings and trials, SA50 continued his frequent visits to the Penner family. The major focus of his ongoing information gathering was the strategy of the Labour Defence Committee (LDC). Penner proved an excellent source for this because of his prominence in its work, and the spy dutifully passed on the LDC's tactics and strategies to the authorities in Ottawa who in turn kept the prosecution informed. So here we have yet another indictment to add to the compelling and ever-growing evidence against A.J. Andrews and his legal co-conspirators who engaged in every imaginable skulduggery to gain guilty decisions in the multiple hearings and trials of 1919–20.[48] Further evidence of RNWMP complicity in the trials can be viewed in their comprehensive coverage of the speaking tours undertaken by the arrested leaders while on bail awaiting trial. J.S. Woodsworth, for example, had complete coverage of his western fundraising tour for the LDC in September and October 1919. Every speech was carefully observed and summarized for Perry, often by multiple undercover agents and detectives, then forwarded to Ottawa, and subsequently to Starnes in Winnipeg with specific instructions to share the material with Andrews. In one such compilation Perry explained: "All meetings are being covered by plain clothes men [redaction but almost certainly "and secret agents"] and copies of reports submitted in connection therewith are being supplied to Mr. Andrews, K.C."[49] Woodsworth often spoke in these speeches about the mounted police, not only in terms of their overt bloody role in Winnipeg but also of their future destiny: "He prophesized that there would be a great deal of unemployment and distress this winter and because of this the Government were rushing in Mounted Police Red Coats. There were no Indians here for them to shoot, so they must be coming to shoot down the workers of this country. By sending these Red Coats the Government was evidently bent on attempting something on repression lines and nothing constructive at all."[50] For these speeches Woodsworth drew the ire of Justice Thomas Metcalfe when the indictment hearing against him and Dixon opened. Mounted police testimony almost culminated in a contempt of court citation, but cooler heads appear to have prevailed and Woodsworth was indicted only for speaking seditious words as well as the original charge of seditious libel.[51] Such surveillance continued throughout the final months of 1919 and into 1920 when the Dominion Police, in their dying days before the takeover by the new RCMP, were able to add their voices to the repressive chorus when Woodsworth undertook an eastern speaking tour.[52]

The degree to which the prosecution depended on the testimony of police agents and spies has been well chronicled by Kramer and Mitchell. Their account of the testimony of SA21, "Poor Harry Daskaluk," demonstrates how questionable the merits of such evidence were.[53] But even more emphatic evidence of the importance of police spies came in "The Speech Bill Pritchard Never Gave." Fifty years after the events of 1919 Pritchard's dominant memories focused on the role of undercover mounties.[54] In his case his secret agent nemesis, like Pritchard himself, played no direct role in the events in Winnipeg. Pritchard, an SPC leader from Vancouver, was in Winnipeg only briefly during the strike. SA10, Frank Zaneth aka Harry Blask, was not there at all.[55] But after Prosecutor A.J. Andrews won a tussle with Commissioner Perry, who did not want his agent exposed in open court, Zaneth did appear in the strike trials. Writing half a century later, Pritchard devoted nearly 40 percent of his text to the testimony of D/Sergeant Reames and "the chief witness for the Crown . . . a young man of many parts and various faces with two names and two nationalities," Frank Zaneth or Zanetti. The secret agent testified about Pritchard's speeches in Calgary in a predictably selective fashion, three minutes out of two hours, according to the defendant. Pritchard's summary comments on Zaneth after alleging he may have planted one particular anarchist pamphlet in the literature seized in Calgary and used in the Winnipeg trial: "Do you suppose that a man who had habituated himself to lying for the better part of a year, as part of his occupation, and admitted having done so whenever he thought it necessary, could be believed when in the witness box he declared: 'I am telling the truth now?'"[56]

Throughout 1919, with the fulsome support of the Borden government, the RNWMP, the Canadian military, the Department of Justice, the Department of Labour, and the Office of the Privy Council were all complicit in these repressive efforts. While I and others have made the argument before, the major institutional beneficiary of the repression of the labour revolt was the new RCMP, conceived in the struggles of 1917–19 and birthed on 1 February 1920. From the day the RNWMP's geographic scope expanded to cover Canada from the Lakehead west to Vancouver Island in January 1919, the critical asset of the force lay in its simultaneously offering the Canadian state two effective elements of repression: first, an overt, demonstrable strength as a trained cavalry force perfect for street actions and capable of enforcing the law in riotous circumstances without necessitating the far less legitimate resort to military aid to the civil power; second, considerable experience with the covert operation of undercover police, secret agents, and informants.

In the discussions in 1918 and 1919 about the future of the RNWMP these two functions proved decisive in ensuring that it would become the predominant component of the new RCMP. In the exchanges between Perry and his minister, Newton Rowell, in late 1918 and early 1919, the commissioner emphasized these two elements as the major rationale for proceeding to create an amalgamated force, "a Canadian constabulary." Such a force should have "rigid discipline and control" and be "armed and trained as a military body so that it can act effectively if it should be required to do so."[57] While this proved a step too far for Borden initially, in the aftermath of the labour revolt he proved far more sympathetic. In early August 1919, with the Winnipeg events and the ensuing nationwide crisis still front and centre, Perry was summoned to Ottawa to meet the prime minister. He did so on 5 August, and with remarkable speed he responded with a scenario, indeed a blueprint, for a new federal police service only two days later.

This letter merits detailed analysis as it provides a synopsis of Borden's charge to Perry and the latter's plan and its rationale, all of which document the centrality of state repression to the future of the new force. Perry commences with a summary of his task: "You informed me that the Government was concerned as to conditions in Canada resulting from general unrest in the World and the pernicious propaganda which is being carried on, distinctly revolutionary in its character." To deal with these threats, the Dominion Police (DP) and the RNWMP were to be amalgamated into a national force under Perry's command. Such a solution would end both the current East/West divided geographic jurisdiction and the split in ministerial responsibility between the minister of justice (DP) and the president of the Privy Council (RNWMP), depicted by Perry as lacking "efficiency" and potentially "disastrous to the best interest of the country." His one-minister, one-police solution allowed for various permutations but any that favoured the Dominion Police he minimized by critiquing their wartime dependence on 1) municipal and provincial police forces; 2) secret agents hired via private detective agencies (often American); 3) other government agencies, such as Immigration and Customs; 4) other American sources; 5) Military Intelligence for alien registration and enforcement of the Military Service Act. These dependencies might have been acceptable while the War Measures Act was still in place, but simply would not work in the postwar world: "The problem has changed. We are now dealing with internal conditions, which are infinitely more complicated, because of the division of opinion among our own people; because of active propaganda carried on with the view of overturning constituted authority, by other than constitutional means; and because Labour Unions and Labour generally are more or less tainted with revolutionary ideas."

The Winnipeg General Strike had demonstrated why unionized local police, "disloyal and unreliable," were not dependable. (As Borden knew: his government in fall 1918 had banned unions in the federal police forces.) Similarly, the Dominion Police's reliance on U.S. detective agencies had resulted in "no large body of loyal expert detectives ... Canadian in nationality and sentiment." The loss of such "invaluable" services was deplorable and necessitated the complete reorganization of the secret service with "greatly increased numbers." The clear recommendation: extend the RNWMP jurisdiction to all of Canada and merge the Dominion Police into the new body under Perry's command. The new, nationwide force would add four eastern districts with headquarters at Toronto, Ottawa, Montreal, and Moncton, each "with as many secret agents as may be required" and a reserve force of at least 160 "in order that those who contemplate disorder may realize that there is force ready to assist local authority."[58]

So, what might easily be regarded as the RCMP's charter document is directly premised on the need for repressive forces focused on a reorganized and augmented Secret Service for spying on labour and the Left and on a paramilitary mounted force for dealing with strikes and riots.[59] Military Intelligence did not disappear either. The new RCMP sat on the Defence Committee of Canada (DCC) from the latter's commencement in October 1920, and the RCMP's intelligence liaison officer, a new position filled by Colonel C.F. Hamilton, chaired the DCC's new Intelligence Sub-Committee from its inception in January 1922.[60] Military Intelligence had not surrendered the field to the new RCMP.[61]

Nevertheless, in addition to the many positive legacies of the labour revolt in general and the Winnipeg General Strike in particular, one must add to its heritage its key significance in the birth of the RCMP with its specific roles as Canada's covert domestic spy agency and as its first line of defence against overt domestic unrest.[62] Whether Jake Penner came up with a new version of his "Rural Nothing Worth Monkey Police" to mock the new force's acronym, we do not know.

Notes

1 Title from Canadian Security Intelligence Service (CSIS), Access to Information (ATI), 89-A-57, PHF437, Jacob Penner, Secret Agent 50, 14 February 1920, Report on Jacob P. Penner and Family. My thanks to Linda Kealey and Margaret Conrad for their helpful comments on this paper.

2 See "State Repression of Labour and the Left in Canada, 1914–20," in Gregory S. Kealey, *Spying on Canadians: The Royal Canadian Mounted Police Security Service and the Origins of the Long Cold War* (Toronto: University of Toronto Press, 2017), 71–105.

3 See Kealey, "1919: The Canadian Labour Revolt," *Labour/ le Travail* 13 (1984): 11–44; and Craig Heron, ed., *The Workers' Revolt in Canada, 1917–1925* (Toronto: University of Toronto Press, 1998).

4 Reg Whitaker, Gregory S. Kealey, and Andrew Parnaby, *Secret Service: Political Policing in Canada from the Fenians to Fortress America* (Toronto: University of Toronto Press, 2012); Steve Hewitt, *Riding to the Rescue: The Transformation of the RCMP in Alberta and Saskatchewan, 1914–1939* (Toronto: University of Toronto Press, 2006); Carl Betke and S.W. Horrall, *Canada's Security Service: An Historical Outline, 1864–1966*, (Ottawa: RCMP Historical Section, 1978), obtained from the Canadian Security Intelligence Service (CSIS) via ATI request 117-90-107. For the concept of "the long cold war" see Odd Arne Westad, *The Cold War: A World History* (New York: Basic Books, 2019) and Kealey, *Spying on Canadians*, 3–13. Readers should be reminded that the RNWMP became the RCMP on 1 February 1920.

5 Reinhold Kramer and Tom Mitchell, *When the State Trembled: How A.J. Andrews and the Citizens' Committee Broke the Winnipeg General Strike* (Toronto: University of Toronto Press, 2010); Dennis G. Molinaro, *An Exceptional Law: Section 98 and the Emergency State, 1919–1936* (Toronto: University of Toronto Press, 2017), 19–56; Kealey, *Spying on Canadians*, 106–66; Hewitt, *Riding to the Rescue*. The Strike's leaders always referred to the Citizens' Committee as the "Committee of Knaves."

6 Mark Humphries, "Before the Strike: Canadian Military Intelligence and the Surveillance of 'Subversive' Labour Groups in Manitoba, 1903–1919" (paper presented at the Canadian Historical Association meetings, Waterloo, ON, May 2012); Kealey, *Spying on Canadians*, 151–57. I would like to thank Dr. Humphries for graciously sharing his paper and his archival research with me.

7 Humphries, "Before the Strike."

8 Mike O'Brien, "Manhood and the Militia Myth: Masculinity, Class, and Militarism in Ontario, 1902–1914," *Labour/ le Travail* 42 (1993): 115–41; Mark Moss, *Manliness and Militarism: Educating Young Boys in Ontario for War* (Toronto: Oxford University Press, 2001).

9 Humphries, "Before the Strike."

10 Ruthenian was an alternative description for what later was normally termed Ukrainian. It is worth noting that MI's preoccupation with "foreign aliens" meant that they focused on the SDP and apparently ignored the more Anglo-Canadian Socialist Party of Canada (SPC).

11 Library and Archives Canada [LAC], RG24, vol. 4611, file 20-22A, vol. 1, Reports of 22–30 April and 3, 11, 21, 27 and 28 May 1915.

12 LAC, RG24, vol. 4611, file 20-22A, vol. 1, General W. Gwatkin to DOC, MD10, Winnipeg, 12 June 1915.

13 Kramer and Mitchell, *When the State Trembled*, 222, 225, 244. In the first reference it appears that the authors thought he was from the RNWMP. In the second he is correctly identified as Military Intelligence.

14 LAC, RG24, vol. 4613, file 20-22A, vol. 7, Campbell to Ruttan, Winnipeg, 6 July 1917.

15 LAC, RG24, vol. 4613, file 20-22A, vol. 7, Sherwood to Ruttan, Ottawa, 23 July 1917.

16 LAC, RG24, vol. 4614, file 20-22A, vols. 9 and 10. There is no direct evidence that the agent is Langdale, and the fact that he appears to speak and read Ukrainian and on occasion act as a translator and interpreter suggests that he is more likely one of the corp's translators.

17 The spelling of this name, like many of the others in these reports, varies frequently. Budiuk also appears as Buduik and Budnik.

18 LAC, RG24, vol. 4614, file 20-22A, vol. 9, Campbell to OC#10, 7 October 2018.

19 Esyllt W. Jones, *Influenza 1918: Disease, Death, and Struggle in Winnipeg* (Toronto: University of Toronto Press, 2007); Mark Osborne Humphries, "The Horror at Home: The Canadian Military and the 'Great' Influenza Pandemic of 1918," *Journal of the Canadian Historical Association*, n.s., 16, no. 1 (2005): 235–60; Humphries, "The Limits of Necessity: Public Health, Dissent, and the War Effort during the 1918 Influenza Epidemic," in *Epidemic Encounters: Influenza, Society, and Culture in Canada, 1918–1920*, ed. Magda Fahrni and Essyllt Jones (Vancouver: UBC Press, 2012); and Humphries, *The Last Plague: Spanish Influenza and the Politics of Public Health in Canada* (Toronto: University of Toronto Press, 2013); Benjamin Isitt, *From Victoria to Vladivostok: Canada's Siberian Expedition, 1917–1919* (Vancouver: UBC Press, 2010). The ironic and tragic intersection of the Siberian misadventure and the great influenza pandemic of 1918–19 merits more attention than I can pursue here. Jones makes a compelling argument that "the community solidarity of the General Strike was prefigured in the epidemic" and "out of this mutual reliance, strong bonds of class and community were formed" (93). Later she argues that "the epidemic had an important role in galvanizing labour's determination to push its agenda . . . and increasing workers' militancy and confidence" (115). For an insightful treatment of the relationship between disaster and utopian visions and transformative potentials, see Rebecca Solnit, *A Paradise Built in Hell: The Extraordinary Communities That Arise in Disaster* (New York: Penguin, 2009).

20 LAC, RG24, vol. 4614, file 20-22A, 20 August–28 October 2018.

21 Kealey, *Spying on Canadians*, 79–83; Jeffrey A. Keshen, *Propaganda and Censorship during Canada's Great War* (Edmonton: University of Alberta Press, 1996), 87–91, 122–26.

22 LAC, RG24, vol. 2543, file 2051, vol. 2, Gwatkin to Major Miller, Military Attache, British Embassy, Washington, 20 January 1919. By "Permanent Force" he means the full, regular Canadian military.

23 Kramer and Mitchell, *When the State Trembled*, 222, 224–25, 244.

24 Writing in 1921, Ketchen is using RCMP to describe the 1919 RNWMP.

25 LAC, RG24, vol. 2656, file 3576, Major General H.D.B. Ketchen, GOC MD10 to Major General J.H. Elmsley, 13 May 1921. Note that this file also contains an anonymous, thirteen-page, plus appendices, unpublished history of the Citizens' Committee of 1000, dated Winnipeg, 29 May 1919.

26 LAC, RG18, ATI 83-84/321, vol. 3, file G-26-22, Lawrence Fortescue, Comptroller to Commissioner, 25 August 1914. See in the same file George T. Hann, "Memo Re Secret Agents," 14 February 1949, which reviews the force's formal history with secret agents. The issue in 1949 was how to maintain secrecy about payments to SAs given more stringent auditing rules. The Treasury Board came up with an effective work-around, much to the delight of RCMP brass.

27 Hewitt, *Riding to the Rescue*, 28–44; Betke and Horrall, *Canada's Security Service*, 305–6.

28 Betke and Horrall, *Canada's Security Service*, 307–8; Kealey, *Spying on Canadians*, 120–23.

29 Betke and Horrall, *Canada's Security Service*, 321–25. I have made a minor correction in the authors' computations.

30 See F. Horrigan, OC Vancouver, to Commissioner Perry, 24 February 1919, printed in Kealey, *Spying on Canadians*, 256–57. The Dominion Police retained jurisdiction only in Canada east of the Lakehead.

31 LAC, RG13, ATI 83-84/321, file G-2-6 (1951), Perry to Comptroller, 14 January 1919.

32 Hewitt, *Riding to the Rescue*, 75–83; Betke and Horall, *Canada's Security Service*, 335–48; Kealey, *Spying on Canadians*, 252–53. Our most detailed understanding of these early police spies is provided in Mark Leier, *Rebel Life: The Life and Times of Robert Gosden*, rev. ed. (Vancouver: New Star Books, 2013).

33 The spelling of this "foreign" name, like so many others, proved difficult for the RNWMP, who used numerous variant spellings.

34 Penner later became a major figure in the Communist Party of Canada and served for twenty-seven years as an elected member of the Winnipeg City Council. He was also the father of Roland Penner, NDP attorney general of Manitoba under the Pawley government, and Norman Penner, a scholar of the Canadian Left and editor of *Winnipeg 1919: The Strikers' Own History of the Winnipeg General Strike* (Toronto: James Lewis and Samuel, 1973). For more background on Jacob Penner, see Roland Penner, *A Glowing Dream: A Memoir* (Winnipeg: Shillingford, 2007) and Norman Penner, ed., "Jacob Penner's Recollections," *Histoire sociale/Social History* 7, no. 14 (November 1971): 366–78.

35 Betke and Horrall, *Canada's Security Service*, 249–50. In their text he is identified only as SA50.

36 On SA50 and Clarke, see Hewitt, *Riding to the Rescue*, 92–93.

37 Hewitt, *Riding to the Rescue*, 54–55. Riethdorf is rendered as Reithdorf in some of the documents.

38 Betke and Horrall, *Canada's Security Service*, 319; RNWMP, General Order 13176, 2 February 1919.

39 SA50's reports are found in Penner's RCMP, Personal History File, P437, acquired via ATI 89-A-57 to the Canadian Security and Intelligence Service (henceforth PHF), and in LAC, RG146, Winnipeg General Strike and Riot, 1919, ATI 1025-9-91035 (henceforth WGSR).

40 Perry to Edwards, 27 May 1919 and 5 September 1919, in WGSR and PHF respectively.

41 SA50 Reports of 12, 29 September and 6 October 1919; Perry to McLean, 18 September 1919; Jacob Penner to "Mr. Alexander," 29 September 1919; A/ Commissioner McGibbon to Starnes, 8 October 1919, PHF.

42 SA50 reports, 14 and 24 March 1919, PHF. For an excellent discussion of the SPC in 1919, see Gerald Friesen, "Bob Russell's Political Thought: Socialism and Industrial Unionism in Winnipeg, 1914–1919," in his *River Road: Essays on Manitoba and Prairie History* (Winnipeg: University of Manitoba Press, 1996), 122–46. Peter Campbell, *Canadian Marxists and the Search for a Third Way* (Montreal and Kingston: McGill-Queen's University Press, 1993) has a fine chapter on Russell. On the theme of revolutionary industrial unionism, see Larry Peterson, "The One Big Union in International Perspective: Revolutionary Industrial Unionism, 1900–25," *Labour/ le Travail* 7 (Spring 1981): 41–66; and Peterson, "Revolutionary Socialism and Industrial Unrest in the Era of the Winnipeg General Strike: The Origins of Communist Unionism in Europe and North America," *Labour/ le Travail* 13 (Spring 1984): 115–31.

43 SA50 report, 19 July 1919, PHF.

44 SA50 report, 3 July 1919, PHF. One interesting outcome of the literature seizure, however, was the fact that among the items removed were two copies of Siberian anti-Bolshevik papers given to Penner as a joke by his conscript brother, John, who had been in the Siberian Expeditionary Force. No doubt the agent's report saved the RNWMP from much confusion. On John's conscript career in the SEF, see LAC, RG150, accession 1992-93/166, box 7718-45, "Penner, John – 3215549," Personnel File; J.E. Skuce, *CSEF: Canada's Soldiers in Siberia, 1918–1919* (Ottawa: Access to History Publications, 1990), 104. My thanks to Ben Isitt for these military references.

45 SA50 report, 24 October 1919, PHF.

46 SA50 report, 5 November 1919, PHF.

47 SA50 report, 14 February 1920, PHF.

48 Andrews's unscrupulous and manipulative behaviour is examined and exposed in loving detail in Kramer and Mitchell, *When the State Trembled*. For a succinct and updated account, see Reinhold Kramer and Tom Mitchell, "'Daniel DeLeon Drew up the Diagram': Winnipeg's Seditious-Conspiracy Trials of 1919–20," in *Security, Dissent, and the Limits of Toleration in War and Peace, 1914–1939*, ed. Barry Wright, Eric Tucker, and Susan Binnie, vol. 4, *Canadian State Trials* (Toronto: University of Toronto Press, 2015), 217–60.

49 J.S. Woodsworth, PHF, 175P/594, obtained from CSIS via ATI 89-A-57. A good example is Perry to Comptroller, 3 October 1919, with enclosed reports from Lethbridge and Maple Creek. It is worth noting that the Regina meetings were covered by the infamous RCMP undercover agent John Leopold, SA30.

50 Woodsworth PHF, Corporal E.C. Newnham, Report on Federated Labour Party, Victoria B.C., 22 October 1919.

51 Woodsworth PHF, D/C W.H. McLaughlin, Report JSW Alleged Contempt of Court and Sedition, 17, 19, and 20 November 1919.

52 Woodsworth PHF, Sgt. B.H. James to Acting Chief Commissioner A.J. Cawdron, 22 December 1919. After F.J. Dixon achieved an acquittal on his seditious libel charges in February 1920, the Crown dropped charges against Woodsworth on the original charge on 16 February and a stay of proceedings against the second charge

on 7 March 1920. Kenneth McNaught, *A Prophet in Politics: A Biography of J.S. Woodsworth* (Toronto: University of Toronto Press, 1959), 125, 128, 135.

53 Kramer and Mitchell, *When the State Trembled*, Chapter 13. In his *Reasoning Otherwise: Leftists and the People's Enlightenment in Canada, 1890–1920* (Toronto: Between the Lines, 2008), Ian McKay describes the show trials and secret hearings as "exercises in ideological manipulation" (497).

54 James Naylor and Tom Mitchell, "The Speech Bill Pritchard Never Gave," *Labour/le Travail* 84 (Fall 2019): 279–301. The best biography of Pritchard is in Campbell, *Canadian Marxists*, Chapter 3.

55 On Zaneth, see Kealey, *Spying on Canadians*, 174–76; Whitaker, Kealey, and Parnaby, *Secret Service*, 84–86.

56 Naylor and Mitchell, "Speech," 291–93, 297–98.

57 Hewitt, *Riding to the Rescue*, 13; and Whitaker, Kealey, and Parnaby, *Secret Service*, 75–80.

58 LAC, RG18, ATI 83-84/321 vol. 1, file 2-6 (1951), Perry to Borden, 7 August 1919. The RCMP act is Statutes 1919 (second session), 10 George V ch.28.

59 Hewitt, *Riding to the Rescue*, 26–27, 106–08.

60 For a discussion of the Defence Committee and its Intelligence Sub-Committee, see Kealey, *Spying on Canadians*, Chapter 5.

61 At least one other spy was present in Winnipeg reporting on the strike for American sources. Fourteen reports were filed between 9 and 26 June, which were particularly concerned with Russian Strike leaders and questions of possible Soviet monetary support. The spy also met with A.J. Andrews and shared his reports with him after gaining permission from his employer. This relationship was reciprocal as the agent subsequently received access to materials seized by the RNWMP in their various raids surrounding the arrests of the Strike leaders. While this source remains obscure, the reports appear to be tied to New York State's Lusk Committee, or at least it had access to these mysterious reports. My thanks to Tom Mitchell for sharing this material with me. It is used in his *When the State Trembled.* University of Regina Archives, Lusk Papers, Joint Legislative Committee to Investigate Seditious Activities, 1919–1920 [1919], Secret Reports, Agent, Winnipeg. Lusk's four-volume report was published as *Revolutionary Radicalism: Its History, Purpose, and Tactics* (Albany, NY: Lyon, 1920). For background, see Todd J. Pfannestiel, *Rethinking the Red Scare: The Lusk Committee and New York's Crusade against Radicalism, 1919–1923* (London: Routledge, 2003.)

62 For a full history of the RCMP SS, see Whitaker, Kealey, and Parnaby, *Secret Service.* The RCMP was ignominiously stripped of its security and intelligence functions with the creation of a civilian agency, the Canadian Security Intelligence Service, in 1984 in the aftermath of the RCMP Security Service scandals of the 1970s.

13

Not by Repression Alone: Defeating the Workers' Revolt by False Promises of Reform

Myer Siemiatycki

It took more than repression to defeat the Winnipeg General Strike of 1919. To be sure, the combined forces of state spies, targeted arrests, and the militarized intervention of "Bloody Saturday"—allied with fierce employer hostility—all had their intended effect. Some 30,000 striking workers in Winnipeg were coerced to capitulate.

Yet the 1919 uprising of Canada's working class ran too wide and deep to be defeated by coercion alone. It would also require an unprecedented tripartite alliance of the Canadian state, employers, and mainstream union leadership, coalescing to promote the illusion that labour's discontents could be remedied without resort to strife and radicalism.

The Winnipeg General Strike was the culmination of escalating labour unrest across the country through the final years of the Great War. State and business leaders now feared for the stability of not only one city, but the entire country. Within the labour movement itself, a veritable civil war erupted. Traditional, cautious craft unionism was now increasingly challenged by an emergent class struggle unionism rooted in workers' support for more militant union structures and strategies—along with more radical views of societal transformation.

If the measure of a social movement's challenge to the status quo is the array of counter forces required to contain it, the Winnipeg General Strike was indeed an unprecedented shock to the system. Labour unrest became so intense that neither the state nor capital believed it could be defeated by repression alone. Nor by them alone—the established, moderate union leadership needed to be an ally in quelling unrest. This collaboration would be secured through an unprecedented co-optation of labour leadership by the Canadian state. Ironically perhaps, historiographic focus on employer hostility and government repression in Winnipeg has blurred any deeper examination of other dynamics that defined 1919: extraordinary rank-and-file worker upsurge, the containment efforts of established cautious unions, and the crucial courting of these unions by the Canadian state.

This chapter examines the national pacification campaign that accompanied outright repression in 1919, "when the state trembled."[1] Measures adopted included bringing labour representation into the federal cabinet, establishing a royal commission into labour discontent, funnelling government and business funds to support embattled established union leadership, and convening a veritable postwar domestic labour peace conference of business, labour, and government leaders. Such a strategy of incorporating capital and labour directly into the state policy-making process is best described as "corporatism." Our memory of 1919 has paid insufficient attention to corporatist pacification as a force in defeating labour's upsurge.[2] What a potent pretense it all was in 1919.

……

The Winnipeg General Strike was not—as proclaimed at the time by screaming newspapers headlines, and leading voices of government, business, and cautious craft unions—an orchestrated attempt at revolution directed by radical extremists. Rather, its messy multidimensionality was the authentic expression of Canadian labour's organic evolution through four years of war, giving way to the uncertain prospects of peacetime reconstruction. Multiple currents, with differing logics, coursed through the six-week showdown.

As a workers' upsurge, the General Strike reflected a range of (sometimes conflicting) impulses among its 30,000 participants. These included: 1) an attempt to extract a peace dividend from labour's wartime sacrifices, through improved wages and working conditions; 2) the belief that only mass working-class mobilization could extract concessions from employers; 3) a desire to exert greater labour influence on a city long dominated by local business interests; 4) an effort, in some fashion, to transition the postwar world from an economic system based on profit to one based on meeting human needs; 5) and for some, the desire through a choreography unknown, to emulate Russia's dramatic revolution of 1917 in the name of the working class.

What all these currents had in common was workers' belief—forged in war—that they deserved better. "At all points across the political continuum," Craig Heron has perceptively noted, "the new vision was about workers' power. It was a revolt against the kind of subordination that workers had hitherto known in Canadian capitalist society."[3] This spirit would propel workers into escalating conflict with employers, government, and their own more cautious union leadership. It would take an unprecedented alliance of these three forces to contain the rank-and-file upsurge of 1919.

The onset of war in 1914 found Canada in deep economic depression. Conditions in Manitoba were particularly severe. As the Manitoba Executive of the national Trades and Labour Congress of Canada informed the 1915 congress convention: "Last year it was our unpleasant duty to report to you that acute misery was afflicting a large army of the working class as a consequence of the slump in industry. We regret to report that conditions are incalculably worse at the present time. . . . As a result of the complete and prolonged distress, financial exhaustion is imposing upon the toilers and their families in the province, the most intense misery."[4] Inevitably, this economic distress also took its toll on the country's labour movement. From 1913 to 1915, union membership across the country fell 20 percent, from 175,799 to 143,343. Unions now represented less than 5 percent of Canadian wage earners. Collective bargaining and mobilization virtually disappeared. The number of strikes dropped to an all-time low; time lost due to work stoppages plummeted. Mass unemployment seemed to render labour resistance futile; employers capitalized by cutting wages of those workers still on the job.

The protection that eluded labour through collective bargaining also proved unattainable in the political arena. The Trades and Labour Congress of Canada (TLC) was the country's largest labour federation and central lobbying voice to government. Its 80,000 affiliated members in 1914 represented half of all union members in the country. Overwhelmingly, TLC affiliates were locals of international craft unions belonging to the American Federation of Labour. Generally, these unions represented skilled craftsmen in a variety of trades. The TLC was the Canadian branch plant voice of American unions committed to a narrow labour vision: organize only the most skilled workers, strive for incremental gains, and demonstrate the benefits of unions to employers by honouring signed contracts and committing to profitable production. In 1919, the TLC and many of its affiliated unions would partner with government and employers to defeat Canadian labour's radical upsurge.

At the war's outset, the TLC leadership petitioned and lobbied the Borden government to alleviate workers' hardships that had resulted from economic downturns. The annual major event in TLC lobbying was its brief, rather ritualistic meeting with the prime minister. As Robert Borden recorded in his diary following both 1914 and 1915 meetings, the views expressed by labour were invariably moderate and sensible, and his own cautious, noncommittal response would close matters until the following year's visit.[5] The Borden government's attentiveness to the TLC would only rise, at war's end, when its efforts were required to stem labour unrest.

Manitoba labour's pleas for provincial government support fared no better. In 1915 the TLC's Manitoba Executive reported that its call for provincial action to assist the jobless had gone unanswered, and concluded: "As it has never since been heard of, it is presumed that it has experienced the common fate of the expression of the hopes of labour—consignment to the waste paper basket."[6] The first year and a half of the war had been an unremittingly bleak time for Canadian workers and unions. Unforeseen was how dramatically the war would revive the Canadian economy and labour movement from 1916 to 1918.

The hothouse war economy was characterized by relentless demand for production, full employment, labour shortages, and workers struggling to keep up with galloping inflation. Workers now had more leverage on the job than ever. They could quit their employer and readily find another job. They could unionize without fear of being fired—employers needed them. They could strike and win—employers needed their production. Yet with inflation running between 50 percent to 75 percent from 1914 to 1919, workers' resentment mounted, as any wage raises inevitably lagged behind rising prices.

Escalating prices prompted a distinct, corollary "inflationary labour" dynamic: more workers than ever joined unions, more engaged in mass strikes, and as Canadian business racked up record profits (denounced by critics as wartime profiteering), so too did workers' resentments multiply. Union membership in Canada rose steadily from a wartime low of 143,343 in 1915 to 378,047 in 1919. The number of strikes climbed even more dramatically from the 1915 total of 63, to 336 in 1919; days lost to strikes over this period soared from 95,042 to 3,400,942.[7] Containing this mounting labour militancy would be a pressing concern not only for government and employers, but also for a cautious union establishment that feared losing control of its own organizations to militant currents.

From early in the war effort, the leadership of craft unions acted as a restraining force against workers' militancy. Addressing the 1915 TLC convention, Canada's labour minister Thomas Crothers praised its union leaders as "reasonable men who take in the broader view that the good of all should be considered. Some people think that the labor leaders wish to foment strikes, but that has not been my experience. They are keenly anxious to maintain peace."[8] There was much truth in this assessment. Canada's craft union leadership was cautious in outlook. They strategized from a position of weakness: relatively small union membership, vulnerable to employer hostility, and enjoying virtually no legislative protection. They came to believe union viability depended not on antagonizing employers, but convincing them that unions could be of benefit in assuring a disciplined, reliable workforce. This outlook, they believed, was in the best interest of unions and their members.

Under certain circumstances, cautious union leadership's commitment to moderation might clash with a more defiant mood among the rank and file. The First World War created precisely such conditions, culminating in calls for mass strike action, and ultimately a campaign from within Canadian labour to secede from international craft unions and form One Big Union instead. The kind of labour movement that emerged in Canada during the second half of the war is perhaps best described as "class struggle unionism." This reflected the sentiment that unions could only make gains if they mobilized the largest number of workers against employers, across occupations and industries. Winnipeg 1919 would be the most potent Canadian expression of class struggle unionism. It was the culmination of a brewing "Workers' Revolt in Canada."[9] From the spring of 1916 to spring of 1919, an escalating arc of strikes and critiques of capitalism reflected both Canadian labour's rising resentments and its mounting confidence in a better world to be won.

The tide first turned from working-class demoralization to class struggle unionism in 1916 on two fronts: Hamilton's munitions plants and western Canada's coalfields. Wartime production needs gave both sites an early economic boost, quickly triggering mass strike action that prefigured the spirit of 1919. In Hamilton, in defiance of their union leadership, some 2,000 workers shut down dozens of munitions plants, in a city-wide strike for better pay and working conditions. Employers formed a united front to oppose concessions, a position supported by government. After five weeks of strike, workers conceded defeat. Many had already quit, leaving for better paying jobs in Toronto.[10]

More successful were three rounds of coalminers' strikes, from July 1916 to January 1917, in the Alberta and British Columbia coalfields represented by District 18 of the United Mine Workers of America. In all three cases, thousands of miners defied their union leadership and their existing collective agreements in order to strike for higher wages. Employers denounced the strikes as illegal work stoppages provoked by radical foreign union agitators disloyal to the country's war effort. Each round ended with concessions to labour as the desperate need for fuel, combined with inability to secure an alternate workforce, greatly enhanced strikers' leverage.[11]

The last two years of war saw this relentless dialectic of working-class aggrievement and empowerment spark intensified labour militancy across the country. Manitoba experienced a veritable rebirth of its labour movement in 1917, as reported by the provincial TLC's executive: "As a general rule conditions have been very favorable for the organizations of labour of all kinds during the current year. Not only have there been unions formed amongst workers who had hitherto remained aloof, but the older organizations which by enlistments and closing down of work, suffered severely in membership following the outbreak of war, have grown to large proportions again. The tendency of wages to lag far behind in the increasing cost of nearly everything which the worker has to buy caused a great deal of unrest."[12]

Winnipeg business leaders lost no time—and would make a recurring wartime habit—of calling for strong government measures to curb labour unrest and work disruptions. In June 1917, the Winnipeg board of trade urged the prime minister to outlaw strikes in essential industries.[13] By then, some 8,000 western coalminers were again on strike in defiance of both their employers and international union leadership. Recouping living standards lost to inflation was again the issue. Borden's government rejected the most repressive options being proposed by exasperated Canadian business interests: a ban on strikes, military supervision of mines, or the mass importation of a foreign workforce.

Instead, the Borden government turned to exercising greater control over essential war industries and courting the support of mainstream union leaders to quell work disruptions. Over the final two years of the war, the state's laissez-faire approach to labour market policy gave way to two different, even contradictory impulses: state capitalism and corporatism. The former entailed a more directive, hands-on economic role for government. The latter involved giving capital and labour a more direct institutionalized role in determining government economic policy. Both strategies were prompted by the same goal—to curb strike activity.

Under the war economy's production imperatives, state capitalism could involve imposing concessions on employers, if their intransigence was prompting strikes and impeding production. Thus, in June 1917, the Borden government effectively took over management of Western Canada's District 18 coal industry, after 8,000 miners launched yet another strike to catch up with inflation—again, against orders from their international union leadership. Rejecting calls to reopen mines under military supervision, the government instead announced a state takeover of mine management. It appointed a director of coal operations, empowered to establish wages, working conditions, and commodity prices. The director's decree of an immediate 22.5 percent wage hike, and regular inflation adjustments, brought an end to the fourth miners' strike within a year.[14] The director's order of higher coal prices cushioned the cost of labour peace for mine operators.

In October 1917, a director of grain operations was appointed to end a strike of close to 1,000 grain handlers in Fort William and Port Arthur (now Thunder Bay). Their job action for union recognition and higher wages effectively shut down the grain trade. Borden's government rejected another emergency appeal from Winnipeg's business establishment to resume production with strikebreakers, under military supervision.[15] Instead, the director of grain operations ended the strike with a decree providing union recognition and wage raises. Given labour shortages, inflation, and urgent production needs, regulation proved a more viable wartime response to labour unrest than did repression.

At the same time, the very different approach of corporatism also came into government favour as a means of reining in labour unrest. Corporatism is typically invoked in times of trouble—when neither a directive state, nor market relations, nor repression alone can restore capitalist economic stability. In 1918 and 1919, trouble came in the form of escalating unionization and strikes, accompanied by reverberating rhetoric of radical societal change. In 1918, these dynamics were regarded as a threat to the war effort; in 1919, they were seen as jeopardizing postwar economic reconstruction.

Leo Panitch has aptly described corporatism as "a political structure within advanced capitalism that integrates organized socio-economic producer groups through a system of representation and co-operative mutual interaction at the leadership level and mobilization and social control at the mass level."[16] It involves the state bringing select leaders of capital and labour directly into decision-making of government policy, rather than regarding them as external "interests." In exchange for this privileged representation inside state institutions, labour leaders are expected to deliver something of value to government. In 1918 and 1919, corporatism meant conscripting moderate union leaders to quell the labour unrest of their rank and file. These union leaders allowed themselves to believe that playing this part would give them the leverage to secure unprecedented concessions from employers and government.

. . . . . .

The Borden government's pivot to corporatism began in the later stages of war, with status and recognition conferred on the Trades and Labour Congress and its leadership. In exchange, union officialdom would be called upon to act as proponents and agents of state labour policy. A first strategic and symbolic step was bringing a union official into government ranks as cabinet minister. The appointment, in October 1917, went to Gideon Robertson, Canadian vice-president of the Order of Railroad Telegraphers International Union. Robertson had been appointed to the Senate by Borden a year earlier, in recognition of his successful resolution of a threatened CPR rail strike. Once Borden announced his intention to bring labour representation into cabinet, Robertson lost no time promoting his credentials to the prime minister. "I have, as you possibly may know," Robertson wrote privately to Borden, "done all possible since 1914 to maintain industrial peace in Canada, which is essential to efficient results in our war work . . . it will be my duty and pleasure to support your war policy, to promote industrial peace in Canada."[17]

Robertson aced the job application with these words, and in October 1917 he joined Borden's cabinet as minister without portfolio, named chairman of the Labour Sub-Committee of the newly formed Cabinet Reconstruction and Development Committee. A year later, he would be promoted to minister of labour. Gideon Robertson would play a leading part in Winnipeg's dress rehearsal general strike of 1918, and the subsequent main event of 1919.[18] Prime Minister Borden understood that containing a labour revolt required the visible handiwork of labour itself.

In January 1918, the Borden government invited thirty labour representatives for discussions on meeting wartime production requirements amidst labour shortages. In return for union leaders' pledge to avert strikes and support a workforce registration campaign, moderate union leaders were appointed to a host of government agencies and boards. In April 1918, the government invited American Federation of Labor president Sam Gompers to deliver an address to Canada's Parliament. Gompers was the prime architect and enforcer of international craft unionism's philosophy of "business unionism," the personification of what government and business officials came to identify as "safe and sane" unionism, in contrast to militant unionism.

Gompers used the occasion to applaud the Allied cause as "the most wonderful crusade ever entered into by men in the whole history of the world," and to stress the critical need for "unity of purpose among the people's of all our Allied nations."[19] Under Gideon Robertson's advice, the government distributed a copy of Gompers's speech to every union local in the country.[20]

The expectations on Canadian unions were not lost on the president of the Trades and Labour Congress of Canada. James Watters declared in 1918: "The war has demonstrated the necessity of co-operation, not alone on the actual field of battle, but in every industrial activity associated with the prosecution of the war. . . . Competition has, therefore, given place to co-operation—co-operation between the State and Capital and Labor."[21] Indeed, Watters confessed himself "surprised to find how much real humanity there is in the employer, if only we go about things in the proper way, and sit down and discuss our problems quietly together."[22] Meanwhile, ever larger numbers of Canadian workers were demonstrating the belief that militancy and class struggle unionism—rather than "quiet" discussion—were the way to make gains.

Internal union conflict between a restive rank and file and restraining officialdom was now commonplace across the country, including central Canada. In August 1918 the membership of Ottawa's street railway union "howled down" advice from an international union executive board member to accept a conciliation board offer, and launched strike action instead.[23] Nor did the president of the International Association of Machinists fare any better a month later in Montreal. W.H. Johnston's speech defending the union's official wartime no-strike policy generated such an outcry from the city's machinists that Johnston was unable to complete his address.[24] Meanwhile in Toronto, the rift within unions now made the local press, when the *Toronto Telegram* reported: "The continued unrest in the labor movement in this city is becoming a serious matter even to the self-appointed leaders of the movement, who are finding themselves now in the position of being unable to control the desire of the rank and file to strike." As one Toronto union official confessed: "The fact is, they [the membership] have got beyond our control."[25]

In turn, international union leadership now regarded the spirit of class struggle unionism as a fatal threat to their organization. As the *United Mine Workers' Journal* editorialized weeks before the end of the war: "Unauthorized and sporadic strikes are the curse of the labor movement."[26] The Canadian state would not lack union allies in its corporatist campaign against workers' unrest.

The sympathetic strike emerged as Canadian labour's wonder weapon in the final year of the war. Perhaps fittingly and prophetically, the first sympathetic strike of 1918 occurred in Winnipeg, when over 15,000 workers from a variety of unions walked off the job in May to support striking, recently unionized civic workers. Again, as in the previous year's grain handlers' strike, Winnipeg's economic establishment besieged the prime minister with calls to declare all strikes illegal. As Tom Mitchell and James Naylor have written, the situation was now highly charged: "Confrontation was in the air. Martial law and arrests were threatened from the outset. Working-class solidarity with the civic employees was palpable and explosive."[27]

Only the direct intervention of trade unionist cabinet minister Gideon Robertson averted escalated strife. He persuaded Winnipeg city council to settle the dispute on the civic workers' terms. Winnipeg labour was re-confirmed in the view that class struggle unionism yielded results. For his part, the usually astute Robertson completely misjudged the significance of the truce he had engineered in Winnipeg in spring 1918. Writing to the minister of labour following the settlement, Robertson informed Thomas Crothers: "I feel sure that greater efforts will be made by them [Winnipeg's workers] in the future to exhaust every effort to reach an adjustment of all disputes by negotiation and conciliation and not to strike in any instance except as a last resort."[28]

Quite the opposite, in Winnipeg and elsewhere, workers were now seized with the allure of the sympathetic strike in "adjusting all disputes." Twice more—in the summer and fall of 1918—Winnipeg and much of western Canada were brought to the brink of general strikes, in support of workers far afield. First was the nationwide strike by letter carriers; second was support for a strike by Calgary freight handlers. In response to both, workers across the country had come to adopt the ethos of the European war theatre. As Calgary strike leader Charles Smitten declared, if it was right for strong nations to come to the aid of weak ones in times of war, then it was equally necessary for strong unions to help young, embattled ones like the Freight Handlers.[29]

Precisely this spirit animated Winnipeg workers again in July 1918 at a special meeting of the city's labour council to discuss sympathetic strike action in support of letter carriers. As the *Winnipeg Free Press* reported: "Almost every delegate who spoke during the three and a half hours the meeting lasted, emphasized the fact that the fight of the postal employees for a union wage and for recognition of their organization was a fight that organized labor could not afford to see lost." In both the letter carrier and freight handler disputes of 1918, threatened sympathetic strike action in several cities prompted government and employer surrender.[30]

What other message could Canadian workers draw from the final year of the war, than mobilization mattered: the more strikes, the better; the bigger the strike, the better. A reckoning was coming in 1919. Labour's defeat that year would stem from a more complex interplay of forces than has generally been recognized.

. . . . . .

Peace in Europe brought immediate economic dislocation on the home front. "A period of severe trial will come to both manufacturer and workman," Prime Minister Borden was apprised just days before the armistice by Joseph Flavelle, the head of Canada's Imperial Munitions Board, which oversaw wartime production.[31] The last months of 1918 through winter 1919 did indeed see recession, mass layoffs, and wage cuts sweep across the country.[32] An entirely different economic climate and labour market suddenly now existed. Workers were desperate to keep their jobs and wartime employment gains. Unionization and strike activity across the country reached record levels that year. Conversely, employers were determined to regain ground conceded in the unusual wartime labour market. Importantly, 1919 should not only be understood as a time of workers' revolt, but equally importantly as an employers' offensive to put labour back in its place. For its part, government now faced massive war-induced debt, and uncertain economic reconstruction.

Prime Minister Borden recognized that in turbulent times to come, a more skilful lead hand was required as minister of labour. In the final days of the war, the redoubtable Gideon Robertson was promoted to the position. His appointment also signalled that corporatism would be a key element of the Canadian state's attempt to restore productivity, profitability, and stability to the country's industrial relations. Repression would deal with workers unduly challenging their place in the economic system; corporatism was intended to reduce their numbers. At a time of escalating labour defiance across the country, corporatism held out the prospect of an alternative, peaceful path to redressing worker discontent. Elite level collaboration between business, labour, and government would deliver meaningful reform. Or so it was signalled.

This corporatist strategy was fronted by Gideon Robertson. By early 1919, the labour minister was coming under intense pressure to crack down on mounting labour unrest. He reported being deluged by "insistent inquiries and requests from various individuals and interests throughout the country to the government and the Department of Labour, urging that something must be done immediately or that Bolshevism may prevail, property and life held lightly, and the country be destroyed."[33]

Rather than repression, Robertson opted for a corporatist response that would have three components in 1919: establishing a royal commission to investigate workplace unrest, providing tangible financial support from government and business to shore up mainstream labour against militancy, and convening a five-day, tripartite National Industrial Conference to set postwar peace terms between capital and labour. Promoting the prospect of betterment through partnership, not strife, was the point of the entire exercise.

In early April 1919, after securing support from the Trades and Labour Congress and the Canadian Manufacturers' Association (CMA), Robertson announced the creation of a Royal Commission on Industrial Relations. Its mandate was to travel the country to hold hearings investigating the causes of workplace strife and to offer remedial recommendations. In true corporatist style, the TLC and CMA would each select and appoint two commission members, with the government appointing two to represent the public and a third as commission chairman. Manitoba chief justice Thomas Mathers was appointed chairman; representing labour were newly elected TLC president Tom Moore and Toronto plumbers' union official John Bruce; representing employers were lumber operator F. Pauze and Carl Riordan, a staunchly antiunion pulp and paper operator; a senator and member of Parliament rounded out the seven-member commission.

From late April to mid-June 1919—overlapping with much of the Winnipeg General Strike—the Mathers Commission visited twenty-eight different cities from coast to coast, to hear testimony from many workers and employers about the causes and cures of workplace unrest. As Chief Commissioner Mathers declared at the opening of the inquiry's first session in Victoria, the commission was seeking advice on how to establish "permanent improvements in the relations between employers and employees," in order to forge "a new spirit of partnership" at the workplace.[34]

Ultimately, the commission's legacy would not be charting historic change, but rather preserving historical voice and memory. In policy terms, nothing would come of the commission's recommendations. However, the testimony presented by hundreds of witnesses—workers and employers—provides an unparalleled portrait of employer and working-class attitudes in the spring of 1919. They were on a collision course.

Testimony from employers made it clear that labour was not alone in championing an assertive postwar agenda. Many employers appeared before the commission to provide their blunt assessment of what ailed the nation's industries—the insatiable, arbitrary designs of workers and their unions were impeding any prospect of economic recovery. Across the country employers assailed labour for its excessive wage demands, its flouting of contractual obligations, its mania for strikes, and its challenge to management prerogatives at the workplace. Employer testimony made clear they were taking "general strike" action of their own in 1919. Employers spoke of closing plants and turning down work contracts until unions and wages were brought back into line.[35] Appropriately, perhaps, the most forceful statement of Canadian capitalism's postwar program came when the Mathers Commission visited Winnipeg just days before the General Strike began. Appearing as a spokesman for the city's employers, J.B. Hugg told the commission on 10 May 1919: "The happiness of the world depends on production: we must get better production." The major impediment to progress, Hugg asserted, was trade unionism: "We think they are interfering with production and setting back civilization."[36] There was no mistaking employers' resolve that any corporatist partnership would be on their own terms.

Turning now to labour testimony before the commission, rarely have the views and aspirations of Canadian workers been publicly articulated with such clarity and forcefulness. Thanks to the Mathers Commission, we have a record of what the Canadian working class was thinking in 1919. Interestingly, labour testimony came from two sources: rank-and-file workers, and international union officials who remained loyal to the TLC. For their part, leaders of the One Big Union (OBU) and radical socialists boycotted the commission as an exercise in deception and manipulation. Montreal firebrand Tom Cassidy declared that the commission's sole purpose was "to devise ways and means for the undisturbed perpetuation of wage slavery."[37]

What stands out in labour's testimony to the Mathers Commission is the extent to which workers—especially in the West, northern Ontario, and Cape Breton—identified the capitalist system as the cause of their discontent. They then proceeded to advocate socialism, usually expressed by the phrase "production for use," as the only solution to industrial unrest. Regina bricklayer James Sanbrook captured the mood, declaring that "a system in which the welfare of capital is the supreme consideration, no matter what may happen to the mass of human beings, that such a system is ripe for radical alteration."[38] Edmonton machinist E.J. Thompson described the view of his fellow workers as follows: "We are the producers and we are not getting what we produce, and that is the cause of our trouble."[39] In Cobalt, Ontario, a miner advised the commission that in order to solve workplace unrest, they should "study the Soviet constitution for pointers."[40] As the *Toronto Star* noted, the Mathers Commission was giving voice to a radical, transformative working-class vision: "One is struck by the emphasis laid upon the control of industry by workers. This idea seems to have made great progress in recent years."[41]

Missing in 1919, however, was any coherent—let alone organized—strategy for establishing socialism out of capitalism. To be sure, a remarkable leadership cadre of worker-militants across the country (including Winnipeg machinist and General Strike leader R.B. Russell) belonged to the feisty Marxist, Socialist Party of Canada. The party itself held to a deterministic view of the inevitable, desirable transition of capitalism to socialism. Accordingly, the party saw its mission as winning workers to this view through education and the not-so-radical practice of running candidates in provincial and federal elections. While the party rhetorically called for revolution, it had no plan for storming the gates of capitalism.[42] Some historians have suggested that labour's revolt of 1919 failed because it was hijacked by socialist and syndicalist radicals.[43] No such heist ever occurred. Rather, Marxist militants in the labour movement were swept up in the class struggle unionism moment of Canada's working class, adapted to it, and led efforts to improve workers' lives under capitalism through mass strikes and advocating for One Big Union.[44]

Workers' testimony before the Mathers Commission gave voice to their accumulated discontents. Everywhere that hearings were held, from Victoria to Cape Breton, workers bitterly recited their full litany of grievances: the high cost of living, rising unemployment, low wages, long work hours, employer hostility to unions, poor housing, and unfulfilled promises of a peace dividend for workers after the war.

As Calgary letter carrier Clifford Nichols made clear, workers were no longer prepared to accept such conditions: "the worker has gotten enormous ideals and he is determined to work them out."[45] The longest-standing labour official to testify at the Mathers Commission could put it all in perspective. John Flett's ties to the labour movement reached back to the 1880s, he served as president of the TLC in the early 1900s, and continued as official of the carpenter's union into the 1920s. Flett told the commission in Hamilton: "I have never seen in my experience, as a man and a boy in this country, such unrest, and among men that heretofore were very conservative."[46]

Testimony before the Mathers Commission laid bare the starkly conflicting postwar agendas of capital and labour across Canada. It was fortuitous for the foes of labour radicalism that the commission conducted its cross-Canada consultation in spring of 1919, precisely when working-class mobilization reached its peak. In all twenty-eight cities it visited, the commission signalled that labour's grievances could be addressed by cooperation rather than conflict. This undoubtedly had some stabilizing effect. Equally important, the commission's tripartite collaboration of state, employers, and mainstream unions facilitated further joint counterattack measures against the General Strike, the OBU, and worker militancy.

Both business and government funnelled financial support to mainstream international unions, for the cause. The executive of the Canadian Manufacturers' Association played a crucial—if discreet—role in launching a moderate "labour" newspaper! In April 1919, the CMA executive reported to its council about the successful culmination of its efforts to establish "a safe and same [*sic*] labour paper, that would denounce Bolshevism, that would support tariff protection, and that would encourage the made-in-Canada idea."[47]

Thus was born the *Canadian Labor Press,* proudly presenting itself as the official organ of labour councils in Ottawa, Hamilton, and Kitchener. The paper's inaugural editorial charted its mission: "The *Canadian Labor Press* proposes to be a Rational, National Labor Paper striving to achieve better things for labor by Peaceful Evolution instead of violent Revolution."[48] Its most notable contribution to Canadian journalism was a brilliant series of full-page posters admonishing workers to forsake radicalism for moderation and harmony. Advertisements from the Canadian Manufacturers' Association and Canadian Reconstruction Association (a CMA subsidiary established in 1918 to advocate business-friendly postwar policies) appeared regularly. Aided by the CMA's tersely described efforts "to secure circulation,"[49] by the fall of 1919 the *Canadian Labor Press* boasted the largest readership of any labour paper in the country.

International unions also received direct business and government funding for their efforts to suppress labour unrest. Support from business was a covert operation. The Canadian Reconstruction Association contributed "thousands of dollars among labor leaders" to secure moderate craft union opposition to the One Big Union and support for continued tariff protection for Canadian manufacturers. A circumspect CRA president John Willison conveyed this news to the president of Stelco, adding it "is a story which cannot be told in a letter."[50] Meanwhile, the Borden government also extended financial support to moderate unions. By order-in-council, labour minister Robertson funded the TLC $1,000 toward expenses at its upcoming 1919 convention, which planned to strengthen powers of the Congress executive to combat the OBU. Authorization for the funding stated, "because of the unusual efforts being made by the Executive of the Congress to stabilize industrial conditions, the Minister recommends that a grant of one thousand dollars ($1, 000) be made for the above purpose."[51] In public statements, Robertson made clear the instrumental intent of state support for mainstream unions: "We are backing the international unions, which believe in the sanctity of contracts . . . we are prepared to see the labor forces built up through the international union so as to make labour an asset and not a menace."[52] As international unions would learn, however, support from employers and government to quell unrest did not mean that support continued once militant labour was contained.

The immediate services rendered by international union officers in 1919 included threats to expel strikers from union membership, to revoke union local charters, and even plans to recruit strikebreakers. All were invoked by Canadian heads of the railway brotherhood unions to prevent a rail shutdown in support of the Winnipeg General Strike. Particularly concerted were the efforts of James Murdock, Canadian vice-president of the Railway Trainmen Brotherhood, whom Gideon Robertson would commend to the prime minister for his "excellent service."[53] In 1921, James Murdock would go on to succeed Robertson as minister of labour in the newly elected government of Mackenzie King.

In July 1919, the Mathers Commission performed its final act—issuing majority and minority reports. Endorsed by seven members including the chief commissioner and both union representatives, the majority report distilled thousands of pages of testimony into ten "chief causes of unrest": unemployment, inflation, working hours, the right to collective bargaining, disenchantment with government, poor housing, freedom of press and speech restrictions, ostentatious displays of wealth, and lack of equal education opportunities. However, the report's remedial prescriptions were a good deal less precise. Generalities and platitudes never transcended the report's concluding statement that "what is required to make the Dominion great and prosperous and its population contented and happy is a spirit of co-operation on fair and equitable lines among all classes."[54]

This was more than two commissioners, Senator White and employer representative Pauze, could endorse. Their minority report opposed union advances at the workplace, rejected shorter working hours, attributed unemployment to workers' refusal to take available jobs, and opposed any consideration of government pension or unemployment plans.

The only tangible outcome of the Mathers Commission was its call for the government to extend the corporatist moment to a final, extraordinary public display of tripartism. The report recommended that a conference of "representative labour men and representative employers," along with government officials, be convened to discuss measures that might ease industrial unrest. The Borden government agreed, and held a five-day National Industrial Conference in Parliament's Senate chambers from 15 to 20 September 1919. Modelled on a February 1919 National Industrial Conference in Britain, as James Naylor has noted, the Ottawa gathering became a forum for "the two great social classes of industrial Canada squaring-off in debate over the shape of post-war 'reconstruction.'"[55] With the Winnipeg General Strike defeated, and the OBU held in check, the irreconcilability of labour-capital perspectives would be on full display.

In true corporatist fashion, eighty-eight labour delegates to the conference were selected by the TLC executive, and eighty-eight employer participants were named by the CMA and various employer associations. The government appointed thirty-four participants to represent the public interest. TLC delegate selection immediately came under fire from labour militants. Toronto's Tom Milleleau complained: "Our members have been hand-picked. There is a lack of Radicals at Ottawa ... it is an attempt to chloroform Labor."[56] Meanwhile, mainstream union leaders arrived with great expectations, confident that "much important legislation will undoubtedly follow this Conference."[57] This would be misplaced wishful thinking.

Gideon Robertson had already made it clear that the government would not impose workplace legislation on employers in efforts to ease workplace unrest: "no legislation of a compulsory character will be of any material assistance in solving a problem of this sort."[58] Corporatism provided the perfect cover for this pro-business stance. The parties themselves would have to consent to any new legislation. What employers would not concede at the bargaining table or on the picket line, they certainly were not prepared to grant in September 1919, when the threat of the Workers' Revolt had subsided.

Indeed, employers privately implored the prime minister to open the conference with a clear call for labour restraint in the cause of reconstruction. They urged "an ungarnished statement of conditions exactly as they are at the moment, as the enunciation of such a condition self-evidently carries with it as the only possible solution the necessity of production on a greater scale as regards volume, and on a less expensive scale as regards costs."[59] Borden's opening address emphasized the economic and fiscal challenges facing the country, citing the prospect of depression and a tenfold rise in the national debt from the war. In these circumstances, only such policies "as will not drive away capital, restrict industry or hinder development" could be considered.[60] Effectively, the conference was over as soon as it began.

The remaining time was devoted to plenary and subcommittee discussion of recommendations from the Mathers Commission. While employers repeatedly stressed the importance of higher production and reduced costs in industry, union officials argued that only concessions to responsible unions could eliminate industrial strife. TLC president Tom Moore was reduced to pleading that an IOU was now due because union leaders had saved capitalism and employers in Canada. "I want to point out very forcefully," Moore declared, "that it was the Trade Union movement that stood as a bulwark between overturning [society] and sensible evolution during this past year."[61]

The National Industrial Conference achieved no agreement on any workplace reforms. Perhaps fittingly, the immediate post-mortem was left to Winnipeg delegate A.C. Hay, vice-president of the city's labour council. "We have not accomplished the ideals of labour for 1919," he declared at the conference.[62] Decades later, the disappointment and sting of betrayal felt by union leaders who had banked on corporatism still burned strong. Almost fifty years after serving on the Mathers Commission, Toronto plumbers union officer John Bruce called the experience "one of the bitterest lessons that ever I learned in political chicanery." Particularly reprehensible to Bruce was the role played by the prime minister himself. Borden personally commended the commissioners for their work, and committed to initiating reforms, declaring that "conditions had to be meliorated . . . [but] still the government refrained from doing anything."[63]

The year 1919 would end without Borden's government adopting any progressive labour or social legislation. Further tripartite collaboration ceased once labour's upsurge had been contained. In 1920, the Canadian Manufacturers' Association refused to participate in another National Industrial Conference, deeming it unnecessary.[64] For its part, the TLC was reduced to its annual cap-in-hand lobbying, reminding government in 1920 of reforms that had been pledged. The most tangible result was a cheery declaration from the CMA that the government's response to labour lobbying "did not contain any very serious concessions."[65] Canadian employers now turned on their erstwhile moderate union allies. Employer offensives drove unions out of industry, postwar unemployment returned to early war-year levels, and strike activity fell sharply.[66] Unions and workers would have to await another world war for their fortunes to improve.

Canada's mainstream union leadership blundered badly in 1919. Union moderates were misguided in believing they could leverage the threat of labour radicalism to extract concessions from employers and government. Neither capital nor the state in Canada would support a reform route to working-class betterment. But the established union leadership did play their part in forestalling a more forceful challenge to constituted class relations in Winnipeg and the country as a whole.

Notes

1 The phrase is from the writing of Antonio Gramsci, evocatively adopted as the book title of Reinhold Kramer and Tom Mitchell's *When The State Trembled: How A.J. Andrews and the Citizens' Committee Broke the Winnipeg General Strike* (Toronto: University of Toronto Press, 2010).

2 Discussion of corporatist interventions in 1919 include Gregory Kealey, "1919: The Canadian Labour Revolt," *Labour/Le Travail* 13 (Spring 1984): 11–44; Myer Siemiatycki, "Labour Contained: The Defeat of a Rank and File Workers' Movement in Canada, 1914–21" (PhD diss., York University, 1986); Larry Gerber, "The United States and Canadian National Industrial Conferences of 1919: A Comparative Analysis," *Labor History* 32, no. 1 (Winter 1991), 42–65; James Naylor, *The New Democracy: Challenging the Social Order in Industrial Ontario, 1914–1925* (Toronto: University of Toronto Press, 1991); James Naylor, "Workers and the State: Experiments in Corporatism after World War One," *Studies in Political Economy* 42 (Autumn 1993): 81–111; Craig Heron and Myer Siemiatycki, "The Great War, the

State, and Working-Class Canada," in *The Workers' Revolt in Canada, 1917–1925,* ed. Craig Heron (Toronto: University of Toronto Press, 1998).

3 Craig Heron, "National Contours: Solidarity and Fragmentation," in *Workers' Revolt in Canada*, 277.

4 Trades and Labour Congress Proceedings, 1915, 25.

5 Library and Archives Canada [LAC], Borden Diaries, 5 January 1914; Ibid., 15 January 1915.

6 TLC Proceedings, 1915, 25.

7 Report on Labour Organization in Canada, 1917, 1919; Morley Gunderson and Daphne Taras, *Canadian Labour and Employment Relations*, 6th ed. (Toronto: Pearson Addison Wesley, 2009), 340.

8 TLC Proceedings, 1915, 5.

9 The best treatment of this nationwide labour upsurge remains Heron, *Workers' Revolt in Canada.*

10 Myer Siemiatycki, "Munitions and Labour Militancy: The 1916 Hamilton Munitions' Strike," *Labour/Le Travail* 3 (1978): 131–51.

11 Siemiatycki, "Labour Contained," 77–87.

12 TLC Proceedings, 1917, 59.

13 LAC, Borden Papers, RLB Series, file 1660, Winnipeg Board of Trade to Borden, 12 June 1917.

14 Siemiatycki, "Labour Contained," 113–21.

15 LAC, Borden Papers, file 1831, Boyle to Borden, 5 October 1917.

16 Leo Panitch, "Corporatism in Canada," in *The Canadian Political Process*, ed. R. Schultz, O. Kruhlak, and J. Terry, 3rd ed. (Toronto: Holt, Rinehart and Winston, 1979), 53.

17 LAC, Borden Papers, OCA Series 79, vol. 137, Robertson to Borden, 23 August 1917.

18 Kramer and Mitchell, *When the State Trembled.*

19 LAC, Flavelle Papers, vol. 22, Gompers Speech to Parliament, 2 April 1918.

20 Martin Robin, *Radical Politics and Canadian Labour* (Kingston: Industrial Relations Centre, Queen's University, 1968), 139–40.

21 LAC, Canadian Brotherhood of Rail, Transport and General Workers Papers, vol. 63, 1918 TLC convention booklet.

22 *Globe,* 29 April 1918.

23 Wisconsin State Historical Society, Amalgamated Association of Street, Electric, Railway and Motor Coach Employees of America Papers, reel 3, General Executive Board Meeting, 1 February 1919.

24 Siemiatycki, "Labour Contained," 213.

25 *Toronto Evening Telegram,* 23 July 1918.

26 *United Mine Workers' Journal,* vol. 29, 1 October 1918.

27 Tom Mitchell and James Naylor, "The Prairies: In the Eye of the Storm," in *Workers' Revolt in Canada*, 180.

28 LAC, Borden Papers, Borden Memoire Notes, vol. 340, Robertson to Crothers, 25 May 1918.

29 *Calgary Herald*, 8 October 1918.

30 A fuller discussion of these disputes is available in Siemiatycki, "Labour Contained," 203–9, 222–27.

31 LAC, Borden Papers, RLB Series, file 2791, Flavelle to Borden, 21 October 1918.
32 LAC, RG 27, vol. 160, file 611.21.
33 Senate Debates, 2 April 1919, 194.
34 Mathers Commission Testimony [MCT], Thomas Mathers, Victoria, 26 April 1919.
35 Siemiatycki, "Labour Contained," 246–48.
36 MCT, J.B. Hugg, Winnipeg, 10 May 1919.
37 *Ontario Labor News*, 1 June 1919.
38 MCT, James Sanbrook, Regina, 8 May 1919.
39 MCT, E.J. Thompson, Edmonton, 6 May 1919.
40 MCT, James Cluny, Cobalt, 1919.
41 *Toronto Star*, 6 May 1919.
42 Ian McKay, *Rebels, Reds, Radicals: Rethinking Canada's Left History* (Toronto: Between the Lines, 2005), 151–52.
43 For such interpretations see, for instance, David Bercuson, *Fools and Wise Men: The Rise and Fall of the One Big Union* (Toronto: McGraw-Hill Ryerson, 1978); Desmond Morton with Terry Copp, *Working People: An Illustrated History of the Canadian Labour Movement* (Ottawa: Denau, 1984).
44 Siemiatycki, "Labour Contained," 302–6.
45 MCT, Clifford Nichols, Calgary, 3 May 1919.
46 MCT, John Flett, Hamilton, 20 May 1919.
47 Canadian Manufacturers' Association (CMA) Papers, Executive Council Minutes, vol. 10, 24 April 1919.
48 *Canadian Labor Press*, 15 February 1919.
49 Ibid.
50 Tom Traves, *The State and Enterprise: Canadian Manufacturers and the Federal Government 1917–1931* (Toronto: University of Toronto Press, 1979), 26.
51 LAC, RG 27, Lacelle Files, vol. 115, file 600.02-108, 13 April 1926, Acland to Minister.
52 *Globe*, 15 August 1919.
53 LAC, Borden Papers, O.C. 564, Robertson to Borden, 31 May 1919.
54 Mathers Commission Report, 19.
55 Naylor, "Workers and the State," 81.
56 *Labor Leader*, 19 September 1919.
57 *Canadian Labor Press*, 13 September 1919.
58 Senate Debates, 2 April 1919, 194.
59 LAC, Borden Papers, O.C. 556, Robertson to Borden, 2 September 1919.
60 National Industrial Conference – Official Report of Proceedings and Discussion, 6.
61 Ibid., 212.
62 Ibid., 226.
63 LAC, John Bruce Papers, John Bruce Interview, 30 March 1963, Transcript, 3–4, 5.
64 LAC, CMA Papers, vol. 10, Executive Committee Report, 28 October 1920.
65 Ibid., 25 March 1920.
66 Siemiatycki, "Labour Contained," 375–401.

14

Remembering 1919: Commemoration and the Winnipeg General Strike

Sharon Reilly

The Winnipeg General Strike has been the focus of a great deal of academic research, writing, and debate for the better part of a century, and today this history is taught in Manitoba's elementary and high school classrooms. As public historians will attest, however, most individuals learn their history through more popular interpretations of the past. Commemorative initiatives from plaques and monuments to works of art, creative writing, music, documentaries, exhibitions, and performances all play a role in this process.

The events of 1919 have been commemorated in all these ways over the years, and the centenary gave rise to an amazing proliferation of new such ventures. In many respects, the development of these public history initiatives has closely followed and been informed by (and has even helped inform and enrich) the Winnipeg General Strike's more academic historiography, which the editors of this volume have detailed in an earlier chapter. Indeed, the relationship between scholarly and popular history is a dynamic one, and the two operate in parallel. Both are driven by broader changes in society and they influence each other. And individuals, not surprisingly, often move between the two, drawn both by the research and reflection emanating from the academy and by the desire to engage with a wider audience. The Winnipeg General

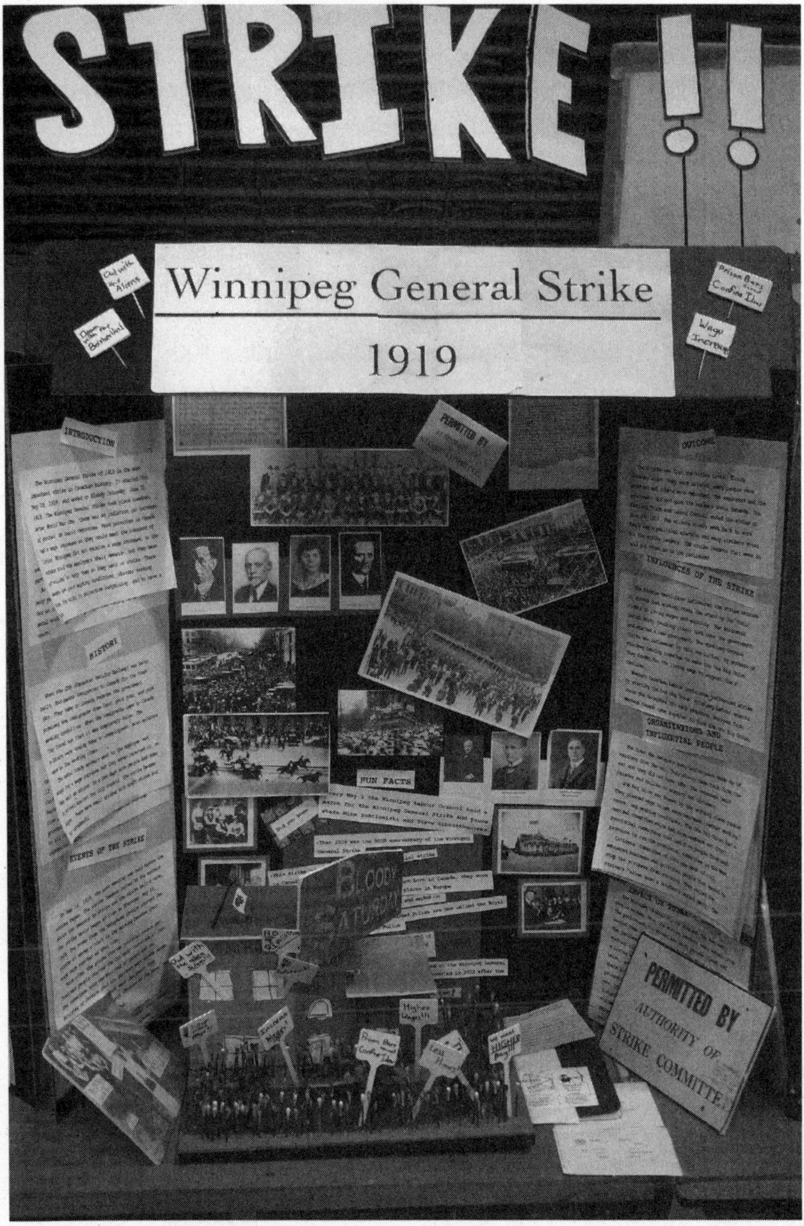

Figure 14.1. *Winnipeg General Strike Student Diorama*, winning entry in the Red River Heritage Fair, 2011. Photo: Sharon Reilly.

Strike provides clear evidence of the fruitful relationship between the academic and popular spheres.

Public history initiatives and their extensive reach have ensured that wide audiences have learned the Strike's history and significance. In their many forms, they have helped keep the Strike front and centre in Winnipeg's history by providing ample, accessible, and varied opportunities to engage in learning and meaning-making activities. Acting as inspirational beacons, these have helped instill in many a strong sense of legacy and pride and demonstrated the potential of working-class and labour activism to help build a better world. The 100th anniversary seemed a fitting time to review these initiatives and to reflect upon the critical role commemoration plays in keeping the history of the Strike alive and relevant to contemporary audiences. As someone who has spent a good part of her career collecting and curating working-class peoples' stories, I am pleased to have the opportunity here to consider and reflect upon both my own work on the Winnipeg General Strike, alongside that of others who, over the past several decades, have helped bring the important history of this labour struggle to the public fore.

Like much of the older historical writing, commemoration has often been used to bolster the power of the dominant elite. This began to be challenged in places like South Africa as early as the 1970s, with attacks on statues commemorating the champions of apartheid. Today, in Canada, a refusal to accept a dominant narrative founded upon colonialism and racism is seen in protests made against the commemoration of political figures who sanctioned the enslavement of Blacks and attempted to eradicate Indigenous people. These protests demonstrate the importance of such commemorative edifices and their power to reflect and uphold, or to negate, controversial aspects of our history. The commemoration of the Winnipeg General Strike—a struggle for justice by working-class and immigrant women and men against a powerful political, economic, and social elite—was an impossibility for many years. This changed over time, however, through the ongoing struggle of those who refused to accept a skewed version of the past—or to cede control over the always contested "sites of memory"—and sought to commemorate their own histories among those of Canadian elites.

Commemorating the Winnipeg General Strike—The First 99 Years

This wall of silent but effective opposition to recognizing the city's labour heritage was breached slowly, only really beginning a half century after the Winnipeg General Strike. One of the earliest efforts to commemorate the Strike was realized in 1967, when R.B. Russell Vocational School was opened and named for Strike leader R.B. (Bob) Russell. A heritage plaque donated by the Winnipeg and District Labour Council recognized Russell's "contribution to the community, as a citizen, a respected labour leader, and an activist for vocational training." Notably, no reference was made to the Strike. As the editors noted in Chapter 1, the Steelworkers' plaque at city hall erected two years later celebrated the Strike, but viewed it narrowly through the lens of a struggle for "collective bargaining." It was, in essence, more a celebration of the post–Second World War attainment of a legal regime that included collective bargaining rights than it was of the events of a half century earlier. The Strike itself, as a massive challenge to the social order, was still off limits for the city's elite and the trade union leadership. It took more years of strenuous lobbying to secure additional monuments to the Strike until, today, heritage plaques in Winnipeg commemorate a wider range of subjects—not only Russell but J.S. Woodsworth; A.A. Heaps; the Ukrainian Labor Temple; the James Street Labor Temple; Victoria Park; and the Winnipeg General Strike itself.[1]

Bureaucratic and conservative gatekeeping was more readily breached through literature, as popular works—including plays, novels, and poetry—not only memorialized the Strike but viewed it more expansively, reflecting the growth of multicultural and feminist sentiments through the last half of the century. *Striker Schneiderman*, by Toronto author Jack Grey, was first performed in Toronto in 1970. Presented from the perspective of an immigrant worker, the play proved popular with audiences and was performed for years by the University of Winnipeg Theatre Department. *Lulu Street*, by Winnipeg journalist Ann Maud Henry, explored the Strike through the tensions that existed between women from differing backgrounds. The production made headlines in 1967 as the first work by a Manitoba author to be performed at the Manitoba Theatre Centre. Published in 1972, the play was performed in Winnipeg and beyond for many years. The Strike was commemorated in 1986 with the publication of *Fox*,[2] a novel by University of Winnipeg professor Margaret Sweatman. *Fox* explored the clash between the elite and working-class communities of Winnipeg through the story of a woman who sympathized with the strikers despite her family's elite status. *Fox* was adapted as a stage production and performed at Prairie Theatre Exchange, Winnipeg, in March 1994.

An impressive opportunity for commemorating the Strike came about in 1970, when the Manitoba Museum of Man and Nature (now the Manitoba Museum) opened at its current location across from city hall. The museum's lifelike Urban Gallery, designed to represent Winnipeg in the aftermath of the Strike, highlighted the social and economic discrepancies that led to the conflict. Developed by a team led by Jim Stanton (Chief of Human History) and curators Rob Gillespie, Steve Prystupa, and David Ross, the exhibit depicted Winnipeg as a city divided. Railway tracks ran through the centre of town, separating the homes and businesses of the elite from working-class Winnipeg. A factory; a boarding house/brothel; warehouses; and an All People's Mission with signage addressing immigrants in half a dozen languages were located on the other side. A Chinese laundry, representing a group of citizens who were even less empowered than British and eastern European workers, backed onto an alleyway. Interpretive text was prepared for the gallery, but never included. Instead, it was decided to prioritize the experiential ambience of the exhibition and offer interpretive tours as needed. For several years, a version of *Lulu Street* was presented in the gallery, and an educational program was developed for school groups. The gallery is highly effective in commemorating the Strike when viewed with such interpretation. Unfortunately, most visitors wander through the museum on their own and see the gallery as little more than a quaint depiction of early twentieth-century Winnipeg. As explained further along, however, exhibitions with full interpretation were mounted in temporary halls for the for the seventy-fifth and ninetieth anniversaries of the Strike, and the Urban Gallery was transformed in 2019 for a 100th anniversary exhibit.

In 1983, the first musical composition to commemorate the Winnipeg General Strike was undertaken by Indigenous and other inner-city youth in the Audio Recording Performance Production Program at R.B. Russell Vocational School. Working under the direction of Albert Kelsch and inspired by University of Manitoba professor

Ken Osborne's publication, *R.B. Russell and the Labour Movement*,[3] the students wrote, performed, recorded, and produced a 45-rpm vinyl recording dubbed *Russell's Tussle*. The project raised awareness that the opportunities for advancement for working-class students offered by the school stemmed from the efforts of progressives like Russell. This message was extended further when the Canadian Labour Congress purchased 300 copies of the record for delegates to their national convention.

Another initiative of 1983 demonstrated the ways in which academic and public history can imaginatively interact. Historian Nolan Reilly and graduate student Gerry Berkowski organized an international Winnipeg General Strike Symposium at the University of Winnipeg, which led to new interpretations of the Strike and the broader Workers' Revolt across Canada, and they presented the first Winnipeg General Strike Driving and Walking Tour. Based on a course developed by Reilly for his students, the tour took participants by bus from Crescentwood—home of Winnipeg's early twentieth-century elite—to working-class and immigrant neighbourhoods in the city's North End, and to the "contested terrain" downtown where many of the events of 1919 took place. Although planned for visitors attending the symposium, the tour quickly proved popular with local audiences, many of whom knew little about the historical geography of their city or had seldom ventured into Winnipeg's North End.

The excursion featured not only extant buildings and locations connected to the Strike, but also places that were at risk of being forgotten because they had disappeared or changed so dramatically since 1919. Victoria Park, for example, the strikers' most important meeting place, was largely erased from public memory when the land was rezoned for industrial development shortly after the Strike. The Winnipeg Industrial Bureau, which served as headquarters for the Citizens' Committee in 1919, was demolished in 1935. Thirty years later, entire blocks that played a key role in the Strike were razed to make way for the Centennial Concert Hall, Manitoba Museum complex, and new city hall. The sites lost at this time included the James Street Labor Temple, Rupert Avenue Police Station, Strathcona Hotel (first location of the Women's Labor League Labor Café), and Hell's Alley—the infamous laneway that linked Market and James, just east of Main Street, where Strike supporters were attacked by specials on Bloody Saturday.

The tour made the commemoration of the Strike relevant by looking beyond the issues of 1919 to explore the contemporary conditions facing working-class and immigrant residents. It was published as a guidebook in 1985[4] and reprinted for the seventy-fifth anniversary in 1994. Whether navigated independently, or taken with a group and led by historians, labour leaders, community activists, or cultural workers, the tour has remained an effective and popular commemorative excursion that has been taken by thousands of students, teachers, trade unionists, heritage enthusiasts, and others over the years.

In 1985 Winnipeg audiences also had their first opportunity to view the work of Winnipeg General Strike artist Robert Kell, when I had the chance to curate an exhibition of Kell's work presented at the Labour Day Festival at Kildonan Park, 2 September 1985, and at the Manitoba Legislative Building for the remainder of the month.[5] Kell began focusing on the Strike after attending a lecture series by historian Charles Lipton on Canadian labour history in Toronto in the early 1970s. He became concerned that the experiences of working men and women were largely ignored—not only by historians—but by artists as well. Kell also met art critic Barry Lord, who explored the class dimensions and American imperialist influences upon Canadian art in his groundbreaking text, *The History of Painting in Canada: Toward a People's Art*.[6] Lord drew attention to Kell and his early 1919 artwork in this book. Later, he introduced me to Kell, leading the way to the exhibition in Winnipeg. At least five of Kell's paintings were purchased for labour and government collections in Winnipeg through this exhibition, and autographed copies of two of Kell's works were distributed widely. One of Kell's lithographs was featured on the front cover of the *Winnipeg General Strike Driving and Walking Tour* guidebook.[7]

At the Manitoba Museum, I also curated an exhibition of archival photos for the 1985 CUPE National Conference in Winnipeg. The display later travelled to schools and other venues in Winnipeg, and a Spanish-language version was produced and taken to Havana, Cuba, by the Canada-Cuba Friendship Centre. In 1990, photos and text from the exhibit were reproduced in an enlarged format and used to add a labour heritage component to the meeting rooms and corridors of Winnipeg's new Manitoba Union Centre on Broadway.

The wider resonance of all of this work was apparent by the time of seventy-fifth anniversary of the Strike in 1994, an anniversary that

Figure 14.2. Robert Kell, *Study for Tryptch [triptych] Painting*, 1983. Watercolour and pencil on paper, 25.75" x 25.75". Photo: Sharon Reilly.

saw a huge upsurge in commemorative activities organized by labour activists, artists, and community groups. These efforts were coordinated by a Manitoba Federation of Labour committee chaired by Winnipeg actor, director, and playwright Rick McNair. Events began on 28 April, with a gathering in recognition of the National Day of Mourning for workers killed or injured on the job. The anniversary of 15 May 1919—the beginning of the Strike—was marked with a festive parade featuring floats, union locals, and bands that marched from Market and Main—near city hall and the events of Bloody Saturday— to the Union Centre on Broadway, where costumed labour leaders, representing the Strike leaders of 1919, addressed the crowd.

One of the most far-reaching of the seventy-fifth anniversary initiatives was the founding of Winnipeg's annual MayWorks Festival of

Labour and the Arts, a month-long program of cultural and educational events that explore the lives, struggles, and aspirations of working people—past and present. This was part of the emergence of a broader movement across Canada and beyond, linking cultural workers, social activists, and the labour movement in broad and imaginative ways. The inaugural Winnipeg MayWorks program reflected the work of historians and included a play by Rick McNair entitled *Labour on Trial*,[8] performed by Wayne Nicklas at the Ukrainian Labor Temple.

The Winnipeg Labour Choir was also created in 1994, founded by Winnipeg Folk Festival cofounder Mitch Podolak. Directed by Ilena Zaramba from 1994 to 1997, and Loa Henry thereafter, the group performed regularly until 2011 and released several vinyl and digital recordings, raising "their voices in support of the struggle for a better life."[9] The Winnipeg Labour Choir held its final performance, under the direction of Loa Henry shortly before her death, at the Ukrainian Labor Temple on 15 May 2019.

The seventy-fifth anniversary of the Strike also saw the production of two commemorative videos by the Manitoba Labour Education Centre. *Telling Our Stories: Winnipeg 1919*, directed by Terry Kennedy, was dedicated to keeping the lessons of working-class history alive for future generations; while *Six Weeks of Solidarity: Winnipeg 1919*, directed by Doug Smith and Victor Dobchuk, focused on the historic and contemporary importance of working-class solidarity.

A major museum exhibition also marked the seventy-fifth anniversary. *Winnipeg 1919: A City in Crisis*, which I curated, opened at the Manitoba Museum 1 May 1994 with a performance by the Winnipeg Labour Choir.[10] The exhibit featured artifacts including a billy club, special constable armbands and badges, and a union ballot box that used black and white marbles to vote "yay" or "nay" salvaged from the James Street Labor Temple before the building was demolished.

The exhibit also featured a rare hand-painted silk parade banner from the International Brotherhood of Electrical Workers, a One Big Union lapel pin, and a Kossuth Hungarian Sick Benefit Society building sign that were acquired as part of a collections development initiative begun in the 1980s. Lifelike vignettes, with mannequins dressed in period costume, were included to convey key themes of the Strike to broad audiences. These vignettes paid special attention to the often underrepresented role of women in the Strike, while members of Earthstory Storytellers presented stories about such women in the nearby Urban Gallery.

Following 1994, the pace of activity continued unabated with significant new productions including three excellent documentaries intended for wide public audiences. *On Strike* (1991), by Joe McDonald and the National Film Board of Canada, offered a concise overview of events that became widely used in high school and university classrooms. *The Notorious Mrs. Armstrong* (2000), by Paula Kelly and Buffalo Gal Productions, brought Helen Armstrong and the Women's Labor League to the forefront for the first time. *Bloody Saturday* (2007), by Andy Blicq and the Canadian Broadcasting Corporation, used the narrative of the *Winnipeg General Strike Driving and Walking Tour* and the drama of the death of Mike Sokolowski as presented in Danny Schur's production, *Strike!* to depict the Strike and its contemporary relevance. All three documentaries were highly acclaimed and remain popular as educational tools today. Public screenings of the latter two productions, along with commentaries by directors Paula Kelly and Andy Blicq, were presented to full houses in 2019 as part of the Strike centenary activities.

In 2011, these documentaries were incorporated into an education package called *STRIKE! 1919: The Winnipeg General Strike Educational Kit*. Produced at the Manitoba Museum under my direction, with assistance from Professor Nolan Reilly, the kit also included the Manitoba Labour Education Centre videos; oral history clips from a project conducted by the museum in the 1970s; artifact replicas; archival photos; and extensive written materials. Funded and produced in cooperation with the Manitoba Department of Education, the kit was distributed to all high schools in Manitoba and continues to be used today.

Unfortunately, projects that commemorate the Strike are not always so long-lived. On 12 September 2012, a mural dedicated to the Winnipeg General Strike—created in 2006 by artist Thomas Andrich—was destroyed in a violent thunderstorm. Located on the south wall of the heritage building at 436 Main Street, the collage featured scenes from the Strike, images of Helen Armstrong and the arrested Strike leaders, and posters from the demonstrations protesting the arrest and trials of the Strike leaders that warned "Prison Bars Cannot Confine Ideas" and "Their Sentence is Our Sentence."

In 2014, a major commemorative work concerning the Strike was lost when a highly acclaimed exhibition at the Canadian Museum of

History—Canada's most frequently visited museum—was simply dismantled. *Meeting Room No. 10, The Winnipeg Labor Temple*, opened in 1999 with the support of the Canadian Labour Congress. Developed under the direction of curator Steve Prystupa, with Nolan Reilly, the exhibit examined the Strike within a re-creation of a room at the James Street Labor Temple—headquarters of the Strike Committee. Reflecting one of the major interpretive trends of Strike historiography, the exhibit argued that the Strike was fought to achieve a living wage, decent working and living conditions, and the right to organize. In 2006, the exhibition was enhanced under the direction of curator Rhonda Hinther with the addition of storytelling and new artifacts. These additions further emphasized the deplorable conditions faced by working-class families and the role played by Helen Armstrong and the Women's Labor League in the fight for greater equity. Although *Meeting Room No. 10* was planned as a permanent exhibition, it was dismantled in 2014 and replaced with a much smaller and less engaging display.

Coincidentally, however, when the Canadian Museum of Human Rights (CMHR) opened in Winnipeg later that year, Hinther, then head of exhibits research, ensured that the Winnipeg General Strike was included as one of the key exhibits in its Canadian Journeys gallery. The exhibit, which I had the opportunity to curate, made it clear that "labour rights are human rights." A nearby display focused on the conditions faced by contemporary migrant farm labourers in Canada, while additional labour-related stories were told using photographs projected on an overhead wall with interpretive text presented at floor-level computer stations.

Commemorating the Strike Centenary

Although not exhaustive, the preceding overview of commemorative projects undertaken in the years leading up to 2019 demonstrates both a steadily growing community appreciation of the significance of the Strike and an interest in exploring, publicly, the issues it posed about the nature of the city's social order. This culminated in a remarkable explosion of enthusiasm by a very broad range of participants intent on marking the Strike's centennial as a formative event in the history of Winnipeg and Canada.

Preparations for the 100th anniversary began as early as 2010, when labour activists started drafting plans, and by 2015 a much broader community was involved. Organizers were inspired by another momentous centenary being planned across the Atlantic. Throughout Ireland, scholars and heritage workers were preparing to commemorate the 1916 Easter Rising—the tumultuous revolt that led to civil war, independence, and to decades of strife. In reflecting upon these preparations, Irish historian Fearghal McGarry noted that commemorating the Easter Rising and studying the history of this event were two different things. While history represents an effort to understand the past in an objective way, he said, commemoration was centred more on the present. Its objective was to ask what values and lessons can be taken from our history.[11]

This conviction was evident in the initiatives that commemorated the Winnipeg General Strike in the years leading up to 2019, and the same philosophy drove preparations for the centenary. From the outset, it was clear that the purpose of the 100th anniversary initiatives was to expose and challenge the social and economic injustices that linked 1919 and 2019. Despite their differing backgrounds and audiences, project organizers declared again and again that understanding the lessons of the Winnipeg General Strike was critical to understanding the present and creating a more equitable future.

Notably, the union movement, including its leadership at the provincial and civic level, as well as individual unions, encouraged and supported the broad range of efforts to celebrate and understand the Strike. This was the product not only of a growing collaboration between historians and organized labour—as epitomized by the work of the Manitoba Labour Education Centre in the 1980s and 1990s—but also of a willingness to use history to think more broadly about how labour could better respond to decades of neoliberal assaults and attempts to roll back trade union rights. President Kevin Rebeck and the small but dedicated staff of the Manitoba Federation of Labour (MFL) led a multipronged, community-based anniversary committee and raised funds from unions across the country to support a multitude of commemorative activities.[12] I was honoured by being asked to cochair the committee along with Rebeck. Federal, provincial, and municipal programs also provided financial support. Union activists and labour leaders; university historians and other academics; museum curators and other heritage professionals; students and teachers; visual artists; playwrights; authors and publishers; filmmakers; musicians; community activists; journalists and other media personnel became involved, exploring the significance of the Strike not only to Manitoba's past but to the issues of today. Commemorative activities too numerous to even list here were promoted online and in print format by the MFL. A detailed program of events was also distributed by the organizers of the 2019 MayWorks Festival.[13]

As the spring of 2019 drew near, even those most involved in the planning were taken aback at the tremendous level of interest generated by the anniversary. The sheer number of activities undertaken to mark the centenary was almost overwhelming. In the key weeks between May Day and 21 June—the anniversary of Bloody Saturday—it was not unusual for two or three different events to take place across the city at the same time. Posters and billboards presented a constant reminder of the anniversary and promoted the many activities. Newspaper reports, radio and television broadcasts, magazines, journals, and social media messaging stirred the flurry of excitement even further.

The extent to which the anniversary spoke to a broad spectrum of community members was demonstrated in an exhibit developed by the United Way of Winnipeg. Entitled *1919: Working Stronger Together*, and displayed at the organization's headquarters at 580 Main Street a short distance from city hall, the exhibit explained United Way's founding in 1919 as a response to the social and economic disparities revealed by the Strike. The founders set out to bring people from diverging backgrounds together to address these injustices and make Winnipeg a better place to live. The display addressed past and present social and economic injustices in Winnipeg, and highlighted efforts to address these problems through the combined efforts of organized labour and the philanthropic movement.[14]

As mentioned previously, the nearby Manitoba Museum transformed its Urban Gallery in 2019 to present *Strike 1919: Divided City*. The exhibition highlighted the social and economic discrepancies of early twentieth-century Winnipeg and explored the differing perspectives of Winnipeggers. It included newsreel footage showing a peaceful demonstration by Strike supporters and contrasted this with a disquieting display of billy clubs, police pistols, and a Lewis machine gun, like the one used to patrol the streets of Winnipeg on Bloody Saturday. Curator Roland Sawatzky made it clear that, in 1919, the state held the monopoly on violence.

The CMHR also marked the centenary of the Winnipeg General Strike with *Rights on the Job*, a temporary display that highlighted the 1974 Elliot Lake, Ontario, miners' strike for recognition of the risks of uranium mining and the need for safer working conditions; the founding of the Canadian Indigenous Nurses Association (CINA) in 1975, with its focus on Indigenous traditions and health-care needs; and the organization of Black railway workers in 1917 as the Order of the Sleeping Car Porters and with the formation of the Brotherhood of Sleeping Car Porters in 1942.

Another temporary exhibition—*Strike 1919: Our Cause is Just*—was developed by Dalnavert House Museum in partnership with the Costume Museum of Canada and the Winnipeg Police Museum. The exhibit explored the ideas of "justice, authority, violence, and how we can change the world." Public programs featured during the exhibit run included a lecture on the role of women in the Strike by University of Manitoba professor Julie Guard. The small Victorian mansion that houses the museum was once the home of Sir Hugh John McDonald, premier of Manitoba in 1900 and a police magistrate who opposed the Strike in 1919.

Archivists in Manitoba commemorated the anniversary by working together to make Strike-related research material readily available for the first time to a wide public. Archivists from the University of Manitoba Libraries, the City of Winnipeg Archives, and the Association of Manitoba Archivists created *Unbreakable: The Spirit of the Strike*[15]—an exhibition of photographs, newspapers, publications, and artifacts presented online and at the archives and special collections section of the Elizabeth Dafoe Library. Content for the exhibit came from the University of Manitoba Libraries, the City of Winnipeg Archives, the University of Winnipeg Archives, the University of Calgary Archives and Special Collections, the Winnipeg Police Museum, and the Jewish Heritage Centre of Western Canada. The project also released resources and finding aids from the Manitoba Archival Information Network, the United Way of Winnipeg, the City of Winnipeg Archives, and the Winnipeg Public Library.[16]

Visual artists also took inspiration from the centenary. A limited edition of 100 prints entitled *Rise* (2019) was commissioned by MayWorks and sold to raise funds to support the year's activities. Created by local artist Lucas C. Pauls, the work quoted Strike leader

Figure 14.3. Yisa Akinbolaji, *For Us*, 2019. Acrylic and mixed media on canvas, 30"x 40". Photo: Yisa Akinbolaji.

William Pritchard, who echoed the words of Irish trade unionist James Larkin (1876–1947) when he proclaimed, "The great appear great to us because we are on our knees. Let us rise!" Pauls also created a 100th anniversary print for the Ukrainian Labor Temple, which opened in 1919 and was raided by the mounted police because its members supported the Strike.

The Manitoba Building Trades (MBT) also commissioned a work for the anniversary of the Strike. Created by Nigerian-born artist and social justice activist Yisa Akinbolaji,[17] *For Us* captured the tension of Bloody Saturday, when workers faced off against specials and the mounted police. Sudhir Sandhu, chief executive officer of the MBT, explained that the painting was meant to invoke "struggle and defiance, both essential underpinnings of the 1919 Strike. The title speaks to the fact that the strikers in 1919 stood for their own generations and all that have followed." Akinbolaji commented, "While creating the piece I felt a sense of presence at the moment of the General Strike. The painting now documents the sacrifice of the men and women of . . . 1919."[18] The artist said the work motivates him to contribute to a more prosperous future for the next generation. *For Us* was featured on the cover of *The 1919 General Strike—A Hundred Year Journey*, the April 2019 issue of the Manitoba Building Trades journal. The publication focused upon the contemporary meaning of the Strike for workers and unions in the building trades. A limited-edition print was distributed, with the original painting slated for installation at the organization's new facility at 225 McPhillips.

Winnipeg artist Kerri Parnell created yet another commemorative painting, *To Hell with the Alien Enemy,* combining the events of 1919 with the unjust treatment of eastern European immigrants who were interned as "enemy aliens" during the First World War. Parnell's painting portrayed the parade of antistrike returned soldiers of 4 June 1919, when "foreigners" were blamed for the high unemployment and economic insecurity that followed the war. She said she chose this theme because "the echoes of this kind of racism are still heard in Canada today." The artist's "canvas" spoke to the inequities evident in early Winnipeg through using 100-year-old tin ceiling tiles from the King's Hotel, which was located across from the former Canadian Pacific Railway Station. The inn lodged newly arrived Eastern European immigrants and stood in sharp contrast to the railway's luxurious Royal Alexandra Hotel. Parnell's painting was created with support from the Endowment Council of the Canadian First World War Internment Recognition Fund and will tour Canada as part of the exhibition *Pause in Plight.*

Members of the Frost Shield Kerfuffle artists collective[19] commemorated the anniversary with an exhibition entitled *REVOLTING! Artworks Inspired by the Winnipeg General Strike* at the Edge Gallery (611 Main Street.) The works displayed included Peter Graham's mini-diorama—*The 100 Year Old Hangover*—which featured a drunken "Iron Golem," a robotic giant from the Vulcan Iron Works that towered above workers, armed soldiers, and "volunteer" firefighters, and the toppled streetcar on Bloody Saturday. One viewer, at least, saw the menacing creature as the "monster of industrial capitalism."

Kenneth Harasym presented *Persistent Resistance*— a montage of social justice activism that combined his photos of the 100th anniversary parade and World Water Day with a 1980s shot of the Winnipeg Walk for Peace by Richard Freedman, and the iconic "Prison Bars Cannot Confine Ideas" image from the 1919 Winnipeg General Strike.

Ukrainian Canadian artist Michael Boss contributed a provocative work entitled *Mike and Steve: Я знаю/Я не знаю – I know/I do not know.*

Figure 14.4. Kenneth Harasym, *Persistent Resistance – Photo Collage*, 2019. Digital print. Photo: Kenneth Harasym.

The installation featured two simple caskets that housed drawings of the remains of Mike Sokolowski and Steve Szczerbanowicz—the two Ukrainian Canadian men who died from injuries sustained on Bloody Saturday. The installation's title reflects the mystery surrounding the deaths of the two men and the confusion surrounding their burial sites. The title also referred to the conflicting emotions immigrants like Mike Sokolowski and Steve Szczerbanowicz must have felt as "aliens" and "undesirables" and to the inscrutability of foreign languages to newcomers. Boss explained, "The tumultuous, landmark Strike of 1919 was about social class hierarchies, unfair wages and dangerous, unhealthy working conditions, 6 day weeks and 12 hour workdays, but it was also coloured by deeply racist views and the fear and the desperation of impoverished workers, many of whom were viewed as foreigners till the day they died. It is worth recalling this mistreatment of newcomers in our new era of mass migration. We can and have done much better (but) even so, today's immigrants are often stigmatized."[20]

Organizations from across the country marked the centenary beginning as early as August 2016[21] by holding their annual or biannual meetings in Winnipeg and asking guest speakers to address their members about the historical and contemporary significance of the Strike. The Women's Committee of Unifor, National Council of Women, and University Women's Club of Winnipeg were among those who held sessions on women and the Strike.

Individuals like union member Leanne Shumka, who addressed gatherings of AESES, the Association of Employees Supporting Educational Services, and the CCU, the Confederation of Canadian Unions, spoke to meetings of their own unions and led them on the Strike tour.

The Prairie School for Union Women, hosted annually by the Saskatchewan Federation of Labour, created a photo display honouring the women of the preceding 100 years, "on whose shoulders we stand." Gina McKay, labour director for the United Way Winnipeg, shared an MFL PowerPoint presentation on centenary events and spoke about the role of women in the Strike and the ongoing struggle for equity.

Public presentations were organized at museums, libraries, and theatres.[22] The Women's Committee of the Winnipeg Labour Council celebrated International Women's Day with a public presentation at Artspace that focused on the women of 1919 and their legacy, and on Indigenous women in today's labour movement. Chaired by Debra Jones, the afternoon included a screening of *The Notorious Mrs. Armstrong* with a commentary by film director Paula Kelly, and presentations by Julie Guard (Labour Studies, University of Manitoba), who discussed women's historical struggle for equality; Molly McCracken (Canadian Centre for Policy Alternatives Manitoba) speaking about *Papergirl*, a new children's novel set in the midst of the Strike; and Jeanna Smoke (Unifor Indigenous Liaison) discussing her role as an Indigenous outreach person in the labour movement.

In February, along with Nolan Reilly, I spoke at the Gaynor Family Regional Library in Selkirk, Manitoba, about the Strike anniversary and driving/walking tour. A few weeks later, Andy Blicq presented his film *Bloody Saturday*. The Henderson and Millennium Libraries in Winnipeg hosted author Mike Dupuis, while the Millennium Library also offered a five-week lecture series that included presentations by Nolan Reilly, Dennis Lewycky, Mitch Podolak with Darry Reilly, Paul Moist, Kevin Rebeck, and Gina McKay (Labour Director, United Way Winnipeg and CUPE 2348 member), who identifies as both a Métis person and a member of the Queer community. McKay stressed that the modern labour movement must be inclusive of, and welcoming to, workers of all identities and backgrounds, and detailed an impressive array of strategies for accomplishing these goals. In October 2021, Gina McKay was elected president of CUPE Manitoba, the province's largest union.

Teachers presented new, Strike-related curriculum projects and signed classes up for the Strike tour. The annual Red River Heritage Fair presented a workshop by Maples Collegiate teacher Sarah Reilly that examined labour rights as human rights. SAGE, the Manitoba Teachers' Society Special Area Groups of Educators professional development day, ran Strike-themed workshops and featured Nolan Reilly speaking about teaching the history of the Strike.

New publications concerning the Strike were frequently accompanied with presentations by the authors to school groups, union activists, and public audiences. A new book of poetry by Ron Romanowski—*If 30,000 Strikers Marched Today*[23]—commemorated the Strike, while former Winnipeg historian and poet Walter Hildebrandt visited Winnipeg to read his tribute to 1919 from his new collection of poems *Documentaries*.[24]

At least three new plays were performed in Winnipeg to commemorate the anniversary. *Bill Pritchard's Address to the Jury*, written by Dale Lakevold and performed by James Forsythe (both faculty members at Brandon University) was presented at the Winnipeg Fringe Festival 19 July 2018. *Bolshie Bash*, a comedy by Bill Harrar, was performed from 8 to 17 May 2019 at the Rachel Browne Theatre in the Exchange District. *Women Strike! 1919–2019, The Winnipeg General Strike*, written and directed by Montreal's Norman Nawrocki, was performed 13 June at the Ukrainian Labor Temple.

Two children's novels were published, both with guidelines for classroom teaching. *Papergirl*,[25] by Melinda McCracken, with Penelope Jackson, was published posthumously by the author's daughter, Molly

Figure 14.5. Winnipeg folk artist Mitch Podolak, founder of the Winnipeg Folk Festival, and Darryl Reilly, cohost of *'Peg City Groove*, CKUW Radio, University of Winnipeg, on guitar, led a singalong session on the protest music of the labour, civil rights, and social justice movements at Winnipeg's Millennium Library, 27 March 2019. Photo: Will Jones.

McCracken. The book tells the story of a ten-year-old girl who helped to distribute the *Strike Bulletin*, while her mother—a striking garment worker—volunteered at the Labor Café. *City on Strike,*[26] by Harriet Zaidman, focuses on a Jewish boy who struggles to help his working-class family during the Strike. The boy's mother bonds with women of differing ethnic and religious backgrounds at demonstrations while his teacher—a young British woman—supports the strikers and loses her job as a result.

1919: A Graphic History of the Winnipeg General Strike[27] by the Graphic History Collective and artist David Lester, used action-filled illustrations and dramatic text to draw young adults and older readers into an examination of the Strike and its broader historical context, and paid special attention to the colonial underpinnings and exploitation of Indigenous people that laid the groundwork for the uprising of 1919.

Long-time Strike tour leader, social justice activist, and creator of the Victoria Park blog Dennis Lewycky drew from his years of experience to write *Magnificent Fight: The 1919 Winnipeg General Strike.*[28] As explained by the publisher on the back cover of the book, "Lewycky speaks to the power of workers' solidarity and social organization, and reveals the lengths the capitalist class and the state went to protect the status quo."

Retired Canadian history teacher and author Michael Dupuis of Vancouver commemorated the anniversary by publishing his own popular history of the Strike—*The Winnipeg General Strike: Ordinary Men and Women under Extraordinary Circumstances.*[29] As the title suggests, the author explores the women and men who made the Strike possible, and the actions taken by the state to suppress it.

The anniversary also saw the publication of a 100th anniversary edition of *1919: The Winnipeg General Strike Driving and Walking Tour*,[30] which incorporates research completed since the guidebook was first published in 1985. The guidebook places the events of 1919 within the context of colonialism, reflecting upon the exclusion of Indigenous peoples from the urban workforce, and discusses the Black trainmen who supported the Strike and the beginnings of the struggle for a racially integrated, gender-inclusive industrial union movement. The brochure highlights several working-class women who made the Strike possible and examines the remarkable depth of class solidarity that emerged during this difficult time. The publication examines the role of firefighters and points out that, although some were blacklisted for joining the Strike, those who remained secured higher wages and better working conditions. The union grew in strength and its members took pride in their accomplishments, founding their own museum and archive in the early 1980s. In 2002, Winnipeg firefighters became the first group of firefighters internationally to win presumptive workers' compensation in recognition of the inherent dangers of the job. This critical win, which can be traced to the struggles of 1919, demonstrated the vital role that the Strike and its commemoration played in shaping the modern labour movement.

The Manitoba Federation of Labour and members of its volunteer 100th Anniversary History and Education Committee coordinated requests for group tours based on the Strike guidebook. Novice and seasoned tour leaders prepared to meet this demand, and hundreds of students, teachers, labour activists, heritage enthusiasts, and others participated in the tour over the course of the year. Thousands of copies of the guidebook, printed in English and in French with the assistance of Manitoba's unions, were distributed to schools, libraries, unions, and individuals. The guidebook also was made available online through the MFL website.

Figure 14.6. *1919: The Winnipeg General Strike Driving and Walking Tour – 100th Anniversary Edition* (2019). Design: Stephanie Whitehouse.

Members of the Winnipeg Repair Education 'N' Cycling Hub (WRENCH) commemorated the Strike by developing a self-guided bicycle tour as a companion piece to the *Driving and Walking Tour* guidebook. Intended as an eco-friendly, accessible, and intimate way to explore key sites of the Strike, the tour highlights the stark social and economic divisions that existed and continue to exist in Winnipeg. *Strike Bike 1919* is available in print from the WRENCH and on the MFL website.

A new Winnipeg labour history tour, focused on individuals with a connection to the Strike whose bodies were interred at Winnipeg's Brookside Cemetery, also was launched for the centenary. Created by Paul Moist, former president of CUPE 500 (City of Winnipeg Workers), and CUPE National, the *1919 Winnipeg General Strike Brookside Cemetery Tour* was offered by Moist as a guided tour beginning in summer 2019 and published in August 2020. It is available in print and online through the MFL.

Two new labour landmarks commemorating Victoria Park and its role as the main gathering place of thousands of Strike supporters in 1919 were installed over the spring and summer of 2019. The first, a bronze Manitoba Heritage plaque, sits in a lighted alcove along the south wall of 339 Waterfront Drive. Victoria Park was located just east of this site. The second landmark, installed by Project Bookmark Canada, recognizes Victoria Park as a site of significance in both the Strike and in *Strike! The Musical* (2015) by Danny Schur and Rick Chafe. Situated along a path on the east side of Waterfront, near James

Avenue, the landmark consists of two plaques—or Bookmarks—which incorporate text from the publication in English and French and form part of a literary trail being created by the organization across Canada.[31] *Strike!* began as a workshop production in 2003 and has been performed in numerous settings and renditions over the years. An enhanced, 100th anniversary version of the musical was performed at Rainbow Stage, Winnipeg's outdoor theatre, in 2019.

The addition of these landmarks to Winnipeg's labour history landscape is particularly important because the story and even the location of Victoria Park remain little known. Attempts by heritage and labour activists to win support for an interpretive centre, including the development of a Victoria Park website[32] and recommendations submitted to the city in 1998 and 2007, were not successful.

The 100th anniversary also saw the unveiling of two statuesque public monuments and the release of a major motion picture commemorating the events of 1919. The first memorial was spearheaded and funded by Winnipeg City Council and awarded through an open competition to Monteyne Architecture. Created under the direction of principal Tom Monteyne, the *1919 Marquee* stands a short distance from the former Victoria Park at the corner of Lily and Market. The illuminated steel sculpture offers both a factual and artistic interpretation of the Strike, challenging viewers to reflect upon the meaning of the Strike today

The second monument, a bronze sculpture entitled *Bloody Saturday*, depicts the streetcar from that fateful day. Created by Noam Gonick and sculptor Bernie Miller, the artwork was made possible through the efforts of the Manitoba Arts Council, with the assistance of the City of Winnipeg, the Manitoba Federation of Labour, and other supporters. The streetcar is depicted erupting into the present and into the consciousness of viewers from the ground below.

The third major initiative, *Stand! The Motion Picture,* was developed from the stage production *Strike! The Musical.* Like its predecessor, the movie is both factual and fictional but, above all, it is passionate about the injustices of 1919 and the issues that connect the Strike to the world today. The big-screen presence and wide audience appeal of the production ensure that the movie and its messages about the Winnipeg General Strike will become known far and wide.

The Winnipeg General Strike Centenary Conference / Building a Better World 1919–2019, held at the University of Winnipeg, invited academics, students, public historians, union activists, and others to explore the events of 1919 in both an historical and contemporary context.

Before launching into three days of academic and activist discourse, the conference began with a session that highlighted the role commemoration and public history have played in keeping the memory of the Strike alive and relevant over the years. Entitled Remembering 1919: Commemoration and the Winnipeg General Strike, the session, chaired by Rhonda Hinther, included my opening remarks from which this chapter was developed. Special guests Tom Monteyne, Noam Gonick, and Danny Schur discussed their respective 100th anniversary initiatives—the *1919 Marquee; Bloody Saturday* (streetcar monument); and *Stand! The Motion Picture*. These projects are discussed in detail in the chapter included in this volume by session commentator David Frank.

These commemorative projects and the others described above drew attention to the fact that the challenges people face today are not so different from those of 1919. The lack of jobs that paid a living wage; resistance to union organizing; discrimination; and poor working conditions that drove people to strike in 1919 are still with us today. The benefits that working people won through years of struggle—including universal health care, daycare, pensions, a strong public education system, pay equity, social security, and minority rights are being threatened. If, as Fearghal McGarry suggests, the role of commemoration is to ask what values and lessons can be taken from our history, it seems likely that these projects will go a long way in helping us to accomplish that goal.

A final labour landmark commemorating the anniversary of the Strike—a public mural entitled *A Century of Solidarity*—was painted on the east side of the Union Centre building at 275 Broadway and unveiled in July 2020. Created by Winnipeg artist Charlie Johnston, the work was commissioned by the Manitoba Federation of Labour with the support of the Union Centre. The dynamic mural speaks eloquently to the power and purpose of commemoration, portraying images from the Strike alongside depictions of twenty-first-century workers and inviting viewers to connect the issues of 1919 to workers' rights, gender equity, and racial justice today.

This description of many of the commemorative events held in Winnipeg to mark the 100th anniversary of the Winnipeg General

Figure 14.7. *A Century of Solidary* mural on Winnipeg's Union Centre. Artist: Charlie Johnston. Photo: Sharon Reilly.

Strike serves to indicate the astounding breadth of activities that were imagined and created by a wide range of progressive groups and individuals. These many initiatives speak to the ways in which the organized labour movement, artists, authors, a diverse array of social movement activists, teachers, journalists, public historians, academics, and others were able to collectively create a unique and valuable public history moment in 2019. Together, they consciously strove to energize today's struggles over inequality and social justice through listening to the echoes of the struggle for liberty and equality in the streets of Winnipeg in 1919. The progressive coalition of that earlier struggle is certainly not beyond criticism, but neither is that of the present day, as we seek to better understand and effectively support Indigenous rights and to grapple with fundamental concerns about systemic racism and other injustices and inequalities in our society. Commemoration of the 1919 Strike was part of our community's challenge of the dominant capitalist narratives of Canadian history and society. The gatherings and events of spring and summer 2019 remind us that—as we saw a century ago—broad, collective action rooted in community coalitions remains the way forward. The public history initiatives documented here, painstakingly created over the past several decades to commemorate the Winnipeg General Strike, have helped to ensure continued resonance, dialogue, and education with respect to this event. Developed parallel to—and, at times, in conversation and cooperation with—academic historians, the Strike's public history and commemoration in 2019 obtained substantial momentum and an astounding level of participation and audience engagement, ensuring that the memory and understanding of the Strike endures.

Notes

1 See municipal, provincial, and national heritage websites.

2 Margaret Sweatman, *Fox* (Winnipeg: Turnstone Press, 1991 and 2017).

3 Kenneth W. Osborne, *We Built Canada: R.B. Russell and the Labour Movement* (Agincourt, ON: The Book Society of Canada Limited, 1978).

4 Gerry Berkowski and Nolan Reilly, *1919, the Winnipeg General Strike: A Walking and Driving Tour* (Winnipeg: Manitoba Culture, Heritage, and Recreation, 1985 and Manitoba Labour Education Centre, 1994).

5 The Manitoba legislature exhibit also featured a series that explored the issue of workplace stress in an office environment entitled *Work Station* by now internationally acclaimed Winnipeg artist Eleanor Bond.

6 Barry Lord, *The History of Painting in Canada: Toward a People's Art* (Toronto: NC Press, 1974).

7 I explained the significance of Kell's works in Sharon Reilly, "Robert Kell and the Art of the Winnipeg General Strike," *Labour/Le Travail* 20 (1987): 185–92.

8 Rick McNair, Pat Martin, Paul Moist, Marla Neikamp, and Ed Rea, "The Significance of the Strike. Then and Now: Winnipeg General Strike, 75th Anniversary," *Canadian Dimension* 28, no. 3 (May–June 1994).

9 *The Red Album* (1995).

10 The Winnipeg Labour Choir returned to the Manitoba Museum in 1998 for the opening of *Stolen Dreams: Portraits of the World's Working Children*, an exhibition of contemporary child labour photos by Minneapolis occupational health physician and photographer David L. Parker. Curated by Sharon Reilly, the exhibit also documented the history of child labour in Canada.

11 The Politics of Remembering, https://youtu.be/0abKnxZUwUI.

12 Winnipeg filmmaker Trevor Gill, creative director at Build Films, Winnipeg, worked with the Manitoba Federation of Labour to produce a three-minute video documenting the many activities organized by Manitoba unions as a part of the year's celebrations. The video, including brief interviews with some of the event organizers, is available online at the MFL website.

13 See Mayworks.org.

14 See https://unitedwaywinnipeg.ca/1919-winnipeg-general-strike/.

15 See http://1919strike.lib.umanitoba.ca/.

16 Archival projects undertaken to commemorate the Winnipeg General Strike include:

Manitoba Archival Information Network (MAIN):
Winnipeg General Strike Guide The MAIN Strike guide provides users with information on how to search for records related to the Winnipeg General Strike and how to gain access to those records through the MAIN online database.

United Way Winnipeg: 1919 Working Stronger Together
This is the digital version of the historical exhibit described above. It commemorates the centennial of the 1919 Winnipeg General Strike and celebrates the United Way Winnipeg's (then known as Community Chest) long-standing solidarity with Labour and its shared communities.

The Winnipeg General Strike: A Guide to Research at the City of Winnipeg Archives
This research guide was created to commemorate the 100th anniversary of the Winnipeg General Strike and facilitate strike-related research at the City of Winnipeg Archives.

The Winnipeg General Strike Recommended Reading List (Winnipeg Public Library)
This Winnipeg Public Library reading list includes works of nonfiction and fiction for all ages related to the Winnipeg General Strike.

17 See yisagallery.com.

18 Personal correspondence, 25 May 2020.

19 Cullen Bingeman, Michael Boss, Evin Collis, Kelly-Jo Dorvault, Patricia Eschuk, Peter Graham, Kenneth Harasym, Chris Simonite, and Diana Thorneycroft.

20 *REVOLTING!* Exhibition Program.

21 Paul Moist and Sharon Reilly addressed the Professional Institute of the Public Service of Canada (PIPSC) at their meeting in Winnipeg, 23 September 2016.

22 Henderson Library; Millennium Library; Selkirk Library.

23 Ron Romanowski, *If 30,000 Strikers Marched Today* (Augustine Hand Press, 2019).

24 Walter Hildebrandt, *Documentaries* (Edmonton: NeWest Press, 2016).

25 Melinda McCracken, *Papergirl* (Winnipeg: Fernwood Publishing, 2019).

26 Harriet Zaidman, *City on Strike* (Red Deer: Red Deer Press, 2019).

27 The Graphic History Collective and David Lester, *1919: A Graphic History of the Winnipeg General Strike* (Toronto: Between the Lines, 2019).

28 Dennis Lewycky, *Magnificent Fight: The 1919 Winnipeg General Strike* (Winnipeg: Fernwood Publishing, 2019).

29 Michael Dupuis, *The Winnipeg General Strike: Ordinary Men and Women under Extraordinary Circumstances* (self-pub., 2018).

30 Nolan Reilly and Sharon Reilly, *The Winnipeg General Strike Driving and Walking Tour: 100th Anniversary Edition* (Manitoba Federation of Labour and the Province of Manitoba, 2019).

31 https://www.projectbookmarkcanada.ca/#your-canlit-trail.

32 www.victoriapark1919.blogspot.com.

15

Putting History to Work: Public History and Commemoration

David Frank

It is more than fifty years now since I wrote an essay on the Winnipeg General Strike for a history class. There was not much to use at the time. A few chapters here and there, but only one scholarly book, and it was published in 1950. I do remember a special issue of some magazine from Winnipeg . . . *Canadian Dimension*, of course . . . but I had to finish the paper in March, so the July issue did not help me at the time. Today's students will find much more at the library—plus a large number of sources that are out there attracting attention in the world of public history. Indeed, in the space of a few days in the spring of 2019 I received a graphic history of the Strike with wonderful narrative drawings by David Lester;[1] and from the folks at *Canada's History*, this country's largest circulation history periodical, an issue with a cover story by Jim Naylor.[2] There is much more, including the 100th anniversary edition of the Strike tour booklet, a labour of love prepared by Nolan Reilly and Sharon Reilly.[3] These are all cases of putting history to work, and my purpose here is to discuss three additional significant public history initiatives that marked the centenary of the Strike.[4]

Before reflecting on these achievements, there are two matters of context to keep in mind when talking about public history. One is about the divisions of labour that exist in historical work, which I refer to as accumulation, production, and circulation. First, there is the accumulation of research materials, the documents of all kinds that make it possible for us to do history at all. Second, there is the production of narratives and analysis that advance our knowledge of the past. And finally, there is the circulation of history, the public performances and popularizations that add to the common sense of the subject. These phases overlap and reinforce each other, and many of us try to do all three. But far too little is said about the work of circulation, even though this is the predominant public face of history. This involves much more than running a conveyor belt back into the warehouses and workshops of historical supply. In this phase we are called on to apply the creative imagination to available resources and knowledge and to use appropriate tools and vocabularies to bring history into general circulation. In doing this, cultural producers perform the magic that is the basis of all art. The Wolastoqi artist Jeremy Dutcher has said this more concisely, in talking about his own experience as a musician who works with history: first you take hold, then you invent, and then you perform.[5]

Let me add something too about the terms of engagement between commemoration and reception. Much has been said about how public memory is constructed, literally so in the case of monuments. The dominant tradition is at least as old as the pyramids. Make people look up, way up—I think I learned this in Grade 4 when a teacher was talking about ancient history—and remember the significance of the rulers of the world and the unimportance of the rest of us. If the Egyptians started it, Canada continued by giving Champlain, Cornwallis, Macdonald and others pride of place on the historical pedestal. The spread of what has been called "statuemania," especially in the age of nation-building, worked to create an iconic narrative in support of state authority and the dominant culture.[6] In the face of this monumental demand for consensus, there has also been a long, slow, often very local, effort not only to deconstruct official narratives but also to create alternative representations of class, gender, region, ethnicity, and other intersectional identities and their shared struggles. Cultural producers have also recognized that monuments in themselves as traditionally constructed have often invited little more than deference and veneration. A major design strategy for addressing this has been the merging of memorials into everyday public space so that they may function as sites of public engagement.[7] But such decisions do not belong to the artists alone, as

Auguste Rodin famously found when his original plans for *The Burghers of Calais* were thwarted by local authorities, who preferred to place the monument on a pedestal and behind a fence in a park rather than at street level in the market as the sculptor had intended.[8] Clearly, any strategy of integration into public space requires the mobilization of support within our public institutions and our social movements.

With these contexts in mind, our first stop is on Winnipeg's Lily Street at Market Avenue, where we see the results of a city competition to design a monument for the Strike—a competition completed three years before 2019, a good sign of the priority the city attached to this centenary. Here, in-between old warehouses and modern playhouses, we encounter a civic space that invites us to stop and consider the history that ran through these same streets more than 100 years ago. This is not a case of tiny text on small plaques, that bane of historical commemorations, but of single words standing on weathered sheets of steel supported by girders as tall as the neighbouring buildings. *The 1919 Marquee* (Figure 15.1) clearly references the promotional billboards of the modernist urban landscape. But here we are challenged to do a little more work than usual to draw meaning from the letters spelled out by these broad-headed brass rivets on the matrix of a giant crossword.[9] As we piece them together, we see a kind of live concrete poetry that speaks one word at a time: 1919 WINNIPEG CRUCIBLE JUSTICE ORDER FREEDOM FORCE FAIRNESS WAR EQUAL LOVE 2019. And as we disentangle those terms and consider their relationship to each other and to us, we notice that a little farther along the block and closer to eye level, we are invited to inspect plates of stencilled steel whose text and map situate us more exactly in the historical and geographic zone of the Strike. Je remarque aussi que ce texte est donné en toutes les deux langues officielles, ce qui souligne l'importance de ces événements pour les travailleurs et travailleuses du pays entier. In conception, then, *The 1919 Marquee* is a long way from that severely limited plaque, posted at City Hall in 1985 by the Historic Sites and Monuments Board of Canada (Figure 15.2). It took me two complete circumnavigations of City Hall even to locate that plaque, which I found on a low wall on William Avenue at the very edge of the block near Main Street. Instead, the Marquee gives us a bold statement in full public view that, like the Strike itself, calls for attention and engagement.

Figure 15.1. Tom Monteyne, *The 1919 Marquee* (2019) (artist's conception).

Figure 15.2. Historic Site and Monuments Board Plaque (1985), Winnipeg City Hall (author photo).

Figure 15.3. Bernie Miller and Noam Gonick, *The Bloody Saturday Streetcar Monument* (2019) (artists' conception).

Next we go back to Main Street, at the corner across from City Hall. The *Bloody Saturday Streetcar Monument* also helps to solve the problem of visibility (Figure 15.3). This steel and glass installation was unveiled in 2019 on the anniversary of the events of 21 June. As conceived by the late Bernie Miller and completed by Noam Gonick, the monument echoes one of the famous Lewis Foote photographs of the culminating moment in the events of the Strike on Bloody Saturday. Those streetcars, which ran from the 1890s to the 1950s, were part of the urban infrastructure that created a network of public transportation operated by a private utility. Like the aqueduct that nourished the city and immiserated an Indigenous community,[10] the streetcar had contradictory effects. It delivered workers to sites of production and consumption, but fares were high and routes never adequate; and for employees, wages were low, hours long, and conditions dangerous. In Winnipeg, as in almost every large North American city of the time, these contradictions produced conflict. It is not surprising to see that the city's first labour mayor in 1923 declared the streetcar company "a direct menace to the interests of the people," and a dozen years later the second labour mayor called for municipal ownership, which was ultimately achieved in 1953.[11] When street railway workers went on strike in such cities, demonstrations of public support were common. Crowds came out to block scab cars, disconnect cables, break windows, and push cars off the tracks. Police and militia were called out. Such things happened in Halifax, Saint John, Montreal, Ottawa, Toronto, London, Vancouver—and so too in Winnipeg in 1906 as well as in 1919—often enough that we can think of the streetcar as a meme, a unit of cultural transmission. When we choose a streetcar to represent the Strike, we are referencing this history of contradictions between public services and private profit, as well as the countervailing solidarities of resistance that make a difference for workers and their communities. Gonick's hope is that the site will serve as a gathering place, much as it did a century ago, adding, "It's like that spot has just been held in place for us."[12] As we approach this stricken car, stopped, tipped, and trapped there in its circle on Main Street, much as the crowds did in 1919, we see that it is partially submerged. Although its cables have been disconnected, it shines with an interior light. This looks like a history that is only temporarily off the tracks. It is ready for correction, ready to go back into circulation.

Finally, on another stage, we have *Strike! The Musical.* I can remember Paul Moist coming to a meeting in Ottawa some years ago and telling us about an outdoor performance of the show on Main Street for an audience of 5,000 people, complete with real horses for the Mounties. The production returned to the outdoor stage again in Kildonan Park in the summer of 2019, where thousands of people once more learned about the progress of the Strike, much as outdoor crowds did at Victoria Park in 1919. The story of this production is a small epic in itself, starting more than twenty years ago, when Danny Schur and his coauthor Rick Chafe embarked on the collaborations and workshops that produced the first performances in 2005.[13]

Labour theatre? There is certainly a tradition of radical theatre in this country, which can be traced back at least to the workers' theatre activism of the 1930s.[14] Not to be overlooked in this history of alternative theatre are the many productions in the Yiddish, Finnish, and Ukrainian labour halls across the country, where RCMP officers attended productions to monitor ideological content and measure audience reception.[15] Or, by the 1970s, a network of workshops and theatres cultivating homegrown, historically informed productions.[16] But *Strike!* is not a literal transcription of history. There are two Ashdowns and two Almazoffs, plus one Gideon Robertson—but no R.B. Russell, no Helen Armstrong, no J.S. Woodsworth. Mostly the production uses what

Figure 15. 4. *Stand!* Poster for the 2019 film treatment based on the original 2005 production by Danny Schur and Rick Chafe, *Strike!: The Musical* (www.stand-movie.com).

cultural historians call "true invention" to create composite characters who embody central themes in the story. As Danny Schur pointed out, the treatment relies to a certain extent on a "Romeo and Juliet" theme calculated to appeal to a general public. In a brilliant stroke, at the centre of the story in *Strike!* we find an immigrant worker by the name of Mike Sokolowski. He is real enough to be in the *Dictionary of Canadian Biography* but his known history leaves room for invention that adds suspense and complexity to the story.

And secondly, of course, *Strike!* is a musical that enters into the conventions of the genre as part of its strategy to awaken emotions and capture space in the public imagination. A labour musical? I think briefly of the pioneering cultural front production *Pins and Needles*, which was sponsored by the International Ladies' Garment Workers' Union and ran on Broadway for more than 1,000 performances in the late 1930s.[17] I can still recall some of those songs—from a later studio recording, by a young Barbra Streisand among others, that included the romantic duet "One Big Union (for Two)." People may also think of *Newsies*, a Disney film based on the 1899 newsboys' strike in New York City. Adapted for the stage, it has had a healthy life in high school productions as an alternative to some of the old chestnuts. Is there such a future for *Strike!*? That aspect of circulation will depend on the imagination and commitment of teachers, students, and communities.

Meanwhile, the potential for circulation was greatly accelerated by the production of a film adaptation (Figure 15.4), released in the fall of 2019 under the title *Stand!* The producers were able to raise a $7 million budget, a substantial sum for any Canadian film. They assembled support from agencies such as Telefilm Canada and Manitoba Film and Music as well as from the Canadian Labour Congress and other unions. Shooting was completed in Winnipeg in 2018, under the direction of the Hollywood-based Canadian director Robert Adetuyi and the American cinematographer Roy Wagner. There were a number of adjustments in the transition from stage to film, including the addition of the feminist reformer Helen Armstrong. But the centre of the film remains the human drama involving the young immigrant couple, one a Jewish activist and the other a Ukrainian worker, whose story revolves around their respective family sagas, their romance, and their relationship to the Strike. Like the stage production, the film utilizes the devices of "simplification," "true invention," and "compression" to fictionalize details and highlight issues while adhering to the standards of "cinematic realism" appropriate for a "mainstream" historical film.[18] While a film like this cannot engage all aspects of the historical discourse, *Stand!* is faithful to an interpretation of the Strike as an urban rebellion by workers and immigrants who expect a greater measure of fairness and equality within Canadian society at the end of the Great War. We see the divisions between ethnicities, genders, and generations play out before our eyes. We also watch the ideals of solidarity come to life in successive moments of illumination. At the same time, we witness the ways the local establishment pursues its mission of pulling strings, dividing the working class, and representing its own privilege as a defence of the public interest. All this is reinforced by an excellent cast, a powerful musicality, and by art direction and production design that earned a Canadian Screen Award nomination. When *Stand!* received its initial run at some thirty Cineplex theatres across Canada in November 2019, the film was favourably reviewed in the *Globe and Mail* as "a spirited new Canadian movie musical" with "a well-crafted score plus Broadway-worthy tunes that stick in your head." Noting the parallels between the world of 1919 and the present, the reviewer added that "it's heartening to see a film that is actually about something, made by people who are expert storytellers."[19] With a life well beyond the original theatrical release, *Stand!* is a polished and professional achievement that should have a permanent place in the limited library of Canadian labour films.[20]

Let me end by repeating the general point that historical commemoration is to a large degree not about the past but about speaking to the present and pointing to the future. Moreover, the general mission of public history is to open doors, and in the case of labour history, to gain access to what Edward Thompson called the "stored cultural energy" embedded in the history of the working class. This field has gained much ground in the last fifty years, and we can take heart from the impressive results in these latest projects of engagement and commemoration. They have put history to work—and into circulation. For sharing their magic with us they deserve our appreciation, and, from all of us in our own ways, our emulation. Once again, Winnipeg has shown the way.

Notes

1 The Graphic History Collective and David Lester, *1919: A Graphic History of the Winnipeg General Strike* (Toronto: Between the Lines, 2019).

2 James Naylor, "Standing Together," *Canada's History* (April/May 2019): 20–30.

3 Nolan Reilly and Sharon Reilly, *1919 Winnipeg General Strike: Driving and Walking Tour* (Winnipeg: Manitoba Federation of Labour, 2019).

4 This text is an expanded version of comments for the sesssion "Remembering 1919: Commemoration and the Winnipeg General Strike" at the Winnipeg General Strike Centenary Conference, 8 May 2019, which featured presentations by the cultural producers associated with the three examples discussed here.

5 This formulation is distilled from my notes on radio interviews with Jeremy Dutcher and a reception for him at the Charlotte Street Arts Centre, 19 October 2018. See, for example, "Jeremy Dutcher: The Polaris Prize-Winning Musician Reflects on His Whirlwind Year," *q* with Tom Power, CBC Radio, 11 March 2019; and "Jeremy Dutcher on Recontextualizing His Indigenous Past through Music and Language," *The Next Chapter* with Shelagh Rogers, CBC Radio, 18 April 2019.

6 See Maurice Agulhon, "La 'statuomanie' et l'histoire," *Ethnologie française* 8, no. 2–3 (1978): 145–72. For a Canadian application, see Brian S. Osborne and Geraint B. Osborne, "The Cast[e]ing of Heroic Landscapes of Power: Canada's Pantheon on Parliament Hill," *Material History Review* 60 (Fall 2004): 35–47.

7 For a wide-ranging discussion of this theme, see Quentin Stevens and Karen A. Franck, *Memorials as Spaces of Engagement* (New York: Routledge, 2016).

8 Richard Swedberg, "Auguste Rodin's *The Burghers of Calais*: The Career of a Sculpture and Its Appeal to Civic Heroism," *Theory, Culture, and Society* 22, no. 2 (2005): 45–67.

9 I visited in daytime. As Tom Monteyne has explained, the installation lights up after dark and highlights the dates 1919 and 2019. He also noted that a key to the words is attached to one of the girders. Under the structure, a small stage or seating area invites additional usage of the site.

10 Adele Perry, *Aqueduct: Colonialism, Resources, and the Histories We Remember* (Winnipeg: ARP Books, 2016).

11 Stefan Epp-Koop, *We're Going to Run this City: Winnipeg's Political Left after the General Strike* (Winnipeg: University of Manitoba Press, 2015), 44, 138, 145.

12 Darren Bernhardt, "100th Anniversary of Winnipeg's 1919 General Strike Will Be Marked with Monument, Movie, Books," *CBC News*, 19 May 2018.

13 See Lynn Carlile's interview with Danny Schur in *Our Times: Canada's Independent Labour Magazine* (December 2009/January 2010): 20–24.

14 Alan Filewood, *Committing Theatre: Theatre Radicalism and Political Intervention in Canada* (Toronto: Between the Lines, 2011).

15 See, for instance, Kassandra Luciuk, "More Dangerous Than Many a Pamphlet or Propaganda Book: The Ukrainian Canadian Left, Theatre, and Propaganda in the 1920s," *Labour/le Travail* 83 (Spring 2019): 77–103.

16 In his comments at the conference, Danny Schur referred to the classic play by Rick Salutin and Theatre Passe Muraille, *1837: The Farmers' Revolt*. He noted that the final comment to Peter Matthews by Samuel Lount—which he paraphrased as "We didn't lose. We just haven't won yet"—was also relevant to the Winnipeg General Strike. The original text for the play reads: "MATTHEWS: Sam, we lost – LOUNT: No! We haven't won yet."

17 Michael Denning, *The Cultural Front: The Laboring of American Culture in the Twentieth Century* (New Haven, CT: Yale University Press, 2002), 295–309.

18 For an influential discussion of the issues at stake in making historical films, see Robert Rosenstone, "The Historical Film," in his *Visions of the Past: The Challenge of Film to Our Idea of History* (Cambridge, MA: Harvard University Press, 1995), 45–79; and Rosenstone, *History on Film / Film on History* (Harlow, UK: Pearson Education Limited, 2012).

19 Neil Weisensel, "Winnipeg General Strike Musical Delivers a Meaningful Message," *Globe and Mail*, 27 November 2019.

20 The discussion here draws in part on my review of the film, "*Stand!* Show and Tell (and Sing)," posted on the website ActiveHistory.ca, 29 January 2020.

16

The Winnipeg General Strike in the Twenty-First Century

James Naylor, Rhonda L. Hinther, and Jim Mochoruk

The catalyst for this volume was the centenary of the Winnipeg General Strike. Half of the contributions to this volume originated, in some form, as papers presented at a conference held in Winnipeg in May 2019 to mark the occasion; the other contributions were solicited elsewhere because they could address, in insightful ways, the questions (as we articulated them in the introduction) that appeared fundamental to understanding the Strike.[1] Attracting over 300 people, the centenary conference brought together unionists, academics, public historians, and activists. Much dialogue centred, of course, on the Strike itself and the broader Workers' Revolt of the time, but presentations also extended to other aspects of labour and working-class history and activism. Beyond this, a focal conversation point was the Strike's legacy and meaning for the present and the future. Roundtables of activists led discussions about the goals of the Strike in the context of present-day challenges—some of which remained depressingly the same while others could never have been foreseen as "labour issues" by the strikers of 1919. All came away with a desire to better understand the Strike itself—reckoning with its successes and failures; unlocking its relevance to the present—as well as parting with a commitment to build broader audiences for such a history. The goal of the conference, to borrow from its title, was to explore this mass, popular event that had aimed at "Building a Better World." This task is no less urgent today than it was 100 years ago; this volume, we hope, helps to continue and further this critical conversation.

Such a goal requires, as we stated in the Introduction, taking stock. This was the aim of the first chapter of the book where we examined the meanings attributed to this extraordinary event by the growing array of books, theses, articles, and public histories of the Strike over the course of the last century. But where are we now in our understanding of the Strike? How has this volume furthered this? And what is to be done next? In what new topical and interpretive directions should we be headed? These are questions we reflect on in this concluding chapter of the book.

As was clearly apparent at the conference, and explored in different ways throughout this volume, the old binary debate—strike or revolution—was always far too limiting. The leadership of the two primary opposing forces, and many of the historians who came after them, ignored the dynamics of social crises. As Gerry Friesen suggested (somewhat puckishly) in 1984, things might have turned out quite differently if the leadership of the Strike and the One Big Union (OBU) had had a Lenin.[2] Indeed, no social crisis is ever easily defined, since consciousness shifts because of the crisis—and evidence of such shifts abound in the Winnipeg of 1919, particularly in regards to the attitudes of returned soldiers and to folks living in their working class enclaves in Brooklands, Weston, the North End, and elsewhere in the greater Winnipeg area. And, to give the Citizens' Committee of 1000 its due, they were not wrong in thinking that many Winnipeggers were willing to go to great lengths to challenge and perhaps even overthrow the existing order. Hard-hitting critiques of capitalism had developed in Winnipeg in the months and years leading up to the great revolt, and it had become clear to many Winnipeggers in a number of ways that capitalism was not fulfilling fundamental social needs. That, combined with the power that workers gained in the context of a tight labour market during the war, increased their activity despite wartime restrictions. The end of the war (but significantly, not of the government-imposed orders-in-council that severely limited the civil liberties of the working class) removed the lid from workers' largely self-imposed restraint, and things began to explode. The very experience of mass mobilization created new feelings of possibility; workers could perhaps remake society in some way—and Winnipeg's working class was well aware that such changes were being made elsewhere by, or at least in the name of, the working class. Not surprisingly, that fact created considerable fear among capitalists and their allies. Although organizations such as the Citizens' Committee of 1000 (and the American groups from whom they took their inspiration[3]) pointed to the rise of socialist ideas to make their case that the Strike was revolutionary, what was truly revolutionary about the situation was not the spread of "Bolshevism" but rather the broad mobilization of workers and their potential desire for a society organized on different premises.

Does this mean that Winnipeg's workers and their families were explicitly fighting for a fundamental change to the social order? Yes and no. As the leadership made clear, they were fighting for concrete demands centred on living wages and collective bargaining, but they were also motivated, as was repeatedly stated at the Mathers Commission hearings, by the desire for a society that valued production "for use, rather than for profit."[4] In the crucial period of late 1918 into early 1919 it was becoming increasingly clear that not only would capital not concede to such a demand but would go to incredible lengths to prevent such a transition. In this sense, the Strike, when it came, unleashed a dynamic, the final outcome of which was unclear. So, without suggesting that the Winnipeg General Strike was a revolution in the making, it should be noted that all revolutions begin with concrete demands that the rulers will not or cannot concede. Certainly, Winnipeg capital was not willing to budge.

It must also be observed that, in a very real sense—despite the claims of the Strike Committee—the Winnipeg General Strike was not a strike in the traditional collective bargaining sense. The majority of those who struck and who supported the strikers had no imaginable immediate vested interest in the specific demands of the metal or building trades workers. These unorganized workers—for a number of reasons—had not been able to form unions let alone get anyone to bargain with them. Their solidarity with their unionized brothers and sisters was broader and almost certainly reflected the multitude of ways in which they had been oppressed and exploited by their employers and as members of the working class more broadly. And this solidarity extended well beyond the workers themselves. Unwaged family members, be they women, children, seasonally unemployed workers, the elderly—even the boarders—who were part and parcel of so many working-class households, not only supported "their striker" but played active roles in the events of 1919—participating in demonstrations, keeping their neighbourhoods free of strikebreakers, and providing the essential safety net for the family and community. This widespread willingness to support the Strike—at great personal cost, given that most workers and their families could ill afford any loss of wages—indicates that they shared that class status with those whose struggle had prompted the vote on the General Strike in the first place. Even more to the point, it indicates the depth of their consciousness of that status.

What does this mean for future work and analysis of the Strike? On one level, it means that we need to explore further the extent to which transitions were taking place. For example, to what extent were Winnipeg workers thinking and acting as a coherent force? There are indications that the historic isolation of British and "non-British" workers was beginning to dissolve. There is no denying the reality of nativist rioting in Winnipeg earlier in 1919, but there were also signs of a growing political convergence between left-wing leaders of the North End immigrant communities and the increasingly radical leadership of the Winnipeg Trades and Labor Council. In this sense, the specific targeting of immigrant communities by the unpopular orders-in-council is important, and specifically the decision of the Ukrainian Social Democratic Party to turn to the *Western Labor News* for help when its newspaper *Robochyi Narod* was shut down by order-in-council underscores this convergence. It is also of some note that the *Strike Bulletin* was actually printed—free of charge—in the North End at the Israelite Press.[5] It must be noted that many of those from eastern Europe cultivated these connections and exhibited this solidarity at great personal and community risk. The potential for raids on their homes and halls, along with their possible arrest, internment, and deportation remained realities as long as the orders-in-council remained in place.

What these collaborations point to is that the leadership of the Left was largely on the same page, and figures such as Helen Armstrong (as she had been throughout the preceding few years) were actively working to break down the ethnic and gender divides of the labour movement.[6] Moreover, while there is no denying that there was discrimination by British and Anglo-Canadian workers and their organizations toward immigrants and people of colour, the labour movement's concern of immigration was not inherently racist: organized labour blamed capitalists for flooding the labour market by importing and exploiting labour—an argument made several times in the pages of the *Strike Bulletin*. In this sense, immigrants—including workers recruited from Britain—were seen as the victims of capital.[7] As immigrants became active in challenging that victimization, unity became—at the very least—a possibility. This possibility became a reality in the aftermath of the Strike as the North End became a labour stronghold, both for Communists and the Independent Labour Party; by definition and self-consciousness the North End transitioned from a set of ethnic zones into a working-class place. The Strike was key to that.

One must also consider the issue of Britishness, particularly as it has been framed by Chad Reimer.[8] In many ways the strikers' use of the language of Britishness was defensive. The Citizens' Committee, in an attempt to delegitimize the Strike through both red-baiting and nativist attacks upon "dangerous foreigners" whom the committee claimed sought to mislead innocent Canadian workers, accused labour of challenging the British constitution and British norms. The official workers' response was that it was labour, itself, that had been denied British justice. In short, faced by the clear-cut hypocrisy of the Citizens' Committee, they turned the accusation back on the accusers. But this is only part of the reason that a discourse of Britishness was adopted. Canada was, of course, governed by a British constitution, and English Canadians of all classes did identify as British. And, as E.P. Thompson pointed out long ago, while motivated by their class experience, workers turn to their culture to understand their oppression and construct an oppositional imaginary. From the Norman Yoke and the Magna Carta to more modern touchstones such as Peterloo, the Chartists, the Todpuddle Martyrs, Keir Hardie, and the Independent Labour Party, there was much in this tradition worth remembering, recognizing, celebrating, and defending. Particularly for the Anglo-Celtic leadership of the Strike Committee, the majority of whom were British immigrants, these traditions were very much a part of their intellectual and cultural baggage. In this context it is quite telling that when the Scottish-born president of the Winnipeg TLC observed the events of Bloody Saturday he immediately equated them to the attack on peaceful protestors at "Peterloo" by the mounted constabulary of volunteer yeomen a century earlier.[9] Thus, their use of "Britishness" was not necessarily an identification with British chauvinism and imperialism, although there is little doubt that for some strikers and Strike leaders this was the case.

Chad Reimer has implied, and Owen Toews has argued, that Britishness cannot be separated from the history of the empire.[10] This is absolutely the case. As several historians have pointed out, it is impossible to understand Britishness "outside of the imperial and post imperial experience."[11] Imperial greatness not only defined Britain, but for those raised in Victorian or Edwardian Britain, as Antoinette Burton points out, "empire and its signifiers were produced and manipulated at home—in music halls, on biscuit tins, through film and other avenues of popular culture."[12] We would suggest the same was true in the colonies and particularly of Britain's "White Dominions." Still, what needs to be more fully explored—a process that Reimer began in the 1990s—is this: what are the various class-based values that the concept of Britishness could carry? Concepts such as "British fair play" and "British democracy," which can easily be dismissed as self-serving rhetoric when one looks at the empire, were tools that could be and were employed defensively by subaltern groups throughout the empire.

The crucial question in this regard is how does one measure the extent to which workers of British origin had an autonomous sense of Britishness, in other words, one quite separate from the version peddled by Britain's ruling class? We might suggest that not only was this generally in question, but that in the political context of international working-class mobilization, this identification with Britishness and empire fed its instability. Certainly, a crucial segment of the political leadership of the Winnipeg labour movement was increasingly internationalist in its orientation. Its international markers were class ones as opposed to any notion of imperial loyalty; at the famed public meeting at the Walker Theatre in December 1918, then at the Majestic Theatre in January of 1919, and perhaps especially at the Western Canadian Labour Conference held at Calgary in March 1919, the Russian and German revolutions stood as exemplars for the future, and foreign interventions in such revolutions were explicitly condemned. It is also worthwhile bearing in mind that for many of the returned men (who were overwhelmingly working class and Anglo-Celtic) the ruling class definition of empire was far from appealing. The wartime experience of these men had not been positive, and no small part of their quite legitimate complaints stemmed from their treatment by British officers and also concerned the use (and abuse) of "colonial" troops by imperial war-planners. The well-known trope of the Great War creating a more autonomous sense of Canadian nationhood may be somewhat overblown, but the resentment of Canadian troops toward imperial leadership was real.[13] Thus, for many in the working class, empires and imperialism, including the British, were in ideological retreat.[14]

This is not to say, however, that certain aspects of "Britishness" were not treasured and actively employed by strikers as weapons against those who sought to oppress them; they did, indeed, seek "British justice" as the Citizens' sought to railroad them after the Strike.[15] Certainly, the experience of the Great War had a powerful impact on the meaning of Britishness. Appeals to empire had great resonance in the context of war, but working-class Canadians also suffered from its tragic consequences and were tired of the hollow promises of its ideologues. Among workers, sentiments were no doubt in flux, but what is clear is that many of the leaders of the Strike embraced a very different British tradition than the one put on offer in London and Ottawa—or in the Winnipeg meeting hall of the Citizens' Committee.

Of course, this sounds very Thompsonian, and that is not unproblematic. E.P. Thompson has been criticized, and quite appropriately, for largely ignoring gender, race, and empire (historians have increasingly recognized the tight interweaving of these three in their discussions of what legal scholar Kimberlé Crenshaw was first to theorize as intersectionality).[16] Joan Scott, quite famously, focused on Thompson's gendered representation of class in *The Making of the English Working Class* as an opening foray in the poststructuralist critique of what she saw as the universalizing and unilinear historical narratives of—in this case—class.[17] While acknowledging Thompson's sense of class as being "indelibly male," Alice Kessler-Harris points out that "in opening the door to a meaning of class that incorporated the daily lives of ordinary people, Thompson introduced a new realm of power that specifically and inevitably included women."[18] For her part, Anna Clark demonstrated the potential of "re-visioning Thompson's narrative to include gender" by building on his focus on communities and culture to critically explore the ways in which gender relations were, in fact, crucial to the potential ways in which class was "made" and contributed to its unmaking.[19] In light of all this, the Winnipeg General Strike is perhaps best seen as a revolt by the city's working class as a whole—constructing class in a Thompsonian sense. Communities and families were at the heart of this astounding social mobilization. We have learned much about the ways in which specific individuals and groups of women organized and supported the Strike. However, as we noted in Chapter 1, while the historiographical lens has widened to include women, we have only begun to theorize the role of gender in the uprising. David Thompson's study of the life of Winnipeg activist Edith Hancox showcases how expanding our understanding of class and community to encompass social reproduction and affective labour can provide routes forward.[20]

It is also the case that the "peculiarities" of North American class formation have forced historians writing in the Thompsonian tradition to confront working-class diversity and racialization more directly. The American scholar David Roediger, in his discussion of "the wages of whiteness," argues that access to whiteness brought both material and psychological benefits to immigrants if they could claim membership in a racial or ethnic elite.[21] And this was certainly true in the Canadian context, where it is particularly useful to think of Britishness as a privileged "racial" category early in the twentieth century. As Stuart Hall argued, it is critical to think of "race," "ethnicity," and "nation" as closely connected and shifting discourses of cultural difference that interact with other identities, such as gender and class, and take on different meanings in different historical contexts.[22] While Roediger focuses on the powerful case in which white free labour could define itself in opposition to Black slavery, the ability to define oneself against workers who would not or could not express autonomy as free labourers was also apparent in Canada. This was certainly evident in the Winnipeg General Strikers' rhetoric. Beyond question, access to "Britishness" brought benefits. That this was more than just a legal category associated with naturalization was demonstrated quite dramatically in 1917 when long-established immigrants' voting rights were snatched away; their presumptive "Britishness" proved tentative. Of course, "British" workers had some real privileges, including access to skills training which provided an entrée into the so-called "aristocracy of labour." The work of skilled "craft" workers often provided them less precarious work lives in terms of seasonal unemployment and underemployment, better pay, the legal protections associated with being a British subject, and several other, more subtle advantages over their non-British comrades. But this was highly contested. Not only were the skills of craft workers under siege, particularly under the pressure of wartime production, but some of the privileges of Britishness were being actively renegotiated during the Strike. A.J. Andrews and other leaders of the Citizens' Committee consciously sought to reduce the majority of the Strike's leaders—who were British-born—to the legal status of "immigrant" by making them subject to deportation under new amendments hurriedly added to the Immigration Act in June of 1919.[23] Notably, the real privileges some workers potentially enjoyed do not seem to have distracted the broader movement from the central issues of the Strike.

All of this leads one to the following observation: central to any understanding of the Winnipeg General Strike is the very high degree of class independence and autonomy that Winnipeg workers exhibited during May and June of 1919; indeed, one can argue that this was precisely what it was all about. It was a "class" event in its composition, ideology, identity, and leadership.

Winnipeg's radical leaders were almost uniformly working class. This is an important point, since Winnipeg was a well-established centre of middle-class progressivism, and there had been a close relationship between some Winnipeg labour organizations and middle-class reformers in the years prior to and even during the Great War. But 1919 was a defining moment in this regard. As Kurt Korneski points out, reformers like John Dafoe—who, by the way, he explains were exemplars of British-identified settler colonialism—fell firmly on the other side of the barricades in 1919.[24] This was clearly the case for the majority of Winnipeg's middle-class reformers. Nellie McClung rather famously cited the Strike Committee's decision to cut off water pressure at a certain point as her line in the sand,[25] while other reformers—such as those who had long supported the work of the nursing missions, orphanages, hospitals, the Children's Home of Winnipeg, and other such social service agencies—were among those who offered their cars and their volunteer services to the authorities to overcome the many inconveniences associated with the Strike. Choices had been made, and they were choices linked to class.

Of course, there were some middle-class figures associated with the prostrike forces, especially William Ivens, J.S. Woodsworth, and Fred Dixon. But here it needs to be observed that they were, effectively, class traitors—certainly as the Citizens' Committee saw matters. They had unapologetically abandoned their earlier middle-class reform affiliations in favour of the labour movement and the working class by 1919. Consequently, Winnipeg workers, for the most part, encountered them only as voices for the cause of labour. The Winnipeg workers who listened to Woodsworth's sermons in Victoria Park were unlikely to have been aware of his musings a decade earlier about the hierarchy of racial types.[26] This was certainly not the content of his talks in 1919 or afterwards; what one finds instead is the discourse of a much broader, far more egalitarian, and infinitely more radical critique of capitalist society. In effect, the events of 1919 in Winnipeg constituted the sort of dividing line that E.P. Thompson had described for English workers in 1832 when the middle-class reformers abandoned their alliance with the emergent working class. Certainly the "politics of class" that dominated Winnipeg's electoral scene for the next quarter century would indicate that class consciousness had not only been heightened during the Strike but had been worked into the DNA of the city.[27]

The construction of a working-class identity helps us understand another important feature of the Strike. While the Strike drew together workers whose origins lay across the Atlantic—an emerging solidarity that was celebrated in the language of the Strike's leaders and its historians—the same cannot be said about the inclusion of Indigenous workers. It is ironic, but incontestable, that despite the Strike occurring at a site of historic importance to Indigenous people and the place of Métis resistance that only fifty years earlier had spurred the founding of Manitoba and its entrance into Confederation, that strikers and their leadership were essentially silent about Indigenous people and the broader context of settler colonialism. It is important to think about why this was the case. The easy answer is that this was a conflict over wage labour and that in the Winnipeg of 1919 Indigenous people were marginal to that relationship. To the extent that this may have been the case, it is still an insufficient answer. Certainly, the federal government had entered into treaty making in the 1870s and engaged in a host of other, often violent, efforts to "clear the plains" of First Nations and Métis peoples. The goal, as much as was possible, was to confine Aboriginal peoples to reserves located far from the supposedly "corrupting" cities, force processes of assimilation, and make way for colonial settlement, agriculture, natural resource exploitation, and the ensuing expansion of wage labour and profit making.[28] Unlike other places in the Americas, colonial settler society on the Canadian prairies did not generally rely on a racialized non-European workforce (a workforce that was often unfree or, at the very least, heavily marginalized) to develop a capitalist social order, at least not in urban industries, although such labour was crucial out on the nonagricultural resource frontier.[29] Overwhelmingly, the strategy was to import Europeans who would have to sell their labour power, even if their goal (or the vision they were sold by immigration promoters) was to become independent producers in the cities or in the countryside.[30]

That said, Indigenous people worked for wages in many places including near Winnipeg, as Adele Perry pointed out in *Aqueduct*, where they competed with Winnipeg-based workers for jobs.[31] That they were forced out of such jobs had to do with a combination of racism and competition for control of the labour market, a feature endemic to the way in which craft unions operated. This was a strategy white workers used to protect their jobs against competition from cheaper labour, which often meant racialized workers: a division that the employer classes were only too happy to foster, since it ultimately promoted a disunity that weakened labour's power overall. Would the new radical leadership of the Winnipeg labour movement that championed a more inclusive movement see things differently? Or would they accept a settler colonial imaginary that did not see Indigenous people as part of a modern economy and labour force?[32] Labour's silence suggests the latter was the case. The Strike challenged many parts of the status quo, but the propriety of settler colonialism was not one of them.

The case of Métis workers and their role in the Strike is even more difficult to ascertain and demands far more research. Winnipeg was the home of a sizable Métis population that sustained itself in large part through wage labour. As Peters, Stock, and Werner explain in *Rooster Town*, the Métis dealt with dispossession by maintaining family networks and developing a number of strategies to deal with economic marginalization.[33] They were, without doubt, part of the Winnipeg labour force.

In order to understand why the Winnipeg labour movement was blind to Indigenous communities it is useful to ask how an essentially "British" labour movement came to see, acknowledge, and eventually ally with immigrant workers in the city's North End. This emerging unity was the product of immigrant workers themselves. Significant radical organizations, well rooted in immigrant communities, schooled on long struggles in central and eastern Europe, and often energized by the revolution in Russia, sparked and led the Strike in their communities. And they did so in their own names, in practice defying the Citizens' attempts to marginalize and demonize them.[34]

By contrast, Indigenous resistance was difficult in the early twentieth century. There were important struggles, of course, against residential schooling and the expropriation of reserve lands for public works, for new settlers, and, in the aftermath of the war, for soldier resettlement schemes. At least 4,000 Indigenous soldiers fought in the First World War; some certainly were in Winnipeg in 1919. But the focus of their struggles, at least from official records, were on the attempts made by military authorities and Indian agents to reestablish them on reserves without even the minimal benefits afforded non-Indigenous veterans.[35] Similarly, the extant racial order made it difficult for the Métis to present themselves in 1919 Winnipeg as a coherent and organized force. There was, at the time, an attempt to form a Métis national movement, L'Union nationale métisse Saint-Joseph du Manitoba, but it was the work of a relatively small group of professionals—not workers—who aimed to rehabilitate the memory of Louis Riel by stressing the community's political loyalty and submission to the church.[36] This was a world remote both from the Rooster Towns in and around Winnipeg and from the sentiments of the strikers. In short, Indigenous populations were not represented by organizations that spoke in their names in ways analogous to some of the immigrant organizations of the city. And, it is because of these organizations we are largely aware of the role immigrants played in the Strike. Indigenous people were doubly invisible. The modernist imagination of settler-colonial Winnipeg did not perceive them as wage workers, and systems and processes of erasure, racism, oppression, and poverty made it difficult for them to gain a collective voice.[37] The course of the war and its aftermath challenged a hegemonic order in a vast array of ways as Winnipeg workers opened to new ways of seeing the world and formed new alliances. This, though, was an uneven process, and there was little in their lived experience in these years that fundamentally undermined the girders of settler colonialism. But certainly, considerable additional work on Indigenous peoples' labour history in the context of this period is needed to help nuance, enrich, and potentially challenge our understanding of the Winnipeg General Strike.

The Strike was, in Thompsonian terms, unquestionably an episode in the making of a working class. Such an approach leads us to seek to identify the cultural resources from which Winnipeg workers drew—although we certainly could know more about non-British workers in this regard—and the moral economy by which they measured the actions of the state and the Citizens. It does not mean, however, that those resources were unambiguous or stable in their meaning. Class can be unmade as well. The wartime cauldron and the Strike comprised a relatively brief episode in a longer process. And the Strike was defeated. What is remarkable was the transformation that took place over a period of mere weeks and months. A vast range of social relations were opened to questioning—some of course more than others. While, in the aftermath of war and with the rising sense of working-class internationalism, many strikers grew critical of imperialism, there is no sign of a questioning of the colonialist displacement of First Nations. And while women's participation in the Strike was significant and for some transformative, such activities remained highly gendered, and the goal of being able to construct prosperous working-class families around a male "family wage" was not really challenged (at least according to research currently available). Still, along the axis that the Strike was fought, with its focus on workplace relations and improving working-class communities, both "British" and immigrant, these events were, indeed, transformative. They opened up avenues toward thinking and perhaps living differently for working-class Winnipeggers. While defeat certainly had its consequences and capital was again safely dominant, it is not clear that ethnic "hierarchies and conventions snapped back into place."[38] After 1919, class relations turned to a war of position, a long struggle to reassert working-class power. The most overt sign of this was at the ballot box, as workers voted for (often different) working-class parties and sat together on city council or in the provincial legislature.[39] Certainly workers generally returned to a world bounded by their individual workplaces, communities, and families. Nonetheless, much remains to be understood about the development of class cultures within and between particular working-class and ethnic communities in the aftermath of the Strike.

In the end, perhaps the central question of the Strike relates to its impressive scale. Across Canada—and beyond—workers rose in anger and hope in 1919. But why were Winnipeg workers able to bring the third largest city in the Dominion to an almost complete halt and carry out the most sustained general strike in North American history? With the important—albeit brief—exception of Seattle, no other group of workers came close to accomplishing such a feat at this crucial moment. In almost every instance movements toward general or sympathetic strikes were derailed by conservative labour leaders.[40] Without downplaying the reality of the larger Workers' Revolt, it is the case that most of the other general strikes of the period were not "as" general. So, what happened in Winnipeg?

On this score, David Bercuson's *Fools and Wise Men* is quite useful, as he notes the existence of various tendencies in the Winnipeg labour movement that help to explain this phenomenon.[41] Without subscribing to western exceptionalism, it must be conceded that Bercuson's case for western and Winnipeg capitalists being particularly uncooperative and highly successful at employing tactics (with the aid of the courts) such as injunctions against picketers is accurate—and certainly, these manoeuvres raised the ire of Winnipeg trade unionists and the Winnipeg working class in general. Thus, the hardline approach of Winnipeg employers led the leaders of some of the craft unions that had not been historically radical, like the building trades, to be willing both to fight en masse and to use the relatively new labour tool of the general or sympathetic strike.

It is also the case that Winnipeg's conservative trade union leadership was nowhere near as well entrenched as was the case in central Canada. There were few people in Winnipeg who were lifelong trade union bureaucrats. The small corps of real bureaucrats in the Canadian labour movement of the time tended to make Toronto and Ottawa their homes. Still, that being said, one has to temper the western exceptionalist implications by noting that Winnipeg in 1919 was actually more "eastern" than "western": it was already a relatively large urban centre and as such had large contingents of the regular urban trades (as opposed to the resource sector workers who dominated along the frontier), and it possessed a sizable manufacturing workforce as well as a large number of service industry workers—both male and female.

In effect, the Winnipeg story of 1919 is one of context. To begin with, it must be recognized that there is not an absolute unity between militancy and radicalism. There was a growing militant tradition among less radical Winnipeg unions. The brief and successful sympathetic strike of 1918—in support of Winnipeg's municipal workers—meant that this tactic had gained considerable traction well beyond the socialists who had been its earliest proponents, and the spectre of a general strike was raised repeatedly that year.

Beyond this, it is essential to consider the concatenation of events in Winnipeg. By 1919 the Left had gained considerable weight in the Winnipeg Trades and Labor Council—certainly far more than it had had in the prewar years or even from 1914 to 1917—and the Left was clearly instrumental in ensuring the rapid referral of the referendum on the General Strike to the city's unions in May 1919. As a result, the next step was going to be determined by the rank and file—the decision was taken out of the hands of the city's union leadership. Winnipeg trade unionists had seen how successful the mere threat of a general strike had been in 1918 and showed no hesitation in employing this tool yet again. The overwhelming nature of the prostrike vote itself (11,112 to 524) meant that the Strike was on.[42] If any of the more conservative union leaders had reservations, they could hardly voice them at this point, as the rank and file had spoken in a clear and uncompromising fashion. The movement for the General Strike was fuelled from below and there was enough unanimity that it proceeded under its own momentum.

Elsewhere in Canada and the United States, there was more time to discuss and debate—which allowed more conservative trade union leaders the opportunity to organize themselves and to curb the enthusiasm of the membership.[43] The two contributions in this volume focusing on Alberta, by Mikhail Bjorge and Tom Langford, reveal the potential schisms that conservative labour leaders could open, even in the "radical" West. Very importantly, in Canadian cities, the general strike issue became mixed up with the OBU question and the attendant matter of secession from traditional trade unions. This was a deeply divisive issue. There were reasons, both among conservatives but also among radicals, to question the strategy of secession. There were many union leaders and members who did not want to undermine the organizations that they had constructed and maintained against tremendous odds. Others saw secession as inevitably leading to working-class disunity and weakness in the face of an increasingly unified front of capital and the state. (This was the view of radical workers who joined the Communist Party when it was formed a couple of years later.) Particularly in other western Canadian cities, antiradicals would paint advocates of the General

Strike as secessionists. The issue of the OBU is a difficult one. The movement that was born in Calgary in March both inspired the general strike movement and undermined it. At the risk of playing "what if" history, it is possible that if the OBU question had never been posed, there would have been considerably more broad-based support, and more general strikes, in 1919 and 1920 as the argument against sympathy strikes was harder to make than was the argument in favour of secession. Be that as it may, once the Winnipeg General Strike was underway, it was clear to almost everyone in Winnipeg's labour movement that it was necessary to stand together or succumb to the Citizens.

What was so remarkable was not just the resolve and solidarity of Winnipeg's organized workers—although that is remarkable in and of itself, for six weeks without pay constituted a huge sacrifice for all working-class families. Rather, as has been remarked upon on so many occasions, what was truly exceptional about Winnipeg in 1919 was the broad working-class support that the Strike enjoyed. Unionized workers constituted perhaps one-third of all those who quit work in the aftermath of the Strike call on 15 May, so the majority of strikers were women and men who had no formal ties to the labour movement. Many of them were recent immigrants who had, at best, an imperfect grasp on English—but perhaps a more perfect grasp on the notions of solidarity and class struggle. Some had been radicalized by circumstances they had left behind in the "old country"; conditions encountered in Canada politicized (or further politicized) others.[44] And beyond this there were the still unemployed "returned men"—the so-called third force—and the large numbers of prostrike protestors, female and male, who came out to Victoria Park and other mass gathering places throughout the city, and who took part in the parades and other acts of defiance against the antistrike forces.

This is what made the Strike "revolutionary," at least in the eyes of the members of the Citizens' Committee. Winnipeg's employers knew how to deal with the trade unions; they had been generally successful in the past in beating them back, although it would be harder this time around given the ability of the unions to grow and rethink their own tactics. But employers had always been able to divide and conquer. They could threaten to use the cheaper labour of those whose place in the labour market was weaker and less secure against the unions. But once it became clear that, for all the nativism that was present in Winnipeg, the Strike enjoyed great support in the North End—Winnipeg's foreign quarter—all bets were off. Few who lived there were in the skilled trades or had any of the benefits of either "Britishness" or union organization. And yet as Trachtenberg, Usiskin, Avery, and several other scholars have noted, the Jewish and eastern European communities were largely in support of the Strike. While it is certainly the case that the leaders of some of the more radical "ethnic halls" and organizations (notably the newly constructed Ukrainian Labor Temple, the Liberty Temple, and the Social Democratic Party's various "language" groupings) had been actively seeking to radicalize and mobilize Ukrainian, Russian, Polish, German and Jewish immigrants to the cause of socialism and organized labour, they had not been universally successful by 1919. Indeed, far larger numbers of these groups belonged to decidedly more conservative religious and secular organizations. And yet, when push came to shove, these ethnic groups tended to support the Strike (regardless of its overwhelmingly "British" leadership); their identification as workers came to the fore. Indeed, as Henry Trachtenberg noted, in the case of at least the Jewish community, workers even pulled businesspeople in their wake. These were working-class communities.

For the Ukrainian speakers their status as "enemy aliens" made them highly suspect and the subject of much negative attention during and immediately after the war. Indeed, most had been forced to register as "enemy aliens" and approximately 8,000 had been interned as enemy aliens during the war—an internment operation (and situation of coerced labour) that was kept alive even after the war had ended. The Jewish population, of course, was subjected to a sustained pattern of anti-Semitism, social and economic discrimination, and the mindless attacks of returned veterans looking for scapegoats. Thus, for almost any non-Anglo family in the North End, to support the Strike was potentially to add fuel to an already smouldering prairie fire of discrimination. And yet most did—at least tacitly. And as we know, the victims of Bloody Saturday included many "foreigners" who had been part of the prostrike crowd.

It would be easy to suggest that the reason for such support was a clear-cut case of working-class solidarity overcoming ethnic divides. But this had not seemed possible only a few short months earlier when returned men rampaged through the streets of central and north end Winnipeg, attacking the businesses, homes, and bodies of "aliens." So, what had happened?

On one level, as the work of Trachtenberg and Avery suggests, the demands of the Strike Committee made perfect sense to any member of the working class and were worthy of support. If the strikers won, many believed all working-class families—regardless of ethnicity or religion—would benefit. Beyond this, although "foreigners"—a term applied, like "ethnic," mainly to eastern and southern Europeans—did not have a leadership role in the Strike, there were clearly some very positive linkages established between the Strike Committee and several influential leaders in the North End. And it is of considerable importance that Strike leaders such as R.B. Russell and both Helen and George Armstrong had established strong credentials as crusaders for cross-ethnic working-class solidarity prior to May of 1919; indeed, Helen Armstrong in particular was a passionate advocate for the "foreign" workers.[45] And with the foreign-born workers' natural propensity to follow events in their former homelands, there was an awareness of the international situation—and the potential for working-class alternatives to existing power structures.

But even this is probably not sufficient to explain the broad-based support of the Strike. Eric Angel's work suggests that there may have been more than a bit of compulsion applied by strikers and their supporters to ensure full-scale compliance with the Strike. There were clear-cut cases of this in Brooklands and Weston. Did similar cases arise in the heart of the North End? We simply do not know at this point. Geoffrey Ewen's contribution to this volume alerts us to mass mobilization and the politics of the street; more work is definitely needed here. So too, Benoit Marsan's chapter reminds us that the role of the unemployed—a significant group everywhere as the war drew to a close—has been all but ignored in the story of postwar Winnipeg's working-class mobilization. Deprived of paid workplaces, their venue was, as well, the street and public square. How did they use it in the context of 1919 and how might this use have been gendered?

This is a particularly important set of questions for Winnipeg. As the crucial railway hub for western (and northern) Canada, the city was a hiring centre for seasonal workers and host to a huge mobile population of temporarily unemployed workers waiting for the next set of unskilled labour opportunities to open up along the resource frontier and in the railway camps.[46] Winnipeg was also a crucial social service and employment centre for all sorts of people coming in from the rural areas. In particular, young women seeking domestic work, factory jobs, or a host of other employment opportunities were constantly moving into the city. To date no work has been done on this floating population and its role in the Strike.

Winnipeg was, of course, only part of a much broader workers' revolt that began during the war and reached a crescendo in its aftermath. Examinations of cities that experienced parallel processes, such as Jeff Stilley's contribution on Kansas City and Cal Winslow's on Seattle in this volume, provide an instrument not only to understand this process more widely, but also alert us to struggles that differed in their specific array of class, racial, and gender dynamics. They provide lenses to look back at Winnipeg since they allow us to rethink those issues in the context of Winnipeg. Joel Wolfe's chapter's much broader survey of the hemisphere brings a full palate of such considerations to play. No matter how exceptional it may seem, Winnipeg can never be viewed as sui generis; its activists were, and saw themselves, as players in a global confrontation.

We also need to build upon the important contribution of David Thompson concerning the role and transitions undergone by so many of the returned soldiers during the course of the Strike.[47] Equally important, we need to follow his lead and attempt to parse the dialectic of radical and conservative ideas within communities and even within individuals. The readily apparent transformation of social consciousness during and after the war must not blind us to the range of inconsistencies and contradictions that persisted in workers' world views. And, of course, as noted earlier on, we have only begun to scratch the surface of the dynamics of Indigenous groups and people of colour in the Winnipeg of 1919. Adele Perry's contribution here should be seen as an invitation for continued research. Not only do we need to know more about the Indigenous populations of the city at this crucial moment, we need to discern much more about non-Indigenous workers' place in, and understanding of, the settler colonial project.

Still, even after sounding this call for more research—and the list could go on and on—the work on the Winnipeg General Strike that has been completed leads one to conclude that this event can only be viewed as one in which class identity was overwhelming. It is this which accounts for the high degree of unity and persistence that Winnipeg's working class displayed over the course of six tension-filled weeks in

1919. Despite the best efforts of the Citizens' Committee to divide the strikers—by ethnicity and gender, by utilizing the rhetoric of "patriotism" versus disloyalty, through the employment of war-derived discourses of masculinity, sacrifice, and "Britishness," and through coercion and violence—class consciousness triumphed. In fact, this distinction between the war, or at least of what it was supposed to be, and the Strike led to the idea that the Strike was revolutionary. Born in war, it proposed a society in which the assumptions behind the war—profiteering, national chauvinism and jingoism, homicidal masculinity, and unthinking obedience—were roundly rejected. The pillars of the existing order of society were shaken, and in May and June 1919—before Bloody Saturday—it was anyone's guess how it would end. Would it spread across Canada? Would Winnipeg become only the first skirmish in a much larger conflict? Canada's political and economic leaders were certainly capable of overblown rhetoric, but in a world where a workers' revolution had taken place in Russia, and similar uprisings seemed to be crossing Europe, this was a serious threat to the world that they were used to dominating. They would mobilize their resources to fight it, locally and nationally. Tom Mitchell and Reinhold Kramer have incisively documented their strategy, particularly that of the Citizens' Committee of 1000.[48] The Citizens, A.J. Andrews in particular, orchestrated the arrests of the leaders, and established show trials aimed at criminalizing not just the strikers' actions, but their ideas. The federal government passed new laws to punish "sedition" and to ease deportations. As Gregory Kealey has explained here, the reorganization of the Dominion's police forces to create the Royal Canadian Mounted Police was central to this effort. Myer Siemiatycki notes the ways in which Canadian business shared this mission. And the state and business worked in league with educators and social leaders as they sought to instill a new kind of Canadian "citizenship" that would eschew ideas critical of the social order.[49] Collectively, they treated the workers' revolt as an existential threat to their way of life. The Winnipeg General Strike was an internationally recognized display of workers' power. That was, at least potentially, revolutionary.

The study of the Winnipeg General Strike, then, still has much to offer and many avenues to travel. The social explosion of 1919 opened up fissures through which historians can examine the nature of Canadian society in the wake of settler colonialism, industrialization, war, and so much more. Scholarly research and analysis have much to offer here. But Sharon Reilly and David Frank also raise the question of who owns the history of this deeply working-class event. The conference that inspired this book had the goal of ensuring that this massive mobilization to build a better world for all a century ago is made accessible to all of those who face the same mission today and in the future. An informed and active public labour history is the best memorial to Winnipeg's workers of 1919. The Strike's legacy lives.

Notes

1 Building a Better World: 1919–2019. The Winnipeg General Strike Centenary Conference, University of Winnipeg, 8–11 May 2019.

2 Gerald Friesen, *The Canadian Prairies: A History* (Toronto: University of Toronto Press, 1984), 360.

3 Reinhold Kramer and Tom Mitchell, *When the State Trembled: How A.J. Andrews and the Citizens' Committee Broke the Winnipeg General Strike* (Toronto: University of Toronto Press, 2010), 168–76.

4 Library and Archives Canada, RG 33, Commission to Inquire into and Report on Industrial Relations in Canada, passim.

5 Henry Trachtenberg, "'Adapt to the Institutions and the Manners of this Country': Winnipeg Jews and the General Strike" (in this volume).

6 On Helen Armstrong's early work at crossing ethnic divides, see Harry Gutkin and Mildred Gutkin, *Profiles in Dissent* (Edmonton: NeWest Publishers, 1997), 229. Other examples demonstrate that nonexclusionary union structures along with an explicitly antiracist leadership can dramatically overcome even deep-seated divisions. Michael Goldfield demonstrates this clearly in the American South in his *The Southern Key: Class, Race, and Radicalism in the 1930s and 1940s* (New York: Oxford University Press, 2020).

7 David Goutor, *Guarding the Gates: The Canadian Labour Movement and Immigration, 1872–1934* (Vancouver: UBC Press, 2007). Goutor notes that Canadian unions actively attempted, for instance, to dissuade British workers from emigrating to Canada.

8 Chad Reimer, "War, Nationhood, and the Working-Class Entitlement: The Counterhegemonic Challenge of the 1919 Winnipeg General Strike," *Prairie Forum* 18 (Fall 1993): 219–37.

9 Norman Penner, ed., *Winnipeg 1919: The Strikers' Own History of the Winnipeg General Strike*, rev. ed. (Toronto: Lorimer, 2019), 199.

10 Reimer, "War, Nationhood and Working-Class Entitlement"; and Owen Toews, *Stolen City: Racial Capitalism and the Making of Winnipeg* (Winnipeg: ARP, 2018).

11 Shula Marks, "History, the Nation, and Empire: Sniping from the Periphery," *History Workshop Journal* 29 (Spring 1990): 117.

12 Antoinette Burton, "Rules of Thumb: British History and 'Imperial Culture' in Nineteenth- and Twentieth-Century Britain," *Women's History Review* 3, no. 4

(1994): 487. See also Anne McClintock, *Imperial Leather: Race, Gender, and Sexuality in the Colonial Context* (London: Routledge, 1995), esp. 207–31.

13 Ian McKay and Jamie Swift, *The Vimy Trap or, How We Learned to Stop Worrying and Love the Great War* (Toronto: Between the Lines, 2016).

14 This was not entirely novel. As Caroline Bessey points out, the very subjects of Thompson's study who were active in the London Corresponding Society of the early nineteenth century had varying degrees of interracial solidarity connected to their antislavery and internationalist connections. Bessey, "Race, Antiracism, and the Place of Blackness in the Making and Remaking of the English Working Class," in *Histories of a Radical Book: E.P Thompson and the Making of the English Working Class*, ed. Antoinette Burton and Stephanie Fortado (New York: Berghahn, 2021).

15 James Muir, "The Demand for British Justice: Protest and Culture during the Winnipeg General Strike Trials," University of Manitoba, Canadian Legal History Project, Working Paper Series, 1993.

16 See, for instance, Robert Gregg, "Class, Culture, and Empire: E.P. Thompson and the Making of Social History," *Journal of Historiography* 11, no. 4 (December 1998): 419–60. James R. Barrett discusses the ways in which Thompson's sympathetic intellectual reception by American labour historians forced a reckoning with the racial and ethnic—and eventually gendered—ways in which class was made and remade in the United States in "Making and Unmaking the Working Class: E.P. Thompson, *The Making of the English Working Class*, and the 'New Labor History' in the United States," in *History from the Bottom Up and the Inside Out: Ethnicity, Race, and Identity in Working-Class History* (Durham, NC: Duke University Press, 2017), 192–207. The literature on gender and imperialism is now voluminous as authors have built on foundational works of Catherine Hall, Antoinette Burton, Anne McClintock, Ann Laura Stoler, and others. For the classic statement on intersectionality, see Kimberlé Crenshaw, "Mapping the Margins: Intersectionality, Identity Politics, and Violence against Women of Color," *Stanford Law Review* 43, no. 6 (July 1991).

17 Joan Wallach Scott, "Women in the Making of the English Working Class," in *Gender and the Politics of History* (New York: Columbia University Press: 1988), 68–90.

18 Alice Kessler-Harris, "Roundtable on E.P. Thompson's *The Making of the English Working Class* at Fifty," *Labour/Le Travail* 72 (Fall 2013): 249.

19 Anna Clark, *The Struggle for the Breeches: Gender and the Making of the British Working Class* (Berkeley: University of California Press, 1995).

20 David Thompson, "More Sugar, Less Salt: Edith Hancox and the Passionate Mobilization of the Dispossessed, 1919–1928," *Labour/Le Travail* 85 (Spring 2020): 127–63.

21 David R. Roediger, *The Wages of Whiteness: Race and the Making of the American Working Class* (London: Verso, 1991).

22 Stuart Hall, *The Fateful Triangle: Race, Ethnicity, Nation* (Cambridge, MA: Harvard University Press, 2017).

23 Kramer and Mitchell, *When the State Trembled*, 130–33 and 143–46.

24 See Kurt Korneski, *Race, Nation, and Reform Ideology in Winnipeg, 1880s–1920s* (Madison, NJ: Fairleigh Dickinson University Press, 2015).

25 This was a bit disingenuous as she had already abandoned her ties to labour over the issue of the war and conscription in 1917.

26 J.S. Woodsworth, *Strangers within Our Gates, Or Coming Canadians* (1909; Toronto: University of Toronto Press, 1972).

27 See, for example, J.E. Rea, "The Politics of Conscience: Winnipeg after the Strike." Canadian Historical Association, *Historical Papers*, 1971; Rea, "The Politics of Class: Winnipeg City Council, 1919–1945," in *The West and the Nation*, ed. Carl Berger and Ramsey Cook (Toronto: McClelland and Stewart, 1976); Stefan Epp-Koop, *We're Going to Run this City: Winnipeg's Political Left after the General Strike* (Winnipeg: University of Manitoba Press, 2015); Brian McKillop, "Citizen and Socialist: The Ethos of Political Winnipeg, 1919–1935" (MA thesis, University of Manitoba, 1970); H.C. Pentland, "Fifty Years After," *Canadian Dimension* 6, no. 2 (July 1969); Donald Avery, '*Dangerous Foreigners': European Immigrant Workers and Labour Radicalism in Canada, 1896–1932* (Toronto: McClelland and Stewart, 1979); Avery, "The Radical Alien and the Winnipeg General Strike of 1919," in *The West and the Nation*; Roz Usiskin, "A Theoretical Reformulation of the Relationship between Political Ideology, Social Class, and Ethnicity, 1905–1920" (MA thesis, University of Manitoba, 1978); and Henry Trachtenberg, "The Winnipeg Jewish Community and Politics: The Inter-War Years, 1919–1939," in *Historical and Scientific Society of Manitoba Transactions*, series III, no. 35, 1978–79 (Winnipeg: Manitoba Historical Society, 1981).

28 James Daschuk, *Clearing the Plains: Disease, Politics of Starvation, and the Loss of Aboriginal Life* (Regina: University of Regina, 2013). For an excellent discussion of how these processes were at play in Winnipeg historically, see Mary Jane Logan McCallum and Adele Perry, *Structures of Indifference: An Indigenous Life and Death in a Canadian City* (Winnipeg: University of Manitoba Press, 2019).

29 See, for example, Jim Mochoruk, "*Formidable Heritage": Manitoba's North and the Cost of Development, 1870–1930* (Winnipeg: University of Manitoba Press, 2004)—especially Chapters 3 and 5; and Frank Tough, *As Their Natural Resources Fail: Native Peoples and the Economic History of Northern Manitoba* (Vancouver: UBC Press, 1996)—especially Chapters 8–11.

30 An illuminating counterexample would be Bolivia, where Indigenous labour was fundamental to developing the local, largely resource-based, economy. The result was a long tradition of left-wing Indigenous labour struggles. See Jeffrey Webber, *Red October: Left Indigenous Struggles in Modern Bolivia* (Chicago: Haymarket, 2011).

31 Adele Perry, *Aqueduct: Colonialism, Resources, and the Histories We Remember* (Winnipeg: ARP Books, 2016), 75; and Perry, "In the Water: Race, Empire, and the Winnipeg General Strike of 1919"—Chapter 2 (in this volume).

32 As a "perceptional transfer" where their presence doesn't register. Lorenzo Verachini, *Settler Colonialism: A Theoretical Overview* (New York: Palgrave Macmillan, 2010), 37.

33 Evelyn Peters, Matthew Stock, and Adrian Werner, *Rooster Town: The History of an Urban Métis Community, 1901–1961* (Winnipeg: University of Manitoba Press, 2018).

34 See, for example, Avery, '*Dangerous Foreigners*'; Avery, "Radical Alien and the Winnipeg General Strike"; Avery, "Ethnic and Class Tensions in Canada, 1918–20: Anglo-Canadians and the Alien Worker," in *Loyalties in Conflict: Ukrainians in Canada during the Great War*, ed. Frances Swyripa and John Thompson (Edmonton: Canadian Institute of Ukrainian Studies, University of Alberta, 1983), 79–98; Usiskin, "Theoretical Reformulation"; Usiskin, "The Winnipeg Jewish Radical Community: Its Early Formation 1905–1918" in JHSWC, comp., *Jewish Life and Times: A Collection of Essays* (Winnipeg: JHSWC, 1983); Usiskin, "The 'Alien' and the 'Bolshevik': The 1919 Winnipeg General Strike," *Canadian Jewish Outlook*, July–

Aug., 1983 (Vancouver: Canadian Jewish Outlook Collective, 1983); Art Grenke, "The German Community of Winnipeg and the English-Canadian Response to World War One," *Canadian Ethnic Studies* 20, no. 1 (1988): 21–44; Grenke, *The German Community in Winnipeg 1872 to 1919* (New York: AMS Press, 1991); Trachtenberg, "Winnipeg Jewish Community and Politics"; Trachtenberg, "The 'Old Clo' Move': Anti-Semitism, Politics, and the Jews of Winnipeg, 1882–1921" (PhD diss., York University, 1984); Morris Mott, "The Foreign Peril: Nativism in Winnipeg, 1916–1923" (MA thesis, University of Manitoba, 1970); Orest Martynowych, "The Ukrainian Socialist Movement in Canada, 1900–1918," *Journal of Ukrainian Graduate Studies* 1, no. 1 (Fall 1976): 27–44 and Ibid., 2, no. 1, (Spring 1977): 22–31; Martynowych, *Ukrainians in Canada: The Formative Years, 1891–1924* (Edmonton: Canadian Institute of Ukrainian Studies, University of Alberta, 1991); and Peter Krawchuck, *Our History: The Ukrainian Labour-Farmer Movement in Canada, 1907–1991* (Toronto: Lugus Publications, 1996).

35 Brian R. MacDowall, "Demobilization and Colonialism: Indigenous Homecomings in 1919," in *Canada 1919: A Nation Shaped by War*, ed. Tim Cook and David J. Bercuson (Vancouver: UBC Press, 2020), 86–101.

36 Gerhard J. Ens and Joe Sawchuk, *From New Peoples to New Nations: Aspects of Métis History and Identity from the Eighteenth to Twenty-First Centuries* (Toronto: University of Toronto Press, 2016), 113–32.

37 Mary Jane Logan McCallum's discussion of modernity and the binaries of tradition and modern are useful here. See her *Indigenous Women, Work, and History, 1940–1980* (Winnipeg: University of Manitoba Press, 2014).

38 Ian McKay, *Reasoning Otherwise: Leftists and the People's Enlightenment in Canada, 1890–1920* (Toronto: Between the Lines, 2008), 479.

39 Epp-Koop, *We're Going to Run this City*.

40 In this regard, see the contributions of Siemiatycki, Langford, and Bjorge to this volume.

41 David J. Bercuson, *Fools and Wise Men: The Rise and Fall of the One Big Union* (Toronto: McGraw-Hill Ryerson, 1978).

42 *Western Labor News*, 16 May 1919.

43 On other Canadian general and sympathetic strikes, see Craig Heron, ed., *The Workers' Revolt in Canada, 1917–1925* (Toronto: University of Toronto Press, 1998), particularly 188–202; Gregory S. Kealey, "1919: The Canadian Labour Revolt," *Labour/Le Travail* 13 (Spring 1984): 11–44; Benjamin Isitt, "Searching for Workers' Solidarity: The One Big Union and the Victoria General Strike of 1919," *Labour/Le Travail* 60 (Fall 2007): 9–42; James R. Conley, "Frontier Labourers, Crafts in Crisis, and the Western Labour Revolt: The Case of Vancouver, 1900–1919," *Labour/Le Travail* 23 (Spring 1989): 9–38; David Bright, *The Limits of Labour: Class Formation and the Labour Movement in Calgary, 1883–1929* (Vancouver: UBC Press, 1998); Glen Makahonuk, "Class Conflict in a Prairie City: The Saskatoon Working-Class Response to Prairie Capitalism, 1906–19," *Labour/Le Travail* 19 (Spring 1987): 89–124; Tom Mitchell, "Brandon 1919: Labour Relations in the Wheat City in the Year of the General Strike," *Manitoba History* 17 (Spring 1989): 2–13; James Naylor, "Toronto 1919," *Historical Papers* (1986): 33–55; Nolan Reilly, "The General Strike in Amherst, Nova Scotia, 1919," *Acadiensis* 9 (1980): 56–77.

44 The impact of the First World War internment operations on the radicalization of many eastern Europeans is well covered in Kassandra Luciuk, "Reinserting Radicalism: Canada's First National Internment Operations, the Ukrainian Left,

and the Politics of Redress" in *Civilian Internment in Canada: Histories and Legacies*, ed. Rhonda Hinther and Jim Mochoruk (Winnipeg: University of Manitoba Press, 2020).

45 Gutkin and Gutkin, *Profiles in Dissent*, 229.

46 See, for example, Alan Artibise, *Winnipeg: A Social History of Urban Growth, 1874–1914* (Montreal and Kingston: McGill-Queen's University Press, 1975) 129–31; and Artibise, *Gateway City: Documents on the City of Winnipeg, 1873–1913* (Winnipeg: Manitoba Record Society Publications, vol. 5, 1979), 17.

47 While the Great War veterans have received some general attention, as in Desmond Morton and Glenn Wright, *Winning the Second Battle: Canadian Veterans and the Return to Civilian Life, 1915–1930* (Toronto: University of Toronto Press, 1987), the role of returned soldiers in the Workers' Revolt across Canada has only recently begun to receive its due. See, in particular, Nathan Smith, "Comrades and Citizens: Great War Veterans in Toronto, 1915–1919," (PhD diss., University of Toronto, 2012). David Bercuson reprises the crucial role that the returned men played in the progress of the Winnipeg Strike in "The Winnipeg General Strike of 1919: The Role of the Veterans," in *Canada 1919: A Nation Shaped by War*, ed. Tim Cook and J.L. Granatstein (Vancouver: UBC Press, 2020), 148–61. Although not reliable about the Winnipeg General Strike itself, Brock Millman offers interesting insight about military authorities' perception of the returned soldiers and disorder in Winnipeg and elsewhere in *Polarity, Patriotism, and Dissent in Great War Canada, 1914–1919* (Toronto: University of Toronto Press, 2016), 229–40.

48 Kramer and Mitchell, *When the State Trembled.*

49 Tom Mitchell, "'The Manufacture of Souls of Good Quality': Winnipeg's 1919 National Conference on Canadian Citizenship, English-Canadian Nationalism, and the New Order after the Great War," *Journal of Canadian Studies* 31, no. 4 (Winter 1996–97): 5–28.

CONTRIBUTORS

Mikhail Bjorge teaches history and political economy at University of Toronto's Woodsworth College and George Brown College. He is primarily interested in the history of capitalism.

Geoffrey Ewen is an associate professor in the Departments of History and Multidisciplinary Studies at Glendon College, York University in Toronto. He has published on the 1919 Labour Revolt in Quebec and on teacher unionism in Montreal.

David Frank is professor emeritus in Canadian history at the University of New Brunswick. He has published extensively in Canadian labour and social history, including *J.B. McLachlan: A Biography* (1999) and *Provincial Solidarities: A History of the New Brunswick Federation of Labour* (2013).

Rhonda L. Hinther holds a PhD in history from McMaster University. She is a history professor at Brandon University, where she teaches western Canadian and public history. She is also an active public historian, working in film and television production, museum exhibitions, and digital interactivity and gaming.

Gregory S. Kealey is professor emeritus in history at the University of New Brunswick. He is the founding editor of *Labour/Le Travail* and author of *Spying on Canadians: The Royal Canadian Mounted Police Security Service and the Origins of the Long Cold War* (2017) and coauthor of *Secret Service: Political Policing in Canada from the Fenians to Fortress America* (2012).

Tom Langford is professor emeritus of sociology at the University of Calgary. He welcomes correspondence (langford@ucalgary.ca) and recently completed a book manuscript, *"The Lights on the Tipple Are Going Out": The Fight against Mine Closures and Economic Ruin in the Crowsnest Pass and Elk Valley, 1945–1968.*

Benoit Marsan is an historian and postdoctoral fellow at the Department of Sociology at McGill University. He is also a lecturer at the Department of Industrial Relations at Université du Québec en Outaouais where he teaches Canadian and Québécois labour and working-class history.

Jim Mochoruk teaches Canadian, British Imperial, and U.S. history at the University of North Dakota, where he is the Chester Fritz Distinguished Professor of History. He is the author of *The People's Co-op* (2000); *"Formidable Heritage": Manitoba's North and the Cost of Development* (2004); and coeditor (with Rhonda Hinther) of *Re-Imagining Ukrainian-Canadians* (2011) and *Civilian Internment in Canada* (2020).

James Naylor is the author of *The New Democracy: Challenging the Social Order in Industrial Ontario, 1914–1925* (1991) and *The Fate of Labour Socialism: The Co-operative Commonwealth Federation and the Dream of a Working-Class Future* (2016). He is a professor of history at Brandon University.

Adele Perry is a settler historian who grew up in British Columbia. Since 2000, she has taught at the University of Manitoba, where she is currently distinguished professor of history and women's and gender studies and director of the Centre for Human Rights Research.

Sharon Reilly promoted the public history recognition of the Winnipeg General Strike throughout her thirty-five-year career, working with the Manitoba Museum and Canadian Museum for Human Rights. She cochaired the Manitoba Federation of Labour 1919 Centenary Committee and organized the session on commemoration at the 1919–2019 Centenary Conference.

Myer Siemiatycki is professor emeritus in politics at Toronto Metropolitan University. His publications have explored labour, urban, and immigration studies. He has promoted a variety of student-centred labour learning projects, was founding director of the university's graduate program in Immigration and Settlement Studies, and received his faculty association's Career Achievement Award.

Jeff Stilley recently earned a PhD in sociology from the University of Missouri and currently teaches at Virginia Tech. He studies the political cultures and organizational networks that contributed to a militant and solidaristic labour movement in Kansas City in the 1910s. His research contributes to the fields of labour movements, social movements, political sociology, and race, class, and gender inequalities.

David Thompson is an activist, union organizer, and independent historian of the left, labour, and social movements. He has a PhD from Queen's University. Thompson is currently writing a book on veterans of the Great War and their participation in radical politics in interwar Canada.

Henry Trachtenberg was born in Winnipeg and educated at the University of Manitoba and York University. He taught Canadian history on and off campus for Manitoba's three universities and was an historian for the Province of Manitoba. His work has been published in scholarly periodicals and several edited volumes.

Cal Winslow is the author of *Radical Seattle, the General Strike of 1919* (2020). His other books include *E.P. Thompson and the Making of the New Left* (2014) and *Labor's Civil War in California* (2010). He is the director of the Mendocino Institute. He lives with his family on the northern California coast.

Joel Wolfe is a professor of history at the University of Massachusetts Amherst. He is the author of *Working Women, Working Men: São Paulo and The Rise of Brazil's Industrial Working Class, 1900–1955* (1993) and *Autos and Progress: The Brazilian Search for Modernity* (2010). His chapter here is drawn from *The Global Twenties*, a book he is writing about the Western Hemisphere in the 1920s.

INDEX

C

D

E

X

Y

Z

For a Better World